AUTOCOURSE

50 YEARS OF WORLD CHAMPIONSHIP
GRAND PRIX
MOTOR RACING

AUTOCOURSE

50 YEARS OF WORLD CHAMPIONSHIP
GRAND PRIX
MOTOR RACING

by ALAN HENRY

HAZLETON PUBLISHING

publisher
RICHARD POULTER
....
editor
PETER LOVERING
....
managing editor
ROBERT YARHAM
....
production manager
STEVEN PALMER
....
business development manager
SIMON SANDERSON
....
sales promotion
CLAIRE FLANAGAN
....
results
DAVID HAYHOE
....
art editor
STEVE SMALL
....
photography
BERNARD CAHIER
PAUL-HENRI CAHIER
LAT PHOTOGRAPHIC

This first edition published in 2000 by
Hazleton Publishing Ltd, 3 Richmond Hill, Richmond, Surrey
TW10 6RE, England.

Colour reproduction by
Barrett Berkeley Ltd, London, England.

Printed in England by
Butler and Tanner Ltd, Frome, Somerset.

ISBN: 1-874557-78-0

DISTRIBUTORS

UNITED KINGDOM
Biblios Ltd
Star Road
Partridge Green
West Sussex RH13 8LD
Telephone: 01403 710971
Fax: 01403 711143

NORTH AMERICA
Motorbooks International
PO Box 1
729 Prospect Ave., Osceola
Wisconsin 54020, USA
Telephone: (1) 715 294 3345
Fax: (1) 715 294 4448

NEW ZEALAND
David Bateman Ltd
PO Box 100-242
North Shore Mail Centre
Auckland 1330
Telephone: (9) 415 7664
Fax: (9) 415 8892

REST OF THE WORLD
Menoshire Ltd
Unit 13
Wadsworth Road
Perivale
Middlesex UB6 7LQ
Telephone: 020 8566 7344
Fax: 020 8991 2439

We've spent years working towards this moment, and it's been a difficult challenge at times. But this is the new face of Formula 1. The WilliamsF1 BMW is the embodiment of everything we believe motorsport should be, powered by a highly sophisticated 10-cylinder BMW engine, designed and built entirely in-house. We have a lot of ground to make up as we return to Formula 1. The competition has the benefit of years of accumulated know-how.

But the BMW WilliamsF1 team isn't just there to win races. The experience we're gaining as a result of designing our own F1 engine will give a powerful boost to our research and development in other areas. When the season opens in Melbourne on March 12, it'll be the first time in thirteen years that a Formula 1 car will have been powered by a BMW engine. And our hearts will be beating a little faster.

The new WilliamsF1 BMW FW22.

Powered by Ferrari, Mercedes, Jaguar etc.

recommends Castrol.

The eight British FIA Formula 1 World Champions – all BRDC members

THE EYES HAVE IT

BRDC

NLY ONE club includes
all the leading British rac-

especially the young champions of
tomorrow.

form the backbone of the sport,
and the ownership of Silverstone

to grow within the motor sport
environment of the Silverstone

CONTENTS

It's not the taking part,
it's the winning...

RENAULT

From victory in the first ever Grand Prix, back in 1906, to six successive constructors' championships and five drivers' titles in the modern era, Renault supplied the power behind the glory. On road that's reflected today in the brilliant new Clio Renault*sport* 172. On track we never said never... For current model range information call 0800 52 51 50. www.renault.co.uk

The power
behind the glory

AUTOCOURSE
50th Anniversary

AUTOCOURSE 2000-2001
Golden Anniversary Edition

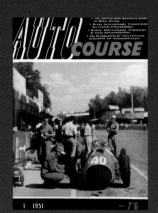

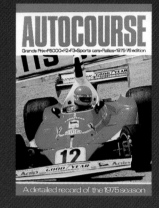

Since the first Formula 1 race was held on a former wartime airfield at Silverstone in 1950, the FIA Formula 1 World Championship has evolved in spectacular fashion, developing from a minority sport followed by a small number of dedicated enthusiasts into one of the biggest sporting spectaculars in the world.

From 1951 onwards, AUTOCOURSE has charted these developments and provided unrivalled coverage of each racing season.

For 2000–2001, Hazleton Publishing is proud to announce its Golden Anniversary Edition of AUTOCOURSE. To celebrate, we shall be publishing a special issue of the definitive annual of motor sport.

As well as special features providing a perspective on the last 50 years of Formula 1, the Anniversary Edition will include:

— incisive, authoritative reports from every Grand Prix race of the season, illustrated by a wealth of superb photographs selected from the best lensmen in the business

— editor Alan Henry's assessment of the top ten drivers (the unveiling of which is as eagerly awaited by the motor racing industry as it is by the motor sport enthusiast!)

— special features and reports covering topical issues

— comprehensive Grand Prix statistics and results.

The coverage doesn't end there. AUTOCOURSE will bring you an unrivalled record of the motor racing year, with reviews of F3000, F3, GT and touring car racing, the American scene, plus an international results round-up.

AUTOCOURSE is the ideal record book for enthusiasts, and the Golden Anniversary Edition is likely to be highly prized by collectors, so make sure you don't miss it.

304 pages, 312 x 232 mm, over 350 colour photographs, hardback with dust-jacket

Available 8 December 2000.
ISBN 1 874557 79 9
Price: UK £35

A special limited leather-bound edition will also be available.
Contact Hazleton Publishing on 020 8948 5151 for more details.
(Please note: book details may alter)

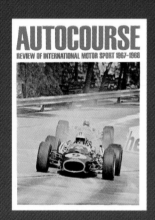

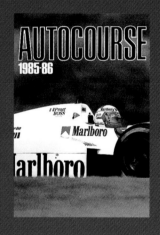

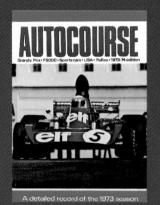

The World's Leading Grand Prix Annual

Golden Anniversary
2000-2001
50th Edition   *Golden Anniversary Edition*

FOREWORD
by Luca di Montezemolo

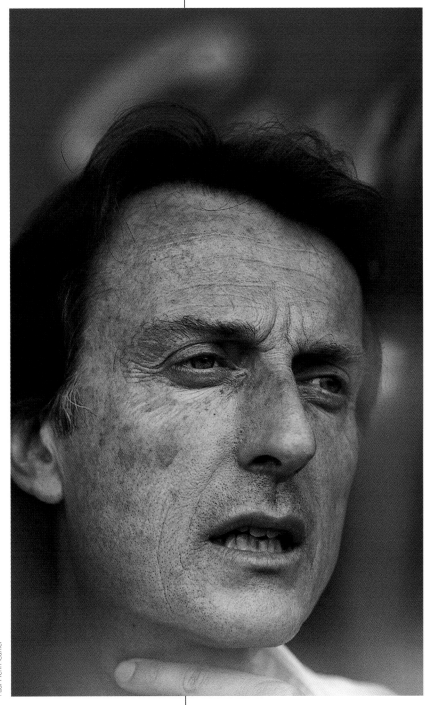

Paul-Henri Cahier

For 50 years, every single World Championship Formula 1 season has guaranteed one thing – there was always a scarlet Ferrari on the grid.

No matter the circumstances – even in the low times – motor sport has always relied on Maranello's long-standing support for Formula 1. It would be true to say there have been occasions in our history when we have stopped and thought about why we have participated and if we should continue.

But, to put it quite simply, Formula 1 would not be the same without Ferrari and Ferrari would not be the same without Formula 1.

It is inherent in absolutely everything we do today, from our road cars to our research and design. This is a significant point and one that often gets overlooked. For, although we are a small concern amidst the massive giants of the modern motor industry, Ferrari is still the only team to make its own car in-house.

We design, test and manufacture everything from the chassis to the engine to the gearbox. We do this in Maranello, not only because we have the knowledge and the expertise but because we have the people who truly understand Ferrari. This is a tradition that we started in 1947 and it's a tradition that I am sure will continue long into the future.

Like us, *Autocourse* has followed the difficult path of Grand Prix motor racing for 50 years, reporting and photographing every facet of the fascinating struggles that have developed during a season or over the years. This book, *Autocourse 50 Years of World Championship Grand Prix Motor Racing*, tells the stories of these historic struggles.

Autocourse has earned a reputation for presenting the world of Formula 1 in an individual and unique way. I sincerely hope that in 50 years' time, *Autocourse* will still be there following our progress and of course our successes.

Luca di Montezemolo
President, Ferrari SpA

13

1965 – Goodyear's first F1 win: Richie Ginther in the Honda in Mexico City

1966 – Goodyear's first F1 World Champions: Jack Brabham and the Repco Brabham

1971 – Jackie Stewart and the Tyrrell, in action at Barcelona, wins his first of three World Championships

GOODYEAR IN F1
368 Grand Prix wins in 34 years of Formula 1 competition

1974 – Goodyear's 50th Grand Prix win: Ronnie Peterson and Lotus at Monaco

1978 – Mario Andretti in the Lotus at the Dutch Grand Prix on their way to another win and both World titles

1991 – Ayrton Senna wins the Hungarian Grand Prix and his third World Championship with McLaren-Honda

1987 – Nelson Piquet in the Williams-Honda, here in Hungary, wins the Drivers' crown

1993 – Alain Prost wins a fourth Drivers' title in the Williams-Renault

1996 – Damon Hill wins the Japanese Grand Prix and the World Championship

GOOD YEAR
#1 in Racing

1998 – Michael Schumacher wins for Ferrari in Argentina

D.C.M Berlin 440/9

There is only one car in Formula 1 that will never be overtaken.

▶ The racetrack is the home of the AMG sports car. Even in Formula 1, the jewel in the crown of motor racing, you will regularly see an AMG car leading the way. We're talking about the CLK 55 AMG, a vehicle that focuses heavily on designs from AMG's motor racing division. A vehicle that offers enhanced performance, superb endurance and a chassis that is even quicker than the engine. Add to that a braking system that keeps this powerhouse in check at all times, and the CLK 55 AMG picture is complete: supreme dynamism and control – both on and off the track.

▶ For more information on AMG please contact: Mercedes-AMG GmbH, Daimlerstraße 1, D-71563 Affalterbach, telephone +49(0)71 44/3 02-0.

AMG. Sportswear for your Mercedes.

Mercedes-Benz

INTRODUCTION AND ACKNOWLEDGEMENTS

THIS BOOK has been hugely enjoyable to write – once I had rationalised the apparently daunting terms of reference implied by its title. From the outset, it was important to emphasise that, while the 50 seasons of the official Drivers' World Championship have been the most high-profile and successfully promoted the sport has known, they are far from the sum total of motor racing history.

With that in mind, the first two chapters are intended to serve as a scene-set, particularly relevant bearing in mind that the key drivers who competed in the early years of the World Championship had already achieved much in the period before the title battle was officially 'codified'.

This is not a race-by-race trawl through post-war Formula 1 history, although you will find detailed results and championship statistics in the substantial appendix at the back of this volume. Instead, I have tried to highlight trends, and focus on star drivers and events of particular significance to the sport itself. The great safety crusades of the 1960s and '70s, and more recent developments on this front, have been charted at some length. They were crucial in shaping the sport as we know it today.

I have also included a number of abbreviated features and interviews from past editions of *Autocourse*, which has developed into the world's leading Grand Prix annual during the half-century since the creation of the World Championship. In 1999 I was entrusted with responsibility for *Autocourse* for the 12th year, and it gives me much satisfaction to be the longest-serving occupant of its editorial chair.

Also, in order to help set the whole story in a wider context, we have included a running diary of major world events which flows in parallel to the main text.

It was also obviously of enormous importance to everyone at Hazleton Publishing that this one-off, prestige volume should be illustrated to a very high standard. With that in mind, I was delighted when we reached an agreement to use photographs from the splendid archives assembled over five decades by Bernard Cahier and his son, Paul-Henri.

Bernard has been a friend ever since I first appeared on the F1 scene in the early 1970s, when he was President of the International Racing Press Association. Extraordinarily well connected, he was a close friend of most of the top drivers from the early 1950s onwards and we believe his very personal photographic style adds enormous character and depth to this book. He has also helped with some splendid anecdotes which enhance the text. Paul-Henri has been a prominent contributor to *Autocourse* for many years and is now its Chief Photographer, so it is highly appropriate that his evocative images of Grand Prix racing in the 1980s and '90s should illustrate the later chapters of this book.

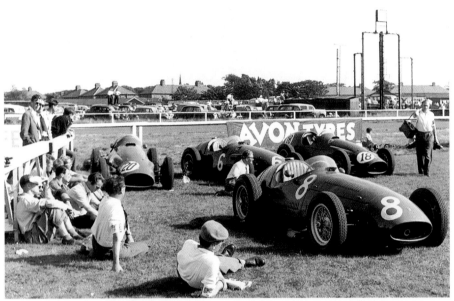

Bernard Cahier

Paul-Henri Cahier

Above: Then and now. Ferraris and Maseratis casually abandoned in the relaxed paddock at Aintree in 1955 (top), and today's thoroughbreds lined up in *parc fermé* after the 1999 Malaysian Grand Prix.

Left: Graham Hill and Bernard Cahier in 1965.

Photos: Paul-Henri Cahier

There are others I wish to thank for their help over the past quarter-century of race reporting who have indirectly contributed to the information contained within these pages. My appreciation goes to contemporary F1 team principals Sir Frank Williams, Ron Dennis of McLaren International, Luca di Montezemolo at Ferrari, Eddie Jordan and Jackie and Paul Stewart and a host of their colleagues and co-conspirators. I would also like to thank Bernie Ecclestone and FIA President Max Mosley for various on- and off-the-record briefings over a long period, many of which have effectively taken me behind the scenes of the F1 political drama at crucial moments in the sport's history.

Among my journalistic colleagues I would like to thank Maurice Hamilton, Doug Nye and Nigel Roebuck for the patience and generosity with which they have provided information and assistance. Everybody at Hazleton Publishing pulled out all the stops to get this job done at a time when all the annuals it produces had to be completed as well. It has called for huge efforts from all concerned. I hope the reader feels it has all been worth while.

Alan Henry,
Tillingham, Essex,
February 2000

Above: A bustling grid at Silverstone prepares for the 1999 British Grand Prix.

Far right: Max Mosley and Alan Henry in conversation in the Monaco pit lane.

BIBLIOGRAPHY

Dreyfus, René with Rae Kimes, Beverley, *My Two Lives: Race Driver to Restaurateur*, Aztec Corporation, 1983

Dymock, Eric, *Jim Clark*, Haynes Publishing, 1997

Ferrari, Enzo, *Pilote Che Gente . . .*, privately published by Ferrari, 1983

Hamilton, Maurice, *British Grand Prix*, The Crowood Press, 1989

Hawthorn, Mike, *Challenge Me The Race*, William Kimber, 1958

Henry, Alan, *The Four Wheel Drives: Racing's Formula for Failure*, Macmillan, 1975

Henry, Alan, *Formula One, Driver by Driver*, The Crowood Press, 1992

Henry, Alan, *Ferrari: The Grand Prix Cars*, Hazleton Publishing, 1984 and '88

Jenkinson, Denis, *The Maserati 250F: A Classic Grand Prix Car*, Macmillan, 1975

Moss, Stirling with Nye, Doug, *Stirling Moss: My Cars, My Career*, Patrick Stephens Limited, 1987

Nixon, Chris, *Racing the Silver Arrows*, Osprey Publishing, 1986

Nye, Doug, *Cooper Cars*, Osprey Publishing, 1983

Nye, Doug, *The Grand Prix Tyrrells: The Jackie Stewart Cars 1970–1973*, Macmillan, 1975

Nye, Doug with Rudd, Tony, *BRM: The Saga of British Racing Motors, Volume I*, Motor Racing Publications, 1994

Orefici, Oscar, *Carlo Chiti: The Roaring Sinfonia*, Autocritica Edizione, 1991

Surtees, John with Henry, Alan, *John Surtees, World Champion*, Hazleton Publishing, 1991

Autocourse

Autosport

Motor Racing

Motor Sport

It's in the
blood

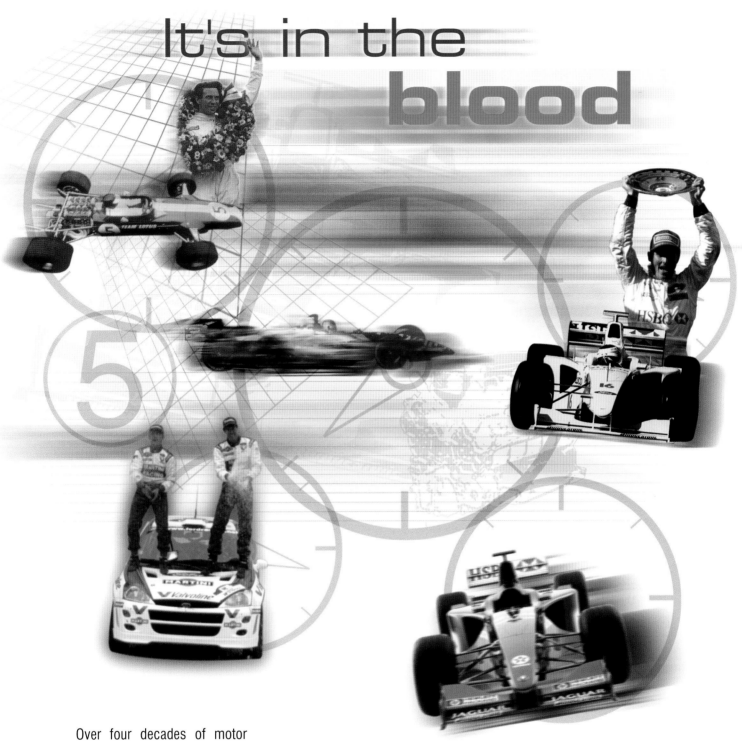

Over four decades of motor

racing heritage has given birth

to some of the world's most

successful racing engines.

Legendary partnerships: high-

performance future.

Visit our website **www.cosworthracing.com** for all the latest updates and info.

Cosworth Racing Limited, The Octagon, St. James Mill Road, Northampton, NN5 5RA
Tel: +44 (0)1604 598300   Fax: +44 (0)1604 598656   e-mail: cmanley@cosworth-racing.co.uk

PASSION IS THE EMOTION THAT HAS SHAPED MASERATIS OF THE PAST AND WILL DETERMINE THE CARS IN OUR FUTURE — A PASSION FOR PERFORMANCE, FOR SOPHISTICATED STYLE AND FOR UNBRIDLED DRIVING PLEASURE. NOW IS THE TIME TO INDULGE YOUR PASSION...

MASERATI 3200 GT. 370 HORSE POWER AND ROOM FOR FOUR

MARANELLO
═SALES LTD═

Tower Garage, The By Pass (A30), Egham, Surrey TW20 OAX Telephone: 01784 436431 Facsimile: 01784 436510
Website: www.maserati.it E-Mail: owen@maranellosales.com

CHAPTER ONE
BEFORE THE WAR

THIS VOLUME celebrates the 50th anniversary of World Championship Grand Prix motor racing, a half-century of a dramatic, colourful and ever-expanding global contest that has evolved almost beyond recognition during that period. As we stand on the threshold of the new millennium, Grand Prix racing is now arguably the world's most prestigious and cosmopolitan sport. More significantly, it is also more structured and regularised than any comparable international sporting spectacular.

With an annual programme of around 16 races across the world, it captures a global audience far more frequently than either the World Cup or the Olympic Games and has certainly not been publicly discredited in the way the latter has. Yet it would be a mistake to believe that Grand Prix history began in 1950 with the inauguration of the official World Championship. As this introductory chapter shows us, motor racing coughed and spluttered into life in the early years of the twentieth century and was already rich in tradition and achievement before everything was put on hold for six years while humanity became embroiled in the Second World War.

The first recorded motorised competition was the Paris-to-Rouen trial in 1894, which was followed by a rash of road races between European capitals. However, the 1903 Paris–Madrid event wrought such carnage among competitors and spectators – the marathon was halted after a succession of accidents, with primitive machines plunging into the crowds who lined the very edge of the route – that international racing subsequently developed on closed, albeit hardly short, circuits.

The first Grand Prix – as such – took place in 1906 when two days' racing was staged on a 65-miles-to-the-lap road course near the French city of Le Mans, with each competitor facing the challenge of completing six laps of the circuit on each of those two days.

The event was won by Hungarian driver Ferenc Szisz, who took over eleven hours to complete the course at an average speed of 63 mph, quite remarkable when one considers how his car's solid tyres and cart-sprung suspension must have reacted to the bumpy, rutted and badly surfaced roads on which the event took place.

All this seems prehistoric by the high-tech, space-age standards of the current era when Grand Prix drivers are as much highly qualified technocrats as committed professional competitors. It is also worth adding another perspective. Today, a full Grand Prix field is regularly whisked around the world loaded into a couple of Boeing 747 jet airliners. By the time Szisz won at Le Mans only three years had passed since Wilbur and Orville Wright had taken their first, faltering powered flight at Kitty Hawk, North Carolina. And the development of the jet engine was still almost forty years away.

Technical development proved as painfully slow and unco-ordinated as the evolution of the rule book in the early years of the century, yet by 1907 the idea of a 'Grand Prix formula' was becoming established. Initially this was based on fuel consumption considerations, with around 30 litres per 100 km permitted.

This was followed variously by a piston area restriction, then a 300 cc 'voiturette' formula and later a 14 mpg fuel consumption limitation. However, not until after the First World War did Grand Prix racing seriously develop an identifiable pattern which would form the foundations on which the subsequent evolution of the sport would be based.

In 1921 Grand Prix racing was revived under a 3-litre/800 kg minimum weight limit which was then reduced to 2 litres/650 kg from 1922 to 1925 inclusive. The 1922 season also saw the construction of the world's first permanent Grand Prix circuit in the former royal park at Monza, on the northern fringes of Milan. Seven years later Monaco would host its first race and names such as Delage, Bugatti, Mercedes-Benz and Alfa Romeo became increasingly familiar thanks to their on-track achievements.

The potential of international motor racing as a vehicle by means of which national prestige could be enhanced abroad was quickly recognised by those two despots with a taste for self-publicity and a tendency to megalomania, Benito Mussolini and Adolf Hitler. Thanks largely

Below: Edmond's Renault is wheeled towards the startline at the first Grand Prix, a gruelling two-day affair held on a triangular road course near Le Mans in France in 1906. The event was won by the similar car of Ferenc Szisz.

Below: Bernd Rosemeyer in the Auto Union on his way to victory in the 1937 Eifelrennen at the Nürburgring. The team's race manager, Dr Feuereissen, signals that he is already 36 seconds ahead of Rudolf Caracciola's Mercedes.

to the splendid achievements of Alfa Romeo engineer Vittorio Jano throughout the 1920s, Mussolini decided that Italy's sporting prowess could be demonstrated to great advantage with the onset of a new 750 kg Grand Prix formula which was introduced in 1934.

MOTOR RACING AND PROPAGANDA

Unfortunately the prospects for the P3 Alfa Romeo and the corresponding 2.9-litre Maserati took a dive when Auto Union and Mercedes-Benz – backed strongly by Hitler's Nazi regime – joined the fray. It had originally been Hitler's intention to pay the massive state subsidy of around 450,000 Reichsmarks (about £40,000, which today would have the equivalent purchasing power of £2.5 million) exclusively to the long-established Mercedes-Benz company, but Auto Union's Chief Designer, Professor Ferdinand Porsche, persuaded the government to split the contribution equally. The subsidy was in many ways symbolic as the overall operating costs

of these teams were several times the total of the individual government backing.

Mercedes would be responsible for this new generation of German Grand Prix cars being dubbed 'The Silver Arrows'. The technical regulations in force at the time of their 1934 debut did not place any restriction on engine capacity, but imposed a maximum weight limit of 750 kg.

While being scrutineered prior to their debut in that year's Eifel Grand Prix at the Nürburgring, the eight-cylinder, 78 × 88 mm, 3360 cc supercharged Mercedes W25s tipped the scales fractionally over the limit. This deeply alarmed the team's racing manager, Alfred Neubauer, but someone – reputedly driver Manfred von Brauchitsch – cleverly suggested that it might be a good idea to strip off the cars' white paint overnight prior to the race.

This inspired piece of improvisation left the W25s, which developed 345 bhp at 5800 rpm, just inside the maximum weight limit, but now sporting bare silver aluminium bodywork. Hence they received their new, informal nickname, which was also applied to the Auto Unions for the remaining years in the run-up to the Second World War. And, indeed, would continue to be applied to Mercedes's Grand Prix representatives well beyond.

The efforts of the Mercedes-Benz and Auto Union teams left precious little room for anybody else to enjoy the limelight, although the Italians picked up a few crumbs from the German table, most notably when Tazio Nuvolari stole victory in the 1935 German Grand Prix from under their noses.

Nuvolari was motivated by a passionate desire to upstage the German teams on their home patch, believing as he did that a conspiracy between fellow-Italian Achille Varzi and German driver Hans Stuck had kept him out of the Auto Union team.

Yet it was Mercedes who came to the 'Ring in confident mood, having already won seven major races that season to Auto Union's one. On a glistening, ominously damp track, the legendary Rudolf Caracciola stormed away into an immediate lead. Yet although the Mercedes driver led at the end of the opening lap, the remarkable Bernd Rosemeyer soon took up the challenge in his Auto Union. But after seven laps he was forced to make a precautionary pit stop after damaging a rear wheel against an earth bank earlier in the race.

It was not long, however, before the focus of attention fell on Nuvolari in the Scuderia Ferrari Alfa Romeo P3. By lap seven in this 22-lap race he was up to third, trading fastest laps with Rosemeyer. Then on lap ten he stormed ahead of Caracciola to take the lead. The crowds fell silent. This was not part of the intended script by any stretch of the imagination.

At the end of lap 12 it was time for the mid-race spate of routine refuelling stops. The Mercedes W25 of Manfred von Brauchitsch now went through into the lead as Nuvolari lost two minutes topping up his Alfa. But the frail-looking Italian had not finished yet.

Having resumed in sixth, Nuvolari climbed relentlessly back to second place and only von Brauchitsch lay between his Alfa and an astounding victory. Nevertheless, it looked as though Mercedes had it made. The German driver went into the final lap just under 30 seconds ahead and it all seemed over bar the shouting.

Regrettably, von Brauchitsch had been caning his Mercedes's tyres in his anxiety to stay ahead. Midway round that final lap the W25's left-rear tyre flew apart

PROFESSOR PORSCHE AND THE AUTO UNION

LAT Photographic

PROFESSOR Ferdinand Porsche started his first technical drawing office in Stuttgart, where he produced two designs for the Wanderer company, which – along with Audi, DKW and Horch – was one of the constituent members of the Auto Union combine.

Prior to that, Dr Porsche had worked for Daimler-Benz where, shortly before he left in 1928, he outlined a new racing car design. With its supercharged, eight-cylinder in-line engine and rear-mounted gearbox it was, in essence, the machine which Mercedes would produce in 1934 at the start of the 750 kg formula.

The new formula set no restriction on power and Porsche, impressed by his business manager Alfred Rosenberger's memories of racing the central-engined Mercedes *Tropfenwagen* in the mid-1920s, decided on a mid-engined concept for his proposed supercharged V16-powered racer for the new regulations. This would become the spectacular Auto Union which was destined to go head-to-head with the Mercedes opposition for six memorable seasons.

The cars were designed at the Porsche headquarters but built at the Horch plant at Zwickau, which, after the war, would be stranded in the eastern zone of a divided Germany. Professor Porsche and his son, Ferry, were passionately involved in the whole project in a very hands-on manner, developing the cars technically at a relentless pace through to the end of 1937 when Porsche Senior's contract with Auto Union came to an end.

For the following two years Porsche worked for Mercedes, developing a Land Speed Record challenger, and, of course, is well known for his contribution to the design of the original Volkswagen, which was very much a pet project of Hitler's. Professor Robert Eberan-Eberhorst, who had been invited by Professor Porsche to join Auto Union in 1933, was now promoted to take charge of the Grand Prix project.

Unquestionably, he was a Porsche fan. 'He was the presiding genius,' he said. 'He seemed to have a sixth sense. He could smell success and knew how to avoid mistakes.'

and the German driver was left a sitting duck. Nuvolari roared past to post possibly the most remarkable victory of his career.

There was an amusing postscript to this episode which aggravated his rivals' embarrassment. The organisers had understandably anticipated nothing but a win for one of the German teams. Consequently, there was no recording of the Italian national anthem available. No matter, said Nuvolari, producing his own, which he carried around with him to all the races. Best to be prepared.

NUVOLARI: THE SPEED-HAPPY LEGEND

Nuvolari was a racing driver cast in the heroic mould. As this volume unfolds, the reader will understand that the role and prestige of the Grand Prix driver changed subtly over the half-century we are reviewing. In Nuvolari's heyday the drivers were motivated by a passion for racing which seems almost reckless and ill-judged by the structured standards of the 1990s. Today a racing driver is regarded as a committed, polished and professional sportsman.

He may have a burning competitive spirit and enormous motivation, but he tends shrewdly to assess the overall equation and judges that, on balance, the risk is worth taking. In reaching such a conclusion he is buttressed by a generally supportive governing body in the sense that today's FIA – under the presidency of Max Mosley – is very aware that Grand Prix racing must be seen to be as safe as possible. Fatal accidents involving racing drivers have become no more acceptable in the public psyche than permitting NATO soldiers to be killed during a peace-keeping operation.

The notion of safety was simply not part of the equation in Nuvolari's day. Born in 1892, he had originally made a living as a motor cycle racer, although his underlying ambition was to race on four wheels. In 1925 he was quite badly injured after crashing on a test run in an Alfa Romeo P2. Yet only a matter of weeks later he ordered his doctors to strap him up into a compromise riding position in order to race his Bianchi in the Italian motor cycle Grand Prix. He won.

In 1930, when they were both members of the Alfa Romeo works team, Nuvolari successfully duped Varzi into losing victory in the Mille Miglia by the simple expedient of closing on to his tail in the dark, having switched off his own headlights. Almost within sight of the finishing line, he pulled out and passed his astonished rival to take the win. Varzi was not amused.

In 1933, the Alfa Romeo works team withdrew from international racing and the Scuderia Ferrari effectively became the Milan car company's nominated team. In 1935 came Nuvolari's attempt to join Auto Union, but Varzi paid him back for the Mille Miglia trick. Not until 1938 did he finally get his break with Auto Union; he duly won the Italian Grand Prix at Monza and the second Donington Grand Prix, an event which had been taken the previous year by his predecessor, Bernd Rosemeyer, who had subsequently been killed during a speed-record attempt on a German autobahn near Frankfurt in January 1938.

The rivalry between Mercedes-Benz and Auto Union was intense. The Auto Union was a central-engined concept, powered by a 4360 cc (68 × 75 mm),16-cylinder engine initially developing 295 bhp at 4500 rpm. By 1936 it would be enlarged to 6 litres, at which point it pro-

LAT Photographic

duced 520 bhp at 5000 rpm, although Mercedes topped this with the ultimate development of its straight-eight-cylinder car – the sensational W125 – which had grown to 5.6 litres by the end of the 750 kg formula in 1937, by which time it was offering 610 bhp at 5800 rpm.

If Nuvolari and Rosemeyer were regarded as the stars of the Auto Union show, then the ace Mercedes exponent was surely Rudolf Caracciola. Despite starting this golden era on a low note, having been out of action for more than a year after fracturing his right thigh and hip during practice for the 1933 Monaco Grand Prix, he went on to win three European Championship titles and no fewer than 15 Grands Prix before the Second World War intervened.

Varzi was another Auto Union great, but his career was almost wrecked prior to the war by drug addiction. He would heroically kick the habit and return to the Formula

Tazio Nuvolari was one of the great racing heroes of the 1930s and won the very last Grand Prix of that golden era, literally with the Second World War already started.

Neubauer with his competitiveness in both an ERA and a ten-year-old Delage.

Seaman was unquestionably destined to become Britain's first world-class driver, scoring a politically rather awkward victory in the 1938 German Grand Prix. He would surely have thrived in the post-war era, but his career was cut tragically short when he crashed in the 1939 Belgian Grand Prix at Spa-Francorchamps and succumbed to serious burns.

There is an anecdote which amusingly puts a social perspective on this era of German motor racing domination: it recalls an occasion when the aristocratic Manfred von Brauchitsch led Caracciola and their team-mate, Hermann Lang, into Berlin's swanky Roxy bar in the late 1930s. Lang was regarded as somewhat working class – having been unemployed during the early '30s, he originally joined the Daimler Benz company as a mechanic – and had previously raced motor cycles.

Von Brauchitsch settled down into a chair and hailed a waiter. 'A bottle of champagne for Herr Caracciola and myself,' he said. 'And a beer for Lang.'

Of course, in setting the scene for what came after the war, no account of European motor racing in the 1930s would be complete without mention of the 'voiturette' categories which thrived during that decade with 1100 or 1500 cc engines. Bugatti and Alfa Romeo competed in this category along with the British-built ERAs with which Raymond Mays and others would lay the foundations for the post-war BRM operation.

Late on the afternoon of 3 September 1939, Tazio Nuvolari took the chequered flag to win the Yugoslavian Grand Prix in Belgrade. The Second World War was already a few hours old and by the time Nuvolari re-appeared in the austere post-war world, he would be over fifty and beset by bronchial problems, a shadow of the man he once was. A golden era for racing was at an end.

Above: Tazio Nuvolari won the 1938 Donington Grand Prix in the Auto Union D-Type.

Below right: The mighty Mercedes-Benz W125 of Manfred von Brauchitsch finished in second place behind Bernd Rosemeyer's Auto Union when the Silver Arrows made their first visit to Donington the previous year.

I front line in the immediate post-war era only to be killed during practice for the 1948 Swiss Grand Prix.

In 1938 new technical rules were introduced that limited supercharged machinery to a capacity of 3 litres, with both German manufacturers opting for the V12 engine configuration. By then Mercedes had secured the services of the dynamic young English driver Dick Seaman, who had impressed team manager Alfred

Opposite, top: Arthur Dobson and Earl Howe in their ERAs at the 1937 Donington Grand Prix.

Opposite, inset: Raymond Mays, whose influence on motor sport in Britain went far beyond his key role in the ERA project.

Photos: LAT Photographic

RAYMOND MAYS AND THE CONTRIBUTION OF ERA

Photos: LAT Photographic

IF THERE WAS a pivotal personality on the British motor racing scene whose influence straddled the war years, then it was unquestionably that of Raymond Mays. A dignified, unstuffy and charismatic man in his own way, he was born in the Lincolnshire fenland town of Bourne in 1899 and never lived anywhere else until his death 80 years later.

Mays served in France in the closing months of the First World War, having been commissioned into the Grenadier Guards in 1918, and began his racing career three years later while still a Cambridge undergraduate. In the mid-1920s he made his name competing with a Bugatti, but then switched to a 3-litre TT Vauxhall, which was suitably updated by distinguished engineer Amherst Villiers.

He then switched to a highly tuned Riley, success with which prompted him to encourage the wealthy Humphrey Cook to fund the construction of the ERA (for English Racing Automobiles) single-seaters to compete in the 'voiturette' category. The company

established its factory in premises adjacent to the Mays family home in Bourne, Eastgate House, where Ray lived in some style together with his mother and Peter Berthon, a former RAF pilot who became an indispensable friend and confidant as well as a key engineer in the forthcoming BRM project.

The Mays family business included the wool, tannery and fertiliser trades. They were certainly comfortably off, if not dramatically rich. Ray was an only child and was brought up insulated from the harsh economic realities of life which blew through the homes of all too many English families during the first half of the century, particularly during the 1930s.

Although ERA sold several Riley-engined cars to private entrants, Mays was effectively the number one works driver and recorded the marque's first Continental victory in the 1935 Eifelrennen at the Nürburgring. The pressure of development and reported poor preparation standards at Bourne meant that Mays did not win another international event until 1937, when he really got into his stride and scored three more victories.

Mays had the ability to charm the birds off the trees, a quality which aided him enormously throughout his adult life when it came to romancing potential backers for his various motor racing projects. Famous names such as Dick Seaman, Pat Fairfield and the enormously talented Siamese prince, 'B. Bira', all purchased ERAs and helped add further gloss to the image of the marque.

Unfortunately it seems that, by 1939, Humphrey Cook was tiring of his role as ERA's benefactor. He had spent around £95,000 – a truly massive sum by the standards of the day which would equate to almost £6 million in today's values – over five years and felt that he was being increasingly taken for granted by Mays and Berthon, who seemed to be hogging all the limelight.

There was considerable acrimony behind the scenes because Cook felt resentful about the way in which he had been treated, although Mays's innate sense of good manners precluded him from making any overt criticism of his former colleague. When Mays published his memoirs, *Split Seconds*, in 1950, he talked about Cook in affectionate terms as a close and valued friend.

Yet there was very real rancour between the two men, as evidenced in the correspondence published in *BRM, The Saga of British Racing Motors* by Doug Nye with Tony Rudd (Motor Racing Publications, 1994).

The whole tone of Mays's letters suggested that he delivered rather more

to the whole equation in terms of intangible prestige than Cook did with hard cash. It was an ultimately irreconcilable issue but Mays's somewhat cavalier approach to financial and organisational matters would resurface when it came to establishing the BRM team immediately after the war.

Some members of the racing fraternity regarded Mays as something of a social butterfly, determined to look after number one. A great fan of the theatre, he was an unashamed 'stage door Johnny', but those who worked with him testified to his loyalty and steadfast friendship. He was not a man to give up easily on any project.

Almost as the war came to an end, Mays was still anxious to float his plan for a British national Grand Prix car, the project which would eventually turn into the BRM and initially establish itself as a countrywide joke, or disgrace, depending on one's sense of humour and the absurd. Mays continued sprinting and hillclimbing throughout the late 1940s until finally retiring in 1949 when the BRM project was getting into top gear.

Mays and the influence and interest prompted by his ERAs have been widely credited for the expansion of interest in the 'voiturette' category during the 1930s. Latterly, his faith in the BRM project seemed dramatically misplaced – as we shall see – but he was ultimately vindicated when Graham Hill won the marque's first and only World Championship title in 1962.

GREAT DRIVERS: DICK SEAMAN, BERND ROSEMEYER

DICK SEAMAN was a rich boy whose family had the resources to fund his progress up the rungs of the motor racing ladder. His mother and father certainly disapproved of his aspirations behind the wheel but they had no joy when it came to influencing him to pursue a career in the diplomatic service.

Even by the time he left Cambridge in 1934 at the age of 21, Seaman was absolutely determined that he was going to become a professional driver and bought the MG K3 Magnette which his fellow-student Whitney Straight – later to become Chairman of the British Overseas Airline Corporation – was all too willing to sell on to him.

Despite parental disapproval, Seaman secured sufficient finance to clinch a deal to drive a factory-prepared ERA in 1935. Unfortunately this coincided with a downturn in the standards of preparation at Bourne and Dick soon decided to cancel the agreement, preferring to have his car prepared by the highly respected Giulio Ramponi, whom he hired as his personal mechanic.

In 1936, frustrated by the ERA's performance, he was coaxed into acquiring the nine-year-old Grand Prix Delage which had been driven in its heyday by Earl Howe. The car was extensively re-worked and lovingly fettled by Ramponi, and Seaman drove it to four prestigious wins in 1936, sealing his reputation as the most impressive 1500 cc driver in Europe. It was on the strength of that achievement that he was offered a place in the Mercedes-Benz factory team for the following year.

Seaman accepted. This was an unmissable opportunity to make the Big Time, but his contract had to be personally rubber-stamped by Adolf Hitler himself, a measure of just how seriously the Nazi government regarded its investment in Grand Prix racing during the 1930s. Hitler, of course, had always been a fan of the English and would clearly have had no reservations whatsoever about approving Dick's appointment.

Little success came Seaman's way during his first season with Mercedes. Indeed, his first test after signing his contract resulted in an accident at Monza from which he was fortunate to escape with relatively minor injuries. By all accounts, Alfred Neubauer, the portly Mercedes team manager, was very philosophical about such incidents, feeling they were something of an occupational hazard.

Later in the year, Dick was involved in a very serious accident in the German Grand Prix at the Nürburgring on the long straight which leads back to the start/finish line running parallel with the main road to Koblenz. His rival, Ernst von Delius, attempted to overtake Seaman's Mercedes with his Auto Union, but inadvertently clipped the dense hedge and was thrown across in front of the Englishman.

Von Delius careered into the opposite hedge and catapulted the Auto Union back through the left-hand hedge, after which it rolled several times before landing in a field on the opposite side of the main

road. Meanwhile, Seaman struck a kilometre post and was thrown out of his Mercedes, taking most of the skin off his nose and breaking a thumb. The hapless von Delius died of his injuries that night.

Later that year Seaman was disappointed not to have posted a good result in the first Donington Grand Prix, being pushed off by a rival Auto Union early in the race. Amazingly, he did not race again until the following year's German Grand Prix at the Nürburgring, which he won. He was then faced with the embarrassing situation of having to give a Nazi salute – which he did, albeit tentatively – on the rostrum.

In December 1938, Dick Seaman married Erica, the 18-year-old daughter of BMW founder Franz-Joseph Popp. They were to have less than a year together as Dick crashed heavily on a rain-soaked Spa-Francorchamps circuit while leading the 1939 Belgian Grand Prix. He succumbed to fatal burns that evening. The entire Mercedes team attended his funeral at Putney Vale cemetery in south London.

Seaman died at the age of 26 and his very real talent would have continued to shine on the post-war racing scene. He would have been just 37 when Alfa Romeo brought their dominant 158s to Silverstone for the very first round of the official World Championship on 13 May 1950. On that occasion Reg Parnell was given the third entry and rounded off a Portello 1–2–3, much to the delight of the organisers. But for that skid on a rain-drenched circuit 11 years earlier, it might well have been driven by Dick Seaman.

If Seaman was the best and most accomplished racing driver to emerge from Britain in the 1930s, then Bernd Rosemeyer was Germany's most dazzling, charismatic star from the same era. Born in 1909, Rosemeyer began motor cycle grass-track racing in 1930 and made such dramatic progress that he had been recruited as a member of the Auto Union team by the start of the 1935 season.

As well as great charm, Rosemeyer had terrific car control and his technique with the daunting rear-engined Auto Unions was truly magical. In only his second race, the Eifelrennen, he acutely embarrassed established star Rudi Caracciola, and the Mercedes ace had to draw on all his considerable experience to keep the new lad back in second place at the chequered flag.

Later Rosemeyer would finish second in the Coppa Acerbo at Pescara and round off the '35 season with victory in the Czech Grand Prix at Brno. The 1936 season would see him win the Eifel GP ahead of Tazio Nuvolari's Alfa and score a hat-trick of wins in the Coppa Acerbo and the Swiss and Italian Grands Prix.

The 1937 season would yield repeat wins in the Eifel GP and Coppa Acerbo and he rounded off the year with victory in the inaugural Donington GP, the first of two memorable occasions which saw the 'Silver Arrows' visit and compete in the UK.

Bernd Rosemeyer married the aviatrix Elly Beinhorn in the summer of 1936 and together they became one of pre-war Germany's most glamorous and attractive couples. Their idyllic life together was torn apart when Bernd was killed during a record attempt in a streamlined Auto Union on the Frankfurt–Darmstadt autobahn on 27 January 1938. To this day, a handsome memorial remains in the woods close to a lay-by on this same autobahn at the point where he crashed more than sixty years ago.

Top: Dick Seaman had become a Grand Prix winner by the time he raced the Mercedes at Donington in 1938.

Left: In just three seasons Bernd Rosemeyer created a legend at the wheel of the Auto Union.

THE POST-WAR SCENE

A S EUROPE dusted itself down and surveyed the destruction wrought by six years of war, one might have been excused for thinking that motor racing would be low on the collective agenda. But that reckoned without the passion and purpose of those engineers, drivers and fans who had been starved of their favourite sport for so long.

Once the heady fever of relief had passed, there was a burning desire to re-establish normality as quickly as possible. Thus the first flickers of racing enthusiasm began to be nurtured in the dying embers of the conflict. But it was still a rough and ready game.

Crash helmets were optional until the early 1950s, safety facilities non-existent. A generation of young men who had become acquainted with suffering and danger in wartime now wanted to compete at their chosen sport. So it was hardly surprising that nobody gave much thought to safety.

Before the war, a change in Formula A regulations – effectively F1 – had been pencilled in for 1941. These rules would call for 4.5-litre unsupercharged or 1.5-litre supercharged engines, and in 1945 the newly titled Fédération

Internationale de l'Automobile (FIA) quickly adopted these regulations for those who felt able to take part.

The Alfa Romeo 158s, the eight-cylinder 1.5-litre supercharged machines which had made their race debut in the 1938 Coppa Ciano at Leghorn – and which had allegedly spent the war walled up in a cheese factory – were the most obvious contenders to re-emerge. There was naturally nothing from Auto Union or Mercedes-Benz, but there were some old French Talbots, the odd Delahaye, British ERAs and Italian Maseratis to fill out the field.

FERRARI TAKES CHALLENGE TO ALFA

More significantly, there was a new name on the block. Enzo Ferrari had forged his reputation by operating what was, in effect, the works Alfa Romeo team from 1929 through to 1938. At this point he had a major breach with the company after falling out on a personal level on matters of strategy with its Director, Ugo Gobatto, and his nominee, the Spanish engineer, Wilfredo Ricart.

Ferrari said of Ricart: 'When he shook hands, it was

Below: An atmospheric view of the pits at the 1947 Swiss Grand Prix at the Bremgarten circuit near Berne.

like grasping the cold, lifeless hand of a corpse.' Ferrari certainly had a way with words, although he would be less appreciative when firm criticism was aimed in his direction over the next two generations by a succession of car-crazy Italian scribes.

In 1938 Alfa wanted to take back control of its works team to the company headquarters at Portello in Milan. Ferrari was having none of this and decided to go his own way, somewhat hamstrung in his ambitions by a severance clause banning his participation in any races with a non-Alfa product for the next four years.

Despite this, by the end of 1939 the new company he had formed, Auto Avio Construzioni, was working on a couple of eight-cylinder sports cars – simply dubbed '815s' – for the following year's Mille Miglia. After Italy entered the war Ferrari concentrated on specialist engineering work, and in 1943 he moved his base from Modena to a new factory which he built at nearby Maranello.

By 1947 Ferrari was free to build cars under his own name. Two Ferrari 125s, fitted with 1.5-litre V12 engines, made their debut in a sports car race at Piacenza, where they were driven by Franco Cortese and Giuseppe Farina. A Ferrari took part in a classic Grand Prix event for the first time the following May, when Igor Trobetskoy, later to gain fleeting celebrity status as one of the many husbands of Woolworth heiress Barbara Hutton, competed with a 2-litre version of the same machine.

Not until September 1948 did the first of the supercharged Ferrari 125s make their race debuts. Driving in the Turin Grand Prix were Raymond Sommer, Farina and the Siamese prince, 'Bira'. The cars had been designed by former Alfa Romeo engineer Giacchino Colombo – the man responsible for the legendary 158 – and Sommer finished third on this occasion behind Jean-Pierre Wimille's Alfa and Luigi Villoresi's Maserati.

The 1949 season saw Ferrari concentrating on the development of the 125s and, crucially, generating extra income by selling a couple of cars into private hands. Both went to British owners; one to privateer Peter Whitehead and the other to Tony Vandervell, the engine bearing magnate who raced the car under the title 'Thinwall Special Ferrari'.

By the mid-1950s, of course, Formula 1 would be well supported by many teams and manufacturers, but this was far from the case in 1949 when Alfa Romeo temporarily withdrew from the Grand Prix arena. The Milanese firm was worried by opposition from the emergent Ferrari and BRM teams.

In addition, Alfa's efforts had been undermined by the loss of three of its top drivers. Achille Varzi had been killed the previous year, while Jean-Pierre Wimille lost his life at the wheel of a little Simca-Gordini in Buenos Aires on 28 January 1949. In addition, Count Carlo-Felice Trossi had been laid low by cancer and would eventually die on 9 May 1949 following a long illness.

Alfa Romeo's decision to stand aside, albeit fleetingly, meant that Ferrari pretty well had the scene to himself. Not that things went smoothly by any means, for Tony Vandervell soon returned his Ferrari 125 to Maranello with a stiff note from the British industrialist to the effect that he was certainly not satisfied with the new car's performance.

Nevertheless, his decision to buy that Ferrari in the first place was not only Vandervell's first step towards building his own Vanwall cars, but a clear signal that he

had tired of his involvement in the complex 'management by committee' BRM project.

The first BRM was a 1.5-litre centrifugally supercharged V16 which was not only late off the mark but beset with mechanical problems almost from the moment of its very first test outing. By the time its complicated and very temperamental engine had been massaged into some semblance of competitive trim, such was the dearth of cars available generally which conformed with the F1 regulations that the 1952 and '53 title battles were turned over to Formula 2 machinery.

As a result the BRM would eke out a faintly pathetic twilight existence in British domestic events and those motor industry backers who had rallied to the cause, energetically supporting the call for a new national British Grand Prix car, suddenly found themselves pilloried for its lack of success.

Eventually the original British Motor Racing Research Trust foundered and the project was bought by the Owen Organisation, one of the country's largest privately owned industrial empires. Its head was a serious-minded, but very human and popular, Methodist by the name of Alfred Owen – later Sir Alfred – whose cars would eventually be pitted against Tony Vandervell's Vanwalls.

Much was made of the personal rivalry between these two very different 'millionaire industrialists'. Yet the reality seems to have been that they enjoyed a formally cordial relationship. They were very different personalities, but both were, in effect, second-generation members of major commercial dynasties. The difference, of course, was that while Alfred Owen accepted the custody of his father's engineering empire, Tony Vandervell – the son of Clive Vandervell, founder of the CAV electrical concern – preferred to strike out on his own.

Meanwhile, back at Ferrari, a great deal of technical consideration had gone into the V12 engine configuration for, although Ferrari admitted that his enthusiasm for this layout had originally been fired by the American Packard V12 engines, there were firm practical reasons not to follow the Alfa Romeo eight-cylinder route.

The short-stroke configuration chosen by Colombo for the Tipo 125 offered potential for higher revs and the additional advantage of a stiffer crankcase, reduced bearing loads and a lighter, lower cylinder block. Alfa Romeo's 158s were clearly the main opposition at this time, although Maserati's supercharged 4CL was regarded as the next best challenger, giving away around 50 bhp to the 'Alfettas', which developed a claimed 275 bhp at 7500 rpm from their two-stage supercharged engines.

Talbot continued to campaign a 4.5-litre unsupercharged machine which was definitely inferior to the Italian opposition, but fields were unpredictable in size and there was no obligation on the part of any individual team or manufacturer to contest any particular race.

In that respect, the development of Grand Prix racing was a distinctly piecemeal affair in those immediate postwar years, with race organisers getting by as best they could while being perpetually dependent on the technical readiness of the competing teams.

There were other aspirants on the F1 stage at the time, yet most appeared only fleetingly. The futuristic Cisitalia-Porsche would never start a race, the French CTA Arsenal was seen briefly in 1947 and '48 before disappearing for good and, as far as Britain was concerned, efforts to build a national racing car resulted in the BRM project getting off the ground, albeit shakily.

Opposite: Alberto Ascari, seen chasing round the bales at Silverstone, initially made his post-war name driving this private Maserati 4CLT/48.

Opposite, bottom: Louis Chiron ensured that he remained in the forefront of attention with some sterling drives in the lumbering 4.5-litre Lago Talbot.

JEAN-PIERRE WIMILLE:
FRANCE'S UNCROWNED CHAMPION

FRANCE WOULD have to wait until 1985 before hailing its first official World Champion driver in Alain Prost. Yet in the first few seasons after the war, Jean-Pierre Wimille established himself as one of the greatest drivers of his era. Had he lived, say his fans, he would have won the first official title in 1950 instead of Giuseppe Farina.

Wimille was the son of a pioneer motoring and aviation journalist. Born in 1908, he was variously described as austere, aloof, withdrawn, stylish and deeply religious. He was accustomed to a wealthy lifestyle. Prior to the war he raced Bugattis, starting as early as 1930, then tried his hand with an Alfa Romeo 8C-2600 before joining the Bugatti works team, for whom he shared victory in the 1937 Le Mans 24-hour race with Robert Benoist.

During the war Wimille served energetically in the French resistance movement, together with his young wife, the 1938–39 ski champion Christiane de la Fressange. Their resistance group was headed by Wimille's racing colleague, Robert Benoist, who was ultimately betrayed to the Gestapo and executed at the Buchenwald concentration camp in the closing months of the war.

Wimille was cheered generously by the crowds who flocked into the Bois de Boulogne in September 1945, where he won the Coupe des Prisonniers meeting at the wheel of his old 4.7-litre Bugatti *monoplace*.

In 1946 Wimille drove an ancient Alfa Romeo 308 Grand Prix car, in which he showed typically

competitive form, and was then invited to join the Alfa factory team for the Grand Prix des Nations at Geneva, finishing third in the final. He then took second in Turin's Valentino Park.

In 1947 and '48 Wimille consolidated his brilliant reputation in the Alfa 158s, winning the '47 Swiss GP at Bremgarten and the Belgian race at Spa-Francorchamps – where he topped 180 mph on the Masta straight.

His Alfa Romeo team-mate, Consalvo Sanesi, would remember him for a particularly symbolic gesture in the 1948 Autodrome Grand Prix at Monza, a race held to celebrate the re-opening of the famous circuit for the first time after the war. Sanesi was the test driver, a mechanic who had been promoted, and it was agreed that he would be the man to win this race.

He recalled watching in his mirrors as Wimille and his other team-mate, Count Trossi, held back, but Trossi eventually could contain himself no longer and shot past into the lead. Wimille followed him through and won, against team orders, to teach Trossi a lesson for overtaking Sanesi in the first place. 'Wimille was a great man,' recalled Sanesi.

On 28 January 1949, Wimille was killed driving one of the 1.4-litre Simca-Gordinis during an early-morning practice session for the Buenos Aires Grand Prix on the Palermo Park circuit. He was 41 years old and, ironically, wearing a crash helmet for the first time in his long career instead of a linen cap.

Photos: LAT Photographic

FRANCE TAKES
A BACK SEAT

Of course, France had made a substantial contribution to the international motor racing scene in the pre-war years. Bugatti had won the inaugural Monaco Grand Prix in 1929 with William Grover-Williams at the wheel and followed that up with a repeat victory thanks to the efforts of René Dreyfus the following year.

Dreyfus later produced one of the most startling upsets in established form at the 1938 Pau Grand Prix, run round the splendid road circuit through the streets of the picturesque town in south-western France. Driving a 4.5-litre naturally aspirated Delahaye against the 3-litre supercharged works Mercedes, Dreyfus took advantage of lower fuel consumption to win the race and beat Rudolf Caracciola into second place.

Forty-five years later, Dreyfus recalled: 'Finally Rudi came in for fuel and got out of his car. His hip hurt, he said, he wanted Hermann Lang to take over. Rudi had suffered a bad accident five years before at Monaco which had left him with a tender hip, but that wasn't the real reason he didn't want to finish Pau. We both knew, without ever saying it, that he just didn't want to be beaten by me.'

That year also saw the Talbot company joining in, buoyed in its optimism after winning the previous year's Grand Prix de l'ACF for sports cars. Despite originally planning an ambitious 3-litre supercharged engine, Antony Lago's factory in Suresnes preferred to develop a 4.5-litre six-cylinder unit which, as things turned out, would see racing action through to the early 1950s.

The French constructors were also very much in at the start of the post-war racing renaissance. Jean-Pierre Wimille won the very first race to take place after hostilities had ceased in 1945, taking the single-seater 1939 Bugatti to victory in the Liberation Grand Prix through the Bois de Boulogne in Paris.

By 1947 there were just four major international Grands Prix on the calendar. Wimille won the Swiss and Belgian races while Count Trossi added a third success for the Alfa Romeo 158s in Italy. But Louis Chiron, 17 years after winning at Monaco in a Bugatti and as old as the century, gave Talbot a historic victory in the GP de l'ACF.

The 1947 season would see Maserati throw its hat into the ring with an uprated version of its 1939-built 4CL. Powered by a four-cylinder, single-stage super-charged 1.5-litre four-cylinder engine, the car was steadily developed to produce the 4CLT that year and later the 4CLT/48 – or 'San Remo' model after the memorable victory posted in its debut race by Alberto Ascari.

ASCARI BIDS FOR
THE BIG TIME

Ascari would become one of the great post-war Grand Prix drivers, although his career would be prematurely ended at the age of 37 in 1955 when he crashed a borrowed sports Ferrari fatally in what was supposed to be a leisurely test session at Monza.

His father was the legendary Antonio Ascari, who was killed when his Alfa Romeo crashed in the 1926 French Grand Prix on the Montlhéry circuit near Paris. Alberto's competition career started on motor cycles just before the Second World War when he raced for the factory

LAT Photographic

The front row of the starting grid for the 1949 British Grand Prix at Silverstone. From the left, the Maseratis of Luigi Villoresi and Prince Bira, Peter Whitehead's ERA, eventual winner Baron de Graffenried's Maserati and Bob Gerard's ERA.

Bianchi team and he also tried his hand at car racing with the first '815' – the very first Ferrari-made car – in the 1940 Mille Miglia.

Ascari also finished ninth in the 1940 Tripoli Grand Prix before the war wrote *finis* to any further motor-sporting activities. During the war, Ascari managed to establish a thriving road transport business with his friend Luigi Villoresi, hauling fuel to Mussolini's army in North Africa. This had the additional benefit of exempting him from military service and Alberto picked up the threads of his racing career after the war with a Cisitalia, winning his first car race with a Maserati sports car at Modena on 28 September 1947.

By this time, Ascari was married with a son and had seriously considered the idea of giving up racing alto-gether, but Villoresi persuaded him to continue. Together they raced under the Scuderia Ambrosiana banner through 1948 in a pair of Maserati 4CLTs and Alberto finished runner-up in the British Grand Prix at Silverstone.

Also in 1948, Tony Lago and his chief engineer, Carlo Marchetti, raised the tempo of the marque's challenge with the production of the new Talbot 26C which, with 240 bhp on tap, was expected to come close to chal-lenging the rival Maseratis, which developed 260 bhp.

That year Maserati and Alfa Romeo carved up the six Grands Prix equally, scoring three wins apiece. Louis Rosier drove the new Talbot at Monaco and the team eventually managed to produce fourth, fifth and sixth places in the Grand Prix de l'ACF.

That season also saw the legendary Achille Varzi killed during wet practice for the Swiss GP at Bremgarten, his Alfa 158 toppling over at relatively modest speed after a spin. Varzi, wearing a linen helmet, hadn't a chance. That race also claimed the life of German driver Christian Kautz, third at Monaco in 1937 for Mercedes, when he crashed his Maserati.

The absence of Alfa Romeo in 1949 left the Formula 1 scene split three ways. Baron Emmanuel de Graffenried won the British Grand Prix at Silverstone for Maserati, then Rosier triumphed in the Belgian Grand Prix at Spa-Francorchamps and Alberto Ascari's Ferrari took the Swiss Grand Prix at Berne. Chiron scored a second Talbot victory in France, then Ascari won again at Monza and Peter Whitehead's private Ferrari 125 clinched the distant Czechoslovakian Grand Prix at Brno.

It would be another 30 years before the French crowd would see their home Grand Prix won by a French driver and an all-French car. For that treat the fans would have to wait until 1979 when Jean-Pierre Jabouille won at Dijon-Prenois with the Renault turbo.

The 1949 season saw Ascari and Villoresi receiving the pay-off for their efforts at the wheels of their private Maseratis when they were invited to join the works Ferrari team. It was then that Ascari's career really began to take off, notably when he led his old friend Villoresi to a 1–2 in the Swiss Grand Prix at Berne's spectacular Bremgarten circuit, thus achieving the Ferrari team's first international success with the 1.5-litre Tipo 125. It was a victory made undeniably easier by the absence of Alfa Romeo from the stage, but it was an important success nevertheless.

A new face had appeared on the international motor racing stage in 1948 who would eventually break all the records and gain legendary status over the following decade. Driving a 1.4-litre Simca-Gordini, Juan Manuel Fangio made his European debut in the Coupe des Petites Cylindres at Reims on 18 July, followed by the French Grand Prix on the same day. The 37-year-old fin-ished neither event, but he would be back in 1949 at the wheel of a Maserati 4CLT/48.

Equipped with this car, which had been purchased by the Argentine Automobile Federation, he won in front of his home crowd at Mar del Plata before coming back to Europe where he won again at San Remo, Pau, Perpignan, Marseilles, Monza and Albi. These successes led to an invitation to join the Alfa Romeo factory team for the 1950 season, the first year of the official World Championship for Drivers.

After that unobtrusive outing at Reims with the Simca-Gordini, Jean-Pierre Wimille invited Fangio to accompany him to the *L'Equipe* newspaper reception at which he was to be interviewed after his victory in the Grand Prix. On this occasion the number one driver of the Alfa Romeo team took the opportunity to introduce the new arrival from Argentina.

'He is the one you'll be writing about one day,' said the Frenchman to the newspaper's editor as he patted Fangio on the back. Later, he added: 'If Fangio ever gets behind the wheel of a good car, he will do great things.'

Wimille was killed barely six months later, ironically enough driving a Simca-Gordini in Buenos Aires, capital of Fangio's homeland. And the not-so-youngster from the provincial town of Balcarce would, by popular con-sensus, emerge as the man who took over the baton from the Frenchman as the finest driver of his era.

Opposite, top: Jean-Pierre Wimille was seen by some as slightly austere, but he had a hugely loyal following of fans who regarded him as one of the greatest drivers of his generation.

Opposite: Wimille in the Alfa 158 on his way to victory in the 1948 Italian Grand Prix in Turin.

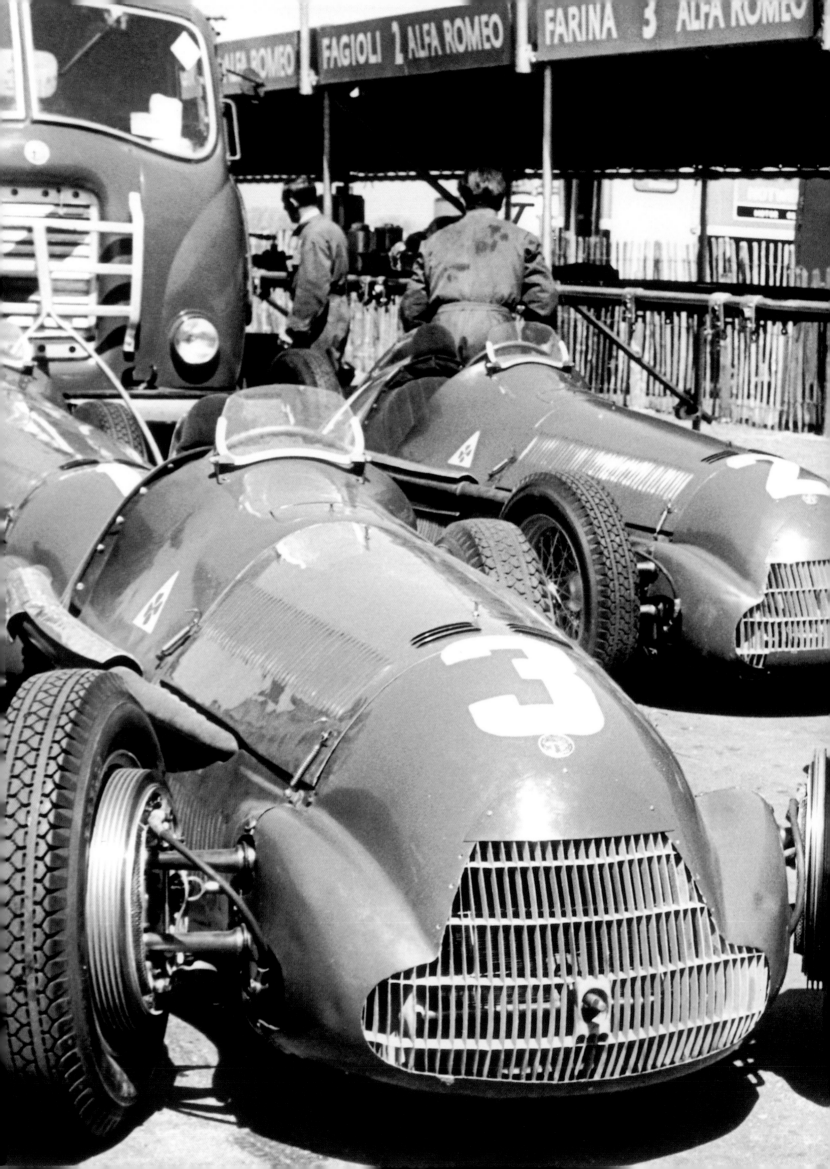

LAT Photographic

Giuseppe Farina winning the 1950 British Grand Prix. The gritty and unsentimental Italian would become the first official World Champion driver that season.

Previous spread: Alfas filled the first three places at Silverstone. The straight-eight-cylinder 1.5-litre supercharged Tipo 158s were the dominant force in Grand Prix racing during the immediate post-war years.

Photo: LAT Photographic

Opposite: The field streams away at the start of the inaugural World Championship Grand Prix. Note the white-painted oil drums decorated with flowers marking the course.

THE OFFICIAL Drivers' World Championship began at the start of the 1950 season. The sport would have to wait until 1958 before the efforts of the constructors were similarly rewarded, so for the moment the men behind the wheel went into battle to sort out who was the Best in the World. If not officially, then certainly mathematically.

The points system rewarded the top five finishers in each qualifying round on a sliding scale 8–6–4–3–2 with an extra point awarded for the fastest lap. This would be amended in 1960 when an additional single point was added for sixth place and the point for fastest lap was dropped; the winner's points were increased from eight to nine in 1961. The practice of drivers being able to share points if they shared a car was abandoned after 1958.

With the exception of the introduction of an extra point for the race winner in 1991, the scoring system has remained the same from 1961 to the present, the only qualification being the number of races which were allowed to count towards a driver's overall total. This has been altered and amended from time to time, as we shall see. Finally, there was another major anomaly from 1950 to '60: the Indianapolis 500 was included as a round of the World Championship even though the cross-fertilisation between F1 and the US 'roundy-round' boys was virtually nil.

It was therefore with Alfa Romeo as the established pacesetters, Ferrari as the challengers and BRM as the no-hopers that the official World Championship kicked off with the grandly titled Grand Prix of Europe – otherwise the British GP – at Silverstone.

This historic event enjoyed the patronage of King George VI and Queen Elizabeth, now the Queen Mother, and much was made of the fact that this was the first time a reigning monarch had attended such an event. With bunting, brass bands and all the panoply of a state occasion, their Majesties were entertained by an Alfa Romeo grand slam and Giuseppe Farina won from Luigi Fagioli and Reg Parnell.

Further back, the elderly Frenchman, Yves Giraud-Cabantous, plodded on his lonely way to fourth place in his 4.5-litre Talbot – two laps behind. It was the sort of domination we would see many years later from the likes of the Honda-engined Williamses and McLarens. Except the Alfas were even more dominant, facing as they were decidedly makeshift opposition.

On race morning the Alfas had been driven to Silverstone on the road from Banbury – strictly illegal, of course, but nobody cared. They managed to avoid getting tangled up in the arrival of their Majesties, who arrived by train at the now long-defunct Brackley railway station, whence a Royal Daimler transported them to the track.

The King and Queen were duly presented to the drivers and every aspect of their behaviour was scrutinised with good-mannered charm by William Boddy, the Editor of *Motor Sport* magazine, who wrote:

Earl Howe sat between the King and Queen, and as the flag was about to fall the King looked up from his programme and eagerly down towards the starting grid. As the cars roared away, he appeared to be heavily interested, but the noise and the smoke took the Queen a trifle unawares as the mass-start of a race does to those close to the course . . . Princess Margaret seemed to want to concentrate solely on what was happening, and to regard conversation as merely incidental. But this is to anticipate.

In the aftermath of the race a Mr A.P. Bird wrote to the magazine commenting that 'the lavatory accommodation was nothing short of disgusting'. Meanwhile, *Motor Sport* commented on the customary Silverstone gridlock which endures to this day.

We feel sure that those who arrived late because of traffic congestion, those who spent four hours or so getting out of the car parks, those who received the wrong passes and those honorary club marshals who had to sleep the Friday night in old tents because the RAC patrols had taken the beds in the huts, will readily concur.

Royal patronage. Among the
drivers presented to George VI
(left) and Queen Elizabeth
(centre) at Silverstone in 1950
was a youthful Stirling Moss
(second right). To his left is
Peter Collins.

"The Motor" Copyright

The Royal Automobile Club

Grand Prix d'Europe

Incorporating
THE BRITISH
GRAND PRIX

Silverstone
Saturday,
13th May, 1950

OFFICIAL PROGRAMME   ONE SHILLING

1950
February: Labour Party wins general election in United Kingdom.
May: Stevie Wonder, US singer, is born.
November: President Truman of USA survives assassination attempt by two Puerto Ricans.
• The first passenger lift with automatic doors is installed in the Atlanta Refining Building, Dallas.

1951
February: Kevin Keegan, England international footballer, is born.
July: The worst floods in US history kill 41 people and leave 200,000 homeless in Kansas and Missouri.
October: Winston Churchill becomes Prime Minister of Great Britain for the second time, at the age of 77.
• The first power steering system is introduced in Chrysler Crown Imperial sedans and convertibles.

First for Ferrari. The 4.5-litre unsupercharged Ferrari 375 of Froilán González heads for that historic 1951 British Grand Prix victory ahead of Giuseppe Farina in the Alfa 159.

BRM'S RIGHT ROYAL EMBARRASSMENT

In an embarrassing and rather contrived footnote, the BRM – still unready to race – was demonstrated for a few laps in front of the Royal Family. Still, at least it turned up, which is more than the Ferrari team chose to do. But Maranello was regrouping, laying a firm F1 footing for the future, which meant developing a naturally aspirated machine in addition to its 1.5-litre supercharged V12s which were being driven by Ascari and Villoresi.

Ferrari engineer Aurelio Lampredi was pressing on with a 4.5-litre non-supercharged engine, reflecting the fact that it would be quite possible to beat the Alfas by the simple expedient of making fewer refuelling stops.

Meanwhile, Alfa had the stage to itself. Fangio won at Monaco, Spa and Reims with Farina adding triumphs at Monza and Berne to his Silverstone victory. The granite-like Farina thus became the first official World Champion driver with 30 points ahead of Fangio (27) and Fagioli (24). Four out of the seven races counted towards his title.

The 1951 season would mark the gloriously memorable swansong of the Alfa straight-eights, which were now heavily revised and designated Tipo 159s. Their power output had now been boosted to a remarkable 404 bhp at 9500 rpm, more than twice the claimed 190 bhp with which they had reputedly competed before the war.

However, there was a distinct downside to this performance increment. The Alfas' consumption of alcohol-laced fuel was now down to a punishing 1.5 miles per gallon, which meant that the 70-gallon fuel load represented almost one-fifth of the car's all-up weight on the Grand Prix starting grid.

Alfa and Ferrari stalked each other in the pre-season

non-championship races at the start of 1951, avoiding any direct confrontation. Ascari's new 4.5-litre Ferrari 375 won at Syracuse, Pau and San Remo, but Alfa's record remained intact when it came to the Swiss Grand Prix at Berne. Fangio won immaculately in pouring rain, but Piero Taruffi's Ferrari took second.

Ferrari consolidated its challenge in the French Grand Prix at Reims, a race extended to 77 laps – 374.9 miles – which evened up the balance between the two Italian teams by ensuring that Ferrari would have to stop at least once. Taruffi was unwell and his place in the Ferrari squad alongside Ascari and Villoresi was taken by the tubby, but immensely tough, Argentine driver, José Froilán González.

Despite his build, González had proved himself to be a well-rounded athlete from a young age. A first-rate swimmer, a crack shot and an accomplished cyclist, he had started motor racing in rough-and-ready open road races like his compatriot, Fangio. His father set him up in the trucking business and by 1949 he was ready to join Fangio on their first European tour together.

After an undistinguished first couple of seasons, González made his name in Buenos Aires at the start of the 1951 campaign. Mercedes-Benz dusted down a trio of pre-war two-stage supercharged W163s and shipped them to Argentina for a couple of high-profile Formule Libre races. But González trounced them all in both events driving a supercharged 2-litre Ferrari 166. This was his passport to the works Ferrari squad.

In the event, at Reims in '51 Ascari had to take over González's Ferrari 375 after his own suffered a gearbox failure and he finished second behind Fangio's victorious Alfa.

There was a fascinating footnote to this race. Enzo Ferrari had actually approached the 21-year-old British

rising star, Stirling Moss, to drive at Reims. However, the telegram inviting him to do so arrived at the Moss family home at Tring, in Hertfordshire, after Moss had left for Berlin's Avus circuit, where he was scheduled to race his underpowered HWM.

Moss's manager, Ken Gregory, knew that Stirling was in Berlin, but he didn't know where. As a result, he telephoned the British consul in the German city, getting him out of bed at some ungodly hour, and he searched around to find Moss and give him the message.

Stirling was enormously flattered but felt he had to decline due to his commitment to the HWM team. That said, most believe that HWM team chief John Heath would have released him from his commitment. It says much for Moss's sense of obligation that he did not even ask.

Another non-starter at Reims was the elusive BRM, prompting *Autosport* Editor Gregor Grant to write in the issue of 6 July: 'The failure of the BRM to come to the line at Rheims (sic) was a bitter disappointment to its thousands of well wishers.

'In the opinion of many people D-day for the BRM is 14 July. If the car fails to appear at Silverstone for the British Grand Prix, there is grave danger that the not inconsiderable amount of support gained for the venture will dwindle to such an extent that it will vanish – for evermore!'

The BRM's failure to appear at Reims was also symptomatic of the difficulties presented to race organisers by the haphazard nature of the F1 business. No promoter could be certain from one week to the next who would turn up for which event.

With that in mind, it's perhaps worth noting that on the same day that Fangio won at Reims, a 21-year-old was competing in the 500 cc F3 race at the old Boreham airfield in Essex. In the first heat he diced wheel-to-wheel with future Ferrari Grand Prix winner Peter Collins, only losing the lead on the last lap. In the final he finished third behind Eric Brandon and Alan Brown. His name was Bernard Ecclestone.

PRANCING HORSE AND THE PAMPAS BULL

Finally, at the bleak airfield waste of Silverstone, Ferrari made history on 14 July 1951. González was still in the team for the British Grand Prix and, despite the fact that he was only allocated one of the earlier 1950 12-plug-specification 375s, he stormed round to take pole by over a second from Fangio's Alfa.

The big and heavy Alfa 159s found the relatively short straights at Silverstone insufficient for them to get fully wound up. Funny how perceptions change – today, even with several extra corners, Silverstone is regarded as a relatively high-speed track.

González consolidated his place at the front of the field, but then Fangio began to come back at him. Ferrari and Alfa Romeo were amazingly closely matched on this occasion and, although Fangio got ahead, González – 'a fat, dark little man, bare arms at full length' – clawed his way on to the Alfa's tail and retook the lead on lap 48.

González went on to score a commanding victory, breaking the mould of contemporary Grand Prix racing for good. Enzo Ferrari sent an emotional telegram to Alfa Romeo's Managing Director, saying, 'I still feel for our Alfa the adolescent tenderness of first love.' What an old actor manager he was!

FARINA WAS the first man to win the official Drivers' World Championship in 1950. He was tough and unforgiving to his rivals out on the circuit and his sheer reckless driving on the road – to which Fangio attested many years later – ended with his death at the wheel of a Lotus Cortina near the French town of Chambéry a few months after his 60th birthday in 1966.

The son of one of the founders of the Farina coachbuilding dynasty, 'Nino' was born in Turin in 1906. After qualifying with an engineering doctorate, he began his competition career in an Alfa Romeo 1500 in the Aosta–Grand St Bernard hillclimb. It was not an auspicious debut, ending with a broken shoulder and facial lacerations.

In 1934 Farina scored his first major victory when he drove his Maserati 4CM to victory in the voiturette race which supported the Czech Grand Prix at Brno. In 1938 and '39 he was recruited to drive the Scuderia Ferrari Alfa 158s and his final victory of the pre-war era came at Tripoli in 1940.

He picked up the threads of his career at the end of the war, racing his own Maserati 4CLT in 1947 and '48. He won the '48 Monaco Grand Prix and then rejoined the works Alfa squad in 1950, when he won the British, Swiss and Italian Grands Prix to beat team-mate Fangio to the first drivers' title.

In 1951 he won a single victory in the Belgian GP and he then switched to Ferrari, where he stayed to the end of his career in 1955, a season in which he drove only a handful of races after battling the after-effects of burns suffered in the previous year's Mille Miglia – an event in which he crashed again during his final season.

In 1956 and '57 Farina made a couple of half-hearted attempts on the Indianapolis 500 and he was later Jaguar importer for Italy before becoming a main agent for Alfa Romeo, the marque with which he had achieved such great success.

Farina was popularly credited with having pioneered the arms-stretched driving style so favoured by Stirling Moss. He was also regarded by more than a few as a ruthless and uncompromising driver whose aggressive style would have been more at home in the 1990s than the 1950s.

JUAN MANUEL FANGIO, 1911–95

Bernard Cahier

A moving tribute to the great Argentine driver was written by the late Denis Jenkinson and published in AUTOCOURSE 1995/96. This is an edited version of Jenks's first-person text.

I FIRST SAW Juan Manuel Fangio race in 1949 when he won the Pau Grand Prix on the street circuit round the Basco-Bearnais city in south-west France, within sight of the Pyrenean Mountains. I had gone to Pau not to see a future five-times World Champion, but to race a motor cycle. The Grand Prix was traditionally held on Easter Monday, with motor cycle racing the day before. We practised on Saturday morning and the Grand Prix cars practised in the afternoon, so naturally I stayed behind to watch.

Fangio did not disappoint, for he was known as a natural winner before he left Argentina, being champion in that country's national races with home-made specials and a winner of marathon stock-car events in which he displayed remarkable stamina and endurance. More important was the impression he made on good European Grand Prix drivers of the time when they went out to the winter races in South America. They returned to Europe with the simple words: 'He is good, a future champion.'

Fangio came to Europe with a pretty good CV, but went back to Argentina about half-way through the '49 season with a much better one! He had won his first three Grand Prix races and totalled six victories in all. It later transpired that before he left his hometown of Balcarce for the first time, he had said to his friends, 'I hope for one victory.'

At the end of that season, I wrote in one of my motor racing books: 'To those of us who have been fortunate enough

to see this Fangio in action, the fact that he scored a hat-trick with his first three appearances in European racing does not come as such a surprise, for he really "motor races" with his Maserati in a manner that is a joy to behold.'

The greatest demonstration of his ability to keep calm in times of crisis was during the 1951 Belgian Grand Prix on the very fast Spa-Francorchamps circuit when he was driving for the Alfa Romeo team. Two stops for fuel and tyres were planned and, after setting a new lap record at over 120 mph, Fangio made his first stop while in the lead.

Drama then intervened when the left-rear wheel would not come off its hub. It was fourteen and a half minutes before Fangio rejoined the race, during which time the Alfa mechanics had to remove the entire wheel, hub and rear brake from the driveshaft, take the assembly into the pits, remove the tyre from the

rim, fit and inflate a new tyre, and then fit the whole assembly back on the rear axle.

Throughout this, Fangio stood by, watching but not saying a word to anyone and displaying no outward emotion, cleaning his goggles, cleaning the windscreen of the car and, above all, not making a fuss like some well-known drivers of that and even the current era.

When he rejoined, all hope of regaining the lead was gone, but he was determined to finish the race and protect his lap record if need be, thus preserving the World Championship point earned by fastest lap in those days. His big handicap now was that he could not make his second scheduled tyre change and had to preserve the rubber on his car for the rest of the race as well as going fast enough to be classified as a finisher. He finished ninth and retained his lap record.

LAT Photographic

In later life, when telling us about this incident, he said, 'That day people said how calm I was in the pits as I saw my chances of a win slipping away. It was not me they were slipping away from. I had done everything as it should be done, and made no mistakes. I believe that someone might well get nervous, or at least uneasy, when he has made a mistake. That was not the case with me. I was calm, even though Farina was at the top of the championship table. The second race of the championship was soon to come.'

I watched that drama from the grandstand opposite the Alfa pits, not on a television screen, and joined in the applause and cheers from the spectators as this remarkable man from the Argentine went back into the race.

During his ten years of racing in Europe, Fangio seemed to create at least one magical legend each year. Many racing drivers would have been content to win one World Championship in that time, but Fangio won five. He entered motor races to win; if you won more than anyone else, you were justified in being called World Champion. He said, 'If you are World Champion, it is up to you to always be the best and to show that you are champion.'

The interesting thing about Fangio during that time was the way in which he would return to Argentina as soon as the Grand Prix season was finished. No world publicity tours, no hype and bullshit in those days. If you did not know who the World Champion racing driver was, then you were not paying attention to your sport. He was born in Balcarce in 1911 and Argentina was his home; when he finished his season of work, he went home. He had no desire to live in Monte Carlo, or in a tax haven, or even in a beautiful part of Europe. It was always 'better in Balcarce, where my friends and family are'.

After he retired, Fangio would often return to Europe on business trips, principally connected with his Mercedes-Benz dealership in Buenos Aires. If it could be combined with a visit to a Grand Prix, he would take the opportunity and arrive at Monza, for example, before Saturday practice, often accompanied by his old sparring partner, Froilán González. Ten or fifteen years after his last race his presence was magical and 'FANGIO!' was the word that rippled through the crowd and along the pit lane.

On such occasions he would make a tour of the pits with various officials, pausing to shake hands with old racing friends or acquaintances, or with current drivers like Jim Clark, Graham Hill or Jackie Stewart, and, more particularly, with mechanics and engineers from his Alfa Romeo and Maserati days.

Fangio was Fangio. There was no need to embellish his name. It was powerful enough on its own.

Thankfully for British fans, the BRM V16s duly made their appearance. Reg Parnell finished fifth, Peter Walker seventh 'suffering intense agony from burns in the latter part of the race. No praise can be enough for their unforgettable performance.'

The effusive *Autosport* editorial was supplemented by the words of its Technical Editor, John Bolster, also a BBC commentator. He wrote: 'In conclusion, I would like to thank Reg Parnell for consenting to give me a broadcast interview when he was in great pain from his burns.'

Another interesting footnote. The British GP supporting F3 final was won in commanding style by Stirling Moss. Into tenth place came B.C. Ecclestone. Forty-five years later, anybody wanting a 'broadcast interview' with any F1 driver would be doing so through Mr Ecclestone's Formula One Administration empire. The 'consent' of the driver concerned would be neither here nor there!

Ferrari could now sense a realistic possibility of actually winning that year's World Championship, a prospect further enhanced by Ascari's dominant victory in the first post-war championship German GP, held at the Nürburgring. Having been defeated by Ferrari twice now, Alfa Romeo was very definitely on the run. Ascari and González scored another 1–2 at Monza, where five Tipo 375s were ranged against the supercharged challengers from Milan.

There was now a single round of the World Championship remaining, the race scheduled for Barcelona on 20 October. Somewhat questionably, given what was at stake, Ferrari decided to experiment with Pirelli tyre sizes for this crucial event and the decision to use smaller 16-in. diameter tyres, rather than the 17-in. covers used throughout the year up to that point, caused the 375s to start throwing treads once the race began.

Fangio therefore won the race for Alfa Romeo, with the gallant González second, and Ferrari missed out on his first title crown. With four out of his eight scores counting, Fangio took the first of his five titles with 31 points (net) ahead of Ascari on 25 and González on 24.

ALFA QUITS, F1 TOTTERS

At the end of the season, Alfa Romeo withdrew from racing after failing to secure any financial support from the Italian government. This left race organisers across Europe in an acutely nervous frame of mind, wondering how many fully fledged F1 cars would actually be ready for the start of the 1952 season.

The proof of this pudding was expected to come at the Turin Grand Prix on 6 April, where it was optimistically believed that the BRM team, which had spent much time over the winter testing at Monza, would attend to offer Ferrari some worthwhile opposition. Yet BRM withdrew at the last moment.

Opposite: Fangio and his long-time companion, Beba.

Opposite, bottom: Fangio in the Alfa 159 at the 1951 British Grand Prix, taking another step towards his first World Championship.

The start of the 1951 Spanish Grand Prix along the wide boulevards of the Pedralbes road circuit. The Ferrari 375s of Alberto Ascari (2) and Froilán González (6) lead the field as Fangio's Alfa makes a more leisurely getaway.

RACING FOR BRITAIN: THE BRM

THE PASSION displayed by Raymond Mays for the ERA project in the 1930s found fresh focus in the post-war years with his plan to design and build a state-of-the-art British national Grand Prix car in order to carry the prestige of British industry to the international race tracks of the world.

Taken at face value, this was an admirable ambition. Yet the BRM project would be dogged by chaotic management, inept engineering and poor quality control almost from the word go. It may have been an idea which captured the imagination of the public, but its actual execution left a great deal to be desired. The concept was just too complicated for the technology available.

Mays persuaded leading figures in British industry to form the British Motor Racing Research Trust, designed not only to fund the BRM but also to help with the sourcing of high-technology components and manufacturing techniques.

The 1.5-litre centrifugally supercharged BRM V16 was an ambitious project indeed. Demonstrated at the 1950 British Grand Prix, the car suffered the embarrassment of breaking its driveshafts on the starting grid for that year's International Trophy race – much to the resigned dismay of its driver, the great Raymond Sommer – and, remarkably, only once finished in the World Championship points, when Reg Parnell was placed fifth in the 1951 British GP.

Towards the end of 1951, rising star Stirling Moss drove the V16 and, while impressed with the sheer, raw power, identified a huge number of shortcomings.

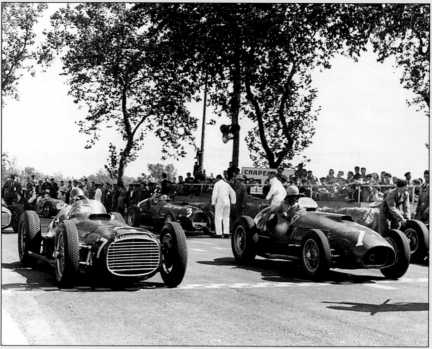

Bernard Cahier

In 1987, Moss would tell author and historian Doug Nye: 'It was a classic example of a small concern convincing itself it was Mercedes-Benz and going into the high-technology racing car business deeper than either its competence or finances would allow.'

While conceding that the BRM engine was a 'fantastic device' he was less complimentary about other aspects of the car.

'Its chassis and suspension design was not really capable of putting its power through to the ground,' he said. 'Its steering was simply dreadful and its cramped-up, short-arm driving position was straight out of the ark . . . [and] its management was a shambles.'

In failing to turn out for the 1952 Turin

Grand Prix, despite an intensive programme of winter testing at Monza, the BRM management effectively scuppered the 4.5-litre/1.5-litre supercharged F1 regulations. It was also a massive own-goal. The star-struck Raymond Mays was more interested in letting Fangio test the car on an airfield in Lincolnshire than in racing in Turin. It was the story of BRM's life up to that point.

The BMRR Trust was unwieldy and difficult to steer. By the end of 1950 a big effort had been made to trim its membership and an executive council was established which consisted of Tony Vandervell, Alfred Owen and Bernard Scott of Lucas in addition to Raymond Mays and Peter Berthon. Soon afterwards,

Vandervell walked out to start his own F1 project. Eventually the entire BRM programme was purchased by the Owen Organisation under its patriarchal Chairman, Alfred – later to become Sir Alfred – Owen.

It would take another decade, but eventually BRM would win the World Championship. That it survived at all was down to Sir Alfred Owen's commitment, loyalty and extraordinarily patient way with people.

The Owen Organisation was one of the country's most diverse and wide-ranging engineering conglomerates. It had been founded by Alfred Owen's hard-working and diligent father, Ernest, in partnership with J.T. Rubery, back in 1893, and the group's headquarters were at Darlaston in Shropshire.

Ernest Owen died at the relatively early age of 61 and left a fortune in excess of £1 million, which, thanks to some shrewd and careful financial husbandry, enabled the group he had founded to ride out the economic slump which followed the First World War. This ensured that his sons, Ernest and Alfred, and his daughter, Jean, would inherit a thriving industrial empire.

Jean and her husband, Louis Stanley, would later run BRM after Sir Alfred Owen was sidelined due to the effects of a stroke in 1969. Stanley was a larger-than-life personality who was no fool. Among his many observations in connection with the team, he once observed that 'had the BRM project coincided with his [Ernest Owen Senior's] heyday, success would have come twice as quickly at half the price'.

THE SAVIOUR OF THE BRM

ALFRED OWEN inherited his father's astuteness and enthusiasm, also showing himself to be a kind and warm-hearted man. Perhaps he indulged his employees too much and that was why it took until 1962 for BRM to win the World Championship with Graham Hill.

In fact, by the start of that season, even Sir Alfred's patience was wearing thin. He informed the team management that unless they won at least two Grands Prix in 1962 they would be closed down. Hill duly obliged with a first win in the Dutch Grand Prix at Zandvoort, scene of Jo Bonnier's first-ever BRM victory three years earlier, after which designer Tony Rudd felt sufficiently confident about the future to pen a note to Sir Alfred raising the subject of plans for 1963.

Back came a letter reminding Rudd that his chairman had meant what he said. Hill subsequently ensured the team's future with wins at the German Grand Prix at the Nürburgring and the South African

race at East London, where he clinched the title.

Thus was Sir Alfred Owen's confidence and support for BRM vindicated at long last. Louis Stanley would later write: 'He showed unbelievable patience, sometimes to the point of weakness, and there were occasions where stern actions would have produced results. But he was reluctant to upset the ties of friendship.'

Reg Parnell's son, Tim, who rose to take over the job of BRM team manager

in 1969, described Sir Alfred as 'quite the most amazing and remarkable man I have ever met in my life'.

He continued: 'He was the chairman of over 1000 subsidiary companies all round the world, yet he also found time to be a committed Methodist lay preacher and a great family man, and worked on many public boards and charities such as Dr Barnardo's and the YMCA. The list was incredible.

'He had an army of secretaries keeping tabs on his appointments and work programme, which used up every minute

of his day. People talk about workload, but, my goodness, he was absolutely unbelievable. He was an extremely nice man and, of course, my family knew him well from the time my father drove for the team.

'Then in the mid-1960s I managed the BRM Tasman team for three consecutive years and Reg Parnell Racing ran what was effectively a "B" team for the BRM factory with people like Richard Attwood, Piers Courage and Chris Irwin driving. But if I ever had to see Sir Alfred on business, it was usually a few moments squeezed into the back of a taxi while he was en route between board meetings . . .'

Sir Alfred Owen died on 29 October 1975. That meant he was spared the embarrassing death throes of the BRM team a couple of seasons later. Yet without his foresight and determination a whole chapter of British motor racing history would have ended in 1952. And the BRM would have been nothing more than a brief footnote in post-war F1 history.

LAT Photographic

It had been the story of the BRM's life ever since the start of the official World Championship. Never confident enough to go head-to-head with Alfa and Ferrari, the BRM spent much of its career in minor-league club races. Take the rain-soaked Goodwood meeting in September 1950 as an example. The car was entered for Reg Parnell to drive and you might have been forgiven for imagining that the crowd would dismiss its appearance with derisive laughter. Far from it.

There was admirably little scepticism among the race fans in those days and the sodden crowds cheered stoically as Parnell won the Woodcote Cup race by 13 seconds from Prince Bira's Maserati.

Supporting the BRM, and its originator, Raymond Mays, was regarded as a matter of faith by some sections of the media and those who scraped the surface of the project to even hint that the whole thing was a disgraceful failure were regarded rather sniffily as being unpatriotic.

It was certainly a sign of the times that Movietone News devoted a considerable amount of coverage to Parnell's Goodwood success in these dank conditions, the flickering newsreel supported by a suitably upbeat commentary.

Yet if the Goodwood crowds really longed for a taste of sophisticated international competition, they certainly got it in 1951 when the September international meeting saw reigning World Champion Giuseppe Farina turn out to drive one of the legendary supercharged 1.5-litre Alfa Romeo 159s. Against makeweight opposition, it was not surprising that Farina won all thee of his races that afternoon, duly receiving the *Daily Graphic* trophy from the Duchess of Richmond and Gordon.

The BRM's failure to perform on an international stage could be viewed as the last straw for motor racing's governing body, the Commission Sportive Internationale (CSI), the sporting arm of the FIA. The decision was taken to hold the official 1952 and '53 World Championships under the 2-litre Formula 2 regulations, leaving Ferrari's Tipo 375s along with the supercharged BRMs to justify their existence with outings in a handful of F1 non-championship events over the next couple of seasons.

In October 1952, the paddock at Goodwood echoed to the raucous crackle of BRM's V16 engines yet again as the *Daily Graphic* International meeting was held for a mixed bag of Formula 1 cars.

The tubby Argentine driver, Froilán González, a great favourite with British fans since scoring Ferrari's first-ever World Championship Grand Prix victory at Silverstone the previous year, won both the Woodcote Cup and the Goodwood Trophy, heading the sister BRMs of Reg Parnell and Ken Wharton across the line in the latter event.

'It was most impressive, but hardly epoch-making,' noted *Autosport*'s founder-Editor, Gregor Grant, referring to the fact that the BRMs were now redundant.

FERRARI'S LONG-TERM PLANNING

Ferrari, of course, had been prepared for every eventuality. Not only had he developed his Grand Prix cars assiduously, but in the 1951 non-championship Bari Grand Prix Piero Taruffi had appeared behind the wheel of a 2490 cc four-cylinder Ferrari. This was followed up by a 2-litre version in time for the Modena Grand Prix, so it was clear

that the Commendatore had things covered for the F2 World Championships in 1952 and '53 as well as having an engine which he could use for the planned 2.5-litre F1 regulations which would kick in at the start of 1954.

Aurelio Lampredi was the man behind these large-capacity four-cylinder engines. Although he knew they would have a longer stroke and a bigger piston area than a corresponding V12, he was more concerned about better torque characteristics and the overall lightness of the unit. In his estimation, a reduction in total engine weight from 400 to 348 lb would equate to an increase in power-to-weight ratio of around 15 per cent.

This new Ferrari was dubbed the Tipo 500 – reflecting its individual cylinder capacity. It would perform sterling service across two action-packed international seasons, during which the list of non-championship races it contested far exceeded the World Championship qualifying rounds. It would also represent the heyday of the brilliant Alberto Ascari, who did far more races than simply the title qualifiers.

Ranged against the Ferraris in 1952 were the new Colombo-designed six-cylinder Maserati A6GCMs to be driven by Fangio, González and Felice Bonetto plus the six-cylinder French Gordinis handled by Robert Manzon and Jean Behra.

Four major non-title races took place on the European

calendar prior to the Swiss GP at Bremgarten which opened the World Championship contest. Three of these events fell to Ascari. The brilliant Italian headed a Maranello 1–2–3 at Syracuse ahead of Taruffi and Farina, while at Pau he led French privateer Louis Rosier's Ferrari across the finishing line.

Next up, Ascari survived to win the Marseilles GP on the Parc Borely circuit, a race notable for Farina's reluctance to acknowledge Ascari's status as team leader. Only when Farina spun off shortly before the finish, lightly damaging his car against the straw bales, could Ascari be certain of victory.

The Swiss Grand Prix saw another works Ferrari demonstration with Farina, Taruffi and André Simon on the driving strength as Ascari was away at Indianapolis and Villoresi convalescing following a road accident. Farina led initially before being sidelined by magneto failure, after which Taruffi had a relatively easy run to victory.

Opposite: Fangio in the BRM V16 at Albi in 1953, flanked by Alberto Ascari in the last derivative of the 4.5-litre Ferrari 375.

LAT Photographic

Piero Taruffi tries to squeeze his Ferrari inside Jean Behra's Gordini at the cobbled Nouveau Monde hairpin during the 1952 French Grand Prix at Rouen-les-Essarts.

Opposite: Alfred – later Sir Alfred – Owen, the saviour of Britain's 'national racing car'.

Right: Familiar vista. The plunge down to Eau Rouge at Spa-Francorchamps has changed very little since the Ferrari 500s of Alberto Ascari and Giuseppe Farina led the pack down the hill on the opening lap of the 1952 Belgian Grand Prix.

Below right: Stirling Moss in the unsuccessful ERA G-type, British Grand Prix, 1952.

Below far right: Mike Hawthorn on his way to an epic fourth place in the 1952 Belgian GP in his Cooper-Bristol.

Bottom: Ascari takes the chequered flag after another dominant performance in the '52 Belgian Grand Prix.

On 8 June, the works 500s appeared at the Autodrome Grand Prix at Monza, sporting a small number of detailed improvements, including revised inlet trumpets and a longer nose section.

This race also saw the debut of the new Maseratis driven by Fangio, González and Bonetto, but Ferrari's rivals received a shattering setback in the first of the event's two 35-lap heats. The reigning World Champion had the previous day competed in the Ulster Trophy at Dundrod with the largely redundant V16 BRM, then missed a lift in Prince Bira's aeroplane and been forced into a gruelling overnight drive from Paris to Monza in order to compete with the Maserati.

Exhausted, Fangio started from the back of the grid without having practised, then crashed badly on the second lap. He fractured a vertebra in his neck. He was invalided out for the rest of the season and his next Grand Prix success would not occur until Monza the following year, when he dodged through a last-corner pile-up to win the Italian GP for Maserati.

The 1952 season also saw the French Gordini marque deliver a rare knock-out blow to Ferrari in the non-title Reims Grand Prix. In the hands of Behra, the blue car out-ran Ascari in highly impressive style, the Italian eventually being forced into the pits with overheating problems after slipstreaming the French machine too closely.

Inevitably, many detractors were quick to suggest that Behra might actually have been using an engine larger in capacity than the regulation 2 litres. Perish the thought! Farina finished second while Ascari sprinted back to third after taking over Villoresi's car.

Ascari won the 1952 Drivers' World Championship with 36 points (net), 12 ahead of Farina. The four best scores from the eight races (including Indianapolis)

counted. He went on to retain the title the following year with 34.5 points (net) ahead of Fangio on 27.5. A race in Argentina was added to the calendar but, once again, only the four best scores counted. However, the real point about Ascari was the fact that he won nine straight *Grandes Epreuves* between the 1952 and '53 Belgian Grands Prix. It was quite an achievement.

MOSS AND HAWTHORN: FLYING THE FLAG FOR BRITAIN

British drivers began to appear with distinction on the World Championship stage at this time. The most famous were Stirling Moss and Mike Hawthorn, who carved their respective paths to the upper echelons of motor sport by two distinctly different routes.

Stirling's father, Alfred, was a prosperous dentist and had raced at Indianapolis as a keen amateur in 1925, while Hawthorn's father, Leslie, moved from Yorkshire to Farnham, where he bought a car repair and sales business, in the 1930s in order to be closer to Brooklands for his motor cycle racing.

Moss started racing in 1948, rising to prominence thanks to his exploits in the closely contested 500 cc F3 category. For his part, Hawthorn started two years later, driving a couple of Riley sports cars owned by his father. Mike hit the headlines in 1952 when a family friend bought him a Cooper-Bristol F2 car. It was his passport to the Big Time.

Mike rocked the establishment on its heels by planting his Cooper-Bristol on the front row of the grid for the first World Championship Dutch GP to be held at Zandvoort. There was no way he could stay with the Ferraris once the race started, even on what people

Bottom: Ferrari's F1 driver line-up for the 1953 season. From the left, Giuseppe Farina, Alberto Ascari, Mike Hawthorn and Luigi Villoresi.

Right: Maurice Trintignant limps his Gordini towards the pits prior to his retirement from the 1953 French Grand Prix at Reims with transmission failure.

Below right: Peter Collins was classified a distant 13th in the '53 French GP in this HWM.

Below: Crouching over the wheel of his Maserati, Froilán González heads for third place behind the Hawthorn/Fangio battle, Reims, 1953.

Photos: Bernard Cahier

regarded as a medium-speed circuit at the time, but he finished fourth, just as he had done earlier in Belgium.

Before the end of the '52 season, Ferrari invited Hawthorn for a test drive. This was scheduled to take the shape of an entry in the non-championship Modena Grand Prix, but Mike rather blotted his copybook by rolling his Cooper-Bristol – which had been brought along for fellow-Brit Roy Salvadori to drive – during an unplanned test run.

Enzo Ferrari was won over as much by Mike's open, easy-going personality as by his talent at the wheel and made it clear that this little incident wasn't going to stand between Hawthorn and a full-time Ferrari Grand Prix drive.

For the 1953 season, the Ferrari 500's power output was boosted to around 180 bhp. Hawthorn had a shaky start to the year, with Ascari again doing the lion's share of the winning, but Mike's great day finally came in the 1953 French Grand Prix at Reims. Yet Hawthorn, and the rest of the Ferrari team, very nearly failed to start at all.

The Grand Prix was preceded by a 12-hour sports car race, from which the 4.5-litre Ferrari of Umberto Maglioli and Piero Carini was unfortunately withdrawn after the organisers announced that no more times would be recorded for it following an apparent rule infringement. Enzo Ferrari responded by threatening to withdraw his cars from the Grand Prix but the cracks arising from this dispute were eventually papered over and the Ferrari 500s duly took up their positions on the grid.

Froilán González set a cracking pace in the opening stages of the race, but he was running a light fuel load and would have to stop for a top-up. Fangio and Hawthorn were wheel-to-wheel for second place, and when González duly made his scheduled stop after 30 laps he just failed to resume ahead of the battling duo.

From then on it was a straight fight between the Argentine driver and the young Englishman, each crouched low down behind his windscreen, almost willing the last ounce of speed from his car. It was clear that the issue would only be sorted out on the final lap and Hawthorn duly timed everything perfectly, slipping through on the inside of the final corner as Fangio briefly struggled to get a gear. Hawthorn duly won what *Autosport* magazine billed as 'the race of the century' by just a single second.

It is fair to say that the Reims win was the making of Hawthorn, but he had to live on that reputation for much of his career. F1 success would come his way infrequently. In fact, his six-year Grand Prix career netted only three victories, including just one – in the 1958 French Grand Prix – during his World Championship year.

Incidentally, Hawthorn's 1958 World Championship success would prompt Vanwall driver Tony Brooks to remark – very many years later – that he 'never felt quite the same about the World Championship scoring system given that in 1958 Stirling [Moss] won four races, I won three and Mike won one – and the championship!' Many people could well understand his point.

Moss, meanwhile, graduated to F1 via HWM, a determined, grossly underfinanced team which was run by John Heath and George Abecassis from their business, HW Motors, in Walton-on-Thames.

In 1950 Moss first drove their dual sports/single-seater car, fitted with an underpowered 2-litre Alta engine which developed around 140 bhp at 5500 rpm. With these cars he raced across the Continent in a wide variety of events

1952
February: King George VI dies after a long illness.
July: Eva Perón, Argentine political campaigner, dies.
September: Christopher Reeve, US actor, is born.
• The first car safety belts are manufactured in the USA.

1953
January: The coasts of Britain and the Netherlands are flooded, killing over 2000 people.
March: The first low-cost disposable pen, the Bic ballpoint, goes on sale.
May: Mount Everest is conquered for the first time by the New Zealand mountaineer, Edmund Hillary, and his guide, Tenzing Norgay.
June: Queen Elizabeth II is crowned in London's Westminster Abbey.

LAT Photographic

On the map. Mike Hawthorn celebrates his emergence as a top-line Grand Prix driver after that momentous Reims victory.

which really enabled him to get to grips with road racing in the raw rather than simply chasing round the straw bales on abandoned aerodromes, which was very much the style of racing available to post-war British competitors.

That year Moss was fortunate to survive a big shunt at Naples, when a brush with a slower car burst one of the HWM's tyres. In the ensuing accident Stirling broke his knee and lost two teeth, but he still had sufficient wit to leap from the car as best he could at the first opportunity.

In 1951 HWM produced a pukka F2 car in which Stirling took part in his first World Championship GP at Bremgarten; he then contested the same race the following year, followed by the Belgian, British and Dutch races with an uncompetitive ERA. He then had two outings in a Connaught and three in a Cooper-Alta in 1953 before getting his big break with a private Maserati 250F in 1954.

Of course, the most celebrated British Formula 1 effort of the 1950s would eventually gel in the form of Tony Vandervell's magnificent Vanwalls, which would win the first official Constructors' World Championship in 1958. The BRM struggled on, dogged with management and technical problems, only to come to full flower after the 2.5-litre era had come to an end. Yet there was another important British F1 project in the mid-1950s which achieved a quite remarkable amount with very limited resources.

CONNNAUGHT'S DRIVING AMBITION

The Connaught grew from modest roots shortly after the war when Rodney Clarke set up business in a small garage on the Portsmouth Road at Send, a few miles behind Guildford. At that time his speciality was the preparation of Bugattis and he made the acquaintance of Kenneth McAlpine, heir to the construction family.

McAlpine was a keen amateur competitor at the wheel of a Maserati but was anxious to expand his involvement in the sport and asked Clarke whether he would be interested in building him a car.

Clarke agreed to the proposal and came up with the design for a two-seater sports car using a 1.7-litre Lea Francis engine which developed 98 bhp at 5500 rpm. The Connaught L3 put the company's name on the map and a total of 24 such cars were built by the end of 1953. But Clarke and McAlpine quickly developed a taste for more ambitious projects and produced their first Formula 2 Connaught 2-litre as early as 1950; it made its race debut at the Castle Combe meeting in October that year, McAlpine finishing a strong second in one of the ten-lap events behind rising star Stirling Moss in an HWM.

Although the main purpose of Connaught Engineering was to provide Kenneth McAlpine with racing cars – reasonable enough, since he had underwritten the whole project – it was also intended to produce Formula 2 cars for sale to private owners. In 1951, a total of nine such cars were sold and over the next couple of seasons the Connaughts tended to confine their racing activities to British domestic events while the rival HWMs and Cooper-Bristols took the opportunity to race abroad.

In 1952 and '53, of course, the World Championship was staged for 2-litre Formula 2 cars and in the '52 British Grand Prix at Silverstone privateer Dennis Poore's Connaught was at one point holding down third place behind the Ferrari 500s of Alberto Ascari and Piero Taruffi. Unfortunately, the need for an extra pit stop dropped him back behind Mike Hawthorn's Cooper-Bristol into fourth place, but the press gave favourable mention to the Connaught as a credible rival to both the Cooper-Bristols and the HWM team, which at that time also enjoyed the services of another rising star in Peter Collins.

The early 1950s were certainly a hectic and busy time for the young British drivers. Moss also found himself invited to drive a Ferrari, at Bari in 1951, where he was due to appear in the 2.5-litre-engined Tipo 500 which was effectively a technical rehearsal for the 1954 F1 World Championship regulations. Unfortunately, after making the trip, he found that he had been replaced without warning by Taruffi. Stirling was furious, and never seriously spoke to Ferrari again for another ten years.

ENZO FERRARI: F1'S LAST LONER

WHEN ENZO FERRARI died at the age of 89 in August 1988, he had not been present to see one of his own cars racing for almost 31 years.

After the death of his first son, Dino, Ferrari vowed never to attend another race. But he made an exception for the 1957 Modena event as it marked the debut of the Dino 246s, named in memory of his son, who had collaborated in their design with the respected former Lancia technician, Vittorio Jano.

For the remaining years of his life, the Old Man lived in the shadow of that grief, his Maranello office regarded by many as a shrine to his much-missed offspring. Yet for many years he would turn up at Monza for final practice prior to the Italian Grand Prix. But never the race.

In the space of 40 years Enzo Ferrari transformed a tiny business making specialist sports cars into one of the most famous brand names in the world. He

achieved this not only by building some of the most aesthetically beautiful and successful racing cars ever seen, but also by virtue of the continuity represented by the distinctive Prancing Horse motif, which had originally been presented to him by the parents of the famous Italian First World War fighter pilot, Francesco Barracca.

The Ferrari image has magical connections back to the pioneering days of motor racing. Ferrari himself ran what amounted to the factory Alfa Romeo team in the 1930s.

In his heyday he was the man in absolute charge. Team managers would often shudder at the prospect of having to telephone him with news of the practice times, particularly when the red cars had done badly. More than one simply told him the incorrect times, simply for a peaceful life.

This dictatorial tone was part of the man's compelling attraction. As the 1950s turned into the 1960s and rival Italian

makes faltered, so Ferrari increasingly became regarded as Italy's international flag bearer on the sporting scene. When Ferrari won, the whole of Italy cheered. When it failed, which it did often, the country was plunged into gloom.

Enzo Ferrari also had an illegitimate son, Piero Lardi, who was born just after the war. Only after Dino's mother, Laura, died in 1978 was Piero formally acknowledged by the Old Man, although he had been working in the company for many years. By the late 1970s he was fully integrated into the senior management with 'Piero Lardi Ferrari' on his office door at Maranello.

Having rebuffed an approach from Ford to buy his company in 1963, six years later Enzo Ferrari was on his financial knees. Fiat Chairman Gianni Agnelli stepped in with a rescue package, shrewdly judging how much the national car company would benefit from an association with what had become a national institution.

In essence, the deal was that Fiat would control the road car business while Enzo Ferrari would continue to have complete control over the racing cars until the day he died. In the mid-1970s Ferrari had its most sustained period of F1 success when Niki Lauda won the Drivers' World Championship in 1975 and '77 while the team took a hat-trick of Constructors' Championships between those two years.

The man who masterminded the revival was Luca di Montezemolo, then a young lawyer, now President of arguably the most famous car company of all. Yet no matter how much Ferrari tries to re-invent itself, it can never be the same.

The heritage remains to this day, but by 1999 there was a raw, almost desperate, urgency about the need to win. Enzo Ferrari always liked winning. Even though his cars were perhaps not as successful as he might have liked to recall.

Top: Jean Behra lasted just seven laps of the 1953 German Grand Prix at the Nürburgring before his Gordini's gearbox broke.

Above: Juan Manuel Fangio's second-placed Maserati in the 1953 French Grand Prix at Reims.

Right: Greater than Fangio? Alberto Ascari celebrates his victory in the '53 German Grand Prix.

Photos: Bernard Cahier

THE 2.5-LITRE FORMULA

THE START of the 1954 season brought with it the new 2.5-litre F1 regulations which opened the doors on one of the most fascinating and diverse periods in Grand Prix racing history. By the time the formula came to an end after the final race of 1960, the sport's senior category would have been revolutionised.

Of the front-running teams in existence at the start of 1954, only Ferrari would endure to the end of this period. Maserati, Mercedes-Benz, Vanwall, Connaught and Gordini would bow off the stage to be replaced by the likes of Cooper and Lotus, who would usher in the central-engined revolution.

On the face of it, Ferrari started the new era in a very strong position, having tested its new 2.5-litre four-cylinder engine for more than two years. With a driver line-up of Hawthorn, Farina, González (back from Maserati) and Maglioli, the team initially relied on its 1953 Tipo 500 chassis powered by the new 94 x 90 mm engine directly derived from its F2 unit.

This evolutionary design was dubbed the 625 and the team also had a totally new machine, the 553 'Squalo' with distinctive side tanks, but this would not make its debut until the Syracuse GP in Sicily during April.

However, there were definitely worries on the horizon for the Ferrari team in the form of the planned Mercedes-Benz F1 return and the much-anticipated Lancia Grand Prix effort. As if that was not enough, Fangio, who had been signed to lead the Mercedes team, was loaned to Maserati for the opening race of the year and duly won the Argentine Grand Prix.

FANGIO SWITCHES HORSES MIDSTREAM

Fangio's mount on that occasion was the elegant Maserati 250F. If any single car came to represent the 2.5-litre Grand Prix formula, it was surely this well-balanced and versatile machine which carried the Trident of Bologna – the Italian city's emblem – as its badge.

Never mind the fact that in the late 1930s the company had been taken over by Adolfo Orsi and moved to Modena. The name, image and reputation survived this reorganisation. The surviving Maserati brothers – Ernesto, Bindo and Ettore – were retained as designers and engineers until 1947, when they left to start their own new company, OSCA, back in Bologna.

Under the stewardship of Adolfo Orsi's son, Omer, Maserati thrived into the 1950s. The 250F was a direct descendant of the A6GCM in which Fangio had dodged through to win the 1953 Italian Grand Prix at Monza. Its six-cylinder engine had a bore and stroke of 84 x 75 mm and, running on a mix of methanol and benzol, developed 240 bhp at 7400 rpm.

Fangio used the works 250F to win the 1954 Belgian GP at Spa-Francorchamps ahead of Maurice Trintignant's Ferrari 500 and the private Maserati 250F driven by Stirling Moss. When Mercedes announced its return to F1 for the 1954 season, Moss's manager had contacted the German company's racing manager, Alfred Neubauer, to see if there was any chance of securing Stirling a drive alongside Fangio.

Neubauer wisely replied that Moss should get some experience in a really powerful F1 car, with the result that his father, Alfred, agreed to purchase a Maserati 250F with the aid of sponsorship from the Shell Mex & BP fuel and lubricants firm, for whom Stirling was contracted to drive.

After the Belgian race, Maserati found itself short of top-calibre drivers now that Fangio was due to make his debut for the emergent Mercedes-Benz team in the French GP at Reims, round three of the World Championship. However, Maserati were certainly impressed by Moss's progress and began to offer tacit factory support, suggesting that he could rev his car up to 8000 rpm and if the engine broke they would replace it free of charge.

This was a fantastic offer for the English privateer, who had, up to then, been driving with something in reserve. Later in the season Moss would become an official factory entry with his private car, being promoted to number one driver on the understanding that, if his own 250F was not ready on schedule for any race, then he would be loaned a works car.

Moss made full use of this unexpected promotion and, although he failed to score any victories, he was well in charge of the Italian Grand Prix until mechanical failure intervened. By the end of the 1954 season, both he and Mercedes-Benz were ready for each other.

By then, of course, the Mercedes W196 had rewritten the parameters of contemporary F1 car design. Although the Mercedes factory had been razed to the ground by Allied bombing during the Second World War, West Germany's economic resurgence in the early 1950s continued at a remarkable rate and nothing symbolised that recovery more graphically than the sight of three sleek 'Silver Arrows' lined up in front of the pits for the 1954 French Grand Prix.

Ranged against the Ferrari 625s and Maserati 250Fs, the Mercedes W196 was an extremely sophisticated and technically advanced machine, perhaps matched only by the Lancia D50, which was at the time still undergoing a protracted development phase and would not make its race debut until the end of that season.

The Mercedes was built round an advanced tubular spaceframe, which carried an in-line eight-cylinder engine that incorporated desmodromic valvegear and was canted over at a 70-degree angle to keep the car's profile as low as possible. The car, designed by a team under

Opposite page: Two ways to win. Top: Fangio in the distinctive Mercedes-Benz W196 streamliner on the car's debut in the 1954 French Grand Prix, where he finished feet ahead of team-mate Karl Kling. Bottom: The Argentine ace in the more conventional open-wheeled version, winning that same year's Swiss Grand Prix at Bremgarten.

The cars set off on their first 14-mile lap of the Nürburgring at the start of the 1954 German Grand Prix.

the direction of Professor Fritz Nallinger, Dr Lorenscheid and brilliant engineer Rudolf Uhlenhaut, featured inboard drum brakes and Bosch fuel injection and, with a capacity of 2496 cc, developed 260 bhp at 8500 rpm as a starting point on what was originally anticipated to be a five-year development programme which would see the W196 developing more than 300 bhp by the end of 1958.

Fangio was the only world-class driver in the Mercedes line-up, which also included Karl Kling and Hans Herrmann. Moreover, time has tended to throw many people's memories into soft focus and the W196s were not quite the all-conquering titans they were expected to be, at least not as far as the 1954 season was concerned.

MERCEDES SETS NEW F1 BENCHMARK

Fangio and Kling finished 1–2 at Reims using cars fitted with streamlined all-enveloping bodywork, but this configuration was certainly not the ideal choice for Silverstone, where concrete-filled oil drums delineated the inside of the corners.

As a result, Fangio could only struggle home fourth, his car's silver bodywork carrying ungainly dents by the time he took the chequered flag, in a race won by Froilán González's four-cylinder Ferrari 625, the uprated version of the type 500 F2 car which had carried Alberto Ascari to the previous two World Championship titles.

For Mercedes's home race at the Nürburgring, Fangio was allotted a W196 prepared to conventional open-wheeled specification. He won this race in commanding style but with a heavy heart. During practice his young friend and compatriot, Onofré Marimón, had crashed his Maserati 250F at Wehrseifen and suffered fatal injuries. González was so distraught that Mike Hawthorn had to take over his Ferrari to finish the race second behind Fangio.

At Monza, Fangio again scraped home the winner in the W196 streamliner, but not before two key rivals had fallen by the wayside. The Ferrari team was determined to do well on its home turf and negotiated for Alberto Ascari to be released from his Lancia contract for this specific event. The Italian driver had been sitting around

Photos: Bernard Cahier

Left: Dramatic contrast.
Amédée Gordini – a long-time
friend of photographer Bernard
Cahier – stands (foreground)
amidst his little French
challengers in the pit lane at
Monza. Beyond, the Mercedes
W196 streamliners wait for
battle to commence.

Above: Alberto Ascari in the exquisitely engineered Lancia D50 during the 1955 Monaco Grand Prix, less than a week before his death.

Right: 'How much for Alberto?' Mercedes team manager Alfred Neubauer gets out his wallet while Ascari (centre) grins broadly and Lancia D50 designer Vittorio Jano (left) looks smugly confident.

for much of the year vainly waiting for the new high-tech Lancia D50 to be readied and now jumped at the chance of displaying his legendary skills.

Driving brilliantly in a Ferrari 625 powered by the later type 553 'Super Squalo' engine, Ascari shook himself free of Fangio and pulled out a nine-second lead before a valve broke. That let Stirling Moss through into the lead in his Maserati, which then suffered a fractured oil pipe, allowing the Merc through to win ahead of Mike Hawthorn's Ferrari.

Hawthorn then gave the Italian team a win in the Spanish GP at Barcelona's Pedralbes circuit, followed home by Luigi Musso's Maserati and Fangio in the Mercedes. It was sufficient to clinch Fangio's second World Championship crown with 42 points (net) ahead of González (25) and Hawthorn (24.5). Five scores out of nine counted.

Hawthorn would remember that race with particular satisfaction. After seeing off an early challenge from privateer Harry Schell's Maserati, he recalled: 'The Squalo was going beautifully, while the Mercedes was giving trouble and Fangio was struggling on, covered in oil and black dust . . . The pit signalled each lap to tell me what the gap was between Fangio and I, but towards the end the Mercedes began to trail a smokescreen and was beaten into second place by Musso's Maserati.'

LANCIA'S LOST CLASSIC

For 1955 Moss duly gained his promotion to the Mercedes works team, but that season the German manufacturer was scheduled to face possibly its most formidable opposition in the form of Lancia's new D50 in the hands of Ascari. It didn't show in the race results, but on the car's debut in the '54 Spanish GP Ascari was pulling away at two seconds a lap before retiring with what was officially described as clutch trouble.

Respected journalist Denis Jenkinson wrote, 'The whole conception of the Lancia Grand Prix car was one of normal Grand Prix design but with great attention paid to detail, excellent finish on the mechanical parts and a keen eye to weight saving.'

The original concept had been approved in principle back in 1953 by Gianni Lancia, after which he left his chief designer, Vittorio Jano, to get on with the project. After a year of speculation the Lancia D50 finally turned out to do battle in the 1954 Spanish GP, where Ascari was absolutely bursting to show Fangio what he was *really* up against.

It was about time. The prototype D50 had first turned a wheel within the courtyard of Lancia's competitions department on Turin's Via Caraglio on 8 February 1954. Just over two weeks earlier Ascari and Villoresi had signed their contracts but, while the car was briefly tested at the Caselle airport in Turin during mid-February, it took another eight months before it was 'signed off' ready to race.

The Lancia D50 was striking indeed. It was powered by a 73.6 x 73.1 mm, 2487 cc, twin-overhead-camshaft 90-degree V8 engine, itself mounted at an angle of 12 degrees within the chassis with the propeller shaft running to the left alongside the driver's seat in order to keep the overall package as low as possible.

The engine itself was a semi-stressed unit, in effect doubling for the upper tube of what would otherwise have been a complete spaceframe chassis, and the car

was distinguished by long pannier fuel tanks fitted between the wheels, the right-hand tank containing exclusively fuel and the left-hand one including an oil cooler towards the front.

Weighing in at 1367 lb (620 kg), the Lancia D50 was one of the lightest Grand Prix cars of its era. The Mercedes W196 tipped the scales at 1587 lb (720 kg) in aerodynamic trim and 1521 lb (690 kg) in open-wheeled form, while the Ferrari 625 weighed in at 1433 lb (650 kg), the 553 'Squalo' at just over 1300 lb (590 kg) and the Maserati 250F at 1389 lb (630 kg).

The history of Mercedes's 1954 'domination' might have been very different had Ascari been able to debut the car at Reims on the same day as the W196, but it was not until Ascari lapped Monza during testing a full three seconds faster than Fangio's best in the Mercedes streamliner that Gianni Lancia gave the green light for its racing debut.

Yet in 1955, Ferrari would inherit the superb D50s when Gianni Lancia's team hit the financial rocks shortly after Alberto Ascari's untimely death in May of that year.

By the time of this disaster, the writing seemed very clearly on the wall for Ferrari. In addition to Moss joining Mercedes, Hawthorn opted to switch to the British-based Vanwall team, reasoning that such a move would enable him to spend more time concentrating on his family's garage business in Farnham, Surrey, in the wake of his father Leslie's death in a road accident the previous year.

Ferrari began the 1955 season in a precarious state, using the two-year-old, now-coil-sprung Tipo 625s equipped with five-speed gearboxes and driven by the journeyman Trintignant and Farina, the Italian veteran now well past his best.

Fangio and Moss scored a Mercedes 1–2 in the Argentine GP season-opener at Buenos Aires, with Trintignant a solid third sharing his 625 with Maglioli and Farina. For the start of the European season there was another revamped machine available, the Tipo 555 'Super Squalo', which was built up round a completely different chassis frame, the new machine making its debut in the Turin GP at Valentino Park.

Ascari, Villoresi and new signing Eugenio Castellotti delivered a 1–2–3 grand slam for the Lancia D50s, and Ascari rammed home the message by winning at Naples and dominating the Pau GP before he retired, allowing Jean Behra's Maserati through to win.

Amazingly, considering how outclassed the 625 had become, Trintignant bagged a fortuitous win at Monaco, but only after the Mercedes of Fangio and Moss retired and Ascari took an unscheduled ducking in the harbour. Castellotti finished second ahead of the Behra/Cesare Perdisa Maserati and the arthritic Farina.

Further back in the field, Piero Taruffi became so fed up with the handling of his 'Super Squalo' that he came into the pits and handed it over to Paul Frère, the Belgian semi-professional racer who was the team's reserve driver.

Frère later shed some interesting light on the way in which the Ferrari team operated, having failed to persuade manager Mino Amarotti that changes should be made to improve the 555's handling characteristics.

'That car was a real beast round Monaco,' he remembered, 'as it just wanted to plough straight on at the two tight hairpins. I hinted that it might be a good idea to disconnect the front anti-roll bar, but Amarotti was

1954
February: John Travolta, US actor, is born.
July: The Boeing 707 jet airliner makes its maiden flight from Seattle.
May: Roger Bannister breaks the four minute barrier for the mile.
July: Rationing ends in UK after 14 years.

1955
April: Albert Einstein, German-born US scientist, dies.
April: Winston Churchill quits as British Prime Minister because of poor health.
June: 85 spectators and a driver, Pierre Levegh, are killed when Levegh's Mercedes-Benz crashes in the Le Mans 24-hour race.
• The first European Cup football competition is held. Scottish clubs participate, but none from England.

action. Stirling Moss in the Mercedes W196 en route to that memorable maiden Grand Prix victory at Aintree, 1955. Head slightly cocked, sitting well away from the wheel, the speed simply flowing from his fingertips . . .

Photo: Bernard Cahier

sure he was really upset by my suggestion.

'He did not want to take the responsibility for modifying something which was part of the original design – for which he was not responsible. If he had taken my advice, and then something had gone wrong, then he most certainly would have been held responsible for it back at the factory. He just wasn't prepared to do it.'

Four days after Monaco, Ascari was killed testing a sports Ferrari at Monza. Lancia's most crucial human asset had been snatched away and Gianni Lancia, together with the entire Italian motorsporting fraternity, was bereft. Although Castellotti was allowed to take a single D50 to the Belgian GP at Spa-Francorchamps, financial problems were weighing heavily on Gianni Lancia's shoulders and he decided that he would have to retire from F1 racing thereafter.

Thanks to the combined efforts of the Italian automobile federation and Fiat, a deal was struck whereby Ferrari took over the entire inventory of Lancia D50s, plus the associated spares, with the promise of the equivalent of £30,000 a year in financial support for as long as the Maranello team continued to race the cars.

Enzo Ferrari may have privately thought this was Christmas for his own team, but did a very good job of imitating somebody who really believed he was doing the Italian federation something of a favour taking over what he would have liked to suggest was an outdated pile of junk – but was far from being that. The old myth-maker had landed on his feet once more.

On 26 July 1955, the formal hand-over of six cars and a host of other equipment took place. Neither Ferrari nor Gianni Lancia was present on this symbolic occasion, Enzo perhaps keenly appreciating his good fortune and not allowing his pride to be publicly dented by what, in truth, amounted to a fairly comprehensive, if oblique, humiliation for his organisation.

Unfortunately, by this stage Mercedes had effectively put an arm lock on the 1955 World Championship. Fangio had opened the season on a successful note by winning the Argentine Grand Prix, but Monaco proved a total disaster. Hans Herrmann crashed in practice, breaking a hip, and his place was taken in the team by the relatively slow French driver, André Simon.

Although the Mercedes team produced several permutations of chassis, with various wheelbases and the choice of either inboard or outboard brake set-ups, neither Fangio nor Moss could win. Victory fell to Maurice Trintignant's reliable Ferrari 625 while Ascari's Lancia ended in the harbour just when it stood poised to take the lead. Within another week came Ascari's fatal accident.

MOSS MAKES HISTORY AT AINTREE

Thereafter, the Mercedes W196s finished first and second in the four remaining races on the World Championship calendar. Fangio led Moss across the line at Spa-Francorchamps and Zandvoort, but in front of Stirling's home crowd in the British Grand Prix at Aintree the positions were reversed. Britain's 'Golden Boy' – who had insisted on carrying the Union Flag on the tail of his silver Mercedes – won by a nose from the canny Argentine ace.

Was it staged? Did Fangio throw the race? If he did so, then it was a performance delivered with such consummate

Opposite: Moss, ready for action, sits on the tail of his Mercedes W196 in the pit at Monaco, 1955.

Below: Sad moment. Alfred Neubauer (left) and Juan Manuel Fangio symbolically cover a W196 with a dust sheet on the company's withdrawal from racing in 1955. Karl Kling is covering the left-rear wheel, flanked by Hans Herrmann and Peter Collins.

subtlety that even Stirling has his doubts to this day. Karl Kling and Piero Taruffi rounded off a Mercedes grand slam by taking third and fourth places.

Transmission problems caused Moss to retire at Monza, where Fangio led Taruffi home to the final 1–2 of the season, thereby clinching his third World Championship with 40 points to Moss's 23, counting five scores from seven races. But it was all over now for Mercedes-Benz, whose management had been numbed by the Le Mans disaster in which Pierre Levegh's 300SLR had collided with Lance Macklin's Austin Healey, triggering the carnage which cost the lives of more than 80 spectators.

Moss's move to Mercedes had frustrated the Maserati team, which was left without a first-rate number one driver for the 1955 season. Instead they had the tenacious Jean Behra as team leader, backed up by Luigi Musso and Roberto Mières. To keep pace with the Mercedes on the fastest circuits, Maserati also developed a distinctive, all-enveloping 'streamliner' bodywork car. As Denis Jenkinson remarked from first-hand observation, 'It was not at all successful, having been designed by intuition rather than according to any aerodynamic theories, and was little faster than the normal 250F.'

Maserati also began experimenting with Bosch fuel injection, a development which would start to pay off in 1956, but the 1955 season also saw extremely important developments on the British F1 scene. While BRM was struggling along developing its 2.5-litre four-cylinder P25, Tony Brooks took the opportunity to write his own distinctive entry in the history books with an unexpected victory. And Tony Vandervell's new Vanwalls were showing the first signs of genuine promise.

BROOKS WINS FOR CONNAUGHT AT SYRACUSE

Two developments were responsible for propelling Connaught into the motor racing spotlight, albeit briefly. The decision was taken to build a proper 2.5-litre Formula 1 car for the new regulations which began in 1954. Then, in 1955, a quiet 21-year-old dental student turned in some impressive drives at the wheel of a privately entered Formula 2 Connaught. This, together with his performances for the factory Aston Martin sports car team, prompted Connaught to give him his first taste of Formula 1. His name was Tony Brooks.

The B-series Connaught Formula 1 car had been designed with the abortive 2.5-litre Coventry-Climax 'Godiva' V8 engine in mind, but since this never materialised as a serious project a four-cylinder Alta unit was used instead. Although this engine had its origins before the war it still produced a respectable 240 bhp at 7000 rpm.

The Connaught was promising, but by international standards it was definitely 'second division'. By the end of 1955 more than £15,000 had been poured into the F1 project by Kenneth McAlpine, and both he and Rodney Clarke were feeling tempted to close down the whole company. But at the end of the season they put in a couple of entries for the non-championship Syracuse GP in distant Sicily. A streamlined B-type was entered for the seasoned Les Leston with Tony Brooks in a regular car. What happened next went straight into the pages of the Formula 1 history books.

'I honestly think they invited me because most of the regulars couldn't manage it,' said Brooks, who'd never so

Left: After the drive which probably sealed his 1955 Mercedes contract, Stirling Moss waits to push his stricken Maserati 250F across the line at Monza, '54.

Right: Before the start of the 1954 French Grand Prix Onofré Marimón offers a drink to Prince Bira, while behind are Kling and Fangio.

Below: Maurice Trintignant and Froilán González await developments.

Below right: Pass on the left! Jacques Pollet signals to Eugenio Castellotti at the 1955 Dutch Grand Prix. ·

Bottom right: Peter Collins hitches a lift back to the pits on the Gordini of Georges Berger at the 1954 Belgian Grand Prix.

much as sat in the cockpit of a Formula 1 car prior to arriving at Syracuse, where he faced stiff opposition from the Maserati 250Fs of Luigi Musso, Luigi Villoresi and Harry Schell.

Yet to the amazement of the onlookers, Brooks planted the Connaught on the outside of the front row alongside the two fastest Maseratis. 'I never even managed a practice start,' he remembered. 'Firstly, I was anxious not to jigger up the 'box and secondly I was very conscious of my instructions not to over-stress the engine.'

Nevertheless, after a poor getaway behind the Maseratis, Brooks took the Connaught through into the lead on lap 11. At a time when the drivers of British cars were only supposed to watch Italian Ferraris and Maseratis disappear into the distance, this was a truly memorable change of script.

Musso tried his very hardest, regularly outbraking the Connaught into the tight hairpin on this challenging road circuit, but Brooks was always in a position to out-accelerate him. In fact, by the finish, Brooks had outpaced the works Maseratis by almost one minute.

Back in Britain it was Motor Show time and the Connaught victory was greeted with remarkably little in the way of editorial attention. Even Brooks was somewhat downbeat about his own achievement.

'Only I knew how easy I had been on the car,' he said. 'In a straight line we definitely weren't faster than the Maserati, but I'd always tended to go rather well on circuits like Syracuse, with long, sweeping corners and brick walls [waiting] if you make a mistake, so I managed to get away.

'There are plenty of other circuits where this just wouldn't have worked. I think everyone was carried away and thought that Britain had a World Championship winner [in the Connaught], but, with respect, I was the best person to know that, unfortunately, we hadn't.'

Yet Rodney Clarke's team remained a great favourite with the fans. In 1956 the Connaught Supporters' Club returned to Syracuse on a package tour to visit the scene of the marque's greatest triumph. Apart from the airline getting its wires crossed and booking the Dakota a day late for the nine-hour flight down to Sicily, the coach bringing the fans – and some of the drivers – back from Syracuse to Catania airport contrived to burst its radiator.

Depressed as they might have been after the best Ivor Bueb could manage was a distant fifth in the race, the sight of Alfred Moss – Stirling's father – lying flat on his back beneath the coach attempting to plug the holes with blocks of wood must have raised more than a few smiles. Meanwhile, the drivers stood in a line down to a nearby stream using their trophies to pass up the water to Stirling, who was sitting astride the bonnet, filling up the radiator. Difficult to imagine Michael Schumacher doing the same today.

Eventually Connaught became overwhelmed by consistent lack of finance, so Clarke and McAlpine agreed to call a halt to proceedings shortly after Stuart Lewis-Evans won the 1957 Easter Monday Goodwood F1 race in the aerodynamic 'toothpaste tube' B-series.

In 1972 Clarke told the author, 'Here I was, having been cut down on expenses ever since 1954, and the team was winning races with a three-year-old car. I got on the phone to McAlpine and said, "Let's stop while we're on top." And we did.' The team's final race was at Monaco a few weeks after the Goodwood victory, where Lewis-Evans's fourth place closed the book on a heroic effort to put Britain on top in Grand Prix racing.

By 1958 the Vanwalls were ahead, but the 'toothpaste tube' and the last of the conventional B-types were acquired by a Bexleyheath-based wheeler-dealer who subsequently sent them to Australia and New Zealand at the end of 1957 for Lewis-Evans and Bueb to drive.

The motor racing entrepreneur would have quite a future ahead of him on the Grand Prix scene. His name was Bernie Ecclestone and he did a few laps at Monaco in the B-type in practice for the 1958 Monaco Grand Prix, where Paul Emery and the American, Bruce Kessler, also took a turn at the wheel. None of them qualified to start.

VANWALLS MAKE THEIR MARK

Tony Vandervell pursued his Grand Prix success with the same zeal and determination as he applied to his business ventures. In 1930, almost by chance, he had discovered that a new replaceable car engine bearing was being manufactured in the USA.

Quickly appreciating its implications for reducing cost and manufacturing complexity in production cars, he hurried across the Atlantic and successfully concluded a deal with the Cleveland Graphite Bronze Company – inventors of the new technique – for its British licence.

With the enthusiastic financial advice and assistance of his father, Tony set up Vandervell Products Ltd in a purpose-built factory on Western Avenue, Acton, on the western fringes of London.

The production of Vandervell 'Thinwall' bearings made a significant contribution to the war effort between 1939 and '45, after which the company's immensely patriotic head quickly became involved with the new BRM project. Yet the vague, rudderless manner in which the

Opposite: The determined Franco-American driver, Harry Schell, tries the Vanwall cockpit for size at Monza, 1956, watched by Ferrari newcomer Wolfgang von Trips.

Below: Guy Anthony 'Tony' Vandervell (left), driving force behind the 1958 Constructors' Championship-winning Vanwalls, and one of his contracted drivers, the great, under-acknowledged Tony Brooks.

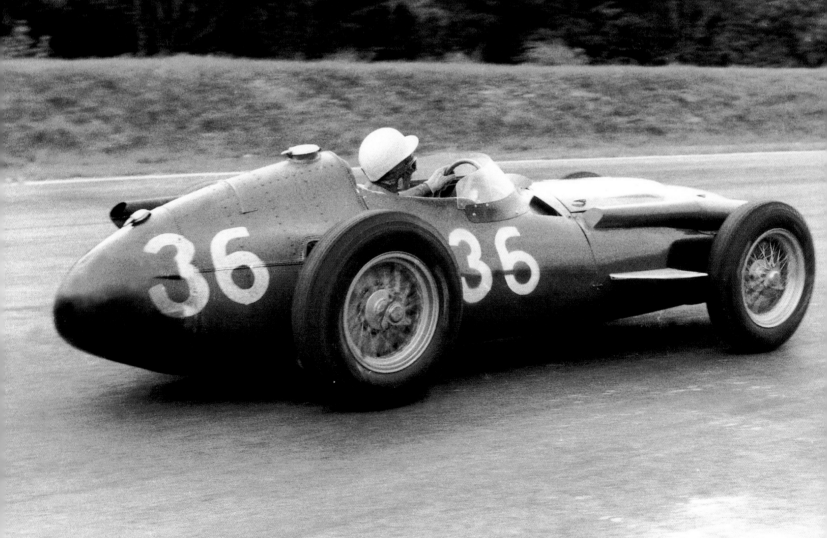

BMRR Trust imposed 'management by committee' on the team grated with Vandervell's direct manner.

It soon became clear to him that the 1.5-litre BRM V16 was going to be hopelessly late, so he struck out on his own. In 1949, as we've seen, he purchased a 1.5-litre supercharged Ferrari 125 as a test bed for the Vandervell Thinwall bearings – racing the car under the title of 'Thinwall Special' – and in 1951 he replaced that with a 4.5-litre Ferrari 375, by which time he had convinced himself that he should go it alone.

Mike Hawthorn was signed to race for the team in '55, but Vanwall was not quite ready for front-line action. As Hawthorn recalled: 'When Tony Vandervell invited me to sign a contract to drive the Vanwall, with a regular retainer as an added inducement, I was very tempted for it would give me the chance to spend more time in England. The Vanwall was improving fast.' Hawthorn was right; but it wasn't improving fast enough.

Things came to a head for Hawthorn at the Belgian Grand Prix, where just a single Vanwall was entered for him to drive. Unfortunately Tony Vandervell exercised his droit de seigneur over the team by driving the Vanwall out to the circuit prior to Saturday practice, with the result that Hawthorn found that the clutch was slipping.

Hawthorn was extremely angry about the whole episode and, after retiring from the race, apparently bumped into team manager David Yorke in a bar, where tempers got heated and Mike made some intemperate remarks about Vanwall's operation. The 'Old Man' had clearly compromised his team's efforts by indulging his own passion and taking a turn at the wheel of his car but it was decided that he and Hawthorn should go their separate ways after this unfortunate débâcle.

Hawthorn commented that, while everybody admired the immense drive and effort which Vandervell had put into his cars, it was difficult for him to accept the fact that they were still not ready for top-line international racing. 'But that was the hard truth and there was still a great deal to be done,' he noted.

By 1956 the 2.5-litre four-cylinder Vanwalls were beginning to show genuine promise. After initial experimentation with chassis designed by Cooper, Tony Vandervell commissioned Lotus chief Colin Chapman to produce a new chassis clothed in a strikingly slippery body conceived by aerodynamicist Frank Costin.

The '56 season saw Ferrari concentrating all its efforts on uprated versions of the Lancia D50 – dubbed the 'Lancia-Ferrari' – although there were already signs that Maranello was starting to make a muddle of the exquisite Jano-designed car which had originated from Turin.

With Mercedes-Benz withdrawing from F1 at the end of 1955, Fangio signed for Ferrari, although he was clearly in two minds about his plans until quite late in the day.

'At the end of 1955 I considered the possibility of retiring,' he later admitted, 'but the Argentine government had fallen during the summer and there were great changes going on in my country. In fact things began to go not-so-well in Argentina, so I decided to postpone my retirement for another year. As Mercedes-Benz had withdrawn, I returned to Europe to race with Ferrari in 1956, but I wasn't very happy about that.

'Since I first raced in Europe I had always been in a team opposing Ferrari. Now I was joining him, with Castellotti, Musso and Collins. But he would never say who was to be number one driver, although the younger men told me, "Juan, you are the leader."

'Ferrari was a hard man. His team raced in every category and his drivers drove always for *him*. He wanted victory primarily for his cars and this suited my attitude, because I have never raced solely for myself, but for the team as a whole. But a driver must have a good relationship with his mechanics and I found this rather difficult to achieve within the Ferrari team. I suppose it was because I had been their opposition for so many years and now here I was as their driver.'

Meanwhile, over at rivals Maserati there was definite optimism in the air with Stirling Moss leading the team and opening the European season with a splendid victory at Monaco with the 250F.

Unfortunately things went downhill from then onwards and the best result Moss could post in the next six races was a second place to Fangio in the German GP at the Nürburgring. In their efforts to satisfy Moss's high standards and at the same time keep their number two, Jean Behra, as happy as possible, the factory spent too much time experimenting with various technical developments on a random and intermittent basis.

These included trying various controlled air-flow concepts, ducting the radiator and improving the flow around the cockpit, a variety of different fuel injection systems and some experimentation with Dunlop disc brakes. However, in the final race of the season, the Italian Grand Prix at Monza, Moss managed another splendid victory and the lessons learned there were incorporated into the very successful 250F derivative for 1957.

Meanwhile, Fangio had won his fourth World

Opposite: Lancia-Ferrari threesome. Juan Manuel Fangio is the closest Ferrari driver to the camera with team-mates Peter Collins and Eugenio Castellotti beyond at the start of the 1956 German Grand Prix.

Opposite, bottom: The personification of front-engined F1 elegance. On the exit to Monza's Parabolica right-hander Bernard Cahier captured this brilliant shot of Stirling Moss's factory Maserati 250F with just a touch of oversteer on his way to victory in the 1956 Italian Grand Prix.

Below: Monza, '56, was a troubled time for the Lancia-Ferraris which threw treads on their Englebert tyres during both practice and the race.

Championship title thanks to the incredible generosity and sporting spirit displayed by British driver Peter Collins. Earlier in the year Collins had taken his Lancia-Ferrari to victory in the Belgian and French Grands Prix and had looked well placed to become Britain's first World Champion driver. At Monza came the grand gesture.

On lap 19 of the Italian Grand Prix, Fangio wobbled into the pits with a broken steering arm on his Lancia-Ferrari and when Collins came in for a precautionary tyre check (after an earlier failure) he unhesitatingly gave his car to Fangio in order to keep open his colleague's title chances.

It was a generous, prompt and open action which attracted a deal of attention at the time, marking Collins out as a gentleman. The fact that he was a Ferrari team driver and was obliged to obey such an instruction from the management was not altogether the point. The nice thing about Collins's attitude was his willingness to oblige without any sort of debate, in contrast to Luigi Musso, who had declined a similar suggestion that he might hand his car over to Fangio.

In the end, Fangio won the 1956 World Championship with 30 points (net) to Moss's 27 and Collins's 25. The Argentine ace then moved to Maserati in 1957, while Moss signed for Vanwall and Hawthorn rejoined Ferrari after a season with BRM.

Moss would be joined in the Vanwall team by Tony Brooks. Connaught had offered Brooks a deal for the 1956 season, but the promising young English driver was being pursued with rival offers. 'I couldn't see the

Connaught being competitive, so it was with considerable regret I refused their offer,' he recalled.

'I joined BRM in 1956. They'd got a tremendously fast car in a straight line, but the only problem was that it was completely undriveable around corners.

'If Connaught had used the BRM engine it would have been a seriously competitive car. But, as it was, the Connaught had a wonderful chassis and an uncompetitive engine, while the BRM had a first-class engine and diabolical chassis – and I *mean* diabolical. It was an absolute danger.'

The BRM P25, designed by Peter Berthon, had a four-cylinder 2.5-litre engine and developed 270 bhp at 8000 rpm. It was extremely fast but painfully unreliable – as emphasised in the British GP, where Hawthorn and Brooks led in the opening stages.

After 30 laps Brooks was running smoothly in fourth place only for the BRM's throttle linkage to come adrift ten laps later. He pulled off at Club Corner, effected a temporary repair and successfully returned to the pits. After losing over nine minutes, Brooks rejoined, but got only as far as Abbey Curve.

There the throttle stuck open and Brooks crashed heavily, being flung out of the BRM, which promptly rolled and burst into flames. 'Which was the best thing that could have happened to that particular motor car,' he told the author some 17 years later.

If BRM was still struggling, then Vanwall was certainly advancing towards maturity. With the gutsy Franco-American driver, Harry Schell, at the wheel, the Vanwall

Opposite: Enzo Ferrari and Fangio after the Argentine driver had clinched his fourth World Championship at Monza in 1956.

Opposite, bottom: Legendary designer Vittorio Jano and his Lancias – now Ferrari badged – at the same race.

Below: The Marquis de Portago pushes his Ferrari towards the pits at Silverstone in the British Grand Prix. He took over the car from Castellotti and it was eventually black-flagged with steering defects.

Photos: Bernard Cahier

Top: Jean Behra led the opening stages of the 1957 French Grand Prix at Rouen-les-Essarts in this factory Maserati 250F.

Above: 'Fon' de Portago showed signs of a promising F1 future only to die prematurely in the 1957 Mille Miglia.

Right: Maserati 250Fs were the ideal 'customer' F1 car during the late 1950s. Here Jo Bonnier lines up to take the start at Pescara, 1957.

drove into the thick of the action in the French GP at Reims, where Schell mixed it determinedly with the Lancia-Ferraris of Fangio, Collins and Castellotti on this ultra-fast circuit. In the event the Vanwall failed and Schell took over the sister car driven by Mike Hawthorn, who was briefly back in the fold, having made up his differences with Tony Vandervell.

Jean Behra stayed on in the Maserati works team for 1957, but this was to be Fangio's year yet again. The 250F was now entering its fourth season of front-line F1 competition and further modifications were incorporated.

Moss's Italian GP-winning car from the previous year was one of two 250Fs which were significantly lower and lighter, this being achieved by setting the engine at an angle of five degrees to the centre-line of the chassis, allowing the prop-shaft to run diagonally across the floor of the cockpit to a revised final drive unit with the input bevel gears more offset to the left. This had enabled a much lower seating position to be achieved for the driver and the frontal area was much reduced.

For 1957 it was decided to go back to the original central engine position and use a chassis frame of much smaller diameter and thinner gauge tubing, while the engine was now developing around 285 bhp at 8000 rpm. Even more importantly, if Fangio had experienced a troubled relationship with Ferrari, he was back in his personal element at Maserati, for the Argentine driver was, if anything, even more popular with the workforce than Moss had been because his association with the team went back to 1948 when he first began racing in Europe.

FANGIO SIGNS OFF ON TOP

The 1957 season started with Maserati posting a remarkable 1–2–3–4 grand slam in the Argentine Grand Prix at Buenos Aires, where Fangio led home Behra, Carlos Mendiréguy and Harry Schell. Fangio then won the Monaco and French Grands Prix – sensationally at Rouen-les-Essarts – before he was stopped in his tracks by a historic victory for Stirling Moss, who won the British Grand Prix at Aintree with the Vanwall.

The Colin Chapman-designed Vanwall, clothed in Frank Costin's very high, distinctively aerodynamic bodywork, had been steadily refined since it first appeared in 1956. Its 96 × 86 mm, 2490 cc four-cylinder engine had been developed by Leo Kuzmicki, incorporating Norton motor cycle cylinder head technology with a Rolls-Royce industrial bottom end.

It was Britain's first seriously competitive Grand Prix car of the post-war, or indeed any, era. Moss would gain great success in its cockpit and the image of the impassive young man sitting far away from the steering wheel with his laid-back – in every sense of the expression – driving position somehow came to encapsulate the best of the front-engined 2.5-litre era.

Yet the Vanwall was not perfect. Its four-cylinder engine was prone to flat-spots, it had a bad gearbox and its handling bordered on the knife-edge, tending towards understeer and requiring the deft touch of a top driver. With Moss and his team-mates, Tony Brooks and the outstandingly talented rising star, Stuart Lewis-Evans, Vanwall certainly had the requisite resources at its disposal during 1957 and '58.

Yet before the British cars could achieve that memorable breakthrough at Aintree, Behra's Maserati had

moved into the lead after Moss's car hit trouble and he took over Brooks's sister machine. Behra was a good number two who somehow felt more relaxed at Maserati supporting Fangio than perhaps he had the previous year with Moss. This may have been because he was closer to Stirling in age and, in any event, all the drivers acknowledged Fangio as the best of his era in much the same way as rivals conceded Ayrton Senna's superior status just over four decades later.

Mike Hawthorn, for his part, was having a good race in the Ferrari 801 and was closing on Behra when the Maserati's clutch blew apart, showering the track with debris on which the Englishman then picked up a puncture. That caused Hawthorn to make a stop for a fresh tyre, so he ended up in third place behind Luigi Musso's Ferrari, allowing Moss a clear run through to his second World Championship victory at Aintree in two years.

The German Grand Prix at the Nürburgring followed, in which Fangio produced what is widely regarded as the most remarkable victory of his career. Qualifying gave a taste of what was to come. Fangio had managed a 9m 41.6s fastest lap with a Lancia-Ferrari en route to victory in the '56 Grand Prix, but when he did a 9m 25.6s to claim pole in the Maserati 250F it was clear that the Argentine ace was in a class of his own.

The best Hawthorn could manage was a 9m 28.4s for second on the grid but he actually got away first at the

Below: Charles (left) and John Cooper (right) with their Indianapolis car in the streets of Surbiton in 1961. Between the pair are driver Jack Brabham and journalist John Blunsden.

LAT Photographic

CHARLES AND JOHN COOPER

A STRONG STREAK of technical and mechanical ingenuity ran through the post-war British motor racing scene like the lettering in a stick of Brighton rock. Nowhere was it more evident than in the achievements of Charles and John Cooper, the father-and-son partnership who rocked the F1 establishment to its core in the late 1950s.

The Coopers had built their first single-seater racer back in 1946 when they produced a creation fashioned from a couple of Fiat Topolino saloons and propelled by a single-cylinder JAP engine. Thus they were in on the ground floor of the 500 cc F3 category, which took off spectacularly as a nursery for future F1 stars such as Stirling Moss and Peter Collins. In the early 1950s, Coopers were everywhere on the F3 scene.

Charles and John provided a uniquely balanced partnership. The son's sometimes over-ambitious and effervescent enthusiasm was tempered by the Old Man's ingrained conservatism and reluctance

to spend money unless absolutely necessary. This conservatism would ultimately lead to the Cooper F1 team's downfall in the late 1960s, but those days were far ahead when Mike Hawthorn started out on his quest for stardom in the Cooper-Bristol F2 car back in 1952.

The Cooper-Bristol indirectly shaped the company's path into F1, but via the experiences of Australian Jack Brabham, who arrived in Britain at the end of 1954 after racing one of these now-ageing F2 cars in his native land. In the 1955 British Grand Prix at Aintree, Brabham debuted an aerodynamically bodied, 2.2-litre Bristol-engined Cooper in the British GP. It marked the company's debut as an F1 constructor.

From the start of 1957, Cooper really got into the swing of things, pitching their F2 Climax-engined cars into the battle for F1 supremacy. They lacked power but displayed splendid agility. Their best result was Roy Salvadori's fifth place in the British Grand Prix at Aintree. But better was to come in 1958.

Above: The breakthrough. Moss scores Vanwall's first victory in the 1957 British Grand Prix at Aintree.

Right: Juan Manuel Fangio rounded off his front-line F1 career with a devastating performance for Maserati in the 1957 German Grand Prix.

1956

January: A.A. Milne, the creator of Winnie the Pooh, dies.
June: Hollywood actress Marilyn Monroe marries Pulitzer Prize-winning playwright Arthur Miller.
October: Martina Navratilova, US tennis player, is born in Czechoslovakia.
November: Dwight Eisenhower is elected US President for a second term.

1957

January: Anthony Eden quits as British Prime Minister.
January: Humphrey Bogart, US actor, dies.
April: First parking meters are put up in London.
October: The Soviet Union launches the satellite 'Sputnik' into orbit around the Earth.

start, pursued by Peter Collins. Second time round Mike did a 9m 37.9s to post a new lap record, but by the end of lap three Fangio – running a light fuel load and intending to make a pit stop – had torn through into the lead and by lap eight he had pulled out almost half a minute's advantage.

At the end of lap 12 he came in with a 28s lead, which was then squandered disgracefully as the Maserati crew shambled their way through the stop, taking 52s to refuel the car and fit two new rear tyres.

That left Hawthorn and Collins swapping the lead together and Fangio spent the next couple of laps getting into the swing of things again. After that, he put the two Ferrari drivers on red alert for a ferocious counter-attack. Down, down came the gap. On lap 16 it was 33s, on lap 17 it was 25.5s, on lap 19 it was down to 13.5s and on lap 20 it was just two seconds.

Fangio then dived past Collins going into the North Curve, shattering one of Peter's goggle lenses in the process. Going down to Adenau he forced his way ahead of Hawthorn, but the British driver fought back magnificently and went into the final lap only three seconds behind the Maserati and dropped just one more second on that final 14-mile blast.

'It was now a straight fight between Fangio and I once again,' said Hawthorn, recalling the French GP four years earlier, 'and I was driving right on the limit as we rushed through the endless tree-lined curves to Hocheichen and on to the Quiddelbacher Hohe, but just as I was going into a slow left-hander, Fangio cut sharply inside me and forced me on to the grass and almost into the ditch . . .

'As we started the last lap he had the vital yards in hand which prevented me from getting to grips on the corners and he crossed the finishing line 3.6s ahead of me. This time the race had been every bit as exciting for the drivers as for the spectators and even though Peter and I had been beaten, we enjoyed every moment of it.'

The Vanwalls had an utterly dismal time at the Nürburgring. They may have performed to splendid effect on the relatively smooth surface at Aintree, but on the bumps and humps of the epic German track they were well off the pace.

Stirling told Doug Nye: 'The Vanwall's taut suspension was totally unsuitable for the Nürburgring, where they took a fearful hammering. Stuart crashed, I finished a distant fifth and Tony was ninth, having been sick in the cockpit. But my engine never missed a beat.'

Moss would follow that up with momentous drives to victory at both Pescara and – perhaps most satisfyingly – Monza, where he finally realised the gruff Tony Vandervell's ambition to 'beat those damn' red cars' and won the Italian Grand Prix in *una macchina Inglese*.

In the face of all this achievement on the part of Maserati and Vanwall, Ferrari faced up to a bleak 1957 season indeed with its type 801, the ultimate bastardisation of the Lancia D50 which now had close-fitting bodywork, no trace of the original pannier tanks and a rear-mounted fuel tank.

Bottom: Mike Hawthorn (right) may have been defeated in the '57 German Grand Prix, but he still congratulated Fangio warmly once the race was over.

Bernard Cahier

Classic car, epic venue, great driver. Fangio swings his Maserati 250F into the Nouveau Monde hairpin at Rouen-les-Essarts during his victorious run in the 1957 French Grand Prix.
Photo: Bernard Cahier

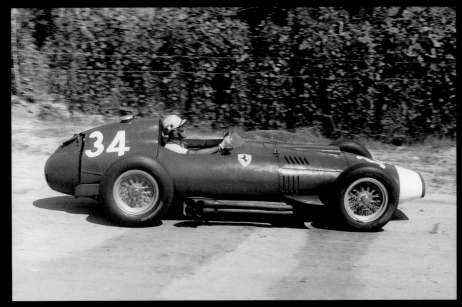

Top left: A quartet of
Ferrari 801s are warmed up at
Rouen-les-Essarts, 1957.

Above left: Luigi Musso in the
'57 Pescara Grand Prix; note the
rear oil tank working loose.

Left: Jean Behra in the
sensational V12-engined
Maserati 250F in the 1957 Italian
Grand Prix.

Above: Fangio's Maserati 250F embroiled in battle with the Vanwalls of Tony Brooks and Stuart Lewis-Evans, 1957 Italian GP.

Left: Moss's victorious Vanwall is sandwiched between Fangio's Maserati 250F (left) and Luigi Musso's Ferrari 801 at the start of the 1957 Pescara Grand Prix.

Above: Mike Hawthorn's Ferrari Dino 246 brakes for Tabac during the 1958 Monaco Grand Prix, in which he failed to finish.

Right: Ferrari team manager Romolo Tavoni (in braces) in discussion with Mike Hawthorn and Luigi Musso.

DINO 246
BOOSTS FERRARI FORTUNES

At the same time, Ferrari was developing a new 65-degree F1 V6, which saw the light of day initially as a 1.5-litre F2 engine but which would later be developed into the engine which would power one of the most famous F1 Ferraris of all time into the 1958 season, the Dino 246.

This, of course, was named after Ferrari's first-born son, Alfredino, who died from nephritis, a kidney complaint, in the summer of 1956 at the age of 24. This personal tragedy was a pivotal moment in Enzo Ferrari's long life and would result in his becoming increasingly reclusive, although no less a showman for that.

By the time the Italian Grand Prix at Monza came around, Fangio had long been crowned World Champion for a fifth time, clinching that unique distinction with his victory at the Nürburgring. This was also a memorable achievement for Maserati, and the famous Italian company was hard at work on a V12 engine project which had originally been started in 1956, when it was envisaged that the powerplant would be installed in a totally new car.

This was re-thought for the 1957 season and the new 60-degree V12 was eventually finalised in time to race at Monza. The 68.5 x 56 mm, 60-degree V12 had a capacity of 2476 cc and was originally designed to run at up to 10,000 rpm with a massive 320 bhp at 9500 rpm being developed during test runs on the dynamometer during the summer of '57. Unfortunately the downside to all this was a very narrow power band and acute lack of torque at anything below peak revs.

Behra agreed to drive the V12-engined 250F in the Italian Grand Prix and for the first 28 laps he was right in the thick of the action, helping Fangio all he could in his battle against the Vanwall team. Unfortunately he overtaxed his rear tyres and had to stop to change them, after which he thrashed his way back through the field only for the engine to fail.

At the end of that memorable Italian Grand Prix Moss and Fangio, separated by 40s, were the only competitors on the same lap. Into third place came Wolfgang von Trips's Ferrari 801 ahead of the private Maserati 250F driven by Masten Gregory.

The final points tally for the Drivers' Championship saw Fangio on 40 (net), comfortably ahead of Moss on 25 and Ferrari's Luigi Musso on 16. Only the best five results out of the eight races – which again included the Indianapolis 500 – counted for the ultimate outcome.

HAWTHORN AND VANWALL
MAKE IT FIRSTS FOR BRITAIN

For the 1958 season the F1 technical regulations were changed, largely at the prompting of the fuel companies, who were anxious to make as much advertising capital as possible out of their involvement in this increasingly prestigious sport.

It was decided to introduce a requirement for pump petrol in place of the alcohol-based fuels used previously, but this posed immediate difficulties when it came to establishing and maintaining minimum acceptable standards on an increasingly global basis. As a result, it was eventually decided that 130-octane aviation fuel (AvGas) would be adopted as the only available fuel governed by the appropriate international standards and regulations.

Adopting AvGas also had the effect of putting the brake on power outputs, at least temporarily. Ferrari would go into battle with the new 85 x 71 mm, 2417 cc Dino 246 V6, which was now developing around 270 bhp at 8300 rpm. The Vanwall four-cylinder engines were now nudging the 290 bhp mark while the BRM P25s produced around 280 bhp at 8800 rpm.

Driver line-ups were broadly the same. Hawthorn, Collins and Luigi Musso were in the Ferrari front line, Vanwall retained its talented British trio and BRM signed

Jean Behra and Harry Schell. Juan Manuel Fangio began the season driving a Maserati 250F in the Argentine GP, but his long-term plans were uncertain.

There was, however, another major factor injected into the F1 equation which would transform the Grand Prix scene in a period of barely 18 months. It was the arrival of the small British Cooper company with its spindly little rear-engined cars.

The 1958 season was scheduled to start in Buenos Aires with the Argentine GP on 19 January, but neither Vanwall nor BRM was ready. Moss had concluded a deal with Rob Walker to drive his Coopers in any race not contested by Tony Vandervell's cars so he drove the 1960 cc Climax-engined Cooper instead. What happened next would change the face of F1 for ever.

The story has been told time and time again. Moss won the race after a non-stop run in a close finish ahead of Musso's Dino 246. Lulled into a false sense of security that Moss would have to stop for fresh tyres, Ferrari's confidence turned first to disbelief and then to anguish as it became clear that he was going through without any delay.

Musso began his counter-attack too late in the day and failed to catch the in-control Moss by just over two seconds. Mike Hawthorn was a distant third and the Ferrari pit was embroiled in a huge row at the end of the race over the Italian driver's failure to get the job done. For his part, Musso shouted back that he hadn't been kept fully informed about Moss's progress, but Peter Collins knew full-well that he himself had held out several signals to his Italian team-mate after retiring his own car. It was all extremely unsettling.

Moss, in fact, had himself inherited the lead on lap 35 of the 80-lap race when Fangio's Maserati stopped for fresh tyres, and Stirling thereafter took things as gently as he dared. He was particularly keen to keep going as he knew only too well that the four-bolt fixing on the

Stirling Moss in the Rob Walker Cooper dives inside Mike Hawthorn's Ferrari Dino 246 to snatch second place in the 1958 Argentine Grand Prix.

1958
February: Eight members of the Manchester United football team are killed in an air crash at Munich airport. Also killed are eight journalists and three club officials.
August: Madonna and Michael Jackson, both US pop musicians, are born.
• The Boeing 707 passenger jet enters transatlantic service with Pan Am for the first time.
• The Lego brick is launched by a Danish toy manufacturer.

Above: Maurice Trintignant would emerge the lucky winner of the 1958 Monaco GP in Rob Walker's Cooper. Here the Frenchman sweeps into Tabac ahead of Tony Brooks's Vanwall and the rest of the pack.

Right: With magnificent precision, Tony Brooks heads for victory in the 1958 Belgian Grand Prix in his Vanwall.

Cooper's wheels would destroy his chances if he had to stop. He held on – and delivered.

The 1958 World Championship developed into a two-horse race between Ferrari and Vanwall. The 1958 Monaco Grand Prix was the second round of the title battle and proved to be a washout for both the front-runners. Hawthorn and Moss both had spells in the lead, but retired, allowing Rob Walker's Cooper – this time driven by Maurice Trintignant – through to win again. The race was also marked by the debut of the distinctive front-engined Lotus 12s driven by Graham Hill and Cliff Allison. It was another starting point for another F1 legend, with Allison managing to squeeze home in sixth place.

Then came the Dutch Grand Prix at Zandvoort, where the three Vanwalls buttoned up the front row of the grid and Moss won easily. The Ferraris were nowhere, Hawthorn wrestling his way home to a frustrated fifth.

The Belgian GP at Spa-Francorchamps should have provided another win for Moss, but he inexplicably missed a gear while pulling away in the lead on the opening lap. The Vanwall's engine failed as a result and Stirling was absolutely aghast at his mistake, which he freely and promptly admitted. But there was to be no joy for the Ferraris here either. Moss's team-mate, Tony Brooks, took over stylishly at the head of the pack and drove away to post Vanwall's second win of the year.

Had the race been another lap longer, it might well have been won by Cliff Allison's Lotus 12. As he took the chequered flag, Brooks pulled off with gearbox problems. Hawthorn's engine blew up as he came down the hill to take second place and Stuart Lewis-Evans's Vanwall wobbled past the chequered flag with a broken steering arm to take third. Allison followed them home in fourth place . . .

TRAGIC TIMES FOR MARANELLO

The harsh reality of the 1958 season was that the Vanwalls were generally superior and, had it not been for their intermittent unreliability, the Ferraris would have been decisively outclassed for much of the season.

Even so, Hawthorn won commandingly at Reims, where Musso, over-driving wildly in the hope that a big payday might enable him to clear his reputed gambling debts, flew off the road and was killed.

'On the eve of the race, he had, in fact, received a message; a few words typed on a buff telegram that urged him to make an all-out effort,' Ferrari would later reflect. Many believe this dark speculation to have been well founded.

Peter Collins, meanwhile, was experiencing some problems with his employer. The Englishman had been one of Enzo Ferrari's favourites, the team chief admiring his open and sunny disposition. However, the relationship changed distinctly after Peter married an American girl, Louise King. Ferrari hinted that the romance had taken the edge off his hunger in the cockpit. Or perhaps he was just jealous that Peter was no longer simply starstruck by the Ferrari team as a whole.

Just prior to the Reims race, team manager Romolo Tavoni announced that Collins would only be driving the Dino 156 in the F2 supporting race. This was absolutely typical Ferrari agitation, but the Old Man found himself up against a tough adversary in Collins.

Supported by his pal Hawthorn, Peter replied that if he wasn't going to be allowed a run in the Grand Prix, then he wouldn't be driving in either race. Tavoni relented, so Collins also drove the F2 race and finished second, before finishing fifth in the Grand Prix.

Cliff Allison in the spindly little Lotus 12 in which he so doggedly drove to fourth place in the 1958 Belgian Grand Prix.

Carlo Chiti later suggested another reason behind Collins's apparent demotion. Mino Amarotti, who had been responsible for managing the works Ferrari Testa Rossa squad at Le Mans in 1958, reported back that Hawthorn and Collins deliberately destroyed their gearbox. Amarotti, who'd been a prisoner of war in East Africa, reportedly hated the guts of the British and somehow got it into his mind that Collins and Hawthorn were trying to help the rival Aston Martin squad, an absurd piece of lateral thinking by any standards.

Hawthorn's victory in France would be the last such success of his F1 career. It was also the last race for Fangio, who finished fourth in his Maserati 250F, Mike

The charismatic Luigi Musso was another victim of the tragic 1958 season, crashing his Ferrari Dino 246 fatally at Reims during the French Grand Prix.

Countdown to a fateful race. Mike Hawthorn checks his watch just before the start of the 1958 French Grand Prix while Luigi Musso, in the other Ferrari in the middle of the front row, is about to start the last race of his life. On the outside of the line-up is Harry Schell in the BRM P25.

Photo: Bernard Cahier

respectfully easing his pace in the closing stages of the race so as not to lap the five-times World Champion.

Collins later scored a beautifully executed victory in the British GP at Silverstone, but was killed a fortnight later chasing Brooks's Vanwall round the Nürburgring in the German Grand Prix.

Moss had taken an early lead at the Nürburgring only for his Vanwall to stop with magneto trouble. That left Hawthorn and Collins running first and second, but Brooks swooped past on lap 11 and began to pull away.

Battling fading dampers and erratic drum brakes on his Ferrari Dino 246, Collins was chasing the leading Vanwall for all he was worth as they came out of the Pflanzgarten dip and into the climbing right-hander which followed.

From third place, Hawthorn saw the drama unfold a matter of yards in front of him. As they went into that right-hander, Collins was slightly off-line, running wide to the left by little more than the width of his car.

The car's left wheel rode up the small bank on the outside of the corner and, just as Mike was preparing to tell Peter what a bloody fool he was, the car flipped over and threw out its driver.

Hawthorn almost stopped, looking backwards to see Collins's Dino bounce upside down in a cloud of dust. Thereafter Mike drove on like a robot, uncaring about the race and worried sick about his friend. Next time round he retired when the clutch expired. Brooks won the race and a shattered Hawthorn later learned that his great friend, 'Mon ami mate, Pete', had succumbed to serious head injuries in hospital.

From here on in, Hawthorn just wanted the season over. He determined he would stop driving at the end of the year and that would be it. Done, decided. No more.

The crucial race in the World Championship battle between Moss and Hawthorn was the Portuguese GP at Oporto on 24 August. Mike led early on, but his Dino's drum brakes were no match for Moss's disc-braked Vanwall and Stirling won easily.

After losing second place to Jean Behra's BRM when he came in to have his brakes adjusted, Hawthorn then set a new lap record as he chased back after the Frenchman. It was at that point that the Vanwall pit signalled 'HAWT REC' to Moss, indicating that Mike had set the fastest lap. Stirling read it as 'HAWT REG' – Hawthorn regular – meaning that Mike hadn't made any progress.

On the last lap Mike shot up an escape road and turned the car round himself, fending off outside assistance from officials (which would have been illegal). There was subsequently a protest to the effect that Mike had pushed his Ferrari against the direction of traffic on the track, but this was rejected thanks to the evidence of Moss, who correctly pointed out that Hawthorn had been on the pavement at the time of the alleged offence. So Mike took second place and that crucial extra point for fastest lap.

Then came the Moroccan Grand Prix on Casablanca's

Opposite: Number one takes number one. The prophetically numbered Dino 246 of Peter Collins heads for victory in the 1958 British Grand Prix at Silverstone.

Opposite, bottom: A delighted Collins poses for his friend Bernard Cahier's camera with the winner's trophy.

Below: Just a fortnight after that glory day on home soil, Collins strives to keep the Ferrari ahead of Tony Brooks's Vanwall at the Nürburgring. Brooks soon overtook – and Peter crashed fatally trying to keep pace.

85

Photos: Bernard Cahier

Left: **Mike Hawthorn strolls across the paddock at Oporto in 1958. After the Portuguese Grand Prix there would be just two more races to go before he could retire from the sport. He duly clinched the World Championship but, five months after Bernard Cahier snapped this informal shot, Mike would be killed in a road accident on the Guildford bypass.**

Bottom left: **Second place for Hawthorn at Casablanca's Ain Diab circuit was enough to nail down his title.**

Bottom right: **Vanwall team-mates Stirling Moss (left) and Stuart Lewis-Evans together with Harry Schell.**

Below: **Mon ami mates. Mike Hawthorn and Peter Collins in morning dress and with pipes, ready for Stirling Moss's marriage to Canadian Katie Molson.**

daunting Ain Diab circuit, where Stirling would again win convincingly for Vanwall. But Ferrari new boy Phil Hill moved over to allow Hawthorn to take second place and become Britain's first World Champion driver by the margin of a single point.

Tony Vandervell's smart green Vanwalls had, for their part, won Britain the first Constructors' World Championship, but the celebrations were muted in the aftermath of another serious accident which left Vanwall driver Stuart Lewis-Evans with 70 per cent burns.

Vandervell realised that motor racing was a dangerous game, but couldn't rid himself of the notion that poor Lewis-Evans wouldn't have been in this terrible state 'if it wasn't for my bloody silly obsession with racing cars'.

Poor Stuart was flown back to Britain in Vandervell's chartered Viscount airliner, the other drivers taking turns to talk to the amazingly cheerful young man who lay in a stretcher at the back of the passenger cabin. He was admitted to the famous McIndoe burns unit at East Grinstead hospital, where he succumbed just over a week later.

Grand Prix racing in those days was nothing if not pre-dictably dangerous. Lewis-Evans was the highest-profile casualty of a race which also saw Olivier Gendebien upend his Ferrari Dino 246, injuring his chest and ribs. François Picard crashed his F2 Cooper and sustained a fractured skull, while British privateer Tom Bridger was lucky to walk away from his wrecked F2 Cooper. Part of the game, part of the risk.

FIA ANNOUNCES 1.5-LITRE LIMIT

There was certainly a sting in the tail of the 1958 World Championship and, after months of rumour and specula-tion, it was delivered on 29 October 1958 within the lofty portals of the Royal Automobile Club in London's Pall Mall.

The occasion was the presentation of awards to Mike Hawthorn and Tony Vandervell, but the President of the sport's governing body, the CSI, Auguste Perouse, threw a time bomb into the proceedings when he announced that a 1.5-litre F1, with a 500 kg minimum weight limit, would supersede the present 2.5-litre rules from the start of 1961. The British constructors were almost apoplectic with indignation.

Autosport responded with a suitably bold editorial. 'The CSI can prattle about safety till they are blue in the face,' boomed Gregor Grant. 'The fact remains that all top-flight drivers maintain the greater the power, the greater the safety.'

They could have saved themselves the breath. The new formula was a *fait accompli*. British race promoters wasted their time supporting a half-baked 3-litre 'Intercontinental Formula' for a couple more years, run-ning various domestic events for this category, but it was real King Canute stuff. Ferrari, meanwhile, settled down to develop a revised 1.5-litre version of the Dino V6 and the British teams, as time would demonstrate, were left behind. For the moment.

Below: Stirling Moss in the shapely Vanwall dancing on the limit during the 1958 Moroccan Grand Prix. 'Stirl' won the race, but Hawthorn came second to take the World Championship.

Bernard Cahier

The Cooper now emerged as the car to beat. Jack Brabham's head-down, opposite-lock style of driving at the wheel of the four-cylinder Cooper-Climax would become an F1 trademark as the little team from Surbiton rose to humble the front-engined Ferrari Dino 246s and BRM P25s which would be their prime opposition in 1959.

Throughout 1959 Brabham would be teamed with the young New Zealander, Bruce McLaren, and the bespectacled Masten Gregory from Kansas City. Brabham would win at Monaco and Aintree while Stirling Moss, driving a Cooper-Climax for privateer Rob Walker, would triumph at Lisbon and Monza. For his part, McLaren would round off the season with his first F1 victory in the US Grand Prix at Sebring, where an exhausted Brabham pushed his out-of-fuel Cooper T51 home in fourth place to clinch the World Championship on a day when it could so easily have gone to Ferrari driver Tony Brooks, who had switched to the Italian team after Vanwall's belated withdrawal from F1.

Brooks, however, was bumped by team-mate Wolfgang von Trips on the run to the first corner and came in to check for damage at the end of the opening lap. Beneath his quiet exterior Brooks had a very strong, unshakeable personal philosophy which was founded on an unobtrusive, but very real, set of Christian beliefs.

'Motor racing was always only part of my life,' he explained. 'I think I was blessed with a lot of natural abil-ity; I tried hard, but I never tried to the point that I might risk killing myself.

'I think that taking an uncalculated risk could lead to what amounts to suicide and I have a religious conviction that such risks are not acceptable. I learned from my accidents at Le Mans with an Aston Martin and at Silverstone with the BRM that I would never try and compensate for a mechanically deficient car.

'In my book, you should never drive to the point where you experience fear. I would drive to the very best of my ability, and persevere with a car if it was mechanically deficient in a non-dangerous way. I was fortunate enough that I could win races without going into that fear zone.'

Part of that philosophy was shaped – or certainly endorsed – by his experience at Le Mans in 1957 when he rolled an Aston Martin after struggling with a troublesome gearchange. Lying under the upturned car was bad enough, but then along came a rival Ferrari which crashed into the Aston, knocking it off Brooks. Under the circumstances, Tony was fortunate to have got away with relatively minor injuries from an accident in which he could so easily have been killed. It certainly made him think.

Brooks had held on waiting to see if Tony Vandervell would continue in 1959 and, by the time the British industrialist decided to quit, the only available competitive seat was at Ferrari. It was a move which undoubtedly

Opposite: Tony Brooks in the rebodied Ferrari Dino 246 during the 1959 Monaco Grand Prix, in which he finished second.

Opposite, bottom: Stirling Moss in the Rob Walker Cooper, 1959, with legendary mechanic Alf Francis looking into the frame from the left.

Below: Jean Behra's Ferrari Dino 246 leads the pack into the old Gasometer hairpin at Monaco just after the start of the '59 Grand Prix.

Bernard Cahier

The 1959 Monaco Grand Prix. Sheer weight of traffic causes a few anxious moments at the first corner as Bruce McLaren, Phil Hill and Maurice Trintignant (32) scramble through side by side.
Photo: Bernard Cahier

put Jean Behra's nose out of joint, but Tony was not the sort of character to fuel personal rivalries.

Moss, meanwhile, judged that driving for Rob Walker's team was the best alternative available following his two seasons with Vanwall. He had a close personal friendship with Rob, who was, and is, one of nature's true gentlemen and an outstanding sportsman-enthusiast.

Unfortunately, while Cooper was all too willing to sell Walker a car, they could not help with a gearbox as they were at full stretch trying to make their ERSA-modified Citroën boxes sufficiently durable to handle the power of their 2.5-litre Climax four-cylinder engines over a full race distance.

As a result of this, Walker and his team had to turn to Italian transmission specialist Valerio Colotti to manufacture a gearbox for them. It proved a real disaster, costing Moss sure victories in the Monaco and Dutch Grands Prix and eventually prompting Rob to suggest that it might be better if he did not race the car until these problems were sorted out.

Moss's failure at Zandvoort had handed the BRM team its maiden Grand Prix victory with Jo Bonnier winning at the wheel of the much-improved P25, so a deal was cut for Stirling to drive a loaned BRM in the light-green livery of the British Racing Partnership – an outfit run by his father, Alfred, and manager, Ken Gregory – in the French and British GPs.

Stirling spun off on melting tar at Reims and an earlier clutch failure meant that he was unable to keep the engine running, but at Aintree he finished second to Brabham's Cooper after a close battle with McLaren.

Moss was impressed with the BRM P25. Ironically, the BRP BRM was then totally destroyed when Stirling's one-time Mercedes team-mate, Hans Herrmann, suffered brake failure at Avus during the German Grand Prix. 'A sad end to a car which was actually vastly better than its results might suggest,' noted Moss.

For this race Moss was back in the Walker Cooper-Climax, but again the gearbox gremlins intervened and he failed to finish. On this occasion, however, he hadn't expected to be a serious contender for victory. The Berlin race furnished Tony Brooks with his second Grand Prix win of the year in the elegant, revamped Fantuzzi-bodied Ferrari Dino 246.

Brooks's previous victory came at Reims in sweltering conditions, where he simply drove away from the pack with a calm as unruffled as it was awesome. This was also the race where his volatile French team-mate, Jean Behra, finally fell out with the Ferrari management.

'I didn't have any problem with Behra,' says Brooks, 'but we didn't communicate much, because I didn't speak French and his Italian was not very good – mine was quite competent – but there were never any nasty words.

'I don't know what Behra's problem was. Perhaps he thought he should have been appointed number one driver. For my part, I just joined the team on the understanding that I was going to get a car as good as everybody else's. And at Ferrari I did get a car which was always the equal of my team-mates' – which is more than I can say for my time with Vanwall.'

Carlo Chiti, Ferrari's Chief Engineer, felt that Behra was cut adrift emotionally by Ferrari, having joined the team believing he would be designated team leader. At Reims, where he threw a punch at team manager Romolo Tavoni, he had got it into his mind that his Dino 246 was somehow mechanically deficient – and even reportedly

made a protest to the sport's governing body to the effect that Ferrari had stitched him up, providing him with a chassis which had recently been shunted by Dan Gurney in testing at Monza.

'Jean was certainly not a very likeable character,' recalled Chiti with brutal frankness. 'They called him "the gypsy" because of his passionate temperament. He also had a particularly vulgar way of expressing himself.

'But the way he died led me, even so, to think deeply about it. We had completely abandoned that man to himself, with his brooding determination to win. We had obliged him to take refuge in his own desperation.'

Behra, who had led at Monaco before blowing up his Dino's engine, worked himself up into a fury of frustration over his disappointment with the season, culminating in his knocking out cold Tavoni in a restaurant at Reims on the evening after he had trashed another V6 engine.

As if that wasn't enough, he also had a major confrontation with a journalist in the same restaurant. 'If you ever say that again, I'll punch you in the face,' Behra threatened. He went to leave the restaurant, paused at the door and then back-tracked to the journalist's table.

'I've just thought about this,' he pondered. 'It's not worth waiting for the next time.' With that he duly punched the hapless scribe in the face.

Enzo Ferrari may have been privately quite amused that a member of the fourth estate should have been subjected to such summary justice. But thumping his own team manager was another matter altogether. The episode cost Behra his place in the Maranello line-up and the gallant Frenchman died soon afterwards when his

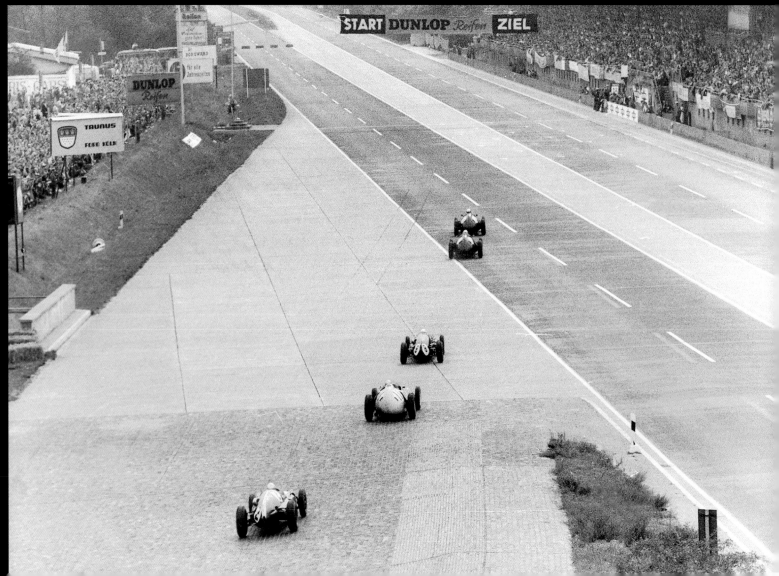

Left: The winning Ferrari of Tony Brooks leads Masten Gregory's Cooper around the steeply banked North Curve at Avus during the 1959 German Grand Prix.

Below left: The leaders sweep off the banking on to the autobahn that formed the basis of the daunting Avus circuit, the opposite carriageway serving as the return leg of the layout.

Right: A welcome swig of bubbly for Jack Brabham after his victory in the 1959 Monaco Grand Prix.

Bottom: Stirling Moss in the Walker Cooper harries the Ferraris of Tony Brooks and Jean Behra in the '59 Dutch Grand Prix. Moss fought his way into the lead after a poor start but the unreliable Colotti gearbox was to let him down once more.

Opposite: Jack Brabham racks up his fifth successive victory in the 'lowline' Cooper T53 at Oporto in 1960.

Opposite, bottom: Innes Ireland in the ground-breaking Lotus 18 at the 1960 Dutch Grand Prix.

Below: Froilán González made his final Grand Prix appearance in Argentina in 1960. Here his Ferrari leads Gino Munaron's Maserati as the pair are about to be lapped by Bruce McLaren's winning Cooper.

Porsche sports car crashed on the Avus banking during a supporting event at the German GP meeting.

Moss then won at Lisbon and Monza, successes that helped clinch Cooper's victory in the Constructors' World Championship, which meant that a British manufacturer had now won this newly instigated award for the second year running.

Although his experience in 1958 meant that Moss wasn't terribly concerned about the significance of the World Championship as a whole, 'Stirl' could still take the title if he won the US race at Sebring and posted fastest lap into the bargain. Six laps in and the gearbox broke again. So that was that.

With the best five results counting, Brabham took the title with 31 points (net), with Tony Brooks second on 27 and Moss third on 25.5.

ENTER THE SENSATIONAL LOTUS

The 1960 season saw the first flowering of Colin Chapman's design talent in the form of the superb Lotus 18, the car which would take the baton from Cooper and progress the rear-engined F1 concept to fresh levels of technical sophistication.

Cooper attempted to match its wind-cheating profile with the new 'lowline' T53 challenger, and this duly carried Jack Brabham to his second straight World Championship with wins in the Dutch, Belgian, French, British and Portuguese Grands Prix in commanding style. Nevertheless, the new Lotus was the class of the field. Light, compact and – unfortunately – horrifyingly frail, the

type 18 was fielded not only by the factory team with Innes Ireland, Jim Clark and former motor cycle champion John Surtees doing the driving, but also by Rob Walker, who immediately purchased a car for Stirling Moss.

The new Lotus 18 had hardly turned a wheel before making its F1 debut in the Argentine Grand Prix, yet Ireland enjoyed a symbolic lap at the head of the field before being overwhelmed by his opposition. He finished sixth. The second race of the season saw Moss win at Monaco, a race which also marked the debut of the front-engined American Scarabs bankrolled by millionaire team owner Lance Reventlow.

The Scarabs were extremely nicely built machines which, like the front-engined Aston Martins which had been introduced the previous year, had missed the F1 boat in the biggest possible way. Ferrari also retained the front-engined Dino 246 for a final season before switching to a rear-engined configuration for the start of the 1.5-litre F1 in 1961.

At Monaco, Moss and the Rob Walker *équipe* gave Lotus its maiden Grand Prix victory – just as they had done for Cooper just two years earlier in Buenos Aires. But while the rugged Cooper would enable Brabham to reel off that succession of World Championship-winning victories throughout the summer, the Lotus squad had an infinitely more stressful time.

Lotus always had a reputation for fragility and this was underlined when Moss's car shed its left-rear wheel midway through Spa's 140 mph Burnenville corner during Saturday practice for the Belgian GP. The car crashed heavily, turning over and throwing Moss out on to the side of the circuit.

Photos: Bernard Cahier

1959

February: John McEnroe, US tennis player, is born.

February: US singer Buddy Holly is killed in an aircraft accident.

May: The first excavations are made for the road tunnel under Mont Blanc, linking Italy and France.

July: The first hovercraft crossing of the English Channel is made.

1960

April: The 'Doc Martens' workboot is launched in the UK.

October: Nigeria achieves independence from Britain.

November: John F. Kennedy is elected US President.

December: National Service for British men ends – the last call-up cards are issued.

Main photo: Jack Brabham's Cooper T53 leads the Lotus 18s of Stirling Moss, Innes Ireland and Alan Stacey on the opening lap of the 1960 Dutch Grand Prix at Zandvoort.

Inset above right: The field surges away through the sand dunes, with Graham Hill's distinctive helmet seen in the BRM on the left.

'Shunt. Nose, Back, Legs, Bruises. Bugger!' read the cryptic note in Moss's diary for 18 June 1960. Yet he was the lucky one. Lotus privateer Michael Taylor was badly hurt when his Lotus 18's steering failed in the same session as that in which Moss crashed. Then in the race itself works Lotus driver Alan Stacey was killed when he hit a bird on the Masta straight and Yeoman Credit Cooper driver Chris Bristow crashed fatally at Burnenville while embroiled in a lurid battle with Willy Mairesse's Ferrari Dino 246 for second place.

Ferrari, meanwhile, was having a disappointing season. Cliff Allison finished second to McLaren's winning Cooper in Buenos Aires, but then crashed spectacularly during practice at Monaco, where he hit the chicane and was hurled from the car. With Brooks having moved to the Yeoman Credit Cooper outfit, this left the responsibility for team leadership on the shoulders of the relatively inexperienced Phil Hill, who at least managed to bag victory in the Italian Grand Prix at Monza.

Not that this amounted to a great deal, as the British constructors were reluctant to risk their cars on the combined banked track/road circuit on which the Italian round of the championship took place.

At an RAC Competitions Committee meeting on 13

July 1960, it was reported 'that the main British constructors had advised the Italian Automobile Club of their unwillingness to participate in the Italian Grand Prix, which is this year the Grand Prix of Europe, as it is to be run over the full circuit at Monza, i.e. the banked track and the road circuit combined. They would be prepared to enter an event on the road circuit only, as has been the case since 1957. So far, no reply has been received.'

The Italians really could not have cared less. They had their beloved Ferraris and went ahead with their own race on their own terms. Hill, Richie Ginther and Mairesse duly delivered a grand slam 1–2–3 victory against makeweight opposition, Giulio Cabianca's Cooper-Ferrari finishing fourth ahead of Wolfgang von Trips in the 1.5-litre Ferrari 156 prototype.

Over two months after that Monza event, the final round of the title chase took place at California's Riverside circuit, where Moss's Walker Lotus won the US Grand Prix ahead of Ireland's works car and the Coopers of McLaren and Brabham, Jo Bonnier's BRM and Phil Hill, driving a borrowed Cooper as Ferrari did not make the trip.

Jack Brabham was comfortably World Champion for the second time on 43 points, with McLaren second on 34 (net) ahead of Moss and Ireland.

Opposite: Stirling Moss displays unflappable cool in the Walker team Lotus 18, winning at Monaco in 1960.

Opposite, bottom: Chris Bristow, pushing too hard and over the top at the wheel of the Yeoman Credit Cooper just before meeting his death in the 1960 Belgian Grand Prix.

Above left: Graham Hill tweaks his moustache as Jo Bonnier and Raymond Mays (right) look on.

Left: Too little, too late. The front-engined Scarab was dismally uncompetitive – and two years after its time.

Bottom: Lotus team-mates Jim Clark (left) and the luckless Alan Stacey, who was killed at Spa-Francorchamps in 1960.

CHAPTER FIVE: 1961–65
THE 1.5-LITRE FORMULA

WHILE THE British teams griped and groaned over the introduction of the new 1.5-litre regulations, Ferrari's engineers got their heads down and pressed on with a suitable engine. Throughout the final three years of the 2.5-litre F1, the Italian team had continued developing a small-capacity version of its 65-degree V6 engine for F2 purposes, and it was this unit which formed the basis of the 1961 challenge.

One of these rear-engined Dino 156 prototypes had been used in the 1960 Italian Grand Prix, where Wolfgang von Trips finished fifth, and preparation for the following season – and the new formula – continued on 2 October, when von Trips took the same car to third place in the non-title Modena GP behind Jo Bonnier's Porsche and Willy Mairesse in a front-engined Dino 156.

Ferrari's Chief Engineer, Carlo Chiti, also produced a 120-degree version of the original 65-degree V6, this revised unit developing around 190 bhp at 9500 rpm. This was more than sufficient to eclipse the 1.5-litre four-cylinder engines from Coventry Climax and BRM used by the majority of the British opposition.

Both Climax and BRM were working flat out on their own V8 designs, but these would not see the light of day until midway through 1961 and would not race competitively until the start of the following year.

The Ferrari V6 engines were installed in spaceframe chassis which were clothed in distinctive bodywork, the main feature of which was the twin-nostril 'shark nose' treatment of the front end. Drive was by means of a five-speed transaxle positioned ahead of the rear axle line – a configuration supposedly adopted to allow sufficient room in the engine bay for a 2.9-litre engine to be installed just in case the Intercontinental Formula should get off the ground after all. Ferrari had all bases covered.

The driver line-up included fellow-Californians Phil Hill and Richie Ginther, the German, Count von Trips, and the Italian novice, Giancarlo Baghetti, whose semi-independent car was fielded under the auspices of a group of Italian racing teams keen to encourage home-grown talent. Later in the year they would be joined by the brilliantly talented 19-year-old Mexican, Ricardo Rodriguez.

It was Baghetti, driving in his first F1 race, who gave the Ferrari 156 a victorious debut in the non-title Syracuse Grand Prix in Sicily. On this occasion the Milanese driver had a relatively easy task defeating what was essentially makeweight opposition. But things would not be so straightforward come the Monaco Grand Prix, the opening round of the World Championship battle.

On the famous street circuit, where chassis agility would inevitably even the balance against an engine power advantage, Stirling Moss and the Rob Walker Lotus 18 were in a class of their own. The team was using one of the later Mark 3 Climax FPF engines, which

benefited from a strengthened bottom end and delivered their performance across a wider torque range.

Moss duly qualified on pole. Shortly before the start there was a very worrying moment when he discovered a cracked chassis tube on the Walker Lotus. No matter, as it turned out; his loyal mechanic, Alf Francis, cool as a cucumber, welded the offending tube on the starting grid – after wrapping the brimming fuel tanks with wet towels! Just in case, you understand.

Despite giving away 35 bhp to the Ferraris, Moss won brilliantly ahead of Ginther. For the rest of his life, the wiry little Californian driver would rate it as the best personal performance of his racing career.

'My car and my effort were stronger than the opposition when I won in the Honda [at Mexico City in 1965], which was just plain faster than the opposition,' he would say, 'but at Monaco both Stirling and I were three seconds below the pole time in the race. Staggering, isn't it?

'I set the lap record very late [16 laps from the finish] but Stirling equalled it next time round. That son of a gun! If you did well against him, then you'd really done something special.'

Phil Hill, who would finish third ahead of von Trips, later likened chasing Moss's Lotus round Monaco to trying to race a greyhound round your living room with a carthorse.

On the same day Baghetti was having an easy afternoon winning the non-title Naples Grand Prix, but von Trips then got Ferrari's World Championship juggernaut seriously rolling with victory in the Dutch Grand Prix at Zandvoort. Hill finished second and then led home a Maranello grand slam in the Belgian GP at Spa-Francorchamps with von Trips, Ginther and Belgian sports car ace Olivier Gendebien – winner of that year's Le Mans classic – following along behind.

FIRST-TIME WINNER

Next up was the French GP at Reims-Gueux, traditionally a sweltering affair under a relentless sun. The '61 fixture proved no exception and Baghetti's FISA-entered 156 supplemented the works entry. Hill, who had learned a thing or two about psyching out his contemporaries, put in a stupendous lap to take pole – over a second faster than the frustrated von Trips.

Ginther led initially, but had an early spin, leaving von Trips and Hill to battle over the lead. Von Trips was out after 20 laps with a stone through the radiator, then Hill spun at Thillois and was clouted by Moss's Lotus. Phil stalled and couldn't restart. All this drama allowed Ginther through into the lead, but his chances were thwarted by fading oil pressure.

Baghetti now found himself embroiled in a frantic battle for the lead of his first World Championship Grand

Opposite: Richie Ginther gives chase to Stirling Moss in the 1961 Monaco Grand Prix.

Opposite, bottom: Giancarlo Baghetti drives into the history books as the only man ever to win his maiden *Grande Epreuve*, the Italian's Ferrari 156 just pipping Dan Gurney's four-cylinder Porsche to the flag in the 1961 French Grand Prix at Reims.

Below: A typical British summer's day for the 1961 British Grand Prix at Aintree. Here Phil Hill's second-placed Ferrari 156 comes up to lap Jack Fairman in the four-wheel-drive Ferguson P99.

Prix with the two powerful four-cylinder Porsches driven by Dan Gurney and Jo Bonnier.

Two laps from the chequered flag, Bonnier dropped from the fray and it was down to Gurney – himself a former Ferrari man – to try and get the better of the Prancing Horse. Coming down the long straight into the final Thillois right-hander for the last time, Gurney slipstreamed past into the lead, staying there as the two cars scrabbled through the turn and made for the line.

In a perfectly judged move, Baghetti then swung out of Gurney's slipstream and surged past to win by one-tenth of a second. The baby of the team had saved the day for Maranello. It was the pleasant Italian's only victory in an international motor race of major consequence.

Von Trips scored his second win of the season in the British Grand Prix at Aintree, an event which was marked by the sole World Championship outing of the technically innovative Ferguson P99 four-wheel-drive car. The machine had been developed primarily as a competition test bed for tractor magnate Harry Ferguson's four-wheel drive systems.

Ferguson Research, established with the technical know-how of former pre-war motor cycle ace Fred Dixon and Le Mans winner Tony Rolt, was at the cutting edge of four-wheel drive technology well in advance of any real interest from the motor industry at large.

Powered by a 1.5-litre Climax FPF engine, the Ferguson P99 was completed in the spring of 1961. It was a front-engined machine with its engine canted over in the spaceframe chassis, a normal clutch taking the

drive through to a bespoke Ferguson five-speed gearbox which had been developed in conjunction with Colotti, the Italian gearbox specialists.

From this point transfer gears stepped the drive sideways towards the centre of the car and propeller shafts then took it to the front and rear, the latter shaft running to the left of the driver's seat, where a small crown wheel and pinion was fitted. At the point where the transfer gears stepped the drive out to the propeller shafts, there was a system of free-wheels and limited slip differentials which made it virtually impossible to spin the wheels.

In addition, the Ferguson P99 was equipped with brake servos operated by hydraulic pressure from an engine-driven pump, incorporating the Dunlop-developed 'Maxaret' braking system, which prevented any wheel locking in wet conditions. Driver controlled, the Maxaret system could be switched on and off from the cockpit.

An agreement was reached for Rob Walker's team to enter the car and the P99 made its debut in the British Empire Trophy race at Silverstone one week prior to the 1961 British GP at Aintree. Jack Fairman was at the wheel on that occasion, but Moss had the option of driving the P99 in the British Grand Prix. Instead, he opted for his regular Lotus 18/21, which eventually retired with brake trouble.

At this point Fairman was called in to hand over the Ferguson to Stirling – and the Ferrari pit immediately advised its drivers of the change, warning them that they

Bernard Cahier

Left: Wolfgang von Trips surges to a stylish victory in the 1961 Dutch Grand Prix at Zandvoort.

Below: Moss's finest win? Great tactical acuity, a clever choice of tyres and precision driving enabled Stirling to take the Rob Walker Lotus 18/21 to victory in the '61 German Grand Prix. Who could have imagined at the time that this would be the final victory of the revered British driver's F1 career?

Above: Dwarfed by the permanent grandstands more familiar as a home for Grand National spectators, the field for the 1961 British Grand Prix at Aintree readies itself for the off.

Right: Phil Hill; few more intelligent and sensitive men ever sat in the cockpit of a Grand Prix car.

Opposite, top: Phil Hill's Ferrari 156 dives through the Karussell 'ditch' en route to breaking the ten-minute barrier at the Nürburgring for the first time during qualifying for the '61 German Grand Prix.

Opposite, bottom: The works Lotus 21s of great rivals Jim Clark and Innes Ireland battle for third place in the '61 French Grand Prix. Jimmy came out on top in the end.

Above: Prelude to disaster. Jim Clark trails the four works Ferrari 156s in the early stages of the 1961 Italian Grand Prix. The Scot would tangle with von Trips (fourth in this group) with catastrophic consequences.

Right: Wolfgang von Trips seems enveloped in his own thoughts after winning at Aintree in 1961.

should not be tricked into thinking it was Fairman if they came across the Ferguson lapping unexpectedly fast.

However, race officials politely pointed out that Fairman had already contravened the regulations by being push-started after a pit stop, but everyone involved was so delighted over the way the car was performing that it was kept running to gain some useful test mileage. Unfortunately, under pressure from other teams, the Ferguson was then called into the pits and withdrawn.

Moss was impressed beyond doubt by the Ferguson's capability in the wet and agreed to drive it in the non-championship Oulton Park Gold Cup meeting later that summer. In patchy wet conditions, he won at a canter from the works Coopers of Brabham and McLaren. The car was then withdrawn from front-line competition, although Peter Westbury would use it to great effect to win the 1964 British Hillclimb Championship.

The frenzied battle for engine power in the first year of the 1.5-litre F1 completely eclipsed the longer-term potential of the Ferguson concept, but the idea would resurface eight years later with a new crop of 1969 four-wheel-drive challengers. As we shall see, by then there were further complications to prevent them from realising their theoretical potential.

Back in the mainstream action, the '61 German Grand Prix at the Nürburgring would go down in history as another fine against-the-odds victory for Moss in the outdated, uprated Walker team Lotus 18/21. Moss also chose to race on the Dunlop D12 'green spot' rain tyres which his old pal, Innes Ireland, had used to such good effect to win the non-title Solitude Grand Prix in the works 21. These tyres gave terrific extra grip and, with rain showers forecast for the Nürburgring, Moss took the gamble of using them even though, in his own words, Dunlop's Racing Manager, Vic Barlow, 'had kittens' and told him that he raced on them at his own risk.

However, the 1961 German Grand Prix was a landmark in that it saw the race debut of the splendid 63 × 60 mm, 1495 cc, two-valves per cylinder Coventry Climax V8 developing 180 bhp at 8500 rpm, installed in Jack Brabham's works Cooper T58. He qualified second to Phil Hill's Ferrari but slid off the road on the opening lap. But it had shown F1 a glimpse of the future.

TRAGEDY AT MONZA

The World Championship was wide open between Phil Hill and Wolfgang von Trips as the Ferrari team arrived at Monza for the Italian Grand Prix. Von Trips took pole from 19-year-old Mexican new boy Ricardo Rodriguez – whose wealthy father had bankrolled his place in the Maranello squad – but, due to running high final drive ratios, the Ferraris were slow off the line. This allowed Jim Clark's Lotus 21 to get in among them on the opening lap.

Coming down to Parabolica for the second time, von Trips was getting into his stride and had just overtaken Clark before the braking area when he apparently moved over on the Lotus before he had completely cleared its left-front wheel. The two cars interlocked and the Ferrari cartwheeled up the bank and along the spectator fence – killing 14 members of the public – before crashing back on to the edge of the circuit. Clark's Lotus spun to a halt and the Scot emerged unhurt, but von Trips had been hurled from his car and lay fatally injured at the trackside.

Phil Hill won the race in the sole Ferrari to make the finish, clinching the World Championship crown ahead of Dan Gurney's Porsche, Bruce McLaren's Cooper and the private Cooper of Jack Lewis. Hill took the title with 34 points to von Trips's 33 with Moss and Gurney sharing third place on 21 points apiece.

Ferrari did not attend the 1961 US Grand Prix, which Ireland won for Lotus just prior to his unceremonious sacking by Chapman. Gurney was second and Tony Brooks third in the underpowered BRM-Climax, a performance which rounded off the career of the 29-year-old one-time Vanwall star, who now opted to retire to concentrate on his expanding garage business back home in Surrey.

Although Brooks never had any regrets about his decision to quit, one is bound to wonder what would have happened in 1962 had he continued racing for BRM. Monza in '61 saw the first appearance of the 90-degree BRM V8 engine, this 68.5 × 50.8 mm, 1498 cc unit developing 185 bhp at 10,000 rpm with an initial 13:1 compression ratio.

The compression ratio was subsequently reduced to 10.5:1 in an effort to protect the pistons from the effects of detonation, and a six-speed gearbox had been designed to complement the V8 when it was installed in the new BRM P56 chassis for the following season.

History, of course, relates that Graham Hill would drive the BRM to the 1962 Drivers' World Championship. Yet had it not been for that retirement decision perhaps the '62 title would have fallen to Tony Brooks, whom many regarded as a much superior driver to the mustachio'd Hill.

Brooks eventually got to drive a BRM P56 some 35 years after Graham Hill's title success. The occasion was the impromptu Basildon Grand Prix – arranged by the enterprising Canon Lionel Webber around the ring roads of the Essex 'new town' in 1997.

'It was the first time that I had ever driven the V8 BRM,' said Brooks, by then 65. 'It made me think that I had retired a year too soon!'

April: Russia's Yuri Gagarin becomes the first man to go into space.
July: Diana Spencer, later Princess of Wales, is born.
August: The Berlin Wall is erected, sealing the border between the eastern and western zones of the divided city.
• In-flight movies are introduced by TWA on the New York to Los Angeles route.
• The E-Type Jaguar, which can reach speeds of 140 mph, is launched.

1962
July: Tom Cruise, US actor, is born.
August: Marilyn Monroe is found dead at the age of 36, after taking an overdose of sleeping tablets.
• Sean Connery lands the role of James Bond in the film *Dr No*.
• The Beatles shoot to success with their first single, 'Love Me Do'.

Tony Brooks in the four-cylinder Climax-engined BRM during the 1961 German Grand Prix. Frustrated and disillusioned with the new generation of 1.5-litre cars, the pleasant Englishman retired from racing at the end of the year.

Bernard Cahier

Bernard Cahier

Bottom: Spirit of 1960s F1. Jimmy Clark and the sensational monocoque Lotus 25-Climax which made its debut at the 1962 Dutch Grand Prix.

Opposite: Graham Hill looks understandably delighted after winning the 1962 German Grand Prix. Not only was it his second win of the season, but his victory also guaranteed the continuation of the BRM team.

END OF THE F1 ROAD FOR MOSS

There were several key elements to the 1962 F1 season: the arrival of the BRM V8 as a front-line challenger, the sensational debut of the monocoque Lotus 25 and the fading fortunes of the Ferrari team, which had been subjected to a wholesale defection of key staff to the ambitious new ATS operation.

However, all these were mere footnotes when compared with the accident at Goodwood on Easter Monday which marked the end of Stirling Moss's Grand Prix career. Driving a Lotus 18/21 'special' powered by a BRM V8 and entered by the UDT Laystall team operated by his father, Alfred, and manager, Ken Gregory, Moss was contesting the Glover Trophy race, in which he had lost time early on with a pit stop to rectify a sticking throttle.

He resumed well behind Graham Hill's leading BRM and, poised to unlap himself from the future World Champion, slammed off the road at St Mary's Corner and crashed head on into an earth bank. It was a miracle that Moss survived at all. The flimsy Lotus spaceframe collapsed around him and it took a seeming age to remove him from the wreckage.

Moss emerged from the twisted shell of his car with deep facial wounds, his left cheekbone crushed, the eye socket displaced, and his left arm, his nose and his left knee and ankle broken. He was unconscious for a month and paralysed down his left-hand side for six months. Thirty-seven years later, Moss acknowledges that he probably retired prematurely, even though he did not make his final decision to quit until the spring of 1963.

Moss effectively relinquished his role to Jimmy Clark, who would be armed with the superb monocoque Lotus

25 from the first Grand Prix of the season, the Dutch GP at Zandvoort. The aluminium 'bathtub' monocoque round which the 25 was built provided compactness allied to torsional rigidity, plus benefits in terms of driver protection, although these were very much a secondary consideration during the early 1960s.

Of course, in introducing the Lotus 25, Colin Chapman was performing a ruthless and lurid commercial juggling act. He had a good business selling F1 cars to private customers, and when it was announced that Innes Ireland was joining the UDT Laystall F1 team for 1962 Chapman confirmed that the customer Lotus 24s — one of which was also going to Rob Walker — would be 'virtually the same' as the factory 25s.

Rob Walker remembers John Cooper making it clear that he knew precisely what Chapman was up to in the pit lane at Zandvoort when he cast an appraising glance over the new monocoque Lotus. Having looked studiously into the cockpit, he said to Chapman, 'Oh yes, I see what you mean; they're exactly the same — you just forgot to put the chassis in this one.'

Chapman smiled weakly. Needless to say, the Lotus 24 wasn't in the same league as the factory cars, although, in fairness, none of the privateer drivers was in the same league as Jimmy Clark either.

Graham Hill had won the Dutch Grand Prix at the start of what would be a crucial year for BRM. From the outset, Sir Alfred Owen had made it clear that the team's future depended on its winning at least two Grands Prix that season. Although Jim Clark got into his stride with victories in the Belgian and British Grands Prix (held at Aintree for what would be the last time), Hill guaranteed the future of the BRM organisation by scoring a close win over John Surtees's Lola and Dan Gurney's Porsche in the German GP at the Nürburgring.

Bernard Cahier

Hill would consolidate BRM's position when he won again at Monza and clinched the World Championship in the South African GP at East London with only two days of the old year still left. Clark's Lotus had seemed on course for the title until sidelined by an oil leak while leading comfortably, but BRM deserved their moment in the sun as the transformation in their fortunes under the engineering direction of the talented Tony Rudd had been quite remarkable.

Hill won the championship with 42 points (net), ahead of Clark on 30 and McLaren on 27.

As for Lotus, Chapman's cars had proved the class of the field but undeniably frail, experiencing some problems with their German-built ZF gearboxes, and there was plenty of evidence that the outfit concentrated primarily on Clark's car to the exclusion of the number two driver, in this case the very talented Trevor Taylor.

For its part, Ferrari had an absolutely dreadful season in 1962. Phil Hill had re-signed with the Commendatore when he was on the crest of an emotional wave in the aftermath of that championship clincher at Monza the previous September which had seen the tragic death of Wolfgang von Trips.

The team continued to rely on uprated versions of the Dino 156 Sharknose, but now the British V8s had parity of power, better chassis and superior drivers. Small wonder that Maranello had to play a supporting role now that Carlo Chiti and most of the engineering team had departed to ATS.

PORSCHE'S LONE F1 SUCCESS

Porsche, which had been competing in F1 with outdated four-cylinder cars, really raised the standard of its game in 1962 with the 66 × 54.66 mm, 1494 cc flat-eight-cylinder Porsche 804, which developed 185 bhp at 9200 rpm. Dan Gurney was the number one driver, paired with Jo Bonnier, and won the French Grand Prix at Rouen-les-Essarts.

It would be the sole World Championship Grand Prix victory to be won by the famous German car maker, which then withdrew from F1 at the end of the season.

The Porsche company's F1 involvement had been inspired by the success of the modified single-seater 1500 RSK sports car that Jean Behra used to win the Formula 2 race at Reims in 1958. Porsche then built a four-cylinder rear-engined F2 car for the following year and by 1961 was an established force in F1 racing, Dan Gurney taking a close second place to Baghetti's Ferrari in the French GP at Reims.

Ferry Porsche, the son of the company's founder, later wrote that he believed that the F1 programme was on the right road, but financial constraints meant that the relatively small German sports car maker could not continue to bankroll such a costly programme.

During 1962 Porsche was also involved in considerable investment when taking over car seat manufacturer Reutter. 'After a thorough study of the situation and lengthy deliberation on the matter, I came to the conclusion that we could not actually afford Grand Prix racing at all,' said Ferry Porsche. Therefore the company withdrew at the end of 1962 and would concentrate most of its future racing efforts on sports cars.

Eric Broadley's Lola company was also struggling to make its F1 mark. Its cars, fielded by Bowmaker Racing,

under the management of the respected Reg Parnell, were driven by John Surtees and Roy Salvadori. Surtees would post the team's sole victory in a non-title race at Mallory Park.

Cooper's star would fade progressively, but McLaren did a grand job to beat Phil Hill's Ferrari into second place at Monte Carlo. It would be the marque's final Grand Prix win under the Cooper company's ownership, their former World Champion driver, Jack Brabham, having gone it alone to build his own Climax V8-engined F1

Bernard Cahier

car, which made its debut in the '62 German Grand Prix.

When it came to marshalling the elements needed to achieve Grand Prix success, the trend towards the small specialist chassis manufacturer, using an engine produced by a separate organisation, was confirmed as the 1960s unfolded. Dynamic individualists like Colin Chapman spawned a new breed of team owner, who would be followed in the fullness of time by the likes of Ken Tyrrell, Frank Williams and Ron Dennis. Only now, more than 35 years after Jim Clark's first win for Lotus at Spa, have the changing commercial circumstances of F1 brought the major motor manufacturers of the world into the Grand Prix arena.

That was never something Chapman could envisage in his early days. The Lotus boss was usually correct, but he certainly made an incorrect prediction about immediate future F1 form in response to a question as to what he was expecting from the BRM.

'I don't think they will offer any really serious opposition,' said Chapman. 'Personally, I think that any firm who tries to build an engine – its own engine – and a chassis is in difficulty from the start.

'Take Ferraris for instance. They have difficulties at the moment. They either get their engines working properly at the same time as they find faults in the chassis – or when they eradicate the chassis faults, they find their engines need improving.

'Besides which, Ferraris never seem to have a chassis working as well as my own or Cooper's do. They are learning and they are copying, but, happily, people who copy are always just that little bit behind the original designer.'

Opposite: Graham Hill accelerates away on his victory lap after winning the 1962 Dutch Grand Prix at Zandvoort, his first World Championship win.

In the mire: Phil Hill (left) and Lorenzo Bandini discuss the Ferrari 156's lack of performance during the '62 season with a youthful Mauro Forghieri, the team's newly promoted engineer.

Opposite: Dan Gurney speeds to victory with the flat-eight-cylinder Porsche 804 in the 1962 French Grand Prix at Rouen-les-Essarts.

JIM CLARK, who died at the age of 32 when his F2 Lotus 48 crashed at Hockenheim on 7 April 1968, is still regarded by his many fans as the greatest racing driver the world has ever seen.

For his fellow-Scot, Jackie Stewart, this is also the inevitable verdict. It is a judgement which comes from a man who not only raced against Clark in F1 regularly from 1965 through to the first Grand Prix of 1968, but also won three World Championship titles to Clark's two. Stewart's assessment also underlines the reality – appreciated by the likes of Stirling Moss and Tony Brooks – that championships alone produce an incomplete index of a racing driver's overall talent.

Clark's racing apprenticeship was played out against a backdrop of considerable anxiety on the part of his parents. His father and mother would have been happier if Jim had been content to channel his energies into the family farm which nestled in the Scottish border countryside close to the village of Chimside. At one point Jim tried to justify his involvement in the sport on the basis that he believed it was a hobby which he could make pay for itself.

'I suppose, in a way, if I had set out to be a Grand Prix driver and made it my life's ambition, then I might have felt a greater sense of achievement,' he once said. 'But, really, I tried to fight against it to a certain extent.'

Clark began racing at club level before dominating the 1960 British Formula Junior Championship in tandem with his Team Lotus running mate, Trevor Taylor. That same season, driving occasionally in the works F1 Lotus 18, he finished fifth on his debut in the Dutch Grand Prix at Zandvoort.

Later that year he was third in the Portuguese GP and, in 1961, armed with the uprated Lotus 21, he finished third at Reims ahead of his team-mate, Innes Ireland. After also using John Surtees and Alan Stacey – who was killed at Spa – in 1960, for the following season Chapman concentrated on the Ireland/Clark combo, even though he realised that they were potentially oil and water.

Robert McGregor Innes Ireland was truly a one-off. Also brought up in the Scottish borders – but in his case in Kirkcudbright, on the opposite coast to Clark's home at Chimside – he was the son of a veterinary surgeon. In his youth he was apprenticed to Rolls-Royce in Glasgow and London, and later, during his National Service, he was commissioned in the King's Own Scottish Borderers and seconded to the Parachute Regiment.

Innes began racing in a vintage Bentley bequeathed to him by an elderly lady friend of his family and hit the headlines in 1960 when his works Lotus 18 twice beat Stirling Moss's Rob Walker Cooper in races at Oulton Park and Goodwood.

Ireland was sufficiently shrewd to appreciate just how superior his machinery had been on those two occasions. He never believed himself to be in Moss's class, but nevertheless posted Team Lotus's maiden World Championship victory in the 1961 US Grand Prix at Watkins Glen. Weeks later, he was fired by Chapman and replaced by Trevor Taylor.

It was a crushing blow to Ireland's morale, kindling a legacy of bitterness which took years to erase. In his own mind, Innes blamed Jimmy for the split with Chapman. Clark, easy-going in some ways yet never privately doubting his own status and ability behind the wheel, felt that Ireland was wrong in blaming him.

Instead of thrashing out their differences and clearing the air, the two Scottish drivers remained at odds until Clark's death in 1968. They never made their peace, although Ireland went some way towards doing so in an emotional yet dignified obituary on his compatriot published in *Autocar*, the magazine for which he was at that time Sports Editor.

Chapman and Clark became a legendary partnership. In 1962, driving the new Lotus 25 powered by a Climax V8 engine, he began a run of domination which was only fleetingly interrupted by the advent of the 3-litre F1 regulations in 1966.

The Lotus founder produced a succession of highly competitive racing cars which were complemented by the tippy-toes driving genius of a man who – like Michael Schumacher more than a generation later – never bothered himself with detailed self-analysis. 'I just get in and drive the car,' said Schumacher in 1997. It was the same for Jimmy Clark.

His old friend, Jabby Crombac, said in 1999, 'Jimmy was the quickest in the world, but he didn't know why. He was just ultimately competitive. The driving just came to him – he didn't have to try.

'One of his main assets was that he was 10/10ths from the start of every race. By the time the others were up to speed, Jimmy had gone.'

The relationship between Clark and Chapman was complex and comfortable. It was founded on mutual trust, although the Lotus boss was probably the dominant partner. It's traditional to depict the pair as something approaching blood brothers, Chapman demonstrating an almost telepathic ability to interpret Clark's comments about the cars' behaviour in order to make specific changes to their set-up.

Despite this, he never let any sentimentality he might have felt towards Jimmy compromise his efforts to get the Scot's services at the cheapest possible price. Chapman always drove a hard bargain.

Clark's first World Championship victory was at Spa-Francorchamps in 1962 in the Belgian Grand Prix, a race he would win for the following three years. His last came barely six years later at Johannesburg's Kyalami circuit in the epochal Lotus 49.

He won just two World Championships, in 1963 and '65. Yet he missed the 1962 and '64 titles by a hair's breadth and the combination of Clark and Lotus dominated that entire era. When Jimmy had a competitive car, the battle was for second place.

The satisfaction Clark derived from his motor racing was deeply personal. 'It's not so much the racing, more the satisfaction of driving a car on the absolute limit and still being in control of it,' he reflected. 'That's the greatest feeling of fascination I get from this business.'

If Jim Clark was characterised as the sport's last great driver from the essentially amateur era, it in no way lessened his professionalism and determination. His death almost literally coincided with the arrival of Lotus's Gold Leaf cigarette sponsorship, a deal that triggered a sea change in the financing of Grand Prix racing which would alter its face for ever.

'By the end of his life Jimmy was becoming much more sophisticated and worldly-wise,' Jackie Stewart told the author. 'I honestly don't think he would have returned to the business of farming when he retired.'

Nobody ever got to know. Clark died at Hockenheim at the peak of his achievement. Author Eric Dymock, an old friend of Jimmy's, summed it up perfectly when he wrote that 'motor racing almost died of a broken heart'.

The success of the BRM in 1962 – and indeed for the remaining years of the 1.5-litre formula – may have been a minor embarrassment for Chapman when one considers these remarks. But in general terms he was correct. The quick response times demanded by the F1 business were such that the sport's most senior category would continue to be ruled by the small specialist chassis constructors. For the foreseeable future, at least.

On the technical front, low-pressure fuel injection became *de rigueur* in 1963 with Lucas systems boosting both Coventry Climax and BRM power outputs to just above the 200 bhp mark. Meanwhile in Italy Ferrari started along the road back to serious success with the recruitment of John Surtees as its lead driver, the former motor cycle ace having apparently found the sort of personal rapport with Enzo Ferrari that he had previously enjoyed with Count Domenico Agusta during his days of two-wheeled competition.

There were also changes on the technical side at Maranello, Carlo Chiti's defection to ATS accelerating the career prospects of a talented young engineer, Mauro Forghieri, whose father, Reclus, had been a pre-war Scuderia Ferrari pattern maker who had worked on the cylinder heads for the first Alfa Romeo 158s.

'I had originally been to see Ferrari at the end of 1960,' recalled Surtees, 'but when I decided to join them at the end of 1962 I judged it had to be the finest time to go there. They were on the floor, but they also wanted to pick themselves up and have a bit of a go. Forghieri had come in, and I got on with him fine.'

Fitted with a specially developed high-pressure Bosch fuel injection system, the initial '63 Ferrari 156 developed a theoretical 200 bhp at 10,000 rpm. 'The problem was that it wasn't safe to rev it where it developed its full power,' said Surtees wistfully. 'There was no comparison with the Climax or BRM V8s.'

Yet there were no ifs or buts about the outcome of the 1963 World Championship. Jim Clark and Lotus fully realised the potential that was clearly lurking the previous year. Armed with the elegant Lotus 25, the shy Scot won the Belgian, Dutch, French, British, Italian, Mexican and South African Grands Prix to clinch the title with 54 points net (counting the best six results – which were six wins!) ahead of Graham Hill and his BRM team-mate, Richie Ginther, on 29 points apiece.

Yet Surtees would put Ferrari back in the F1 winner's circle for the first time since Monza in 1961 when he took the latest 156 to victory in the German Grand Prix at the Nürburgring. Clark strained every sinew to keep up with a misfiring Lotus 25 which was running on only seven of its eight cylinders for much of the distance. It was Ferrari's sole win of the season, but it did much for the team's morale.

Back in Maranello this success was greeted with considerable satisfaction. In particular it served as a dramatic counterpoint to the efforts of ATS, the new Italian F1 operation founded by Count Giovanni Volpi de Misurata, industrialist Giorgio Billi and Jaime Ortiz Patino, the millionaire heir to a Bolivian tin fortune.

Under the technical guidance of Carlo Chiti, ATS set up shop in opposition to Ferrari, designed and built its own V8 engine and signed up fellow-Maranello refugees Phil Hill and Baghetti to drive. The whole project was an absolute and utter disaster. The money quickly ran out and ATS vanished, almost without trace, at the end of the season.

Elsewhere on the F1 grids Cooper was in steady decline just as the new Brabham team began to emerge as a force to be reckoned with. After Porsche withdrew from F1 at the end of '62, Dan Gurney signed to drive for Jack Brabham's new outfit and would stay there for three seasons. It was a partnership which would yield two Grand Prix victories, both in 1964, and confirmed the lanky American driver as one of the few drivers capable of giving Clark a decent run for his money.

Yet Clark remained easily the man to beat into the 1964 season. Early that year the Japanese Honda company decided on an F1 involvement and sent its Chief Engineer, Yoshio Nakamura, to Europe to make contact with the competing teams and find one which might be prepared to use its engine.

Nakamura was impressed with Brabham, but Colin

Bernard Cahier

Chapman then muscled in on the deal. A mock-up of Honda's transverse V12 engine duly arrived at the Lotus headquarters at Cheshunt, Hertfordshire, but no more was heard of the project. The ever-resourceful Chapman had been using the possible Honda connection to put pressure on Coventry Climax to continue development of its own V8. It worked a treat and Honda, slightly irked that it had been used in such tawdry fashion, pressed on with the development of its own car.

FERRARI PICKS UP THE PACE

During the second half of the 1963 season Ferrari produced a 64 x 57.8 mm, 90-degree, 1487 cc V8 engine, developed under the direction of Angelo Bellei, but although it was exhaustively tested the new unit did not make its race debut until the following year's non-title Syracuse Grand Prix in Sicily.

The power output was claimed to be in the order of 210 bhp at 11,000 rpm, which was enough to keep Maranello in play with the opposition from BRM and Coventry Climax. Predictably, Ferrari's customary preoccupation with its Le Mans sports car programme meant

Opposite: One of the few races which consistently failed to yield to the Clark touch was Monaco. Here Jim accelerates out of the old Station hairpin during the '63 event, from which he retired while leading in the closing stages.

John Surtees in the revamped Ferrari 156 leads Clark's misfiring Lotus 25 during the 1963 German Grand Prix. This would be Surtees's first *Grande Epreuve* victory.

Opposite: Dan the Man. Gurney joined the Brabham team for 1963 and is seen here at Silverstone.

that the V8 was beset by reliability problems and didn't really get into its stride until the second half of the year.

Lotus, meanwhile, was determined to sustain its World Championship momentum. The type 25 reached its ultimate development in the shape of the type 33 derivative, which was a broadly similar concept, with a stiffer monocoque and suspension geometry specifically designed to cater for the new 13-in., wide-track Dunlop tyres.

The Lotus 33 was powered by the latest flat-crank Mk 2A Climax V8, which was now developing 204 bhp at 9800 rpm while the rival BRM delivered 208 bhp at 11,000 rpm. BRM also concentrated its efforts on the new monocoque P261 chassis, which first hit the headlines when Graham Hill drove it to his second straight Monaco Grand Prix victory.

On the driver front, Clark was now partnered by Peter Arundell, Colin Chapman having ditched the amiable Trevor Taylor, who – although very quick – seemed to have become dangerously accident prone during the 1962 and '63 campaigns. This was unfortunately ironic, for Arundell's promising season as Lotus number two came to a premature end when he was involved in a horrifying crash in the Reims F2 race. It would take him 18 months to recover and, while Chapman kept his drive open for 1966, the pleasant Essex driver was never quite the same competitor again.

Taylor would join fellow displaced Lotus man Innes Ireland driving the superbly crafted Tony Robinson-designed, BRM V8-engined cars produced by the British Racing Partnership. For his part, Ireland was absolutely determined to get his own back on Chapman and Clark and there would be at least one occasion during the 1964 season when Innes made it extremely difficult for Clark to lap him, a strategy which merely served to heighten the tensions between them.

BRABHAM EMERGENT

By the start of the 1964 season it was also clear that the Brabham F1 team was becoming a serious force to be reckoned with, particularly now that Dan Gurney was getting into his stride as its *de facto* number one driver.

Jack Brabham was a shrewd operator. He knew that the initial promise displayed by the fine-handling works BT7s during the 1963 season had prompted a considerable degree of interest among the substantial body of privateers within F1 racing, most of whom had hitherto relied on second-hand Lotus or Cooper machinery in order to take part.

However, by the end of the '63 season Cooper's level of competitiveness was fading fast and independent teams were continually finding themselves frustrated by Colin Chapman's avowed policy of never allowing the customers to have equipment anywhere near as good as that available to the works drivers.

Several private entrants had been more than slightly put out when Chapman sold them Lotus 24s at the start of 1962, having assured them he was supplying them with up-to-the-minute machinery, and then equipped his works team with the new monocoque Lotus 25s, justifying this on the basis that these were the 1963 cars 'under development'.

Interestingly, if anything, Brabham took the opposite view and made sure that most of its 1964 customer BT11s were supplied to their purchasers before the works cars were built up. One of the converts to

Brabham ownership in 1964 was none other than Rob Walker, who had experienced much sadness over the previous couple of seasons, Stirling Moss's Goodwood accident having been followed all too soon by the deaths of both Ricardo Rodriguez and former motor cycle ace Gary Hocking at the wheels of his Lotus 24-BRMs at the end of the 1962 season.

Unhappily Walker's new Brabham-BRM, driven by Jo Bonnier, was burnt out in an unfortunate fire during practice for the '64 Silverstone International Trophy race, an event which marked the Brabham marque's maiden F1 success after Jack lunged round the outside of Graham Hill's BRM on the final lap at Woodcote Corner.

Jack and his highly regarded Chief Designer, Ron Tauranac, gained much wry amusement from the fact that the spaceframe Brabhams with their outboard front spring/dampers were fully competitive with the monocoque BRM and Lotus, both of which sported inboard front suspension neatly tucked in out of the airflow.

Tauranac attributed at least part of the effectiveness of those early Brabham-Climaxes on fast circuits to the aerodynamic lessons learned from his links with no less a company than Jaguar.

'I knew Malcolm Sayer, who had done the aerodynamics of the Jaguar D-type, and we went to the MIRA wind

Opposite: Chris Amon at the Nürburgring in 1964 with the Parnell Racing ex-works Lotus 25 powered by a BRM V8 engine. One of the factory BRMs is seen in the background.

Opposite, bottom: John Surtees's Ferrari 156 chases Graham Hill's BRM out of the Station hairpin during the '63 Monaco Grand Prix.

Below: The ever-amenable, supremely popular Daniel Sexton Gurney.

Bernard Cahier

tunnel under his auspices,' Tauranac told the author. 'From that we learned to run the nose of our cars as close to the track as possible in order to prevent too much air getting underneath and generating lift. I think this was the problem with the Lotus 24 which Jack had complained about at Spa in 1962.' Jack had briefly raced his own private Lotus while waiting for the first Brabham F1 chassis to be readied that year.

Graham Hill may have won in Monaco, but Gurney put the Brabham on pole at Zandvoort for the Dutch Grand Prix, only to retire with a broken steering wheel. Clark won that race commandingly for Lotus, but Dan then ran away with the Belgian GP at Spa-Francorchamps before experiencing a heart-breaking retirement in the closing moments of the race.

After only five laps round the daunting Belgian track, Gurney was 12s ahead of a battle between Clark, Hill and Bruce McLaren's Cooper for second place. John Surtees's Ferrari was an early retirement and Gurney piled on lap record after lap record, finally leaving it at 3m 49.2s, a stunning average of 137.60 mph. This would have been quick enough 30 years later, but this was being achieved by a tiny spaceframe Brabham running on tyres narrower than one finds in 1999 on the average super-performance road car.

Clark was experiencing quite severe overheating with the Lotus 33 and came in to top up with water on lap 28, only for Gurney suddenly to slow. On lap 30 Hill tore past into the lead as Gurney's Brabham hurtled into the pits, its driver crying, 'Fuel, fuel!'

However, this wasn't the highly disciplined and organised world of Grand Prix racing, 1990s-style. No fuel was immediately available and, rather than wait for the churns to be humped round from behind the pits, he resumed the chase. He had almost ground to a halt on the previous lap as the Brabham spluttered low on fuel, but the mechanics were convinced he had sufficient to make it to the flag.

Into the last lap, therefore, the order was Hill, McLaren, Gurney and Clark, but Dan never made it round to the finish, rolling to a halt with dry tanks at Stavelot. Hill ran out shortly afterwards and McLaren was left to stagger on in the lead, his Cooper misfiring ominously with a flattening battery.

Just as it looked as though the Cooper might score an incredibly lucky outsider's victory, Clark came as if from nowhere and surged by Bruce within yards of the flag to take one of the most unlikely wins of his career. Ironically, his Lotus 33 then ran out of fuel on the slowing-down lap and he coasted to a halt alongside Gurney's silent Brabham. Neither knew the true outcome of the afternoon's events and they commiserated with each other until they were told that Jimmy had, in fact, emerged the winner.

Gurney's big day finally came in the French Grand Prix at Rouen-les-Essarts. Two years after winning there for Porsche, he now scored the Brabham team's first World Championship victory. Clark hit trouble after leading initially, but Gurney had been the class of the field at Spa and certainly deserved this consolation prize.

1963
June: George Michael, British pop musician, is born.
August: An armed gang hijack a train and escape with more than £2.5 million in a raid dubbed the 'Great Train Robbery'.
November: The push-button telephone is introduced for the first time in the USA.
November: American President John F. Kennedy is shot dead by a hidden assassin as he drives through the centre of Dallas.

Opposite: Dan's day at Rouen. Gurney wins the 1964 French Grand Prix to score the Brabham team's most important win to date.

Below: John Surtees drives in to celebrate victory in the '64 German Grand Prix at the wheel of the Ferrari 158.

Right: **Sign of things to come. Honda's new transverse-engined F1 challenger in the paddock at Zandvoort during testing prior to its race debut.**

Below: **US sports car driver Ronnie Bucknum debuts the new Honda in the '64 German Grand Prix, where it spun off the road.**

Photos: Bernard Cahier

Brands Hatch hosted the British Grand Prix for the first time in '64 and Clark won his home race for the third year in a row, beating Graham Hill's BRM by just over a couple of seconds. John Surtees was third in the improving Ferrari 158 and would go on to score his second straight win in the German Grand Prix at the Nürburgring, the next round on the title schedule.

Surtees edged out Clark's Lotus 33 to take pole position, and while Jimmy led the opening lap Surtees was soon through into the lead. Both Clark and Gurney hit trouble, allowing the Ferrari team leader to storm home first by over a minute from Graham Hill's misfiring BRM, Lorenzo Bandini in the earlier Ferrari 156 and Jo Siffert's private Brabham-BRM.

HONDA MAKES ITS F1 BID

After that earlier rebuff from Colin Chapman, Honda's new RA271 F1 challenger made its debut in the 1964 German Grand Prix. Its 58.1 x 47 mm, 1498 cc four-overhead-camshaft V12 was mounted transversely in the chassis, and it was claimed that this latest F1 machine produced in excess of 200 bhp on its debut outing.

That may well have been the case, but the Honda engineers directed by Yoshio Nakamura certainly needed to polish up their chassis engineering technology. The tale of how the team's driver, Ronnie Bucknum, came to drive the car on this occasion remains one of the strangest stories of post-war F1 history. An SCCA sports car driver from California, he was plucked from relative obscurity to debut the new Honda following the somewhat convoluted logic that, since the Japanese company did not have any F1 experience, it made sense to recruit a driver who was correspondingly raw to the challenge. Needless to say, the car ran right at the back of the pack.

Nürburgring '64 was the start of a good run for Maranello. Later in August the Zeltweg military aerodrome turned its runways over to racing cars as the venue for the first F1 Austrian Grand Prix. By the mid-1990s the airfield would be crammed to bursting point with the executive jets owned by F1's new glitterati, but in 1964 F1 was indeed a much more primitive affair.

Although the 3.2-km, straw bale-lined perimeter road/runway track looked pretty crude, even by the fairly tolerant standards of the day, most people praised the initiative and enthusiasm of the organisers in having managed to stage a World Championship qualifying round at all. The race also marked the F1 debut of Austrian rising star Jochen Rindt, who drove Rob Walker's Brabham-BRM only a couple of months after stunning the British racing community with a dazzling win in the Whit Monday Formula 2 international at Crystal Palace at the wheel of his own Brabham-Ford.

Dan Gurney's Brabham led off the line but John Surtees nipped ahead in the Ferrari 158 on the second lap, only for the Italian car's rear suspension to become one of the first casualties of the dramatically bumpy track surface a few laps later. Gurney looked set for an easy win – Clark having retired with a broken driveshaft – but a front suspension radius arm pulled out of the Brabham's chassis. All this drama and mechanical mayhem allowed Ferrari number two Lorenzo Bandini through to post the sole Grand Prix win of his career.

The Austrian race marked another twist in the downhill spiral in which Cooper seemed to have been locked

Honda engineer Yoshio Nakamura with Ronnie Bucknum, Nürburgring, 1964.

for over a year since John Cooper had been involved in a road accident which left him badly bashed about. For the 1964 season it had been planned to run the very promising young American driver, Timmy Mayer, as Bruce McLaren's team-mate, but tragedy intervened early in the season when Mayer – whose elder brother, Teddy, would later become a director of McLaren Racing – was killed during practice for one of the Tasman races at Longford, Tasmania.

His place in the factory Cooper team was taken by '61 World Champion Phil Hill, but the pleasant American was beginning to run out of enthusiasm for the business. Emotionally bruised by the ATS experience, he now found himself behind the wheel of another less-than-totally-competitive Grand Prix car. It just didn't work out.

At Zeltweg he crashed heavily in practice, then again in the race with the team's spare car. On the second occasion the Cooper burst into flames. In the aftermath, strong words were exchanged between Phil and John Cooper and the American driver was fired, only to be reinstated in the team in time for his home race at Watkins Glen, the next race but one on the World Championship schedule. Sadly, while his son and the team were away in America, Charles Cooper died suddenly at his home in Surrey at the age of 71.

After Bandini's win in Austria, Ferrari attempted to raise the tempo of its challenge for the Italian Grand Prix at Monza with the introduction of its new Mauro Forghieri-developed flat-12-cylinder engine. This 56 x 50.4 mm, 1489 cc unit was claimed to develop 220 bhp at 11,500 rpm, giving it quite a performance increment over its contemporary V8 rivals.

Bandini briefly tried the 1512 – as the flat-12-engined car was designated – in wet practice on the second day of the Monza meeting, but Surtees used the 158 to take pole position a full 0.8s ahead of Gurney's Brabham. In the event Surtees would win commandingly after his key opposition failed, most notably Graham Hill's BRM lurching

1964
February: 'Beatlemania' seizes the USA as the British pop group arrives in New York.
March: Radio Caroline, a 'pirate' station, begins broadcasting from a ship in the North Sea.
May: Jawaharlal Nehru, Prime Minister of India since independence in 1947, dies at the age of 74.
June: Nelson Mandela is jailed for life after being convicted of conspiring to overthrow the South African government.
October: Britain elects a Labour government for the first time in 13 years, with Harold Wilson becoming Prime Minister.

to a halt on the grid when its clutch thrust mechanism seized at the start.

Bandini finished third behind Bruce McLaren's Cooper, just beating Richie Ginther's BRM to the line in a photo finish, while Ludovico Scarfiotti finished ninth in one of the earlier 156s.

Before the teams then moved on to North America for the final two races of the season, Ferrari fell out with the Italian automobile federation over the disputed homologation of the 250LM sports car. In a fury, the Old Man announced that he would be relinquishing his entrant's licence and would not be fielding cars in his name on home soil again.

To underpin this latest melodramatic outburst, Ferrari's works entries for the US and Mexican Grands Prix were turned out in the blue and white racing colours of the USA and entered by his loyal American importer Luigi Chinetti's North American Racing Team.

Clark, Graham Hill and Surtees all crossed the Atlantic knowing they could win the World Championship. Jimmy was favourite; he qualified on pole at Watkins Glen and was just beginning to get the upper hand in a battle with Surtees when he dropped from contention with fuel injection problems.

Surtees's chances of victory were wiped out by a spin while lapping a slower car and so John had to settle for second behind Graham Hill's winning BRM.

Hill now looked likely to take the title, but in Mexico City Bandini pitched him into a spin as they jostled for position into one of the slowest hairpins and Graham had to make a pit stop to have his BRM's squashed exhaust tailpipes prised open after making smart contact with the guard rail.

'That won Surtees the World Championship,' recalls Tim Parnell, son of Reg. 'I suppose Lorenzo was embarrassed to a certain degree. He was typically Italian in that, having done something like that in the heat of battle, he would then be apologetic and *simpatico* in the aftermath. But he certainly robbed poor old Graham of that title.'

John Surtees also recalls the episode from his own perspective: 'In the aftermath of the accident, a lot of people started gunning for Lorenzo, suggesting that he had driven recklessly in order to help me. Most of these critics were, of course, a good way from the incident and in no position to judge it for themselves.

'Lorenzo may have occasionally tended towards over-exuberance, but he never indulged in dirty tactics. He and Graham shook hands over the whole business very soon after the event and there was no lasting animosity between them.'

Yet this was only part of the story on that sweltering afternoon. While all this drama had been going on way down the field, Jimmy Clark was again in complete control at the head of the pack. Unfortunately for the Scot, his car was losing oil in the closing stages and what should have been a dominant, flag-to-flag, title-clinching victory was snatched away on the final lap when the Lotus's Climax engine seized.

Gurney went through to win for Brabham while Bandini dropped behind Surtees to give the one-time motor cycle champion his first and only F1 drivers' title with 40 points to Hill's 39 and Clark's 32.

Opposite: Wearing an unfamiliar livery, Ferrari's flat-12-powered 1512 was given its race debut in the two transatlantic events at the end of the 1964 season in the hands of Lorenzo Bandini.

Opposite, bottom: The way we were. From the left, Dan Gurney, Jim Clark, John Surtees and Phil Hill before the start of the '64 Mexican Grand Prix.

Below: Graham Hill's '64 title chances were scuppered at Mexico City after his BRM was rammed by Bandini's Ferrari at this point on the circuit and pitched into a spin.

Bernard Cahier

Below: Jackie Stewart and Graham Hill, BRM team-mates, at Monza, 1965, where JYS would score the first of 27 career victories.

GOODYEAR AND STEWART ARRIVE ON THE SCENE

The 1965 season was the last under the 1.5-litre regulations and was marked by two arrivals on the Grand Prix scene which would have enormous future significance for the sport. On the driver front the appearance of the young Scot, Jackie Stewart, as Graham Hill's team-mate at BRM would have huge ramifications on several fronts.

Not only would Stewart, the winner of the 1964 British F3 Championship at the wheel of a Tyrrell team Cooper-BMC, emerge as one of the finest F1 drivers of his era, he would also become a powerful influence in making Grand Prix racing a much safer sport.

The other significant development was the arrival of the US tyre company, Goodyear, to challenge Dunlop's supremacy, which had lasted ever since 1958, when Peter Collins won the British Grand Prix for Ferrari on Belgian Englebert rubber.

Goodyear had returned to motor racing in the mid-1950s after a lay-off of more than 30 years, initially with sports cars and stock cars, and it was during this period that the Akron-based company pioneered the semi-slick tread pattern. The company also made a preliminary, almost unnoticed, foray into F1, supplying tyres for Lance Reventlow's Scarab project, and then began to raise its commercial profile with a first foray to Indianapolis in 1963.

Goodyear tyres were next raced in Europe in 1964, when Frank Gardner competed at Pau in a John Willment-entered Lotus 27. The company then graduated to Grand Prix racing with Honda, and for 1965 it also supplied the works Brabham team.

BRP FORCED TO CLOSE ITS DOORS

As Honda ramped up its F1 efforts, so Ken Gregory and Alfred Moss found themselves forced by commercial pressures to close the doors of the British Racing Partnership.

This was one of the very first examples of F1 teams acting as a cartel to squeeze out one of their own. BRP had been running their Tony Robinson-designed, BRM-engined cars since the start of 1963, but now they fell foul of the Paris Agreement – a cosy deal between BRM, Lotus, Cooper, Brabham and the Grand Prix organisers.

This amounted to a relatively simple predecessor of the present Concorde Agreement by which the commercial dimension of the sport is governed in the 1990s. In essence, the terms of the Paris Agreement were that each of the signatories would get £800 starting money per car in each Grand Prix – on top of which the drivers concerned would get starting money of between £150 and £450 per race, depending on their points score from the previous year.

However, BRP was not a signatory of the Paris Agreement and found itself progressively squeezed throughout the 1964 season. Towards the end of the year they applied for 'membership' of the agreement, and at the US Grand Prix at Watkins Glen Tony Robinson announced that the cars were ready for inspection at any time.

The outcome of this process was that BRP was not permitted to join the Paris Agreement as it was decreed that it did not make a sufficiently large proportion of its own car. Faced with a loss on the season of £7000 – a huge amount of money in 1964 for a private venture – the BRP operation was forced to close down.

Innes Ireland never minced his words when it came to the subject of the British Racing Partnership. Perhaps he hadn't enjoyed the success he felt he deserved during his two years driving for Ken Gregory and Alfred Moss. Perhaps he was too much of an enthusiast in an increasingly intense, professional sport.

Yet nobody could deny the fact that Innes was a racer to the core of his soul. He also had a very well defined sense of right and wrong. And the treatment meted out to the British Racing Partnership deeply offended the Scot's sense of propriety.

'How ludicrous it is that a large and properly organised outfit like BRP cannot afford to race,' he wrote. 'I feel it is an indication of how much "sport" is left within the sport when there is so little concern that a fine team like BRP has had to go to the wall.'

Innes was certainly becoming embittered and recounted in his excellent autobiography, *All Arms and Elbows* (Pelham Books, 1967), how he had once had a chat with another driver who began questioning him about the financial details of motor racing. Innes admitted, rather sniffily, he hadn't a clue about these things.

Reading between the lines it would be all too easy to

Bernard Cahier

conclude that the driver he was referring to was the commercially astute Jackie Stewart. Ireland had his enthusiasm for Jackie well under control for many years, but his feelings definitely mellowed towards the end of his life. By the time Innes died – far too young at 63 – in 1993, he had developed a grudging respect and admiration for his younger compatriot.

Meanwhile, for Stewart, the decision to join the BRM team in 1965 was not a difficult one. In fact, he recalls it as one of the best moves he ever made during his racing career.

'I was being courted heavily by Colin Chapman and it was a very intoxicating thought to go and join Jim Clark, another Scot, whom I admired enormously,' he said. 'I was very much in awe of his talent, but it wouldn't have worked for me and I was certainly aware of that. I could [also] have gone to Cooper' – the berth alongside Bruce McLaren was eventually taken by Jochen Rindt – 'but I chose BRM because it was a good team and I knew that I needed a team that wouldn't push me too hard too soon.

'They had Graham Hill as a number one driver and anybody who came along as number two was going to be just that. Nevertheless, I saw in Graham a talent not as great as Jim Clark's, in sheer driving skill, but also an enormous determination and a wealth of knowledge I could learn from.

'Funnily enough, I didn't think there was much I could learn from Jimmy because his natural talent was so great that sometimes I don't think he knew how he did it.'

Stewart proved to be an outstandingly promising F1 novice. He finished sixth on his World Championship debut in the South African Grand Prix, beat reigning title holder Surtees into second place in the Silverstone International Trophy and then outfumbled team-mate Graham Hill to win the Italian Grand Prix at Monza. He was clearly going to be quite a player.

Yet it was Clark who dominated the 1965 season with his trusty Lotus 33, clinching the World Championship as early as the German Grand Prix at the Nürburgring, a race which he utterly dominated. He wrapped up the title with three races remaining despite the fact that he had not taken part in the Monaco Grand Prix as he was away winning the Indy 500. That left Graham Hill to score a hat-trick of victories for BRM. 'Wish Jimmy had been there to see it,' remarked Hill laconically.

Both the Lotus and Brabham teams were supplied with uprated 32-valve versions of the Climax V8, now nudging the 215 bhp mark at 10,800 rpm, but somehow Dan Gurney's unit always seemed to be running into technical

Below: My turn next! Jackie Stewart congratulates Graham Hill after the Londoner had completed his Monaco Grand Prix hat-trick in 1965.

Bernard Cahier

Bernard Cahier

1965
January: Winston Churchill dies.
February: US President Lyndon B. Johnson orders the US Air Force and Navy to start bombing military targets in Vietnam.
October: The Post Office Tower is opened in London, and becomes the city's tallest building.

After more than six seasons with Cooper, Bruce McLaren decided to strike out on his own at the end of 1965.

trouble. Clark's tended not to, of course, and it was more than enough to keep the brilliant Scot in play at the front of the pack even though the rival BRM and Honda engines were reputedly developing more than 220 bhp.

The Brabham team's 32-valver never worked properly after Jack himself blew it up during the Monaco Grand Prix. 'It never ran well from that day onwards, even though Climax tried hard to repair it,' said Gurney. 'My best run with it was at Clermont-Ferrand, I suppose, when I set fastest race lap quite early on. Then the dam thing broke, as usual, and Jimmy went faster anyway . . .' And on that day Clark was using the Team Lotus spare type 25 – fitted with an earlier-spec 16-valve Climax V8!

At the same time Coventry-Climax was planning a last hurrah in the form of the FWMW flat-16, a complex 54.1 x 40.64 mm, 1495 cc unit which employed a central gear train driving its eight overhead camshafts (four on each bank). In fact, the engine ran into all sorts of problems during dynamometer testing, most of them due to the use of its central power take-off, and although there were tentative plans for it to be raced at Monza another major failure on the test bed a few days before it was due to be shipped consigned this novel engine to the F1 history books.

Although mechanical unreliability thwarted Dan Gurney's efforts through 1965 to the point where the Brabham number one was unable to add to the marque's victories the previous year at Rouen and Mexico City, Honda really began to make its presence felt now that former BRM ace Richie Ginther had been signed to lead the team.

For the British Grand Prix at Silverstone Ginther qualified third on the front row of the grid, just 0.5s away from Clark's pole-position Lotus 33, and briefly led through the first corner before dropping back steadily, later to retire.

At Zandvoort, Ginther again made the front row with third-fastest time and led the opening lap, eventually scoring Honda's first World Championship point with a sixth-place finish.

Finally, on 24 October, the curtain rang down on the 1.5-litre F1 when Ginther walked away to win the Mexican Grand Prix. 'I looked in my mirror at the end of the first lap and just didn't see a soul until I was clear past the end of the pits,' he recalled. 'I thought that I had dropped a gallon of oil and they had all spun out behind me.'

Ginther maintained an iron grip on the race – aided by a combination of sticky Goodyear rubber and the Honda

Opposite page: Men at work. Top: Lorenzo Bandini in the Ferrari and (bottom) new boy Jochen Rindt in the works Cooper-Climax.

Opposite: Richie Ginther steers the Honda to victory in Mexico City, 1965, in the final race under the 1.5-litre regulations.

Opposite, bottom: A delighted Ginther accepts the plaudits of the crowd.

Below: Forghieri looks gloomy sitting in the Ferrari cockpit at Silverstone surrounded by the chaps in sports jackets.

technicians' success in making the transverse V12 perform well at the Mexico City circuit's 7000 ft altitude – and came home the winner by 2.7s from Gurney's similarly shod Brabham.

With this victory, Honda had grasped a prize beyond the reach of Brabham and Ferrari, both of which had failed to win a Grand Prix during the course of the 1965 season. For its part, Maranello had concentrated on the development of its flat-12 engine and this never really came right until the Italian Grand Prix at Monza, where revised cylinder heads really enabled Surtees to pile on the pressure.

He qualified the Ferrari 1512 on the front row of the grid alongside Clark's Lotus 33 and, although hydraulic problems with the clutch caused him to get away slowly and complete the opening lap down in 14th place, he clawed his way back up into the leading bunch. After he had contested the lead for a few laps the clutch slipped out of business for good.

It was John Surtees's final outing at the wheel of a 1.5-litre F1 car for he crashed his own Team Surtees Lola-Chevrolet sports car at Toronto's Mosport Park circuit only a few weeks afterwards. John was very seriously hurt and hung between life and death for a few days before starting out on a recovery which would see him back behind the wheel of an F1 Ferrari the following season.

The final points tally at the end of the year confirmed that Clark had won the World Championship again with 54 points to Graham Hill's 40 and Stewart's 33.

Now it was a question of planning ahead for the future. In the Lotus line-up, Peter Arundell was poised to return and displace stand-in Mike Spence as Jim Clark's team-mate for 1966, the first season of the new 3-litre F1.

Bruce McLaren was off to start his own F1 operation, leaving Jochen Rindt to lead the once-famous Cooper team, and, while Bandini would remain partnering Surtees at Ferrari, Dan Gurney decided he would leave Jack Brabham to start his own All American Racers Grand Prix programme. Dan admitted he was moving with more than a sliver of regret.

'I felt at home on the team and Jack had gradually come to rely on my driving as the strongest,' he said. 'However, I had the chance to do it with my own Eagle. That was too good a prospect to turn down, so I had to say goodbye with regrets.

'I always admired Jack and enjoyed working with him. We were a very small team, but we always seemed to be in the hunt. Jack was a very good engineer and a great man to fix things in the field, despite the fact that we might not have the proper tools or facilities.

'He was also tighter than a bull's ass in fly season. Those were the days!'

Bernard Cahier

MARANELLO
SALES LTD

CONSTRUCTORS CHAMPIONSHIP

1 9 6 1

1 9 6 4

1 9 7 5

1 9 7 6

1 9 7 7

1 9 7 9

1 9 8 2

1 9 8 3

1 9 9 9

F 1 WORLD DRIVERS CHAMPIONSHI

Alberto Ascari

Juan Manuel Fangio

Mike Hawthern

Phil Hill

John Surtees

Niki Lauda

Jody Scheckter

MANUFACTURERS TITLES

1953

1954

1956

1957

1958

1960

1961

1962

1963

1964

1965

1967

1972

CHAPTER SIX: 1966–74
THE HEYDAY OF THE COSWORTH DFV

TOWARDS THE end of 1963, the CSI announced technical regulations for the new Formula 1 which was scheduled to start on 1 January 1966. At the time there was a feeling inside motor racing that a move to more powerful cars would probably be appropriate when it came to the next change of rules, so it was decided that from the start of 1966 engines would be 3 litres unsupercharged or 1.5 litres supercharged.

This latter provision was implemented as nothing more than a stop-gap measure to help those teams who wanted to continue in F1 but lacked access to a 3-litre engine. It was felt that supercharging the old 1.5-litre V8 BRM or Climax units might be a short-term solution. In reality, this was a somewhat fanciful prospect; Coventry Climax had announced its withdrawal from F1 at the end of the 1.5-litre era and nobody pursued this complicated option. It would, however, come back to bite the Grand Prix world more than a decade later – as we shall see.

As far as Enzo Ferrari was concerned, the 3-litre rules were just fine by him, but the speed with which he produced the prototype of his first car for the new formula, the V12-powered 312, helped create a false impression as to the potential for Maranello domination in 1966. Nevertheless, he was first out of the box.

The first 312 was unveiled at Maranello in December 1965. Frankly, it looked a very large machine indeed. Its 60-degree, 77 × 53.5 mm, 2989 cc V12 engine was closely related to the 3.3-litre Le Mans engine, reputedly developing 360 bhp. This subsequently turned out to be rubbish.

Similarly, it was claimed that the Ferrari 312 tipped the scales at 548 kg at a time when the minimum weight limit was set at 500 kg. However, when it was scrutineered at Syracuse for its first race, it tipped the scales at 604 kg. Put simply, Ferrari was set for a fall.

Ranged against the Maranello brigade was what, in retrospect, one can only describe as a rag-bag of improvised machinery. At the start of 1965 John Cooper had sold out to the Chipstead Motor Group for around £200,000. This relieved John, who was still feeling the after-effects of that 1963 road accident, of the business worries of running the company while allowing him to retain his hands-on involvement with the racing team.

Chipstead had been concerned at the costs involved in using the Climax engines during that final season under the 1.5-litre regulations and eventually struck a deal to use a 3-litre Maserati V12 which was an uprated version of the unit fitted to Jean Behra's Maserati 250F a decade earlier.

Maserati engineer Giulio Alfieri revised the engine with 70.4 × 64 mm, 2989 cc dimensions, developing around 340 bhp at 9000 rpm. The first Cooper-Maserati tested at Goodwood in November 1965 and eventually the works team would be supplemented by customer T81

chassis for Rob Walker (driven by Jo Siffert) plus owner-drivers Jo Bonnier and Guy Ligier.

The works Coopers would be driven by Jochen Rindt and Richie Ginther, the latter waiting for the new 3-litre Honda V12 to be race ready, although Denny Hulme briefly tried the car during an early test. In fact, Hulme would remain with the Brabham team, for whom he had driven in F1 on an intermittent basis over the previous 18 months or so.

Jack Brabham opted for what turned out to be the most successful route for the new formula. The Australian Repco company was developing a new V8, based on General Motors' abandoned linerless engine programme for a projected 3.5-litre Buick 'compact' saloon, with the intention of providing a Tasman-formula power unit to replace the elderly 2.5-litre Climax four-cylinder engines which had been the mainstay of the Antipodean category for many years.

However, designer Phil Irving concluded that the F85 Oldsmobile cylinder block which was the basis of the Repco V8 could easily deal with the stresses and strains of running in 3-litre form. With just a month or so to go before the opening race of the new formula, the first type 620 Repco V8 was installed in the Brabham BT19 chassis which had originally been earmarked for the still-born flat-16 Climax engine.

With a bore and stroke of 88.9 × 60.32 mm, the 2995 cc engine developed 315 bhp at a relatively leisurely 7250 rpm. And it was just the ticket.

Some motor racing historians portray Jack Brabham as little more than a driver-cum-mechanic who got lucky. Such judgements are extremely wide of the mark. Objectively, when preparing for the 1966 F1, he and Ron Tauranac were the only people who stuck to what has always been the most basic tenet of racing car design – namely, that the machine involved should always be as light and agile as possible.

Colin Chapman can be excluded from this blanket criticism because, as we shall see, he had already taken steps to guarantee Team Lotus's future with the Cosworth Ford DFV programme. Yet that was only in its fledgling stage at the start of 1966, leaving Jim Clark to go about defending his World Championship with a 2-litre Climax V8-engined Lotus 33. Until, that is, the BRM H-16 engine was made available to Lotus on a customer basis.

The H-16 was the brainchild of BRM engineer Tony Rudd, the man who had masterminded the British team's rise to consistent competitiveness during the halcyon days of the 1.5-litre formula. His idea was, effectively, to couple together two of the 1.5-litre V8s – but with their cylinder banks redesigned to create two horizontally opposed eight-cylinder units, allowing the crankshafts to be geared together.

This 69 × 48.8 mm, 2998 cc engine reputedly gave

1966
June: The first British credit card, the Barclaycard, is introduced.
July: England win the football World Cup final at Wembley Stadium, beating West Germany 4–2 after extra time.
October: 116 children and 28 adults are killed when a rain-soaked colliery tip slides down into the Welsh village of Aberfan.
December: Walt Disney, US cartoon producer, dies.

Opposite, top: Jack Brabham shrewdly judged that a light and nimble package using the Repco V8 engine would be competitive at the start of the new 3-litre formula.

Opposite: Jochen Rindt wrestles one of the Cooper T81-Maseratis round Monaco, 1966. The engine was descended from the 2.5-litre V12 used in the factory Maserati 250F eight years earlier.

400 bhp at 10,750 rpm from the outset. Yet its supposed competitiveness was undermined by its weight and a level of technical complexity which meant that it was hideously unreliable.

Nevertheless, the media greeted the arrival of this new engine with customary deference. Writing in *Autosport*, John Bolster noted: 'An extremely high standard of engineering will be called for to make the units fully interchangeable without upsetting the suspension adjustments, but fine engineering is right up BRM's street.'

At the same time as developing the H-16, BRM commissioned a parallel V12 engine programme, which was carried out by former BRM Chief Engineer Peter Berthon, now working in conjunction with Harry Weslake's company at Rye in Sussex.

Installed in the works BRM P83s, the H-16 never delivered a seriously worthwhile result in 1966, although Jim Clark would drive an H-16-engined Lotus 43 to a lucky victory in the US Grand Prix at Watkins Glen. Ironically, on that occasion Clark was using the BRM works team spare engine, loaned to Team Lotus prior to the race after the Scot had suffered an earlier engine failure. To this day, F1 insiders believe that the key factor in this lone victory for the H-16 engine was Clark's extraordinary mechanical sensitivity.

Elsewhere on the F1 landscape the trusty old Climax four-cylinder engines – enlarged to 2.7 litres – were used by privateers and Dan Gurney's AAR Eagles, whose bespoke V12 Weslake units would not be seriously race

ready until 1967. On the tyre front Firestone had joined the F1 party with deals for Lotus, Ferrari and McLaren; Brabham, Honda and Eagle were on Goodyear while Cooper remained on Dunlop. BRM didn't have a tyre deal and used either Dunlop or Firestone products during the course of the year.

The opening race of the 1966 season was at Syracuse, where John Surtees won easily in the Ferrari 312. Then came the Silverstone International Trophy race – an even more important curtain-raiser – where Surtees was thrashed by Jack's new Brabham-Repco.

The F1 fraternity seemed stunned, but the result came as no surprise to Surtees, who had been deeply concerned about the Ferrari 312's apparent lack of performance since he drove it at Syracuse. It had also been two and a half seconds slower round Modena than the compact Dino 246 which had originally been built for Surtees to contest the '66 Tasman Championship, but had not been used following John's accident in Canada.

'Everybody was saying, "Poor old Jack Brabham has only got 290/300 bhp from his Repco engine," and this bloody Ferrari V12, which weighed God knows how much, was really only giving about 270 bhp,' he noted years later.

Surtees led at Monaco, eventually being sidelined with transmission failure. Jackie Stewart won in the 2-litre Tasman BRM P261 which the team was using until the H-16 was race ready – was it ever? – and Lorenzo Bandini finished second in the little Dino 246.

That year's Monaco Grand Prix also marked the debut of Bruce McLaren as a driver/constructor. In 1965 he had decided to go it alone and signed a promising young designer called Robin Herd to build his new team's first F1 car.

The resultant McLaren M2A was a fascinating, if somewhat over-complex, machine. Herd took the ambitious step of building the chassis from a composite laminate of special aluminium sheet bonded over a sandwich filling of balsawood. The material was known as Mallite and had originally been developed for internal panelling in the aviation industry. Light and torsionally rigid, it was also quite complicated to repair in the event of an accident.

The McLaren M2A was powered initially by a 4.5-litre Oldsmobile V8 prepared by engine specialists Traco Engineering and was employed as a development vehicle for Firestone's F1 tyres. The car was then fitted with a pushrod Ford Indianapolis V8 engine which had been reduced from 4.2 to 3 litres at Traco's Californian workshops. This was something of a stop-gap, hardly providing McLaren with a realistic long-term answer to his needs for a seriously competitive F1 power unit.

The Ford V8 engine transmitted its reputed 300 bhp power output through a rather basic four-speed ZF gearbox and it didn't take long for Bruce to conclude that a lot more development work would be required if his F1 effort was to be taken as seriously as he planned. The McLaren-Ford F1 debut ended when an oil pipe union came undone in the nose section, dousing lubricant all over Bruce's feet and the track surface. He switched off before the engine broke.

The Ford V8 was withdrawn for further development, leaving McLaren to find a replacement engine. He turned to Count Volpi's Serenissima company, which had available a sports car-based 3-litre V8 which had been produced by Alberto Massimino, the man who'd designed some of the very earliest Ferraris.

Bernard Cahier

Left: Jackie Stewart drives the 2-litre Tasman BRM P261 to victory in the 1966 Monaco Grand Prix.

Below: A motley collection of largely interim cars at the start of the '66 French Grand Prix at Reims, the final occasion on which this race would take place on the classic road circuit in champagne country. Lorenzo Bandini's Ferrari 312 (left) just gets the jump off the line ahead of John Surtees's Cooper-Maserati, Mike Parkes's Ferrari 312, Jo Siffert's Rob Walker Cooper-Maserati, Jack Brabham's Brabham-Repco and the factory Cooper-Maseratis of Chris Amon and Jochen Rindt.

Bernard Cahier

No motorhome luxury for former World Champion John Surtees back in 1966!

Unfortunately the Serenissima V8 produced only about 260 bhp, but it was better than nothing and was duly installed for the Belgian Grand Prix at Spa-Francorchamps. The first experience of the Italian engine proved to be substantially worse than the Ford outing at Monaco. Once coaxed into firing on all cylinders, it ran its main bearings inside a lap and had to be withdrawn from the race.

The McLaren-Serenissima made its next F1 appearance in the British Grand Prix at Brands Hatch, where Bruce ran in the top six during the early stages, finally finishing sixth to score the marque's first World Championship point.

Surtees then won the Belgian Grand Prix at Spa-Francorchamps brilliantly. But this wasn't good enough for Ferrari's Machiavellian team manager, Eugenio Dragoni, who felt he should not have spent so much time behind Rindt's Cooper-Maserati.

Yet the 1966 Belgian Grand Prix would be best remembered for a first-lap cloudburst which saw the field decimated by a succession of accidents within a mile or

so of the start. Cars skated off the track in all directions, but by far the most serious accident involved the BRM driven by Jackie Stewart, then one of the sport's most promising young rising stars.

'I must have been doing around 165 mph when the car aquaplaned and I lost control,' said Stewart. 'We just ran into a wall of water in the way it can rain only in southern Belgium.

'First I hit a telegraph pole, then a woodcutters' cottage, and I finished up in the outside basement of a farm building. The car ended up shaped like a banana and I was still trapped inside it.

'The fuel tank had totally ruptured inwardly and the monocoque [chassis] literally filled up with fuel. It was sloshing around in the cockpit. The instrument panel was smashed, ripped off and found 200 metres from the car, but the electric fuel pump was still working away. The steering wheel wouldn't come off and I couldn't get out.'

Stewart was eventually helped from the wrecked car by his fellow-BRM drivers, Graham Hill and Bob Bondurant. He sustained four broken ribs, a broken shoulder and pelvic injuries in what was the worst accident of his professional career. It also prompted the Scot to recalibrate his approach to his chosen sport. Racing drivers, he reasoned, should be paid to demonstrate their skill, not simply their bravery in what now seem prehistoric conditions.

Although people perhaps did not appreciate it at the time, this was a seminal moment in the history of Grand Prix motor racing. For his part, Denny Hulme recalled: 'I think it put me off motor racing in the rain for the rest of my life.'

Brabham then got into his stride with the lightweight Repco-engined car, winning the French, Dutch, British and German Grands Prix in splendid style. Surtees, meanwhile, had a terminal breach with Enzo Ferrari after Dragoni had effectively tried to demote him to 'second driver' status for the Le Mans 24-hour sports car classic.

Surtees went straight to Maranello for a face-to-face meeting with Enzo Ferrari, as a result of which he left the team with immediate effect. Cooper promptly signed Surtees up for the balance of the season, a partnership which yielded victory in the Mexican Grand Prix.

Meanwhile, Ferrari's fortunes slumped dramatically. Dragoni's somewhat naïve contention that his team's cars were so superior that he could employ second-rate drivers and win anyway was so absurdly wide of the mark that one could hardly credit it.

However, after a summer of acute embarrassment at the hands of its rivals, Ferrari produced a revised three-valve (two inlet, one exhaust) cylinder head which gave them around 370 bhp in time for the Italian Grand Prix at Monza. That was sufficient for Ludovico Scarfiotti and Mike Parkes to finish in 1–2 formation, a morale-boosting performance for the famous Italian squad on its home circuit.

Clark qualified the Lotus 43-BRM on the front row at Monza, running quickly, but fruitlessly, after an early delay. He then scored that fortuitous lone victory for the H-16 engine in the United States Grand Prix at Watkins Glen. In the same race, the Indy-based Ford V8 powered McLaren to a fifth-place finish, but it then failed again in Mexico City.

It marked the end of that particular project, but Ford's name would soon be writ large in the Formula 1 business. The Cosworth DFV was coming.

Left: Mike Parkes in the underpowered Ferrari 312 at Zandvoort, '66. Its V12 engine was based on a sports car unit.

Below left: The 1966 Honda was heavy, noisy – and very quick.

Bottom: Jack Brabham (left) and Denny Hulme look pleased with their efforts during a successful year as they pose for the camera at the final race of 1966 in Mexico.

Photos: Bernard Cahier

Opposite: The Ford Cosworth DFV was so far advanced compared with its rivals that it effectively consigned all other contemporary F1 power units to the scrapyard in 1967.

Below: Jim Clark in the sensational new Lotus 49 at Zandvoort in 1967: a superbly integrated piece of motor racing architecture.

A NEW ENGINE FOR A NEW ERA

The Cosworth Ford DFV V8 F1 engine, introduced in the middle of the 1967 season, was not simply the best power unit in the business. It would be responsible for an expansion of interest in the sport which gave it added momentum throughout the following decade and beyond.

Designed by the brilliant Keith Duckworth as part of a £100,000 package funded by the Ford Motor Company, it was the bargain of the post-war F1 age. For its investment, Ford became instantly recognised as the sport's benefactor. From the start of 1969, here would be an off-the-shelf, commercially available F1 engine for anybody with £7500 to spend.

The new engine's design reflected Duckworth's own personal philosophy. Apart from being an intuitive engineer, he was a firm believer that race engine designs should be as simple and uncomplicated as possible.

Duckworth had worked from 1957 to '58 as a transmission development engineer with Lotus before establishing his own business. The very first Ford design to which Cosworth contributed any technical input was the 1963 Cortina GT, which used an inlet manifold and camshaft design that emerged from the Edmonton-based specialists.

Yet even by this stage Cosworth had used Ford engines as the basis of its racing units, most notably in the 1.1-litre Formula Junior category which came to an end in 1963. The engines were then re-worked for the new 1-litre

Formula 3, which took over as the training ground for future Grand Prix stars; the MAE ('Modified Anglia engine') was developed into a winning unit which would be successful right through to the end of the 1970 season when the formula was superseded.

Duckworth was one of the very first designers to appreciate that, although an engine may be sufficiently powerful to fulfil its intended purpose, its potential can be fully harnessed only if it can be integrated with the chassis. This was also one of Lotus founder Colin Chapman's abiding principles and it was therefore no surprise when the DFV-engined Lotus 49 became such a spectacular trend-setter.

The spark which produced the partnership between Ford and Cosworth was initially kindled by Walter Hayes, a former Fleet Street journalist who had joined Ford in 1962 at a time of great expansion of the company's ambitions. It was believed, correctly as it turned out, that the new Cortina saloon would transform Ford's image.

In his new role as director of public affairs, Hayes immediately decided that in the Cortina Ford had the ideal vehicle with which to enter motor racing. Hayes knew very well that Cosworth had amassed much experience developing those production Ford engines for racing purposes, so when Coventry Climax withdrew from F1 at the end of 1965 it seemed an opportune moment for Ford to fill the breach with a totally new Grand Prix engine.

The DFV package also included the development of a four-cylinder Formula 2 engine, which became the highly successful 1.6-litre FVA that dominated motor racing's second division single-seater class from 1967 to '71.

HILL AND CLARK: FI'S FIRST SUPER-TEAM

With the Ford Cosworth DFV in the pipeline for Team Lotus and the all-new type 49 under construction as the first absolutely bespoke engine/chassis combination of the 3-litre formula, Ford bankrolled Graham Hill's switch to the Lotus team as Jim Clark's running mate for the 1967 season.

This was F1's first 'super team' of the post-war era, pre-dating the great Prost/Senna partnership at McLaren by 21 years. Hill once said he had become so identified with BRM over the previous seven seasons that he was worried he would be 'sprayed dark green and stood in the corner of the workshop' if he stayed much longer. He was paid handsomely for the switch, a move which also had the effect of dramatically boosting Clark's salary to a commensurate level – probably to around £30,000.

Lotus began the '67 season racing the Lotus-BRM H-16s, but after the South African Grand Prix – won by the Cooper-Maserati of Pedro Rodriguez (the older brother of the late Ricardo Rodriguez) ahead of local hero John Love's Cooper-Climax 4 – Chapman decided the BRM rebuilding fees were too expensive, with the result that the team back-tracked to using the old 2-litre-engined type 33s until the 49s were ready to race.

Elsewhere on the F1 scene Brabham and Hulme remained together in the Brabham-Repco squad, Rindt was joined by Rodriguez at Cooper – where a newly recruited 19-year-old mechanic by the name of Ron Dennis was just starting his racing career – and John Surtees moved across to Honda.

Richie Ginther joined Dan Gurney briefly in the Eagle F1 squad, now using its new Gurney-Weslake V12 engine, and in the Ferrari camp the promising young New Zealander, Chris Amon, joined Lorenzo Bandini. 'In 1967, Ferrari paid me nothing – just a share of the prize money,' said Chris, 'which was fine by me.'

BRM continued with its P83 H-16 development programme, with Jackie Stewart now partnered by Mike Spence, and the V12 BRM unit was earmarked for McLaren, who made do with a 2-litre Tasman BRM V8 installed in an uprated M4A Formula 2 chassis until the new engine was ready mid-season.

Ferrari did not attend the South African Grand Prix, but Bandini finished a strong second to Dan Gurney's victorious Eagle-Weslake in the Brands Hatch Race of Champions. Then came the Monaco Grand Prix, where the popular Italian driver made a fatal error while chasing Denny Hulme's winning Brabham-Repco.

On lap 82, as Bandini took the chicane on to the harbour front, his Ferrari 312 clipped the inside wall with its right-hand wheels. It ran wide to the left, climbing up the straw bales. A wheel came off, the car turned over on to the track – and erupted into a horrifying pillar of flame. The Italian succumbed to terrible burns three days later.

Certain people believed that Bandini was under some stress just prior to the 1967 Monaco race. According to Ferrari, Lorenzo wanted to take things steadily at Monaco and didn't want Scarfiotti to be at the race. If Ferrari's analysis of the situation is to be believed, Bandini was envious of Scarfiotti's patrician status – he was a second cousin of Fiat patriarch Gianni Agnelli – which so dramatically contrasted with his own humble background.

Enzo Ferrari recalled 'the Bandini who looked up to

Surtees's insufferable pretensions and later the Bandini who begged for tranquillity' before that fateful 1967 Monaco race.

He claimed that he had accommodated Bandini's worries by including Chris Amon in the team for that race, although on the face of it this seems demonstrable nonsense on the part of the Old Man, who had signed the young New Zealander simply because he was regarded as a much better driver than Scarfiotti.

If Bandini was worried, he certainly didn't show it to Amon, who recalls the two of them stopping on their way down into the Principality after a quiet lunch together up in the mountains on the Wednesday before the race. Lorenzo just wanted to savour the view and reflect on things. Chris would later allow himself to wonder whether this was some sort of premonition.

The New Zealander, who shared the winning Ferrari 330P4 sports car with Bandini at both the Daytona 24 Hours and the Monza 1000 Km just before his death, remembers his old team-mate with affection.

'I have to confess that I was a little wary about him when I first joined the team,' he said. 'I suppose his reputation had rather gone before him from the occasion when he knocked Graham [Hill] off in Mexico back at the end of 1964, so I suppose I thought he might turn out to be a little aggressive towards me.

'But he was utterly charming. He was so pleasant and really helpful when it came to sorting out problems with the car. He really was one of the nicest guys I ever came across, and the greatest tragedy of the whole affair is that he was just beginning to emerge from behind the shadow of John Surtees. He really was maturing into a first-class number one in his own right.'

The Cosworth Ford DFV, installed in the beautiful Lotus 49 chassis, made its debut in the third round of the World Championship, the Dutch Grand Prix at Zandvoort. At a stroke, it rendered obsolete every other Formula 1 car on the starting grid.

The 90-degree, 85.7 x 64.8 mm, 2993 cc V8 developed 400 bhp at 9000 rpm. It wasn't the most powerful engine in F1 at that time, but it was the only one to be so beautifully integrated with its chassis. It had been designed to be used as a stressed member, acting as a load-bearing part of the chassis rather than simply sitting within a supporting structure. The Lotus 49 was light, compact and elegant. It was also brittle, only averagely reliable and delivered its power quite abruptly. Nevertheless, it was the class of the field.

Graham Hill led the opening stages of the Dutch Grand Prix, retiring only after a timing gear broke, and Clark took over to score the new car's maiden victory on its debut outing.

That was effectively the whole story of the 1967 season. Ferrari struggled with lack of power, Gurney's Eagle-Weslake scored a glorious victory in the Belgian Grand Prix and the Brabhams and Cooper-Maseratis were consigned to the supporting cast.

John Surtees's Honda – the heaviest car by far on the grid at 1500 lb (680 kg) – posted a terrific last-lap win at Monza in a wheel-to-wheel sprint to the line with Jack Brabham's Brabham BT24. But neither of them would have been in with a chance had not Clark's Lotus 49 spluttered, low on fuel, in the closing moments of the race. Jimmy, lest it be forgotten, had earlier made up a full lap on the entire field after an early stop to change a punctured tyre.

1967
January: Donald Campbell is killed when his boat crashes as he attempts to beat the world water-speed record on Lake Coniston.
August: The Dartford Tunnel beneath the River Thames is opened.
December: The first prototype of the Concorde supersonic airliner is launched in France.
December: A human heart is transplanted from one person to another for the first time.

1968
April: US civil rights leader Dr Martin Luther King is murdered in Memphis.
May: Students riot in Paris.
August: Warsaw Pact forces invade Czechoslovakia, ending the 'Prague Spring'.
November: Richard M. Nixon is elected US President.

Opposite, top: Denny Hulme's Brabham-Repco leads the ill-fated Lorenzo Bandini's Ferrari 312 along the harbour front on the second lap of the 1967 Monaco Grand Prix. Lamp posts and bollards were all part of the game in those days. But the tragic events of that afternoon would mean that things would never be quite the same in F1 again. Thankfully.

Opposite: Dan Gurney's finest hour came at Spa-Francorchamps where his elegant Eagle-Weslake won the 1967 Belgian Grand Prix.

Opposite: Jim Clark took four wins in 1967 with the standard-setting Lotus 49 but the car's unreliability cost him the title.

Opposite, bottom: Team owner, engineer and driver, Jack Brabham takes a keen interest in the preparation of his BT24 in Mexico, 1967.

Below: Brabham (16) scraps it out with the Honda of John Surtees at Monza in 1967. Victory went to Surtees when Brabham ran wide on the final corner of the race.

The writing was very clearly on the wall: anybody without a Cosworth DFV was wasting his time in front-line F1. Cosworth initially built the DFV for Ford to supply on an exclusive basis to Team Lotus. However, when it became clear that the V8 would effectively make all other F1 units uncompetitive, Walter Hayes had a word with Colin Chapman, who most generously agreed to relinquish his exclusivity agreement in the wider interests of the sport.

Jim Clark was not happy about this. 'I'm not terribly keen,' he admitted, 'particularly as we haven't really scored when we should have done.

'One way and another the car hasn't quite lived up to its original promise, though it's difficult to pin the blame anywhere because the things that have gone wrong with my car have been different every time.

'At Spa a plug popped out. At Le Mans the final drive housing wasn't stiff enough. At the Nürburgring I got a puncture, at Mosport I got water in the electrics and at Monza I ran out of fuel.

'It was just like 1962. The car didn't quite come up to expectations there either – and all because of a lot of stupid little faults.'

Jimmy also confirmed that the DFV's power came in with a rush at around 6500 rpm and, while it wasn't ideal allowing the revs to drop to that level in the first place,

with the fixed-ratio ZF gearbox fitted to the Lotus 49 this wasn't always easy to avoid.

He also conceded that it might be an advantage to 'soften' the DFV's power curve 'but as the season [has] progressed we have learned to cope with the power and it was nothing like as bad as I had expected in the wet at Mosport.

'I must admit that before the start of that race I was convinced that I was going to be dropping right to the back of the field, but it was possible with very judicious throttle control to get the car through this period.

'I'm not saying it wasn't difficult to drive – it was very difficult when the track started to dry out and there were still some wet patches – but this wasn't so much to do with the engine as with the tyres and chassis.'

Once the DFV became available for other teams, Bruce McLaren put his money down immediately. The BRM V12 may have allowed his McLaren M5A to lead in the rain at Mosport Park, but those were freak conditions.

Yet at the end of the day it was Denny Hulme who won the World Championship with two wins and a consistent string of results to Clark's four victories. The New Zealander wound up with 51 points to Brabham's 46 (net), while Clark was third on 41. Hulme would now move off to McLaren where he, too, would benefit from the Cosworth DFV's power.

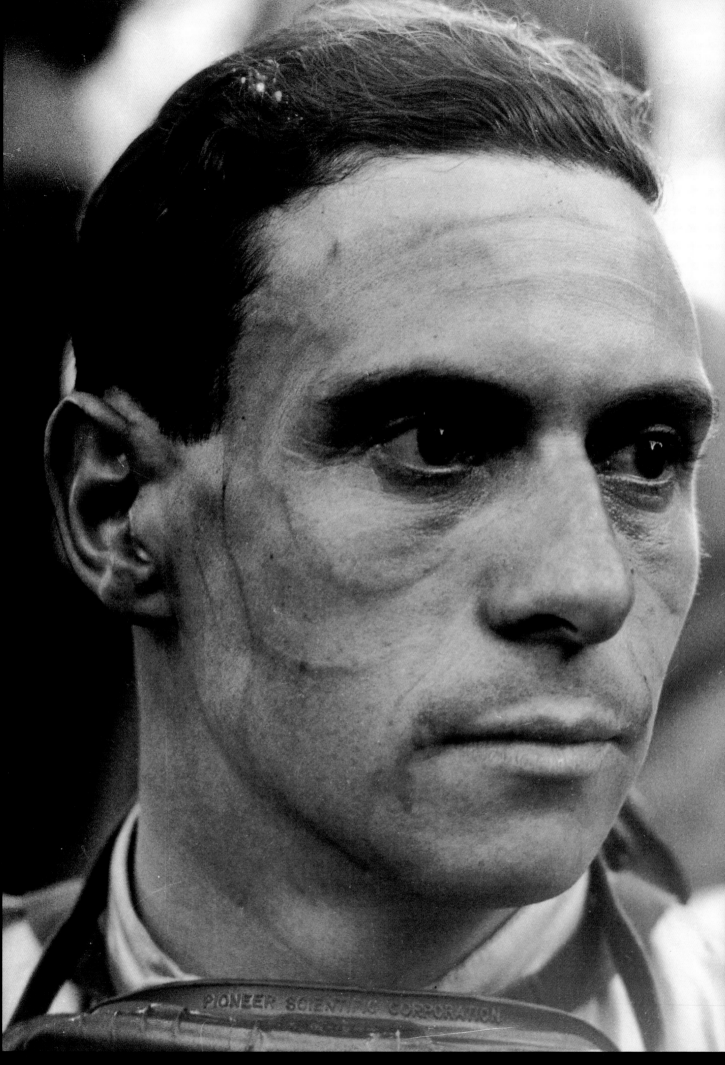

The 1968 season saw the arrival of commercial sponsorship in the form of major backing for the factory Lotus team from the Player's Gold Leaf cigarette brand. It was estimated as being of the order of £60,000 for the season and this included identification on the F2 and sports cars in addition to the factory Lotus 49s.

Yet the 1968 season would not be remembered for the first steps towards the big-money era which would see Grand Prix racing attain a position of unimaginable international status and wealth over the following generation. Instead, it would be remembered as the season which cost the lives of Jimmy Clark, Mike Spence and Jo Schlesser.

Clark would be killed in a minor-league F2 race at Hockenheim on 7 April. It was such a momentous event that it forced everybody to recalibrate their attitude towards the sport. If it happened to Jimmy, nobody was safe.

Then Mike Spence was killed testing a Lotus turbine car at Indianapolis and Schlesser, a veteran 40-year-old making his F1 debut in front of his home crowd at Rouen-les-Essarts, died horrendously when the air-cooled Honda RA302 crashed on the third lap of the French Grand Prix and burst into flames. The implications and consequences of this human mayhem and misery are dealt with in more detail within the accompanying essay on the subject of safety in F1.

After Clark's death, Graham Hill pulled the Lotus team together to win the World Championship, yet the Lotus 49 was no longer in a class of its own. Ken Tyrrell had started his own Grand Prix team, using French Matra chassis and Cosworth Ford DFV engines, with Jackie Stewart doing the driving. Jackie very nearly won the championship in his first year with the team, but in the end Hill took the crown by a comfortable margin with 48 points to Stewart's 36.

The '68 season was also highlighted by a superb British Grand Prix victory at Brands Hatch for Jo Siffert, now driving an elegant dark-blue Lotus 49B for privateer Rob Walker's team. It was one of the most emotionally satisfying days for F1 in a season otherwise blighted by disaster, for it represented a memorable comeback for the famous private team after a disastrous outing in the Race of Champions at the same circuit earlier in the year.

Rob had purchased a Lotus 49 for Siffert to drive in that early-season race, but he crashed heavily in testing. The wreckage was taken back to Walker's Dorking race headquarters, only for a stray spark to ignite petrol vapour as mechanics were stripping down the wreckage.

Within seconds, the Walker race shop was ablaze and, while the workforce escaped unhurt, all Rob's priceless archives and memorabilia were destroyed in the inferno which followed. Yet Rob would be back in business; the Walker team's brand-new Lotus 49B was delivered only days before the British Grand Prix.

McLaren also enjoyed the benefits of Cosworth DFV use. Bruce McLaren scored his first Grand Prix victory since Monaco '62 when his M7A inherited a win at Spa-Francorchamps after Stewart's Matra MS10 ran out of fuel in the closing stages. Later in the season, Denny Hulme would win in both Italy and Canada.

Opposite: Jim Clark was Grand Prix racing's leader. His death in April 1968 was almost more than the motor racing community could comprehend.

Below: Jo Siffert heads for victory in the 1968 British Grand Prix at Brands Hatch in the dark-blue Rob Walker Lotus 49B. It was an emotional occasion and the last GP win for a genuine privateer with a customer car.

Bernard Cahier

Right: Jacky Ickx at speed in the pouring rain at Rouen-les-Essarts, winning the 1968 French Grand Prix in the elegant Ferrari 312.

Below right: Bruce McLaren drove the crisp orange-liveried McLaren M7 to a lucky victory in the '68 Belgian Grand Prix.

Bottom: Graham Hill inherited the Lotus leadership on the death of Jim Clark and lifted team morale with a fine win in the '68 Spanish Grand Prix.

Photos: Bernard Cahier

Brabham, meanwhile, had faded dramatically. After winning two back-to-back championships they had high hopes for 1968 with Jochen Rindt joining the team from Cooper as a replacement for Hulme and a new four-cam Repco type 860 engine installed in the latest semi-monocoque Brabham BT26 chassis. But the whole season turned into an absolute fiasco.

By the end of '68 it had become abundantly clear that the Repco F1 engine programme's salvation would depend on an almost unimaginable turn-round in technical reliability. It was a forlorn hope. There was no way in which the 12,000-mile supply route between England and Australia could survive another season like this. Formula 1 was changing.

Brabham made what was tipped as a short-term, stopgap switch to Cosworth DFVs for 1969, but everybody knew it was the death knell for the Australian V8s.

'I think, given time, we could have sorted out the mechanical problems on the Repco 860,' said John Judd, the Brabham engineer responsible for liaising with the Australian company, who is now a respected F1 engine designer in his own right. 'But the DFV was a good package which could be used as a stressed member, and our engine couldn't. At the end of the day the Cosworth DFV was far ahead in terms of design. So many things they did for the first time. And did them right!'

FERRARI OPENS THE AEROFOIL ERA

At the 1968 Belgian Grand Prix, Ferrari arrived with fixed aerofoils above the gearboxes of their 312s for Chris Amon and new star Jacky Ickx, who had been recruited at the start of the season.

'People reckoned that I'd copied the Chaparral [sports car] concept,' said chief designer Mauro Forghieri, 'but that wasn't really the case. I'd got my inspiration from the ideas tried by Swiss engineer Michael May, who'd tried an aerofoil on a Porsche sports car more than ten years earlier. May had worked informally as a fuel injection consultant to Ferrari for some years [most notably on the 1963 1.5-litre V6] so there was already a line of communication.'

Amon reckoned he should have won that race easily, but Surtees's Honda kicked up a stone which holed the Ferrari's radiator. It was the story of the brilliant New Zealander's career. 'That Honda was a bloody nuisance, actually, both in 1967 and '68,' he recalled. 'It was very quick in a straight line, but always got in the way on the corners.'

On the basis that bigger is better, Colin Chapman soon eclipsed the modest wings on the Ferraris. For the French Grand Prix at Rouen-les-Essarts the works Lotus

Below: Chris Amon's winged Ferrari 312 heads team-mate Jacky Ickx and John Surtees's Honda on the opening lap of the 1968 Belgian Grand Prix.

Bernard Cahier

Bernard Cahier

49Bs of Graham Hill and Jackie Oliver appeared with tall, strutted rear aerofoils working directly on the rear suspension uprights.

Chapman and his colleagues calculated that these appendages developed 400 lb of downforce at 150 mph, but Oliver demonstrated the dangers of loss of such downforce when he pulled into the slipstream of a rival car during practice.

Approaching the pits, Oliver spun into a very substantial gatepost which split the car in two and catapulted its hapless driver out on to the road, standing upright and without a scratch.

'I thought I'd arrived in heaven,' he remembered.

Throughout the '68 season the development of movable aerofoils continued apace. In time for the Italian Grand Prix Forghieri had equipped the Ferrari 312s with a very sophisticated system activated by engine oil pressure and braking effort. The principle was that the wing angle was steeply inclined in first, second and third gears and when the drivers went on to the brakes in fourth and fifth. It feathered in fourth and fifth when the driver was on the throttle.

All this seemed a little too complex to Amon, who preferred to use the manual override system in the cockpit. Lotus, meanwhile, had a feathering wing – operated by a fourth pedal in the footwell – ready in time for the '68 Mexican Grand Prix. The unfettered development of these high aerofoils continued into 1969, with several teams supplementing them with similar structures mounted on the front suspension.

This latest spiral in Formula 1 technology came to an abrupt end after massive accidents caused by wing failures befell both Graham Hill and Jochen Rindt during the Spanish Grand Prix at Barcelona's Montjuich Park. Rindt, who had joined Lotus from the Brabham team at the start of the season, was seriously unnerved by this episode, which left him with a hairline fracture of the skull. From then on he never shied away from expressing his concerns to Colin Chapman over the possible frailty of Lotus equipment.

Rindt wrote: 'I have been racing in F1 for five years and I have made one mistake (I rammed Chris Amon at Clermont-Ferrand) and I had one accident at Zandvoort due to gear selection failure. Otherwise I stayed out of trouble. This situation changed rapidly since I joined your team.

'Honestly, your cars are so quick that we would still be competitive with a few extra pounds used to make the weakest parts stronger. Please give my suggestions some thought. I can only drive a car in which I have some confidence and I feel the point of no confidence is quite near.'

Meanwhile, faced with mounting concern over these aerodynamic developments, motor racing's governing body, the CSI, made a move on the issue after first practice for the Monaco Grand Prix.

After a lengthy debate on the subject, the CSI decided on an immediate ban on these wings, although the use of small fins mounted on the front suspension was permitted as long as these did not project beyond the inside edge of the wheel or above the highest part of the bodywork at that point.

Several of the constructors were quite happy with this ruling, but Ken Tyrrell protested strongly, saying that the Matra MS80 had been designed around these wings and could well be dangerous without them. He also pointed out that the CSI had broken its undertaking that the rules would not be changed without adequate notice, but was in turn reminded that changes could always be made in the interests of safety. As a result of the ban, all the first day's practice times were invalidated.

Thereafter, the F1 teams would develop a generation of lower rear wings mounted on the engine covers, working in conjunction with nose wings. It was the start of aerodynamic development down a path which was still recognisably the same at the end of the century.

Left and below: Horror show at Barcelona's Montjuich Park circuit, 1969. Jochen Rindt's Lotus 49B has suffered a collapsed rear aerofoil on the hillcrest after the pits and crashed heavily out of the Spanish Grand Prix. Helpers eventually right the upturned car and team-mate Graham Hill – who'd earlier had a similar accident at the same point – helps extricate Jochen from the wreck. The Austrian survived with a hairline skull fracture.

SAFETY AND SECURITY: THE BIGGEST LEAP FORWARD OF ALL

THE FATAL accidents which befell Roland Ratzenberger and Ayrton Senna during the 1994 San Marino Grand Prix meeting catapulted the issue of motor racing safety into the headlines around the globe, focusing the spotlight on what had become the most media-intensive sport in the world.

Twenty-six years had passed since Jim Clark's death at Hockenheim had grabbed the newspaper headlines in the same way as Senna's. Yet the world – and the public's attitude towards motor racing – had changed dramatically during the intervening generation.

Essentially, Clark lived, raced and died at a time when the prevailing attitude could be summed up rather frivolously as 'you pays your money and you takes your choice'. When his Lotus 48 smashed into the unprotected trees at Hockenheim on 7 April 1968, only 29 years had passed since Dick Seaman's Mercedes-Benz had been wrapped round a tree at Spa-Francorchamps on the eve of the Second World War.

Racing drivers crashed and died, it was as simple as that. The philosophy endured through the immediate post-war years and into the 1950s. The three Grand Prix regulars who lost their lives in 1958, for example, Peter Collins at the Nürburgring, Luigi Musso at Reims and Stuart Lewis-Evans, after an excruciating struggle against burns sustained when his Vanwall crashed in the Moroccan Grand Prix at Casablanca, were all victims as much of their time as of the physical injuries they sustained.

Consider Lewis-Evans's plight. Today an injured driver can expect to receive state-of-the-art medical attention at any circuit in the world. More than that, the provision of such facilities is a fundamental prerequisite of a track's being permitted to hold a Grand Prix in the first place.

Yet for Lewis-Evans, who was informally managed by 27-year-old Bernie Ecclestone at that time, the situation was very different. A 1990s-style flameproof driving suit would probably have enabled the young driver from Kent to have survived the inferno which erupted after his Vanwall slid into a tree following an engine seizure. But Lewis-Evans was wearing nothing so sophisticated.

There were no medical facilities on hand to deal with the burns he sustained and he faced a painful flight on a stretcher in Vanwall boss Tony Vandervell's chartered Viscount airliner back to Britain. There he was taken to the East Grinstead burns unit which had been established by eminent surgeon Sir Archibald McIndoe to treat the horrific burns suffered by wartime fighter pilots. There was a cruel irony here. Racing drivers were just that in the 1950s: fighter pilots contesting what amounted to an undeclared war.

'When they took Stuart to the hospital at Casablanca they just sat him in a chair with a blanket around him,' said Ecclestone. 'It wasn't because they were particularly neglecting him, that was just how things were there.

'It seems difficult to imagine, looking back from the 1990s, but you got used to people being killed. It was just part of the sport. One expected it.'

Notwithstanding the tragedies at Imola in 1994, today's F1 stars have to be pretty unlucky to be killed at the wheel. A stark statement, perhaps, and arguably tempting fate.

'When I raced, the batting average was that you had a three out of five chance that you were going to die in a racing car if you survived five years,' said Jackie Stewart.

The Scot's attitude towards F1 safety had been shaped in 1966, when he crashed heavily on the opening lap of the Belgian GP at Spa-Francorchamps. He was driving a 2-litre Tasman BRM in this first season of the 3-litre F1 regulations. These were relatively sophisticated cars by, let's say, pre-war standards, yet the Belgian track was virtually unchanged since Dick Seaman's fatal accident in 1939. It was the equivalent of trying to operate a Boeing 747 from a grass airstrip.

By the time Jackie returned to the cockpit for the British Grand Prix at Brands Hatch his car was fitted with a spanner taped to the steering wheel, the better to facilitate his escape if he was to experience another major accident. Later in the season his car would also be fitted with seat belts at his request.

'This was not because of the Spa accident,' he explained, 'but because I'd driven a Lola in the Indianapolis 500 the previous week and it was fitted with belts. Admittedly they were a bit basic, but it struck me they made a lot of sense. If anybody at the BRM team thought this was a little eccentric, they suffered in silence. As far as I was concerned, they were very receptive to my request.'

Yet many people did regard Stewart's request as distinctly odd. An amazing number of drivers still clung to the notion that being flung out of a car was probably the best way to survive a major accident.

This was at best questionable, at worst nonsense, of course, as Ferrari driver Michael Parkes would demonstrate when he was tipped out of his Ferrari on the second lap of the following year's Belgian Grand Prix. The English driver suffered severe multiple leg fractures which effectively ended his front-line motor racing career. Ironically, he went off on oil dropped by Jackie Stewart's BRM H-16, a real gusher on four wheels if ever there was one.

However, seat belts would not have helped Lorenzo Bandini when, on 7 May 1967, he suffered burns which were to prove fatal after upending his Ferrari 312 in the Monaco Grand Prix. The darling of the Italian motor racing community, Bandini was poised on the verge of greatness when a momentary lapse of concentration cost him his life.

The Italian was chasing Denny Hulme's winning Brabham in the closing stages of the race when his car clipped the chicane, bounced on to the straw bales on the opposite side of the track and rolled over. Instantly, it exploded into a fireball.

Eventually extricated from the wreckage, Bandini was mortally injured. He died from his burns, and from serious internal injuries, three days later, shortly before his heavily pregnant wife, Margherita, suffered a miscarriage in the same hospital. It was one of F1's most gruesome episodes and helped kick-start the sport into directing its thoughts towards improved safety standards.

Back in the pits, Stewart watched the smoke rise above the chicane with a sense of foreboding. He had also led in the opening stages until his BRM broke its transmission.

'I was far enough away from the accident not to realise that the driver was still in the car for 90 per cent of the fire,' he said. 'I just saw the intensity, the smoke, the turmoil of it all. I just thought, "Oh no, this is a big one."

'But keep in mind that the real frequency of fatal accidents seemed to come the following year, 1968, when they were dropping like flies with the deaths of Jim Clark, Ludovico Scarfiotti, Jo Schlesser and Mike Spence. Putting it harshly, the Bandini accident represented the reality of the business at the time. No more than that.

'The racing driver is a peculiar animal with regard to observing accidents, dealing with them and despatching the issues from his mind. [Drivers] are incredibly capable of doing that.'

Jim Clark's death was front-page news in most European newspapers. Scarfiotti was killed at the Rossfeld hillclimb in Germany, thrown from his Porsche. Schlesser died when his Honda became an inferno after crashing in the French Grand Prix at Rouen-les-Essarts. Spence hit the wall at Indianapolis and a wayward wheel smashed his skull.

A year later, Lucien Bianchi, although carried from his wrecked Alfa sports car alive, wide-eyed and shaking, succumbed to burns, internal injuries and massive shock after slamming into a telegraph pole during testing for the Le Mans sports car race.

Yet somehow the Bandini tragedy was different. The aforementioned accidents took place almost anonymously. Somehow, without reels of gruesome cine-film recording these painful episodes, the reality of death was easier to confront.

Bandini's accident briefly pulled aside the curtain protecting violent sports from media intrusion. The paying public got a taste of what they would see played out, live, on prime-time television at Imola a quarter of a century later.

The Bandini crash – and the events which followed in 1968 – further strengthened Stewart's resolve to step up his personal campaign for better safety. Racing drivers, he reasoned, should be paid to demonstrate their skill, not simply their bravery in what now seem prehistoric conditions.

'The Monaco disaster was yet another nail in the coffin of the traditionalists who didn't think they needed safety,' said Stewart, 'and there wasn't a more graphic example of their inadequacies and inabilities to change things fast enough.'

Yet those traditionalists went for his jugular. In particular, Denis Jenkinson, the respected Continental Correspondent of *Motor Sport* magazine, derided Jackie and his colleagues as the 'milk and water' brigade.

On 13 June 1972, Stewart felt moved to reply to Jenks's latest invective in a letter to the magazine. 'What Denis Jenkinson thinks or says concerns me little,' he wrote. 'To me he is a fence-sitter, doing little or nothing to secure a future for our sport.

'All Mr Jenkinson seems to do is lament the past and the drivers who have served their time in it. Few of them, however, are alive to read his writings.'

Nor were the drivers the only ones at risk. It is almost too frightening to consider what the consequences might have been at Barcelona's Montjuich Park circuit had there not been at least a single-height guard rail to restrain the Lotus 49Bs of Graham Hill and Jochen Rindt from plunging into the crowd following the failure of their strut-mounted rear wings in the 1969 Spanish Grand Prix.

Thanks to Stewart and many others who subsequently picked up the torch to campaign for improved safety after his retirement in 1973, today's F1 drivers enjoy levels of personal security which seemed unimaginable 25 years ago.

Their medical requirements are dealt with by Professor Sid Watkins, one of the world's most eminent neuro-surgeons, who is employed as the FIA Medical Delegate. Back in 1969, Stewart was regarded as almost eccentric when he hired his own doctor to accompany him to every race.

'Prof Watkins has made such a terrific contribution to all this because he hasn't been a team owner, he hasn't been a driver or even been part of a national governing body,' he said. 'That neutrality has helped him considerably, but still to this day I feel that the drivers do not have enough authority and enough say in what goes on.

'By the same token, the drivers can be incredibly lethargic about safety. They don't want to sacrifice the time to make the improvements required. But if they did that, they would be able to sleep more comfortably.

'I'm clearly not a believer in the syndrome which suggests that motor racing should be dangerous. It will never be safe, but there is absolutely no reason for the competitors to be exposed to unnecessary hazards. It wouldn't happen in any other business.'

Yet the carnage would continue. In 1970 Piers Courage died when his Frank Williams de Tomaso crashed and burnt in the Dutch Grand Prix at Zandvoort. Then Jochen Rindt, the World Champion-presumptive, died horrendously at Monza during practice for the Italian Grand Prix.

In 1973 Roger Williamson's March suffered a tyre failure during the Dutch Grand Prix at Zandvoort, somersaulting to a halt upside down and then bursting into flames. Despite the brave efforts of his rival, David Purley, Williamson was asphyxiated. Then, at Watkins Glen, Jackie Stewart's Tyrrell team-mate, François Cevert, was killed when he slammed into a guard rail during practice.

Surtees driver Helmuth Koinigg was decapitated at Watkins Glen the following year when his Surtees slid beneath inadequately secured guard rails. In 1978 Ronnie Peterson died from injuries sustained when his Lotus 78 crashed accelerating away from the startline at Monza during the Italian Grand Prix.

Four years later the F1 fraternity was numbed by the death of Gilles Villeneuve when his Ferrari 126C2 somersaulted over the back of Jochen Mass's March during qualifying for the Belgian Grand Prix at Zolder. Only weeks later, Osella F1 team novice Riccardo Paletti was fatally injured when he slammed into the back of Didier Pironi's stalled pole-position Ferrari on the startline at Montreal.

Two years after that, Elio de Angelis, the charming and courteous Roman, died after crashing his Brabham BT55-BMW during a test session at the Paul Ricard circuit near Bandol. Yet by this point safety had improved dramatically. After de Angelis's sad loss, another eight years would pass before the double May Day disasters at Imola.

The accidents to Ratzenberger and Senna further accelerated safety moves, but nothing could ever entirely eliminate the danger element. On Sunday, 10 March 1996 television viewers across the world could have been forgiven for thinking this was the day 35-year-old Martin Brundle's luck had finally run out. On the opening lap of the Australian GP at Melbourne, the King's Lynn driver's Jordan-Peugeot somersaulted off the track at around 180 mph after being launched over the back of a rival's car.

Yet the only injury he sustained was a badly bruised foot – incurred as he jogged energetically back to the pits to take over the Jordan team's spare car in time to drive in the restarted race.

Yet it was not by chance alone that Brundle emerged unscathed. Obviously luck plays a part in the outcome of any accident, whether on road or race track,

but for the past decade or more Grand Prix car design has been tailored to offer the occupants of these precision-built, high-speed projectiles the best possible chance of survival in the event of a catastrophic accident.

'Performance and safety are probably the two most important concerns in your mind when you sit down to design a car,' said Gary Anderson, the Jordan F1 team's Technical Director at the time, after Brundle's escape. 'You want your driver to be as quick as possible, and as safe as possible.

'Motor racing does have inherent dangers, as was demonstrated in Australia. The difference between Martin hurting himself in that accident, and not hurting himself, is partly down to luck. You never know where bits of the car are going to end up, or whether another driver is going to hit you in that situation.

'You can, however, devise regulations

to ensure that the drivers are safe in as many situations as possible, hence the new regulation concerning cockpits [designed to provide added lateral protection against head and neck injuries in the event of a side impact, which was brought in for the 1996 season]. As far as our cockpit sides are concerned, safety was the first thing we looked at because that, after all, is the reason that the latest regulations were introduced in the first place.'

There would be many more close shaves over the years that followed. Grand Prix racing, said the critics, was going soft. Yet that wasn't the case. It was simply running slightly ahead of public opinion. The concept of willingly risking one's life in a reckless fashion was no longer really acceptable. So the sport worked hard to keep a safety net beneath its high-wire exponents for as much of the time as conceivably possible.

As the end of the millennium approached, Grand Prix racing had become big business. And multi-national sponsors were not accustomed to losing their biggest investments – that's to say, the drivers – in avoidable accidents.

One only has to consider the furore surrounding Michael Schumacher's fractured right leg, sustained in the 1999 British Grand Prix at Silverstone, to get the point. To judge by the reactions of some people in the F1 paddock one could have been excused for thinking this was a disaster of monumental proportions.

The only man with a realistic perspective on the whole business was Schumacher himself. 'Hello, Sid, it's just my leg – it's not a big problem,' he said when Prof Watkins arrived at the side of his shattered Ferrari. Within three months he was back again on the Grand Prix starting grid.

The 1968 season was particularly tragic. French veteran Jo Schlesser lost his life on the third lap of his F1 debut at Rouen-les-Essarts when his air-cooled Honda RA302 was engulfed in flames after hitting an earth bank.

Opposite: Ken Tyrrell in animated discussion with Jackie Stewart. Behind on the pit counter are Jackie's wife, Helen (centre), and Derek Gardner.

Below: Jackie Stewart in the superb Bernard Boyer-designed Matra MS80 which, fielded by Ken Tyrrell's team, gave him the means to take the 1969 World Championship by storm.

STEWART TAKES A TITLE FOR TYRRELL AND MATRA

The partnership between Ken Tyrrell and Jackie Stewart was based on mutual respect and genuine affection. It lacked, perhaps, some of the mystique which has retrospectively been credited to the relationship between Colin Chapman and Jim Clark, but it was arguably even stronger.

After two years wrestling with the BRM H-16, Stewart was ready for a change by the end of the 1967 season. Tyrrell made an approach and Jackie accepted, privately wondering whether or not Ken could raise the £10,000 retainer he was asking for.

It wasn't a new partnership. Tyrrell had first seen Jackie testing a Cooper F3 car in 1963 at Goodwood. 'Within three laps he was going faster than Bruce McLaren in the same car, and by the end of the day I was convinced that he was going to be a great driver,' said Ken.

'I offered him £3000 to sign with me, on condition that I took ten per cent of his earnings for the next five years. But he declined. Pity, that.'

Nevertheless, Jackie won the British F3 Championship for Tyrrell with a Cooper the following season and stayed on the Tyrrell F2 team long enough to have his first taste of the French Matra chassis in the second division category. By the time the F1 offer came, Stewart was convinced of their potential.

Tyrrell's cars were prepared in an unprepossessing wooden hut in the family timber yard, which drew the memorable remark 'What a dump!' from Ford's Walter Hayes on first acquaintanceship. 'Nobody bothers us, and we can get on and do the job properly,' said Tyrrell mechanic Roger Hill by way of defence.

For the 1969 season the Matra MS10 was replaced by a new chassis, the Bernard Boyer-designed monocoque MS80. Jackie used the MS10 to open the season with a win in South Africa, then won the Spanish, Dutch, French, British and Italian races, clinching his first World Championship at Monza after pipping Jochen Rindt's Lotus 49B into second place. Brabham's Jacky Ickx was runner-up in the final points table with two wins.

Ferrari was now fading fast as a competitive F1 force, the company being so overwhelmed by the cost of its Grand Prix and sports car racing programmes that Enzo Ferrari had to seek the help of Fiat patriarch Gianni Agnelli to keep the show seriously on the road. He succeeded, but his problems meant that every race of the 1969 F1 season was won by a Cosworth DFV-engined car.

That said, increasing the DFV's operational rev limit to around 10,000 rpm might have produced another 30 bhp, but the engines remained brittle. Camshaft failures were quite frequent along with valve spring breakages and lubrication problems. Despite all this, the DFV was unquestionably the engine to have.

In 1969 Frank Williams also made his first appearance on the F1 stage, running a car for old Etonian Piers Courage. The ever-enterprising Williams had managed to pull a flanker on Jack Brabham by acquiring an ex-works Brabham BT24 chassis at the end of 1968. The plan was to race it in the Tasman Championship, a lucrative series of races in Australia and New Zealand which was really a winter Grand Prix series by another name, but Frank eventually decided to make the logical progression and contest the '69 F1 World Championship with Piers driving the car.

Much to the annoyance of Jack Brabham, whose works

KEN TYRRELL: THE GREAT SURVIVOR

Bernard Cahier

EXCEPT FOR a few months, Ken Tyrrell had never worked for anybody but himself since he was demobbed from the RAF with a £30 gratuity in 1946 when he sold his family's F1 team to British American Racing at the end of 1997.

He was retained by the new owners, but acting out the role of a hired hand in the company he'd founded was always going to be a non-starter, said the pundits. Sure enough, it did not take long for Ken and his son, Bob – the company's Business Development Director – to clear their desks at the Ockham headquarters of the Tyrrell Racing Organisation.

'Originally I didn't follow motor racing, but in 1951 the local football team, for which I used to play, got a coach trip together to go to Silverstone,' he recalled, 'but it could just as easily have been a trip to the seaside at Brighton or Bognor.

'The supporting race was for 500 cc F3 cars and one of the competitors was a guy called Alan Brown, who I saw from the programme came from Guildford, where I lived at that time. So when I got home, I went round and knocked on Alan Brown's door and said, "I saw you racing at Silverstone, Sir – could I see your car?"

'Well, he kept his car in a large garage in the garden of a nursery which his mother ran. So he showed me round the car, told me a little bit about it, and at the end of the year I bought it from him.'

Ken raced through much of the 1950s, eventually going into partnership with Alan Brown and Cecil Libowitz in 1958 to run a pair of Cooper F2 cars on an international basis. 'When eventually I discovered I could only finish fifth, sixth or seventh at this level, it didn't satisfy me,' he recalls. 'Then on one occasion I loaned the car to Michael Taylor at Aintree and he drove much better than I did. So I decided that team management was my particular slot.'

Ken remains self-effacing when it comes to his reputation as a talent-spotter. 'It's not really true, you see,' he grins broadly. 'It sounds all right when you read it in print, but it's not really like that.

'If you go back to 1960, when I started running my own Formula Junior team with loaned Cooper chassis and BMC engines, I had John Surtees and Henry Taylor and we won races all over Europe. But most of the people we were racing against were owner/drivers competing for fun, while I was free to sign up whoever I thought was the best driver.'

Jackie Stewart's relationship with Tyrrell was heaven-sent. Ken recalls they fell out only once. 'It was at an Oulton Park Gold Cup when Jackie was complaining bitterly about the March 701,' he recalls, 'and I do remember we had a few words. But we never fell out over money!

'He drove for me in F3, F2 and then F1, but the only year we had a written contract was the first year.'

Jackie won three World Championships for Ken, the first in the Tyrrell-entered Matra in 1969, the second and third with Ken's own cars in 1971 and '73. Tyrrell had hoped to sustain the momentum of that great partnership into 1974, promoting Jackie's team-mate, François Cevert, to the team leadership after Stewart's retirement. Sadly, Cevert was killed practising for the 1973 US Grand Prix at Watkins Glen and the link was broken.

'François absolutely worshipped Jackie as his idol,' recalls Ken. 'I remember Jackie's last F1 win, in the '73 German GP at the Nürburgring, where they finished in 1–2 formation. At the end of the race he stepped out of the car and said, "François could have passed me any time he liked. He was flat quicker than I was."

'But the point was that François stayed in his wheel tracks because he still felt he had a lot to learn from Jackie. And, of course, he knew that Jackie was retiring at the end of the year, and that his time would come.

'But it was all a long time ago. It's much too early to say what I will be doing now, but I'm certainly going to find it strange.'

Jackie Stewart was the only rival F1

team chief who could be bothered to issue a press statement paying tribute to Ken Tyrrell on his departure from the Grand Prix scene. It was perhaps strange – even untypical – that neither Ron Dennis nor Frank Williams, both of whom stood shoulder-to-shoulder with Ken in refusing to sign the 1997 Concorde Agreement, should take the same opportunity.

Ken's exit left Dennis and Williams as the sole remaining representatives of the F1 Old Guard. 'Yes,' said Tyrrell with great satisfaction, 'and isn't it wonderful that they are both at the top of the tree?'

Despite Ken's protestations that he was no talent-spotter, plenty of fine drivers served their apprenticeship under the Tyrrell banner. They included François Cevert, Patrick Depailler, Jody Scheckter, Didier Pironi, Michele Alboreto, Martin Brundle, Stefan Bellof, Jean Alesi and Mika Salo.

'Ken Tyrrell has shaped my personality in racing, and he's given me all the knowledge and experience which have made me what I am today,' said Jackie Stewart on his retirement from driving in 1973.

Twenty-five years later, Jackie would write: 'He has been an immense contributor to motor racing, introducing and nurturing more drivers than anyone else in the sport.'

As usual, Stewart was right on target.

1969

March: The Concorde makes its first flight at Toulouse, France.
July: Neil Armstrong becomes the first man to set foot on the Moon.
September: A group of radical officers led by Muammar Gaddafi seizes power in Libya.

1970

January: The UK age of majority is reduced from 21 to 18.
April: The break-up of the Beatles is confirmed in the High Court in London.
May: The planned South African cricket tour of England is cancelled because of the likelihood of anti-Apartheid protests.
June: Brazil beat Italy 4–1 in the final of the football World Cup in Mexico.

1971

January: 66 football fans are killed in a crush when barriers collapse at Ibrox Park football ground in Glasgow.
February: Britain adopts a decimal currency, replacing the old system of pounds, shillings and pence.
May: The first video cassette recorder (VCR) designed for use in the home becomes available in the shops.

cars ran on Goodyear tyres, the Williams Brabham was contracted to race on Dunlops. Piers really came of age that season, second places in the Monaco and United States Grands Prix testifying to his growing ability.

4WD FORMULA FOR FAILURE

The 1969 Formula 1 season was highlighted by a spate of four-wheel-drive cars from Lotus, Matra, McLaren and Cosworth. Yet it proved a frustrating blind alley for all concerned.

McLaren engineer Robin Herd left his post with the team to design the Cosworth 4WD challenger, which was never raced. The basis of Herd's new design was a pair of sponsons between the wheels on each side joined by a stressed-steel floor, the whole chassis achieving its rigidity from the engine and box-like structures front and rear.

The side sponsons carried the fuel and the front and rear boxes the suspension and differentials. The Cosworth DFV engine was turned through 180 degrees so that the clutch faced forward. From there a Cosworth gearbox containing Hewland gears side-stepped power to an angled bevel differential on the right, which then shared the torque between front and rear wheels.

'It was possibly rather shallow thinking,' said Herd. 'If we'd all thought a little bit longer, then we would probably have realised that, with the trends going the way they were, four-wheel drive wasn't going to be practical.'

In the case of the Lotus 63, the car's Cosworth DFV engine had again been turned through 180 degrees, with a five-speed Lotus/ZF gearbox stepping the drive to the left-hand side of the chassis, a design legacy of the Indianapolis 4WD turbine Lotuses, which were built with a weight bias to that side.

The Matra MS84 4WD machine was built round a spaceframe chassis for reasons of maintenance and economy. Its five-speed gearbox, central differential, control unit and stepped take-off drive were all Ferguson components loaned to Matra for the project.

Designed by the late Jo Marquart, the four-wheel-drive McLaren M9A appeared at Silverstone for the British Grand Prix with Derek Bell in the cockpit. It had already undergone tests in the hands of Bruce McLaren and Denny Hulme but, despite a barrage of encouraging reports in the media, by the time the team arrived at Silverstone it was clear they were barking up the wrong tree.

Bruce himself coined perhaps the most apt description of the sensation of four-wheel drive: handling the M9A was like 'trying to write your signature with somebody jogging your elbow', and after those preliminary trials he looked glum and said 'why bother?' to his team.

That pretty well summed up the general feeling towards this generation of four-wheel-drive racers. The only World Championship point ever scored by a 4WD car came at Mosport Park, where Johnny Servoz-Gavin finished sixth in the Canadian Grand Prix driving the Matra MS84.

As for the rest, the development of aerofoils – even in their newly truncated form – meant that two-wheel-drive cars were quicker as well as less complex than their four-wheel-drive rivals. It was the end of the road.

Well, not quite. Two years later, Lotus brought out their four-wheel-drive Lotus 56B turbine car for several events. Much trouble was experienced reducing the turbine's throttle lag, but during the soaking-wet 1971 Dutch Grand Prix at Zandvoort the smooth characteristics of the turbine motor allied to four-wheel drive opened the door just a fraction for a possible renaissance.

F1 novice David Walker was picking off seasoned runners with no trouble at all in the early stages of the race until he overdid things and crashed at the end of the main straight.

Colin Chapman reflected some years later, 'That was the one race that should, and could, have been won by four-wheel drive.'

The unloved Lotus 63 was just one of a crop of 4WD cars which simply couldn't get the job done.

Bernard Cahier

FERRARI RESCUED BY FIAT

As we have seen, by the start of the 1969 season, Ferrari finances were getting pretty stretched. The Commendatore was finding it extremely difficult to pay for programmes for Formula 1, Formula 2, sports cars, Can-Am and hillclimbing from budgets culled exclusively from traditional motor industry sources.

Firestone and Shell were both putting a lot of money into the Italian team, but this was not in the same league as that which would soon be provided by the tobacco barons. In any case, Ferrari was involved in a far more ambitious overall racing programme than any rival team and it was quite clear that, at the start of 1969, the Prancing Horse had its back to the financial wall.

The company's long-term salvation and security were finally achieved on 18 June 1969 when Enzo Ferrari forged a deal with Fiat overlord Gianni Agnelli to guarantee the marque's future. The racing cars were to remain under Ferrari's personal guidance and control for the rest of his life – he would live another 19 years to the age of 89 – while the road cars would fall more directly under the control of Fiat.

Fiat thus became a 50 per cent shareholder in the Ferrari organisation and their nominee, Giuseppe Dondo, became Managing Director, with another Fiat appointee, Francesco Bellicardi, also appointed to the board. Bellicardi had previously been a director of the Bologna-based Weber carburettor company and was a long-standing friend of Enzo Ferrari.

The arrangement with Fiat was concluded *in vitalizio*, which meant that Fiat effectively paid Ferrari an annuity over the remainder of his life for the privilege of using his property and facilities. On Enzo Ferrari's death in 1988, the whole manufacturing facility was ceded to Fiat. They certainly paid their dues for a long time!

The Fiat/Ferrari alliance would undoubtedly stand the test of time, having been agreed some six years after Henry Ford II made a bid to purchase Ferrari. The Commendatore backed out of the deal at the last minute, which resulted in Ford building its own cars to take on Ferrari at Le Mans.

Gianni Agnelli, at 49 more than 20 years Ferrari's junior, was an altogether more sensitive visionary. He handled Enzo Ferrari with the respect and caution which the Old Man rightfully believed was his due, and was quick to understand that Ferrari was not only a valuable public relations tool for Fiat, but also a standard-bearer for his country as a whole. To this day, Agnelli remains passionate about Ferrari and takes a keen interest in all its activities.

MARCH MAKES ITS F1 BOW

In many ways the car of the 1970 Grand Prix season was the Robin Herd-designed March 701, produced by the newly established Bicester-based constructor which had committed itself to building machinery for F2 and F3 in addition to the sport's most senior category.

March Engineering was an ambitious new company. One of its founders was Max Mosley, the son of former British fascist leader Sir Oswald Mosley, who had been a keen amateur racer in his own right. A highly qualified barrister, Max had gained a reputation for being shrewd and

far-thinking, perhaps even a touch ruthless. Twenty-three years later he would be elected President of the FIA.

Max's fellow-directors were Robin Herd, former racer Alan Rees, who'd run top F2 team Winkelmann Racing for much of the 1960s, and Graham Coaker. Initially they tried to coax Jochen Rindt to join their team. 'That's just something you've knocked up together in Graham's shack,' said Rindt scornfully in his richly Austrian-accented English. Mosley was so amused that he registered 'Gremshek Engineering' as a company name. But they didn't get Rindt's services; he stayed with Lotus.

The March 701 was a very basic, Cosworth DFV-engined 'kit car', two of which would be fielded by the STP-backed works team for Chris Amon and Jo Siffert and two others – amazingly – for Jackie Stewart and Johnny Servoz-Gavin under the Elf Tyrrell banner.

Ken Tyrrell had finished the '69 season with a World Championship title – and a major problem on his hands. Matra would no longer supply chassis for Ken's team to use with Ford engines. Jackie Stewart tried the French constructor's Matra V12-engined car at Albi, in southwest France, late in 1969, but couldn't convince himself. Sure enough, the chassis was fine, but the engine felt strangulated alongside the Cosworth DFV.

Tyrrell therefore had no alternative but to look around for another car. March was the only option and he purchased three of the 701s. Mosley wanted to charge Tyrrell £6000 per chassis, a reasonable enough price, he reckoned, since the cars had cost about half that to build.

'I told them they would soon be out of business if they didn't price the cars higher than that,' said Ford's Walter Hayes. So March increased their price and Ford ended up paying £9000 each for the two Tyrrell race cars. This was nickles and dimes if it was what had to be done to keep Jackie Stewart on the Ford books, although Mosley

Instant racer. Chris Amon swings his works March 701 through Tabac ahead of Jack Brabham's Brabham BT33 and Jacky Ickx in the flat-12 Ferrari 312B1 early in the 1970 Monaco Grand Prix.
Photo: Bernard Cahier

Bernard Cahier

Jochen Rindt, the sport's only posthumous World Champion, at the wheel of the dominant Lotus 72 during the summer of 1970.

recalls making Tyrrell squeal like hell by billing him direct for another £9000 for the team's spare chassis.

'But since Ken couldn't really tell me that Ford had already agreed to buy the cars – but only two of them – he couldn't do much more than grizzle,' laughed Max. 'But Walter's advice made the difference between staying in business and going under. At the end of the year we finished up with a nominal profit of £2000. If we'd sold the seven customer 701s we produced for £6000 each, we'd have lost over £20,000 and that would have been that.'

But Ken Tyrrell wasn't happy. Right up to the start of the season he'd been hoping that Matra might relent and build his team a car to take the Ford engine. He also toyed with the possibility of doing a deal with either Brabham or McLaren, but both those teams had Goodyear tyre contracts and Ken's cars ran on Dunlops. There was no choice but the March.

But Tyrrell quickly concluded this could only be a stop-gap. 'Here we were with the reigning World Champion signed up, yet our racing future was to depend on what we could buy from other manufacturers.

'Until that time I'd had no ambition to build my own car. I'd been happy running a semi-works team, bearing the cost of engines and transmissions and their breakages, while Matra took care of the chassis. The cost of rebuilding a wrecked chassis could have been enormous and it was a responsibility I didn't want. Now I had no choice.'

Even as the first March 701s were being unveiled to the media at Silverstone in February 1970 the first Tyrrell was being designed. The man recruited for the task was

former Ferguson engineer Derek Gardner, and he began work in a converted bedroom at his home in Leamington Spa. The first Tyrrell chassis, Ken had told him, must be ready for the Oulton Park Gold Cup race on 22 August. It was a tall order.

March also provided a 701 for their personal protégé, Ronnie Peterson, the dynamic young Swede who'd so memorably won the previous year's Monaco F3 supporting race. Mosley and Herd did a deal for Ronnie to run his March 701 under the Antique Automobiles banner, this being the historic car dealing company owned by the enthusiastic Colin Crabbe.

The other March 701s, meanwhile, were having a halfway decent run. Amon's Firestone-shod factory car won the Silverstone International Trophy while Stewart scored lucky wins in the Race of Champions at Brands Hatch and the Spanish Grand Prix.

Yet the March 701 was effectively living on borrowed time. It was struggling to look good against its opposition, which included the Brabham BT33 and the promising new BRM P153. And this was before Colin Chapman's new challenger seriously got into its stride.

BRM, meanwhile, had undergone a major administrative shake-out the previous season. The P139 had proved uncompetitive in the hands of John Surtees and the team's chief engineer, Tony Rudd, decided he could take no more of the high level of management interference from Louis and Jean Stanley, respectively brother-in-law and sister of Sir Alfred Owen, who were taking an increasing hand in running the team.

After 19 years with the organisation, Rudd went off to become director of powertrain engineering for Colin Chapman's road car company and BRM designs were now entrusted to a young engineer named Tony Southgate. With the 73.6 × 57.22 mm, 2998 cc P142 V12 engine now developing 435 bhp at a maximum of 11,000 rpm, it was almost on a par with the Ford Cosworth DFV.

The BRM V12 was slightly heavier, of course, but Pedro Rodriguez drove the latest P153 chassis brilliantly round Spa-Francorchamps to beat Chris Amon's March and win the Belgian Grand Prix.

In the Brabham camp, 'Black Jack' had not originally intended to drive the new monocoque BT33 in 1970. He made it quite clear that he would have retired if he could have persuaded Jochen Rindt to rejoin the team.

Eventually, Bernie Ecclestone – Jochen's business manager – got in touch with Goodyear to see if there was any way a half-way serious financial deal could be put together in order to get Rindt back in a Brabham. But Chapman eventually trumped these negotiations with an offer of more money and a supplementary F2 programme. So Jochen stayed with Lotus.

Leo Mehl, then Goodyear's Racing Manager, recalled the negotiations. 'Jack was very interested in doing this deal because he would have liked to retire,' he said. 'I had been quite a good friend of Jochen's and was very keen about the proposal, although I feared money would be the big problem.

'Jochen, Jack and I had talked about the deal, but nobody had really mentioned any hard figures. But Colin Chapman came up to me with a very serious look at one of the races and whispered, "I don't care how much you are going to offer him because it won't be enough . . ." I was young and innocent, and Colin was old and forceful, so I never pursued the matter any further with my management.'

Brabham won the opening race of the season at Kyalami at the wheel of the BT33. He would have won the British Grand Prix at Brands Hatch had his car not run short of fuel in the closing moments of the race. Legend has it that chief mechanic Ron Dennis forgot to put in the final churn, but Ron Tauranac was not so sure.

'It's possible all the fuel didn't go in,' he mused, 'but the people concerned were very reliable and marked off their churns and so on. We could have used more fuel; this is possible because the car did appear to be running rich during the race, but the other possibility is that we had a leak. We did find a suspect bag which was wet when we pulled it out of its carrier after the race, although we haven't got any proof that it leaked.'

As for Lotus, the team began the 1970 campaign with the outdated Lotus 49, now in its fourth season of racing, which had been updated to use the latest 13-in. front wheels. But the car was now entering the sunset of its competitive life and Colin Chapman knew it.

The charismatic Lotus boss had originally laid plans for the radical type 72 after the 1969 Lotus 63 had sadly been numbered among that season's crop of four-wheel-drive failures. The classic Lotus 49 had thus been doing yeoman service ever since its debut at Zandvoort in mid-1967, but now Chapman decided it was time to take another giant step forward.

Developed in conjunction with Firestone, the Lotus 72 was designed to have low unsprung weight and pitch-free ride characteristics which would allow it to get the best out of the softest rubber compound available.

To ensure the optimum performance as its fuel load was consumed, Chapman and his chief designer, Maurice Phillippe, decided to employ rising-rate suspension by means of torsion bars, the car's wedge profile guaranteeing its aerodynamic efficiency and the side-mounted radiators preventing the driver's feet from becoming uncomfortably roasted.

From the outset, the car was hampered by problems with its inboard front brakes. Practising at Jarama, Rindt suffered a failure which left him with braking on only three wheels, pitching him into an abrupt spin. He walked back to the pits and told Chapman he wasn't 'ever going to get into that bloody car again'.

As Rob Walker later recalled, he asked Graham Hill what would happen now. Hill, an experienced Lotus campaigner who was now driving Walker's private Lotus 49C, replied: 'Colin will put his arm round Rindt's shoulder and lead him away for a friendly little chat – and Jochen will eventually get back into the car.' That was precisely what happened.

After a disappointing debut in Spain, Rindt reverted to the works Lotus 49C with which to score a stupendous last-corner victory at Monaco. He used the old car again for the Belgian GP before a reworked Lotus 72 broke cover for the Dutch GP at Zandvoort. A suspension redesign had, in Rindt's view, given the car a 'better feel' – its anti-squat characteristics had been reduced – and he trampled the opposition underfoot to score his second win of the season, a success scarred by the death of his friend Piers Courage when he crashed the Frank Williams de Tomaso. This tragedy marked the beginning of the end for Rindt's enthusiasm for F1 racing. At Clermont-Ferrand, the venue for the 1970 French GP, Rindt was still regarding the 72 with a justifiable degree of paranoia. Chapman fumed, 'What am I going to do

Jochen Rindt looks sombre and desolate on the victory rostrum after hearing that his friend, Piers Courage, has been killed in the 1970 Dutch Grand Prix.

Bernard Cahier

Above: Ron Tauranac (left) and Jack Brabham (right) confer with their youthful chief mechanic, Ron Dennis, at the 1970 British Grand Prix.

Above right: Brabham consoles himself with a cup of tea in the motorhome after losing the race on the last lap when his car ran out of fuel.

**Opposite: Two contrasting views of the start/finish area at Monza during the 1970 Italian GP.
Top: Jacky Ickx's pole-position Ferrari 312B1 nudges ahead of the BRM P153 of Pedro Rodriguez as the race gets under way.
Bottom: The winning Ferrari of Clay Regazzoni is about to be swamped by the delirious *tifosi* at the completion of its slowing-down lap.**

with this bloke? He has lightning reflexes, is bloody quick, but keeps telling me how to design my cars.'

Jackie Stewart was possibly Rindt's closest friend for much of his racing career. 'Colin's approach was just a little too slapdash for me,' he admitted, 'and that's why I never drove for him. By the time of his death I think Jochen was certainly talking in terms of retirement. He told me, "I can't get on with his car – it's going to break," but he just had to drive it because it was so fast.'

Herbie Blash, Jochen's mechanic on the Lotus 72 and today FIA Grand Prix Race Director, vividly remembers that Jochen was becoming increasingly preoccupied over Chapman's obsession with saving weight and bulk at any cost. Despite this, Rindt would win in France, then again at Brands Hatch and Hockenheim. He retired from the first Austrian GP to be held at the Österreichring, yet seemed poised to clinch the World Championship at the Italian Grand Prix.

Yet Rindt's alarming prophecy for the Lotus 72 was to be fulfilled. On Saturday, 5 September 1970 he went out to practice at Monza in preparation for the Italian race. At Chapman's insistence, he was running the car without nose wings or aerofoils in an attempt to match the straightline speed of the powerful Ferrari 312B1 flat-12s.

His Lotus team-mate, John Miles, was told that he had to do the same, but reported to Chapman that the car felt 'horrifyingly unstable' in this configuration. Going into Parabolica, Rindt had just overtaken Denny Hulme's McLaren M14A when his car began weaving under heavy braking and speared left into the inadequately secured guard rail.

Rindt succumbed to neck injuries sustained when he 'submarined' deep into the cockpit. It would take another seven years of investigations before it was decided that a front brakeshaft failure had caused his loss of control, but the unsecured barrier was cited as the cause of his death.

Rindt's championship points lead was by this stage almost unassailable. Ferrari team leader Jacky Ickx would have to win all three of the remaining races to take the title. He managed to win two, but when Emerson Fittipaldi took the Lotus 72 to victory at Watkins Glen – in only his fourth Grand Prix outing – Jochen became the sport's only posthumous title holder with 45 points to Ickx's 40.

FERRARI STARTS FIGHT-BACK

Meanwhile, Ferrari was on its way back. By the end of the 1969 season the Italian team could reflect on just a single Grand Prix victory over the past three years, Jacky Ickx having taken a superb win in the rain at Rouen-les-Essarts during the summer of '68.

For his part, Chris Amon had endured enough. It wasn't a question of whether or not Ferrari regained its competitive edge, it was simply that he was running out of patience. Even though he had tested the new 312B1, powered by its sensational 180-degree, 12-cylinder engine, he wasn't about to be seduced into staying.

'For three years I had been driving cars with super chassis that handled well, but couldn't hold a candle to their rivals when it came to power. Then, suddenly, here was the 312B1 with its flat-12 engine.

'The moment I tested it for the first time I knew this was a completely different proposition. But three times I drove it at Modena, and three times it blew apart, always something drastic like breaking its crankshaft. I thought, God, I can't stand another season of this.'

In his view, Mauro Forghieri had produced a gem. But despite his faith in Ferrari's extrovert and volatile Chief Engineer, Amon decided to leave the team. It is a decision he regrets to this day.

Forghieri and his colleagues had produced a remarkably compact power unit of 78.55 × 51.55 mm, producing a total capacity of 2991.01 cc. Its four chain-operated overhead camshafts ran on needle rollers, operating 48 valves, and the crankshaft ran on four main bearings.

Its reputed 460-plus bhp at an 11,700 rpm maximum was judged to be more than enough to deal with the car's Cosworth DFV-propelled rivals, even though the Ferrari was clearly thirstier and needed more fuel. Some of that fuel was contained within a rearward-extending pontoon under which the flat-12 engine was neatly slung. It was a cleverly executed package.

'I decided on the 180-degree engine configuration for two reasons,' recalls Forghieri. 'There was a slight weight saving as compared with the earlier V12s and the centre of gravity would be significantly lower in the chassis. There was the added benefit of a smooth upper surface

Below: Piers Courage in the Frank Williams de Tomaso 505 prior to the start of the fateful 1970 Dutch Grand Prix at Zandvoort.

to the rear bodywork and we decided to hang the "boxer" from beneath a rearward extension of the monocoque which could also be used to carry extra fuel.

'The 312 engine had four main bearings, the crankshaft was machined from a special alloy billet imported from the USA and it had four chain-driven overhead camshafts running on needle rollers. To cure those early crankshaft failures, we had specially developed coupling between the crankshaft and flywheel, the purpose being to transfer flexing stresses along the length of the crankshaft.'

Forghieri had developed the engine during a spell in 1969 when he had been 'banished' to Maranello's special projects department. 'I began to think of the "boxer" configuration at the end of 1968 after a year of pole positions, leading races and disappointing retirements with Chris Amon,' he said.

Despite the advent of the Lotus 72, the Ferrari 312B1 acquitted itself magnificently throughout its first full season. New signing Clay Regazzoni was able to lead a Grand Prix for the first time at Hockenheim, where Ickx battled with Rindt for the entire distance, just finding himself outfumbled on the final lap. In fairness, Rindt commented: 'A monkey could have won in my car today.'

As we have seen, Jochen failed to finish his home race at the Österreichring, where Ickx and Regazzoni put on a convincing demonstration run to finish in 1–2 formation. Rindt was then killed at Monza, where Regazzoni took victory – his first – and Ickx retired with a broken clutch.

It was a dark weekend for the international motor racing fraternity, but there remained the tantalising prospect that Ickx, after all, just might beat his dead rival for the World Championship crown. Ickx finished the Italian GP weekend with a total of 19 points, way behind the total of 45 which Rindt had accumulated prior to his death.

The mathematics were simple. If Ickx could win the three remaining races – in Canada, the USA and Mexico

– he would pick up another 27 points and take the title by a single point. On the face of it, this seemed like a long shot, but he almost did it. He kept the battle open by winning the Canadian race at St Jovite, near Montreal, but a fuel line sprung a leak at Watkins Glen two weeks later and he could only scramble home fourth.

This now confirmed Rindt as World Champion, but it was a close-run thing as Ickx went on to round off the season with a victory in Mexico City. He had thus won a total of four Grands Prix during the course of the season, only one short of Rindt's total, but the Belgian acknowledged that it was only right that his Austrian rival should have emerged as champion.

DE TOMASO VENTURE ENDS IN TRAGEDY

During the course of the 1969 season, Frank Williams had made the acquaintance of Alessandro de Tomaso, the dynamic and successful Argentine businessman whose marriage to the wealthy American, Isabelle Haskell, had spawned an ambitious business partnership. At the time the couple were already manufacturing Ford-engined high-performance road cars – the Mangusta and the Pantera were two of their best-known products – in a bid to challenge Ferrari and Lamborghini in this prestige sector of the market.

De Tomaso had already produced an F2 car which showed a degree of promise, designed by Gianpaolo Dallara, who would go on to become a leading F3 chassis maker in his own right some 25 years later. For 1970, de Tomaso proposed that his company should build a new Grand Prix car which Frank would prepare and enter for Piers Courage to drive.

Williams's contribution to the equation would be to furnish the engines, driver and organisational expertise,

Bernard Cahier

Bernard Cahier

such as it was. Courage duly agreed to drive the Cosworth DFV-engined de Tomaso 505, turning down a £30,000 offer to join Jacky Ickx at Ferrari. Instead he stayed with Frank on a nominal £3000 retainer, topped up with a fee of £22,500 from the Autodelta Alfa Romeo sports car team.

But the de Tomaso 505 was far from the taut, easy-handling Brabham BT24 which Piers had driven the previous year. Courage struggled from the outset, Frank even asking Jackie Stewart if he would do a few laps in the car in practice for the Silverstone International Trophy meeting, just to provide an objective third-party view as to precisely what he'd got Piers involved with.

Gradually the team's efforts improved the de Tomaso, but on 21 June 1970 Piers crashed while running midfield in the Dutch Grand Prix at Zandvoort. The car caught fire and its driver perished in the ensuing inferno. With this disaster coming barely three weeks after the universally popular Bruce McLaren had been killed testing one of his own Can-Am sports cars at Goodwood, the F1 fraternity began to wonder just how much more tragedy it could bear.

TYRRELL READY TO RACE

The Tyrrell 001-Ford was easily the best-kept secret in motor racing in 1970. It was formally unveiled at Ford's London showrooms in Regent Street on Monday, 17

August, where the press members saw a car which bore something of an inspirational resemblance to the previous year's Matra MS80.

Ken Tyrrell reckoned that first chassis had cost £22,500 to build – about two and a half March 701s, in other words. It was the bargain of the age.

Derek Gardner had concentrated on producing the best possible aerodynamic profile, good weight distribution and the lowest permissible weight. The first monocoque was manufactured by Morris Gomm's specialist sheet metal works at Old Woking, a few miles from the Tyrrell headquarters, and the car was topped off with distinctive bodywork which included a full-width, flat nose wing.

Stewart instantly recognised that here was a car in which he could achieve things. Its outing in the Gold Cup race was blighted by teething troubles, including a jammed throttle and an oil pick-up problem which caused the engine to blow up. But Jackie came away from the weekend with a new Oulton Park lap record and the feeling that this was a car which was as sharp and responsive as the March 701 was dull and ponderous.

Although Stewart raced the March 701 to an emotionally draining second place at Monza the day after his close friend, Jochen Rindt, had died, for the remaining three Grands Prix of the season – in Canada, the USA and Mexico – he would drive the Tyrrell. It never finished, but it did convince him that he could challenge for the World Championship in 1971.

Jackie Stewart at the wheel of the Goodyear-shod Tyrrell-Ford en route to his second World Championship in 1971.

Stewart also had the last word on the March 701. He played golf with Robin Herd shortly before practice at the Canadian Grand Prix. Robin suggested that if Jackie won the game, he should drive the Tyrrell. If he did not, he would drive the March.

With three holes to play, Herd was one up and, with practice starting shortly, suggested that they call it a day there and then. Stewart fixed him with a horrified expression. 'Robin,' he said, 'never has anyone had such an incentive not to lose a golf match.' They played it out. Jackie finished one up and raced the Tyrrell.

Partnered by his talented young team-mate, François Cevert, who had replaced Servoz-Gavin in the middle of the '70 season, Jackie posted the first Tyrrell victory in 1971 at Barcelona's Montjuich Park circuit, then followed that up with his second Monaco victory. But this was something very special, even by his standards.

Despite suffering from a badly upset stomach, he qualified his Tyrrell-Ford on pole position only to find the brake balance bar broken as he took his place on the grid, leaving him with braking on the front wheels only. Unconcerned, he led from start to finish, only to be sick on the winner's rostrum. With a touch of false modesty, he plays down the magnitude of that achievement. 'Although you might not think so, Monaco is not particularly hard on brakes because you are never slowing from really high speed,' he said.

'But it was a good race. To do it with only two-wheel braking was quite something. It's also worth remembering that we had manual gearboxes in those days – and that meant a maximum of 2800 gearchanges during the course of the race with the six-speed box we had on the old BRM. You always ended the race with your gearchange hand badly blistered.'

Thereafter, Stewart sped remorselessly towards his second World Championship, adding victories in the French, British, German and Canadian Grands Prix to his tally. To round off the season Cevert won the US Grand Prix at Watkins Glen, where Stewart had tyre troubles, scooping the $50,000 first prize for Ken Tyrrell's team.

Tyrrell had run the '71 season on Goodyear tyres after Dunlop's withdrawal from F1 at the end of the previous year and, with the advent of this new partnership, Jackie began to gain a reputation for tyre testing and development which has stayed with him to this day. F1 was becoming increasingly scientific.

Elsewhere in the field, Jack Brabham had finally retired at the end of 1970 and sold his shareholding in the Brabham team to long-time partner Ron Tauranac. But Ron was also losing interest and, after a rather indifferent '71 season, would sell out to Bernie Ecclestone.

'There was a change of emphasis,' said Tauranac. 'In the old days, I would stay at the circuit with Jack and the mechanics and we used to work on the cars, knock ideas about and discuss things. Then we'd knock off and go back to the hotel and eat, perhaps a little bit before the mechanics, but still not very early.

'Then Jack retired and things were different. The fun had gone out of it and, by 1971, we were having a rather fraught time. As far as Graham Hill [who had joined the team that season] was concerned, I think whatever talent he may previously have had as a driver had drifted away and only his determination was left.

'I was no good at getting sponsorship, and although Goodyear was paying the lion's share of the budget in

no position to take that on, particularly as I was still paying back Jack the money he lent me to buy his shares. So I started talking to Bernie Ecclestone and eventually sold it to him.'

Ecclestone remembers: 'Ron had initially spoken to me as early as the 1971 Monaco Grand Prix about the prospect of getting involved with him in the Brabham team, but negotiations were not completed until later that year. Ron initially asked me if I could give him some help on the business side, but later he said, "I think I want to sell, do you want to buy half?" I told him that I didn't particularly want to buy half, but if he wanted to sell then I would be prepared to buy the whole business. Which is what I eventually did.'

The original idea was that Tauranac should stay on in a consultancy role, but Bernie found that it just didn't work out. 'Ultimately, you couldn't really employ anybody who had once owned the company,' he reflected. 'It wasn't good for him and it wasn't good for me.'

In his new role as a team owner, Ecclestone would soon emerge as a leading light in the Formula 1 Constructors' Association (FOCA). Grand Prix racing reached a crucial fork in the road at around this time and, together with March's Max Mosley, the Brabham boss would be instrumental in guiding it in the direction of commercialisation. It didn't take long for Max and Bernie to form a shrewd, if informal, alliance within FOCA. In due course, Ecclestone would be elected the organisation's President, handling all the time-consuming negotiations with race promoters. Bernie could see that the commercial potential of Grand Prix racing was dramatically under-exploited. He would rectify that state of affairs over the next 25 years.

Meanwhile, motor racing was still enduring more than its fair share of tragedy. BRM's season was overshadowed by the death of Pedro Rodriguez, who lost his life when he unwisely used a weekend off from F1 to drive a private Ferrari 512M in what amounted to a German club race at the Norisring. Jo Siffert restored morale by giving the BRM P160 a fine victory in the Austrian Grand Prix, which was followed by a similar split-second triumph for Peter Gethin at Monza, but then Siffert, too, was killed at Brands Hatch in an end-of-season non-title F1 outing.

Ferrari, meanwhile, was dropping off the pace. The multi-talented Mario Andretti – who had originally made his F1 debut at Watkins Glen in 1968, where he qualified a works Lotus 49B on pole position – romped away with the South African Grand Prix at Kyalami. He was driving the elegant Ferrari 312B1, but this was soon superseded by the tricky-to-drive B2, in which Jacky Ickx could manage only a single win in a rain-soaked Dutch Grand Prix, where his Firestone wet-weather tyres gave him a significant advantage. Jackie Stewart's Goodyear-shod Tyrrell was lapped in the same race.

At the same time March was thriving with its very distinctive, Frank Costin-styled 711, with which Ronnie Peterson would score four second places to end the year as World Championship runner-up behind Jackie Stewart. The Scot scored 62 points with Peterson gaining 33 and François Cevert 26.

This was certainly the era of the F1 Cosworth 'kit car', which would continue through to the end of the 1970s when another major sea change saw a crucial shift of emphasis within the Grand Prix business.

The original Tyrrell F1 design had been regarded by

Right: Emerson Fittipaldi celebrates victory in the 1973 Argentine Grand Prix at Buenos Aires. With only a handful of laps left, he sliced his way ahead of François Cevert (right of shot) to take the win.

Below: Understated elegance: the black and gold John Player Special Lotus 72 carrying Fittipaldi's number one for his 1973 season as reigning World Champion.

during 1971 he completed the preliminary outline of a second-generation concept that finally saw action the following year as the lower and shorter 005/006 range, which had originally been designed to use inboard front brakes as a means of further reducing unsprung weight.

Unfortunately in 1972 Jackie Stewart's high-pressure lifestyle finally caught up with him and a duodenal ulcer was diagnosed. This forced him to miss the Belgian Grand Prix and it would not be until the Austrian race that Jackie finally gave the Tyrrell 005 its race debut, the car now fitted with outboard brakes after the original inboard configuration had produced quite severe vibration problems.

LAST WIN FOR BRM

The 1972 season also saw BRM relinquish its Yardley sponsorship in favour of the Marlboro cigarette brand just as the Lotus 72s were repackaged in the distinctive black and gold colours of the John Player Special brand. In pouring rain, Jean-Pierre Beltoise took the BRM P160 to an impressive win at Monaco. It would be the last Grand Prix victory for the famous British team, which by now seemed preoccupied with its somewhat shaky historic status rather than pressing on with imaginative ideas for the future.

Chris Amon had moved to Matra at the start of 1971, but although the French team decided to concentrate on running just a single car for the New Zealander the following year Amon's atrocious luck never deserted him. He ran away with the '72 French Grand Prix at Clermont-Ferrand, only to sustain a punctured tyre and drop to third. Jackie Stewart won the race, the Scot making a return to the cockpit after missing the Belgian Grand Prix.

For its part, Lotus was now recovering from the aftershocks caused by Jochen Rindt's death. After finding his feet in 1971, Emerson Fittipaldi drove into the history books as the sport's youngest World Champion at the age of 25. The dynamic young Brazilian won the Spanish, Belgian, British, Austrian and Italian Grands Prix to clinch the title with 61 points to Stewart's 45, with McLaren driver Denny Hulme on 39.

Fittipaldi would put Brazil firmly on the international racing map. The son of a respected motor sport journalist and broadcaster, Wilson Fittipaldi, Emerson was born in São Paulo on 12 December 1946. He and his elder brother, Wilson Jnr, raced motor cycles and karts in their early teens, and Emerson won the 1967 Brazilian Formula Vee championship before coming to Britain to race in Formula Ford two years later.

His progress through Formula Ford, F3 and F2 was to prove meteoric. Offered his Grand Prix debut by Lotus in the 1970 British Grand Prix at the wheel of an outdated type 49C, he kept out of trouble to finish eighth. He then finished fourth at Hockenheim and was finally propelled into the team leadership after Rindt's tragic death at Monza.

Eighteen months later he was ready for the Big Time, and watching him reel off five confident victories that season was to see at work an unflustered natural talent which many were tempted to compare with Jim Clark's.

By the start of 1972 there would be no fewer than three Brazilians contesting the World Championship, Wilson Fittipaldi having secured a place in Bernie Ecclestone's resurgent Brabham team while Carlos Pace was signed up by Frank Williams and would later join Team Surtees.

At the beginning of the 1973 season Jackie Stewart confided to Ken Tyrrell that he was going to retire at the end of the year, but he nevertheless embarked on that final season with some gusto. Again using the 005/006-series cars, the monocoques of which were clad with the now-mandatory deformable structures from the Spanish Grand Prix onwards, the jaunty Scot won the South African, Belgian, Monaco, Dutch and German Grands Prix on the way to his third and last World Championship.

Bernard Cahier

Colin Chapman and Emerson Fittipaldi struck up a rapport which many were tempted to compare with that between the Lotus chief and the late Jim Clark.

Main photo: Paul-Henri Cahier.   Inset: Bernard Cahier

Tragically, his team-mate, François Cevert, was killed at Watkins Glen practising for the United States Grand Prix and Tyrrell withdrew his two other entries for Stewart and Chris Amon. With Jackie's retirement a great partnership had come to an end and the Tyrrell team would never again scale such peaks of achievement.

Meanwhile Emerson Fittipaldi had grown restless after Colin Chapman had brought the brilliant Swede, Ronnie Peterson, into the Team Lotus fold for 1973. The pair scored a total of seven victories that season but the wins were split between them in a tactically questionable manner which allowed Stewart to take the drivers' championship and the frustrated Brazilian opted to switch to McLaren for 1974 and '75.

McLAREN'S M23 PICKS UP THE WINNING PACE

Fittipaldi would win a second World Championship in 1974 at the wheel of the McLaren M23, another outstanding machine from the mid-1970s crop. It had made its debut in the 1973 South African Grand Prix at Kyalami, where Denny Hulme had gained the sole pole position of his Grand Prix career.

The car had won a total of 14 World Championship Grands Prix by the time it made its last appearance in 1978, although during the last two seasons of its career it was displaced as a front-line challenger and was mostly seen in the hands of privateers, having had its last outing

Opposite: Jackie Stewart regarded his comeback drive to fourth place in the 1973 Italian Grand Prix as one of the best performances of his career. Inset: Jackie and his protégé, François Cevert.

Below left: Peter Revson delivered a beautifully controlled performance in the works McLaren M23 to win the '73 British Grand Prix at Silverstone.

Bottom left: Moody brilliance. Carlos Reutemann brooding in the cockpit of his Brabham BT44.

Bernard Cahier

Paul-Henri Cahier

for the factory team with Gilles Villeneuve in the cockpit in the 1977 British Grand Prix at Silverstone.

The M23 was Gordon Coppuck's first complete Formula 1 design. It was also one of the first F1 cars tailor-made to the new technical regulations, introduced for 1973, which required a deformable structure along the side of the chassis to provide added protection to the fuel tanks in the event of a lateral impact.

The new McLaren inherited the rising-rate front suspension of the earlier M19 while conventional rear suspension, with outboard spring/dampers, adjustable top links, reversed lower wishbones and twin radius rods, was fitted. The car had a centre fuel cell behind the driver's seat and the Cosworth Ford DFV V8 engine transmitted its power through a Hewland FG400 transaxle.

During its first season the M23 won three Grands Prix, the first being Hulme's victory in the Swedish Grand Prix at Anderstorp, where he snatched the lead from Ronnie Peterson's Lotus 72 in the closing stages. Peter Revson then went on to win at Silverstone and Canada's Mosport Park track, while Hulme started the '74 season with a lucky win in Buenos Aires after Carlos Reutemann's Brabham BT44 had run out of fuel.

For 1974 the M23s were revamped with revised weight distribution achieved by means of a 3-in. spacer between the engine and the gearbox which lengthened the wheelbase. The rear track was also wider, but new team leader Emerson Fittipaldi was not totally convinced about these changes and experimented with different wheelbase lengths as he worked his way to the '74 title. The Brazilian won only three of the season's 15 races,

but impressive consistency allied to the outstanding reliability of his Marlboro-liveried McLaren enabled him to hold off the challenges of Ferrari's Clay Regazzoni and two drivers who scored their first Grand Prix victories during the course of the year, Jody Scheckter of Tyrrell and Regazzoni's Ferrari team-mate, Niki Lauda.

For the start of the 1975 season Fittipaldi appeared in a car with heavily revised front suspension, Gordon Coppuck having taken a leaf out of Brabham's book by adopting a fabricated top rocker arm configuration with pullrod activation of the now semi-inboard spring/damper unit. This was later modified to move the spring/dampers totally inboard again and a variety of secondary suspension modifications were incorporated progressively over the balance of the season, in which Fittipaldi took second place in the championship.

For 1976, Fittipaldi switched to the Brazilian Copersucar team which had been established the previous year by his elder brother, Wilson. That brought the extrovert, public school-educated James Hunt into the McLaren line-up as number one driver, the Englishman successfully exploiting the M23's continuing development potential to beat Lauda to that year's World Championship.

Into 1977 there was still precious little indication that the McLaren M23 was at the end of its competitive life. The new M26, introduced mid-season in '76, was proving difficult to sort out and it was not until after Monaco that Hunt abandoned the M23 and switched to the new car. His final race win with the M23 came in the Race of Champions at Brands Hatch, the non-title curtain-raiser to the European season.

Opposite: Emerson Fittipaldi in the works McLaren M23 at Monaco, 1974, on the way to his second World Championship.

Below: The first win for Niki Lauda, who waves to the crowd from the top step of the rostrum at Jarama after the '74 Spanish Grand Prix. On the left is second-placed finisher Clay Regazzoni with Emerson Fittipaldi, who was third, on the right.

THE LOTUS 72: THE MOST ENDURING F1 CAR OF ALL TIME?

Paul-Henri Cahier

O N 19 APRIL 1970, a pair of Lotus 72s rolled out to make their F1 competition debuts in the Spanish Grand Prix held at Madrid's Jarama circuit. Strikingly elegant and purposeful in the distinctive red, white and gold livery of Gold Leaf Team Lotus and distinguished by their sleek needle noses and hip-mounted water radiators, they were driven on that occasion by Jochen Rindt and John Miles.

On 5 October 1975, Ronnie Peterson and Brian Henton finished fifth and twelfth respectively in the US Grand Prix at Watkins Glen on the 72's last competition outing. These straightforward facts surely endorse this remarkable car's claim to be the most enduring F1 design of all time, for, although one must acknowledge that Maserati's remarkable 250F raced across the seven years of the 2.5-litre F1 from 1954 to 1960, for the last three seasons of its life it was competing in the hands of privateers.

By contrast, the Lotus 72 was the factory team's front-line challenger in its first race and its last. That said, it was not meant to be in service for that length of time. It started out with Jochen Rindt

regarding it as a death-trap – an unfortunately prophetic judgement, as things turned out – developed into one of the most formidable winning machines of its generation and then suffered a gradual decline into a depressing old age.

After that promising, but bruising, first season, Team Lotus marked time in 1971. Emerson Fittipaldi was obviously a man of the future, but the after-effects of a mid-season road accident left him distinctly below par for much of the year. Not until 1972 was the young Brazilian able to exploit the 72's terrific potential. With his car now wearing the steely black and gold John Player Special livery, Emerson stormed to victory in the Spanish, Belgian, British, Austrian and Italian GPs to become the sport's youngest-ever World Champion.

In 1973, Chapman decided to create a super-team by signing up the dynamic Ronnie Peterson as Fittipaldi's partner. Lotus switched from Firestone to Goodyear tyres, but the 72s were still the class of the field in the opening races of the year. Chapman now briefed his designer, Ralph Bellamy, to start work on a replacement chassis, the Lotus 76,

which the chief decreed should be a Lotus 72 'but 100 pounds lighter'.

At the start of the '73 season, insiders began speculating as to what might happen when Peterson got his hands on a Lotus 72. Perhaps, they mused, he might learn to drive smoothly and tidily, a lesson the car had, in the last few months of his life, taught Jochen Rindt.

Those who watched Ronnie – grappling with an intermittently sticking throttle – yowling through Woodcote on his way to second place in the '73 British GP at Silverstone might have thought otherwise. But Ronnie won four Grands Prix that season in brilliantly disciplined fashion. With Emerson bagging another three, it was good enough to retain the constructors' title for Lotus, but dividing the wins allowed Jackie Stewart to take his third drivers' crown.

Fittipaldi, piqued that his position at Lotus had been undermined by Peterson's arrival, switched to McLaren in 1974 and duly won his second World Championship. Meanwhile, Lotus had a dreadful time with the new 76, which incorporated provision for left-foot braking, an accessory which neither

Ronnie nor team-mate Jacky Ickx could make much sense of.

The new car also rather defeated the point by winding up heavier than the 72, broke with alarming frequency and ate its tyres. Small wonder that Peterson suggested rolling out the old 72, which he then used to win the Monaco, French and Italian GPs, although by the end of the year the cars were suffering from near-terminal understeer on the latest generation of Goodyear rubber.

Ferrari, Brabham, Tyrrell and McLaren took the lion's share of Goodyear's development effort in 1975, leaving the Lotus 72s now struggling to keep pace. Experiments with varying wheelbase and suspension configurations reflected a team in disarray, but good old Ronnie barnstormed his way through from 14th to run as high as fourth in the closing stages of the car's final race at Watkins Glen.

Only when the Swede locked up a brake two laps from home did James Hunt's Hesketh 308C nip ahead of the gallant old Lotus, which, fighting a desperate rearguard action to the very end, at least drove into the history books with all its guns blazing right up to its final chequered flag.

since 1967 this is what
we've done in our spare time

Above: Niki Lauda in the Ferrari 312T leads at the start of the 1975 German Grand Prix. Immediately behind are Carlos Pace (Brabham) and Patrick Depailler (Tyrrell).

Right: Carlos Reutemann was an increasingly competitive force to be reckoned with in 1975 with the Gordon Murray-designed Brabham BT44B.

FERRARI FIGHTS BACK

FERRARI'S FLAT-12 engine powered three World Champions during the second half of the 1970s, Niki Lauda winning the title in 1975 and '77 and Jody Scheckter recapturing the crown for Maranello in 1979. However, although James Hunt's championship victory in 1976 with the McLaren M23 owed much to Lauda's near-fatal crash in Germany, Mario Andretti's success in 1978 for Lotus proved that technical innovation – specifically the development of ground-effect aerodynamics – could allow the British teams to remain competitive despite their continued reliance on the Cosworth V8. Meanwhile Renault took advantage of a legal loophole to introduce a 1.5-litre turbocharged engine, which established a trend others would soon be obliged to follow.

From the moment Lauda first tried the Ferrari 312T – 'T' for *trasversale*, signifying that the car was equipped with a transverse gearbox – it was clear to the 25-year-old Austrian driver that here was a car in which he could win the 1975 World Championship.

So it proved. The brilliant 3-litre 180-degree flat-12 had been the cornerstone of Ferrari's technical armoury since the start of 1970, but the addition of that transverse gearbox to the package helped make the 312T one of the most consistent, neutral F1 cars of its genera-

tion. It was also superbly rugged and reliable, while its engine was powerful enough to keep Ferrari in play as a leading light right through to the end of 1979.

The Ferrari 312T was the making of Lauda's reputation. Together with its derivative, the 312T2, it won a Constructors' Championship hat-trick between 1975 and '77, during which time the design scored 16 Grand Prix victories.

But just how good was the 312T family set against its opposition?

Lauda joined the Ferrari team at the start of 1974 and won two Grands Prix that season with the Mauro Forghieri-designed 312B3. This had a conventional, longitudinal gearbox and, Lauda remembers, was always prone to a touch of understeer. But Niki admits that when Forghieri took the wraps off the new 312T immediately after the '74 United States GP he was a worried man.

Forghieri's avowed intention was to pursue the lowest possible polar moment of inertia by packaging as much of the car as possible between the front and rear wheels. The new transmission cluster was positioned across the car ahead of the rear axle line, the shafts lying at right angles to the centre-line of the car, the drive being taken via bevel gears on the input side of the gearbox.

'When I was first shown the drawings of the 312T I

Below: Niki Lauda signs an autograph for a young fan from the back of the Ferrari transporter. He is watched by team manager Luca di Montezemolo and Clay Regazzoni.

Bernard Cahier

Bernard Cahier

Rivals and close friends, James Hunt (left) and Niki Lauda competed against each other in F1 from 1973 through to James's retirement after the 1979 Monaco Grand Prix.

1975

February: Margaret Thatcher becomes the first female leader of the British Conservative Party, replacing Edward Heath.
April: 40 people are killed by avalanches in the Swiss, Italian and Austrian Alps.
December: Tiger Woods, US golfer, is born.

1976

January: Agatha Christie, British author, dies.
February: The National Exhibition Centre is opened in Birmingham.
March: The British Prime Minister, Harold Wilson, quits in a surprise announcement.
July: Swedish tennis player Bjorn Borg wins the first of his five Wimbledon men's singles championships at the age of 20.

felt indifferent about the whole project,' recalls Lauda. 'I didn't really appreciate the advantages that it would offer, because it seemed such a very big change from a chassis about which we knew everything.

'Then, when I got to drive it at Fiorano, I quickly appreciated that it was a much more competitive proposition. The problem with the B3 had been its inclination towards understeer; no matter how you tried to tune the chassis, it always understeered very slightly. We had also used up all its potential, so we had to switch to the new car. There was no choice.'

However, Lauda firmly believes that the 312T offered only a slight power advantage over the rival Cosworth Ford DFV-equipped machines from McLaren, Lotus, Shadow and Tyrrell. What it *did* provide was totally neutral handling and a wide torque curve from the superbly flexible flat-12 engine. Driveability was the key.

In 1975, Niki won five Grands Prix to take his first World Championship crown. At the start of the following year he won the Brazilian and Argentine races with the 312T, then his team-mate, Clay Regazzoni, triumphed at Long Beach. Not long afterwards Lauda scored further victories in Belgium and Monaco with the evolutionary 312T2. Then came a spate of engine failures caused by a machining error which produced infinitesimal cracks at the point where a flange taking the drive to the ignition was pressed into the end of the crankshaft.

However, in 1976, Lauda faced strong opposition from James Hunt, an old sparring partner and rival from his F3 days. Hunt had driven Lord Hesketh's Harvey Postlethwaite-designed type 308 to victory in the '75 Dutch Grand Prix, beating Lauda in the process, and was the logical choice for the McLaren team when it became clear that Emerson Fittipaldi was leaving at the end of that year.

In Holland the race had started in the wet and James had timed his switch to slicks perfectly, vaulting ahead of Lauda, who was unable to find a way back in front.

'James drove beautifully,' remembers Lauda, 'and there was understandably a great deal of excitement among the

British press about his achievement, although, if I am honest, I would have to say that I took things a little easier than I might have done, as my main priority that day was to keep scoring points to add to my World Championship tally. Nevertheless, James's success took him through a psychological barrier, which was bad for me.'

No sooner did McLaren director Teddy Mayer hear that Fittipaldi was yesterday's news than he put a call through to Hunt, recently made redundant after Hesketh Racing had closed its doors as a front-line F1 operation. Hunt had been in the throes of negotiating with Lotus boss Colin Chapman but both parties were making heavy weather of the talks.

Chapman still clung to the belief that people ought to be honoured to drive for Lotus and that it was better to invest money in the car's technology than in the driver's retainer. James replied that this was all very well, but he was a professional racer and Lotus was poised on the outer rim of competitiveness. The bottom line was: he needed paying.

Mayer immediately told him to stop talking to anybody until they had had time to talk seriously together. The net result was that Teddy got James's signature on a 1976 contract for a reputed £40,000. This was chicken feed, even by the standards of the time, and for McLaren it would prove one of F1's all-time bargains.

James was partnered by Jochen Mass, the pleasant German driver who had been drafted into the McLaren squad in the middle of 1974 after Mike Hailwood had suffered severe ankle injuries when he crashed heavily during the German Grand Prix at the Nürburgring. Mass privately believed that he might be in a position to assert an advantage over his incoming rival, but Hunt quickly showed who was boss by qualifying on pole position for his first race in the M23, the Brazilian GP at Interlagos.

Lauda may have won the World Championship in 1975, but it soon became clear that he was going to have his work cut out if he was going to retain it in '76.

'From the moment he got into the McLaren M23, James was predictably quick,' said Niki. 'The 1976 season

Left: James Hunt wins the 1975 Dutch Grand Prix for Lord Hesketh's independent team in the Harvey Postlethwaite-designed 308.

Below: Carlos Pace on the podium after winning the 1975 Brazilian Grand Prix at Interlagos. Silhouetted to the left is Emerson Fittipaldi (second) and to the right Jochen Mass (third).

Photos: Bernard Cahier

Bernard Cahier

Japan, 1976. Three of the finest F1 drivers of the 1970s: from the left, James Hunt, Niki Lauda and the still much-missed Ronnie Peterson.

has now gone down in motor racing history as one of the most remarkable of all time, but I have to confess I still felt very confident about the Ferrari's performance in the opening races of the year.

'Then both James and I began to encounter our troubles. I damaged a rib when a tractor rolled over on top of me while I was in the garden of my new home at Hof, near Salzburg. Then James won the Spanish Grand Prix for McLaren, beating me in the process, only to be disqualified when his car was found to have a fractionally too wide rear track.'

The McLaren team seriously believed it had got the raw end of the deal in that race at Jarama. They felt that Ferrari somehow represented 'The Establishment' and that the sport's governing body was showing a degree of partiality towards the famous Italian team. It was a theme which would emerge regularly over the years.

Eventually James's race win in Spain was reinstated, which left Ferrari, on this occasion, feeling a bit miffed. Personal tensions began to build between Hunt and Lauda, although they were on a pretty mild level compared with some of the internecine strife between rivals which would follow over the ensuing decades. 'We were rivals, but we respected each other totally, whatever the circumstances,' said Niki.

Hunt then won the French Grand Prix at Paul Ricard after both Ferraris had encountered engine problems. Then came more controversy in the British Grand Prix at Brands Hatch. Lauda and his team-mate, Regazzoni, touched wheels accelerating away from the start into Paddock Bend, causing the Swiss driver to spin, and then James's McLaren was pitched on to two wheels when it rode over Regazzoni's right-rear wheel.

The race was red-flagged to a halt and Hunt eventually

took the restart in his repaired race car, although McLaren initially wheeled out its spare car for him, which was clearly against the rules. Technically he shouldn't have been allowed to take the restart at all, but it seemed to many onlookers that the race officials were so overwhelmed by the fans' vocal support for James that they relented.

'I suppose I was cast in the role of the villain in their eyes, although I have to confess this didn't really bother me in the slightest,' said Lauda. 'Having said that, in the later years of my career – particularly when I returned after my break to drive a McLaren – I tended to find the British fans extremely hospitable towards me, especially after I won at Brands Hatch in 1982 and '84.'

Hunt's McLaren M23 stalked Lauda relentlessly after the British Grand Prix had been restarted and eventually sliced past into the lead with a bold move going into the Druids hairpin. However, he would be disqualified from that win later in the season, by which time Lauda was fighting back to health after his Ferrari had been transformed into a fireball when he crashed in the German Grand Prix at the Nürburgring.

Lauda hung between life and death for several days and, while his old friend was enormously concerned about his condition, his absence nevertheless gave Hunt a golden opportunity to close the points gap on the Austrian. James won the restarted German GP – before the extent of Niki's injuries was fully appreciated – finished fourth in Austria and scored another victory in Holland, by which time it was happily clear that Lauda was well on the road to staging a remarkable recovery.

'By the time I got back in the cockpit for the Italian Grand Prix at Monza, I was only two points ahead of James at the head of the World Championship table,'

Niki would recall. 'I finished fourth there and James didn't score, so now I was five points ahead with three races to go. Then James got disqualified from the British Grand Prix, promoting me to the win, and went into the Canadian Grand Prix 17 points behind.

'People have often asked me whether I felt sympathy for James on this, and I suppose I would have to say no, even though there was quite a bit of tension between the McLaren and Ferrari teams. We were locked in pretty fierce competition for that championship, we were both professionals and didn't allow our personal friendship to get in the way of that rivalry. But I would say that James drove the last few races of 1976 – and the first of 1977 – about as well as at any other time in his career.'

At the same time, McLaren had really piled on the development of the M23, which, although not quite as powerful as the Ferrari, was certainly a tried and tested car with a well-proven competition record behind it. Lauda paid the price for Ferrari's lack of progress with a distant eighth in the Canadian Grand Prix and then third place in the US GP, both races being won by Hunt.

Then came the electrifying finale to a quite remarkable season. In the Japanese Grand Prix at Mount Fuji Lauda pulled out of the race on the second lap, convinced that driving in the prevailing conditions of torrential rain was absolute lunacy.

Some people said that Niki had taken a calculated gamble that James wouldn't finish the race, but that was unfair. Lauda had nothing to prove after that incredible return to the cockpit. For his part, Hunt looked as though he had the race in the bag, only to be sent scurrying into the pits to change a deflated tyre. He resumed the chase, throwing caution to the wind, and stormed back to third place – enough to give him the World Championship crown by a single point ahead of Lauda.

There was still an element of sportsmanship to the Grand Prix business in those days. Hunt made some very public remarks which were supportive of Lauda in the weeks immediately after the Japanese Grand Prix, at a time when the Austrian was being put through the mill by an unforgiving Italian press after being seen to throw in the towel and lose the title at the final gasp.

Unfortunately, Ferrari's chassis development programme had been allowed to drift during the weeks Niki was in hospital. For 1977, the Austrian turned things round and bounced back to take his second title. Yet there was a gradual, almost imperceptible, deterioration in the Ferrari 312T2's performance in 1977 which served as a reminder that F1 cars are complex technical packages.

The Italian team was also slightly irked that Goodyear's latest tyres seemed better suited to the rival McLaren M26, a state of affairs which resulted in Ferrari switching to Michelin radials from the start of 1978.

That incredible flat-12 reliability continued to underpin Lauda's 1977 efforts. In the South African GP, his 312T2 ran over debris from the tragic accident which claimed the life of Shadow driver Tom Pryce and the flat-12 lost all its water and most of its oil as a result. But the car still finished, cockpit warning lights flickering, to post yet another victory.

Below: The frantic first corner of the US Grand Prix West at Long Beach, 1976, with Clay Regazzoni's Ferrari 312T just slipping through in the lead with James Hunt's McLaren and the Tyrrell 007 of Patrick Depailler wheel-to-wheel right on his tail. Niki Lauda's Ferrari and Tom Pryce's Shadow are next up.

Niki Lauda took another decisive step towards winning the 1977 World Championship with this victory in the Dutch Grand Prix in the Ferrari 312T2.

TYRRELL PRODUCES AN F1 NOVELTY

For the 1976 season, the Tyrrell team produced one of the most surprising single technical developments of the decade. Chief Designer Derek Gardner came up with the sensational six-wheeler Tyrrell P34, which some cynics believed was a practical joke when it was first unveiled prior to the start of the season.

The Tyrrell P34 featured four, 10-in. diameter steered front wheels, which were intended to offer reduced aerodynamic resistance and much improved turn-in. It was quite an impressive one-off development, which had its big day at Anderstorp in 1976 when Jody Scheckter and Patrick Depailler finished first and second in the Swedish Grand Prix.

The team persisted with the six-wheeler concept into 1977, when Depailler was partnered by Ronnie Peterson, but the car gained added weight and, if anything, lost its competitive edge. By 1978 this novel exercise had been shelved and in its place the team raced the more conventional four-wheeled Tyrrell 008, with which Depailler scored a superb victory at Monaco.

LOTUS GETS IN ON THE ACT

If it hadn't been for the success demonstrated by Colin Chapman and his team in reversing the declining fortunes of Lotus, Ferrari would have ruled pretty well unchal-lenged from 1975 to the middle of 1979. Instead the British team restored its reputation for technical ingenuity and imaginative thinking by producing probably the most outstanding single quantum leap forward in F1 car performance ever seen at the start of the 1977 season.

By the close of 1975, Lotus was on its knees. The type 72 was at the end of its career and its planned replacement, the type 76, had proved to be a disaster. Chapman's design group now set about consolidating its position with a series of technical deliberations which would catapult Britain's most famous F1 team back into the limelight with dramatic effect.

During 1975 Chapman had produced a 27-page concept document in which he sought to reappraise the team's whole approach to Grand Prix car design. He then handed it to his newly established research and development department and told them to come up with the answers. This group was under the control of Tony Rudd and worked at Ketteringham Hall, a country house situated in tranquil surroundings a couple of miles from the main Lotus factory.

For 1976, the team produced the 'all adjustable' Lotus 77, which offered a theoretically unlimited number of wheelbase, track and weight distribution combinations. Yet all this project did was to publicly announce just how much at sea Lotus had become. By touting the car as all adjustable, Chapman gave the impression that most of its development would take place during the course of the racing season. Which is precisely what happened.

If one compared the Lotus 77 as it appeared at the

start of '76 with the end-product which carried Mario Andretti to victory in the final race at Mount Fuji, it was clear that there had been much progress. The first race of the season saw an ungainly creation taking to the tracks, its front brake discs and calipers mounted awkwardly in the airstream between the wheels and the monocoque. Driven by Andretti and Ronnie Peterson, the two cars managed to collide with each other during the Brazilian Grand Prix.

Peterson left soon afterwards, taking the decision to rejoin March, which, he hoped, would provide him with a simple and straightforward car. After a brief return to the American Parnelli outfit, Andretti would commit himself to Lotus and prosper with the team.

Lotus and Andretti had originally been thrown together in 1968, when, after an abortive outing at Monza, Chapman invited the talented and versatile American to take the wheel of a Lotus 49B for the United States Grand Prix at Watkins Glen. He qualified on pole and led initially, but then Jackie Stewart's Matra went by, leaving Andretti eventually to retire while running second. In 1969 he was signed to drive for Lotus on a restricted basis, when his USAC commitments permitted, but failed to finish any of the three Grands Prix he started.

Unquestionably, Andretti was Formula 1 material yet, while he loved the world of European open-wheelers, there was never any way in which he would abandon Champ cars.

'In the early Seventies, I was really torn between staying in Champ Car racing and concentrating on Formula 1,' he later remembered. 'I recall saying to Peter Revson [the American McLaren F1 driver] that I really envied the hell out of him. He was doing just a couple of 500-milers in the States each year, and spending the rest of his time in F1. It was exactly the programme I wanted.

Below: Swede Gunnar Nilsson drove a great race to win the 1977 Belgian Grand Prix in the works Lotus 78. Tragically, he succumbed to cancer eighteen months later.

Photos: Bernard Cahier

Above: Majestic champion. Mario Andretti on his way to the 1978 title in the elegant Lotus 79 ground-effect wonder.

Right: Jody Scheckter at Silverstone, '77, in the Wolf WR1 which so nearly carried him to that season's World Championship.

Below right: Patrick Depailler in the six-wheeler Tyrrell P34 took second place in the rain-soaked '76 Japanese Grand Prix at Mount Fuji.

Opposite: Carlos Reutemann, seen here at Kyalami driving the Ferrari 312T2, won four races during the '78 season following his move from Brabham.

BRITAIN'S LOST F1 GENERATION

BETWEEN JACKIE Stewart's victory in the 1973 German Grand Prix and Nigel Mansell's maiden F1 win in the Grand Prix of Europe at Brands Hatch 12 years later, only two British-born drivers won races at international motor racing's most exalted level.

Yet the achievements of James Hunt, who won the 1976 World Championship, and Ulsterman John Watson might well have been supplemented by those of Roger Williamson, Tony Brise and Tom Pryce had not fate and ill-fortune taken the trio to an early death between 1973 and '77.

Williamson was a tough, hard-driving protégé of Donington Park circuit owner Tom Wheatcroft. He had originally starred at the wheel of a club racing Ford Anglia prepared with the help of his father, and then moved into F3 and F2 with distinction. Shortly before he died, Williamson won the prestigious F2 Monza Lottery race in a March-BMW fielded by Wheatcroft Racing. Then Tom did a deal for him to race a works 731 in the '73 British Grand Prix.

Roger crashed out of that race, a peripheral victim of the huge first-lap accident triggered by Jody Scheckter. A fortnight later he went to Zandvoort for the Dutch Grand Prix in the same car, settling down to run in close company with the similar private March 731 driven by his old sparring partner, David Purley.

In the early stages of the race the two Marches circulated in 13th and 14th places. Then came tragedy. Midway round the eighth lap, both Purley and Williamson were missing. Way across the sand dunes an ominous pall of smoke began to rise. The old hands, who had seen all this just three years earlier when Piers Courage died, shuddered.

Williamson had gone off the road on a long fifth-gear right-hander and slammed into the guard rail. Unfortunately the rail, mounted directly into the sand, distorted to form a launching ramp. The works March was flipped into the air, flew for about eighty yards and then crashed back down on to the track. Upside down, it then caught fire.

The Williamson débâcle was one of the most disreputable episodes Formula 1 has ever delivered for public consumption. As Purley wrestled in vain to right the upturned March, the rest of the field passed the spot time and time again. Nobody else stopped to help. The late Mike Hailwood later confided to me that he felt 'sick with guilt' that nobody else had given Purley a hand.

Purley, a former paratroop officer who had seen service in Aden and who seemed totally without fear, was rightly awarded the George Medal for his selfless bravery.

Williamson had raced against Tony Brise, the overwhelmingly talented then 21-year-old son of John Brise, a well-known 500 cc F3 racer from the mid-

1950s, who dominated the British F3 and F/Atlantic scenes before moving into F1 with Frank Williams's team at the 1975 Spanish Grand Prix.

Brise had the confidence and audacity of youth, but beneath a thin veneer of arrogance was a huge natural talent. Graham Hill recognised this and signed him to drive for his Embassy Hill F1 team, from which the veteran twice former World Champion stood down in the middle of that season. From now on, Graham vowed, he would tutor Brise to become a future Grand Prix winner.

On 29 November 1975, those dreams were ended with a brutal finality. Flying back from a test session at the Paul Ricard circuit in the South of France, six members of the Hill team – including Graham and Tony Brise – were killed when Graham's

Piper Aztec aeroplane crashed on Arkley golf course while attempting to land at Elstree, north of London.

The third member of this ill-starred trio, Tom Pryce, was the gentle, reticent son of a Welsh policeman. He won a Lola Formula Ford car in 1970 through a competition in the *Daily Express* newspaper and soon became an accomplished Formula 3 contender.

At the start of 1974 he made a false start in F1 by accepting a deal to drive the Token-Ford special which was financed by shipbroker Tony Vlassopulo and Lloyd's underwriter Ken Grob, but the Monaco Grand Prix organisers declined their entry and Pryce instead drove a March 743 in the supporting F3 race, winning easily.

Soon afterwards he was signed to

drive for the Shadow F1 team, showing tremendous skill and flair, and in 1975 he won the Race of Champions at Brands Hatch and started the British Grand Prix at Silverstone from pole position in the promising DN5 challenger.

His best Grand Prix placings were third in the 1975 Austrian and 1976 Brazilian races. He was killed when he hit a marshal crossing the track in the 1977 South African Grand Prix at Kyalami in one of the most bizarre motor racing accidents ever seen.

By cruel coincidence, the mild-mannered boy from the Welsh hills died literally yards from the point where Shadow driver Peter Revson had been fatally injured during a testing crash three years earlier. Effectively, Tom had taken his place in the team.

Bernard Cahier

'There isn't much security in this business, but my Firestone tyre contract represented a lot of that for me. I dropped Formula 1 pretty much in 1973 and '74. I had run for Ferrari the two previous years, but they quit Firestone at the end of '72, like Lotus did. They didn't really need me in F1 because they had their own guys in Europe.'

Yet Andretti was a popular addition to the F1 scene on a personal level. He has great charisma. When he walks into a room you are conscious that here is somebody special. He is civil and articulate. The man has always radiated star quality underpinned by a firm sense of values.

In the early 1970s Andretti freelanced for the Ferrari F1 team, and he eventually found his way back to Team Lotus by a somewhat convoluted route. He had returned to Formula 1 with the new Parnelli team towards the end of 1974 and missed only a couple of Grands Prix the following year. Three races into the 1976 season, however, both he and Chapman were battling against the tide. So they cut a deal.

'Let's see if we can help each other, we decided,' said Mario. 'And I guess it worked out.'

The next six seasons would see him lead a hectic life as he divided his time between his two loves, jetting back and forth across the Atlantic sometimes as often as a couple of times each week at the height of the season.

Chapman had effectively decided to start at technical base camp, to evolve a whole new concept of F1 car design. Many of the aerodynamic developments were tried on the Lotus 77 and Mario ended the 1976 season with that victory in the Japanese Grand Prix at Fuji, the race at which James Hunt clinched his World Championship.

Lessons learned with the Lotus 77 proved crucial to the successful evolution of the superb Lotus 78. Up to this point, aerodynamic downforce had been achieved largely by the effect of front and rear aerofoils. Now Chapman proposed to use the chassis itself as a means of generating downforce, the dramatic side pods on the type 78 featuring inverted aerofoil profiles. The airflow beneath the car was accelerated beneath them, thereby producing an area of low pressure which literally sucked the car to the track.

Throughout the first part of 1977, Lotus did a good job of concealing the true secret behind the car's advantage, attributing its outstanding performance to a preferential tank-draining system and a rather special differential. The opposition seemed only too ready to accept this explanation, much to Lotus's satisfaction.

Andretti's sympathetic driving style was also a major factor in the equation. He won at Long Beach, Jarama, Dijon-Prenois and Monza while his team-mate, Gunnar Nilsson, triumphed in the rain-soaked Belgian Grand Prix at Zolder after Mario's impetuosity saw him collide with John Watson's Brabham and spin out on the opening lap.

There were minor problems to be surmounted with the Lotus 78, of course. It had an aerodynamically cluttered rear end, with the airflow spilling out from beneath the two side pods into a tangle of outboard-mounted rear suspension components. In addition, its centre of pressure – the point at which maximum downforce was generated – proved to be slightly too far forward, providing better grip at the front than at the rear. This was balanced by using slightly more downforce from the conventional rear wing than might have been ideal, the resultant drag taking the edge off the car's straightline speed.

The start of the 1978 Swedish Grand Prix at Anderstorp. Andretti and Lauda have already accelerated out of view. Leading the pursuit are Riccardo Patrese's Arrows (35), John Watson's Brabham fan car (2) and Ronnie Peterson's Lotus 79 (6).

Opposite, top, from the left: Tom Pryce, Roger Williamson and Tony Brise, three British drivers whose rich promise was sadly to remain unfulfilled.

Opposite: Pryce established himself as a man to watch in 1975 with his spirited performances for Shadow.

Right: Nightmare at Monza. Gilles Villeneuve's Ferrari leads down to the first chicane on the opening lap of the 1978 Italian Grand Prix as all hell erupts in the background.

Below right: A pall of smoke hangs over the Monza startline after the accident, which left Ronnie Peterson (below) suffering serious leg injuries from which he later died.

Alfa Romeo's Carlo Chiti hugs Brabham boss Bernie Ecclestone after Niki Lauda's victory in the '78 Swedish Grand Prix.

Photos: Bernard Cahier

Nevertheless, Mario should have won the '77 World Championship, but a spate of engine failures intervened to thwart his ambitions. He had agreed to stay with Lotus for 1978, but then Ferrari appeared on the scene and offered to double whatever Chapman had proposed in an attempt to recruit the American as Niki Lauda's successor. Andretti was absolutely straight with Chapman, who proved sufficiently shrewd to match Ferrari's offer without complaint. Neither really wanted to fracture their partnership, but Colin could see his driver's viewpoint.

There was another side to this, of course. In order to partly fund Andretti's pay rise, Chapman re-signed Ronnie Peterson as his second driver for 1978. The blond Swede was recognised as one of the very quickest men in the F1 business, but his career had been in the doldrums for several seasons and he now jumped at the chance to revive it. Peterson also came virtually for nothing: his salary was paid by sponsorship from well-known racing philanthropist Count 'Googhie' Zanon and commercial backer Polar Caravans.

Peterson replaced Gunnar Nilsson, who had signed for Arrows, yet before the start of the season the younger Swede was stricken with what proved to be terminal cancer and he did not survive 1978.

For this new season, Chapman took the 'ground effect' concept one stage further, producing the sensational Lotus 79. It was the car which produced that immortal quote from Andretti: 'If it hugged the road any closer, it would be a white line.'

With inboard suspension front and rear, springs and dampers well out of the airstream, and a single central fuel cell which also kept the side pod area uncluttered, the new car was certainly a classic and clean concept by any standards.

Mario won the Belgian, Spanish, French, German and Dutch Grands Prix with the Lotus 79 in addition to the season-opener in Argentina which he had bagged using the earlier type 78. Peterson proved to be every bit as quick as his team-mate, but stuck by his deal to play second fiddle. 'The Lotus 79 is the car it is largely because of the development effort put in by Mario,' said the Swede. The two men quickly became close friends.

Although Mario benefited on paper from the contractual stipulation that Peterson had to defer to him out on the circuit, the American driver had too much self-respect simply to cruise round at the front of the field, secure in the knowledge that his position guaranteed him precedence.

'I didn't want Ronnie to feel he was letting me win races,' said Mario, 'so I ran as hard as I possibly could and he worked really hard to keep up in many places, of that I'm sure.

'Take the French Grand Prix at Paul Ricard as an example. I know a lot of people believed we were just cruising round ahead of Hunt, but that McLaren was chasing Ronnie really hard and I, in turn, was having to run my engine up against the rev-limiter to stay ahead of him on the straight. Hell, that was one flat-out motor race, whatever it looked like from the outside.'

Yet the season's domination ended on a tragic note. A multiple pile-up at the start of the Italian Grand Prix left Peterson with broken legs. Despite initial assurances that he would make a complete recovery, he died in the small hours of the following morning. Mario was bereft. He had lost one of his soulmates.

BRABHAM THRIVES THROUGHOUT THE DECADE

Throughout the 1970s, the Brabham team continued to thrive under Bernie Ecclestone's control. By 1973 the young South African designer, Gordon Murray, was in firm charge on the technical side and for '74 he developed the BT44 'pyramid monocoque' cars which would win races over two seasons in the hands of Carlos Reutemann and Carlos Pace.

Bernie could be a difficult employer, insisting that the race shop at the Brabham factory should be kept as tidy as possible. Sometimes he would pick up a broom and do a bit of sweeping himself, but more often somebody would be in deep trouble if they did not get the job done to his high standards.

He was also the master of the shrewd one-liner. When the author asked him many years ago why he didn't change the name of the team, he shot back: 'Look, if you and I went into business and bought Marks and Spencer, we wouldn't rename it Ecclestone and Henry, would we? Brabham is a good name with a good reputation.'

On the other hand, he was astute enough to realise that Murray was an unusually talented designer and he was always prepared to spend money to make the Brabham cars go faster. In that respect, Bernie was extremely pragmatic; the better the cars went, the more success they would achieve and the richer he would become on the back of that success.

Today's F1 television coverage has achieved global levels of exposure which would have seemed remarkable – perhaps even unbelievable – two decades ago. Did he really anticipate the potential of this hidden F1 asset when he bought the Brabham team in 1971?

'No, definitely not,' he explained many years later. 'I wasn't thinking in those terms at all when I bought Brabham. It was only when I began to get fully involved in the whole scene that I appreciated just how fragmented the television coverage had been. Some people covered a few races, some people none at all. My initial motivation was to get the whole business grouped together in an effort to get some decent overall coverage.'

By the start of 1976 the Brabham team had subtly changed its emphasis. No longer did Ecclestone pay for customer Cosworth DFV engines, but had instead forged a deal with Alfa Romeo to use its powerful but heavy flat-12. Alfa also paid handsomely for the privilege of supplying Brabham – and the following year Ecclestone replaced the team's title sponsor, Martini, with the Italian dairy company, Parmalat. They would remain on the flanks of the Brabhams for almost ten years.

At the end of 1977, Lauda quit Ferrari and joined Ecclestone's Brabham-Alfa squad. The 77 × 53.6 mm, 2995 cc Alfa flat-12 may have developed 510 bhp at 12,000 rpm, but it needed every ounce of that power to compete with the Cosworth V8s – given the aerodynamic and fuel consumption penalties it imposed on the Brabham chassis.

Lauda was fascinated by the prospect of working with Gordon Murray, and the high-tech BT46 with its 'surface cooling' radiators looked precisely the sort of project to attract his unwavering attention. Unfortunately, it just didn't work, so Murray had to go back to the drawing board in an effort to uprate the car's performance.

There was no question of building a conventional ground-effect car because the Alfa flat-12 was simply too

1977
March: Hundreds die in a collision between two Boeing 747 jumbo jets at Los Rodeos airport in Tenerife.
April: The British racehorse, Red Rum, wins the Grand National for the third time.
August: Elvis Presley is found dead at his Memphis home, aged 42.
October: Pele, arguably the world's greatest-ever footballer, retires.

1978
June: Argentina win the football World Cup in front of their own fans in Buenos Aires, beating Holland 3–1 after extra time.
July: The world's first 'test-tube baby' is born in Oldham, weighing 5 lb 12 oz.
September: A historic breakthrough in the Arab–Israeli conflict is achieved when a peace accord is signed by the leaders of Egypt and Israel.
• Among the films released this year, *Superman* and *Grease* are two of the most popular.

Photos: Bernard Cahier

Above: Jody Scheckter gave the Ferrari flat-12 a last hurrah in 1979, taking Maranello's third drivers' title in five seasons with the dependable 312T4.

Opposite: Much was expected of the partnership between Brabham Chief Designer Gordon Murray and reigning World Champion Niki Lauda.

wide to permit the necessary aerodynamic tunnels down either side of the chassis. Instead, Murray and his colleague, David North, came up with an altogether more radical concept.

After rejecting the idea of a conventional water radiator, fed by ducting, atop the engine, Murray finalised an arrangement which employed a large water radiator mounted horizontally on top of the engine, but with the whole engine/gearbox assembly sealed off from the outside air by means of flexible skirts and a large, gearbox-driven extractor fan to suck out all the air from beneath the engine/gearbox bay.

The Brabham designer was killing two birds with one stone here, much to the orchestrated disapproval of his rivals. The cars, driven by Lauda and his team-mate, John Watson, made their debut in the Swedish Grand Prix at Anderstorp, where they practised – at Ecclestone's insistence – carrying full fuel loads in an effort to throw the opposition off the scent as far as their race potential was concerned.

Despite this, the Brabham 'fan cars' were visibly quicker off the corners than their rivals, many of whom complained bitterly about all the debris which they were allegedly sucking up off the circuit and shooting out behind them. In addition, the Brabhams were being challenged under the provision in the F1 rules which stated firmly that 'aerodynamic devices – that is, any part of the car whose *primary function* is to influence aerodynamic performance – must comply with the rules relating to coachwork and must be firmly fixed while the car is in motion.'

A total of five teams objected on the basis that the

primary function was surely to generate downforce. Not so, replied Murray, who made the point that, if the fan was disconnected, the car would overheat. The long and the short of it was that Lauda won the race brilliantly, overtaking Andretti's Lotus 79 with ease.

'I tell you, it was the easiest win I ever had,' said Niki. 'You could do *anything* with that car. I was pressing Mario really hard when one of the Tyrrells, [Didier] Pironi, I think, dropped oil all over the racing line and the track became very slippery.

'Mario's Lotus was sliding all over the place and my Brabham was just sitting there, like it was on rails. Then Andretti made a small mistake coming through a corner, I pulled over to the inside and just nailed him coming out. No problem at all.'

Lotus and Tyrrell immediately protested the Brabham BT46B after its win, but the race stewards eventually decided not to adjudicate on the matter and the whole affair was referred to the CSI, the sport's governing body, which decreed that fans were banned from that point onwards. The thing to note here is that the Brabham fan car was never declared illegal at the time it raced, nor was it disqualified from that Anderstorp victory.

Despite this moment in the sun for the Brabham-Alfa, it was the Ferrari flat-12 which posed the main threat to Lotus in 1978, with Carlos Reutemann and Gilles Villeneuve notching up five more victories. Then, in 1979, Jody Scheckter won the World Championship with the latest 312T4 design, winning three races, a tally matched by Villeneuve. But that was effectively the end of the story.

In designing the new car, Forghieri and his colleagues had made great efforts to incorporate the ground-effect

LAUDA OFFERS AN INSIGHT

aerodynamics pioneered by Lotus, but the width of the flat-12 inevitably hampered their attempts to harness the airflow beneath the car. Reliability and consistency would play crucial roles in Ferrari's championship victory.

In contrast to the partnership between Andretti and Peterson, the personal relationship between Scheckter and Villeneuve in 1979 looked likely to be intensely competitive from the outset. Villeneuve had been a member of the Ferrari squad for a year – and had already won a race for the team – by the time Scheckter joined at the start of 1979.

The highly experienced South African had been one of F1's most spectacular new stars in the early years of the decade, producing some wild performances at the wheel of a McLaren M23 – most notably his contribution to the first-lap multiple pile-up which resulted in the '73 British Grand Prix being flagged to a halt.

Nevertheless, Jody quickly settled down when he joined Tyrrell in 1974 and he then switched to the newly refurbished Walter Wolf Racing outfit in 1977, winning three Grands Prix and finishing second in the World Championship. During the summer of 1978 Jody was given the opportunity to test the new Wolf WR5 ground-effect challenger at Ferrari's Fiorano test track. The Italian team monitored his progress and decided that he looked a likely lad.

It said much for Scheckter's maturity that he did not become downcast when Villeneuve won the Long Beach and South African Grands Prix early in 1979. 'I knew just how quick Gilles was,' said Jody, 'and although in terms of sheer speed he was faster than me, I could recognise he was still prone to making youthful errors just as I'd done in my early years.'

As it turned out, the two men had a well-matched season, winning those three races apiece. Yet Gilles faced the ultimate test of character when he found himself running second to Jody at Monza, knowing that all he needed to do to keep alive his chances of becoming World Champion was to overtake his team-mate. Yet his deeply principled nature meant that he adhered to established Ferrari team orders and did not make an attempt to pass.

'I must admit that I just kept hoping that Jody's car would break down,' Villeneuve said. It was a remark which reflected his underlying self-confidence and assurance.

Away from the circuits, Jody and Gilles were both Monaco residents, sharing each other's social life to a degree without ever living in each other's pockets. Scheckter quickly learned that Villeneuve was a madman when it came to road driving and always said, 'I'll drive,' when Ferrari secretary Brenda Vernor telephoned to tell the duo they were needed for testing at Fiorano.

Subsequently, Villeneuve acquired a helicopter and Jody refused to ride with him after one nerve-racking flight during which a warning light flickered ominously on the instrument panel for the entire journey. Jody staggered away from the machine, calling Gilles a 'mad bastard'. Which he certainly was.

They raced together again in 1980, but that season's Ferrari 312T5 was a hopeless waste of time and Jody retired from driving at the end of the season. A revised version of the championship-winning 312T4, the car was completely outclassed by the latest ground-effect designs from Williams, Brabham and Renault. Add to that a succession of engine failures and Maranello was relegated from champ to chump in a single season.

It was time to move on into the F1 turbo era.

Niki Lauda was one of the most perceptive and intelligent drivers in motor racing history. In the 1977/78 edition of AUTOCOURSE, the Ferrari driver, who had just won his second World Championship, reflected on his racing philosophy – and his impending move to the Bernie Ecclestone-owned Brabham-Alfa Romeo team for 1978. What follows is an edited version of his words.

'ONE MORNING I just found myself not feeling about Ferrari as I'd felt in the past. Like painters, we racing drivers have an artistic inclination and are individualist. Our task is to have a free head, come to the race and do more than normal people can manage. But it became like being married to a bad woman.

'As far as Enzo Ferrari was concerned, things began to change this year. Political problems, aggravation, Italian press. In the past I'd have done anything he wanted me to do. Suddenly, my freedom had gone and I felt I didn't want to do more than normal.

'But only to do that would mean not to win; I knew that I *had* to work hard to be successful. So I realised that if I didn't do what I did in the past then we wouldn't be successful.

'The Brabham [BT46] is a brand-new car. One day I went to England to negotiate with Bernie. We spent an afternoon talking. Talking about how we'd get the money together, about my contract.

'Then he said, "Come out to the back, I've got something to show you." And there it was. The BT46, complete and ready to go. I was so excited I knew that I just had to drive that car.

'So I think logically about Gordon Murray [the Brabham Chief Designer]. All his cars have been fast from the word go. He's not just good, he's fantastic. Each car has been an excellent machine.

'I reckon the BT46 must be as good as it looks. So then you say, "It's not reliable." But what *is*

reliability? It's the easiest thing in the world. Just *run* the car. Get the thing working, look at it logically.

'Take, for example, the brake pedal is getting soft. There is no point accepting it. Get it working *properly*. It shouldn't be soft, so make some ducting that *works*. Then, when you come to a place like Zolder – which is hard on brakes – it might get a little bit soft, but it still brakes well. And if it's only all right at Zolder, you know it will be fantastic everywhere else.

'People believe sometimes that I'm a great driver, that I know all the answers. This is complete rubbish, because I don't know everything. It's stupid. But you've got to know yourself.

'Take, for example, when you crash a car. Eighty per cent of the time you know immediately why you've crashed. But for the first ten seconds after the shunt you think, "What can I do to make things look better? Let's look for an excuse."

'You look at the tyres; they're flat. But the rim is broken, so you can't say it's a puncture. Damn. After a moment, you have to shake yourself mentally and say, "Listen, you idiot, what are you doing? You made a mistake, think about it."

'Then it's quite hard to be realistic, forget it and go home admitting to yourself that you made a mistake.'

Lauda also tended to shrug aside the element of danger involved in F1 racing. 'I don't doubt that motor racing is dangerous,' he said, 'but it is the technique of racing which I find stimulating. I don't feel the risk is so important and I don't get excited by it.

'Take a fast lap, for example. I'm satisfied when I've managed one really quick lap because I've *performed* well, got it together. It's this, not the risk, that I like.

'To know that you've got on top of the car, despite banging the guard rail, getting sideways, going on the grass. It is the satisfaction I find stimulating, not the danger.'

55 YEARS OF INNOVATION
IN MOTOR RACING PHOTOGRAPHY

Camedia C-2500 Zoom, a pioneering 2.5 million plus pixel digital camera from Olympus.

Since the launch of the digital revolution, Olympus has led the way with a pioneering range of award winning cameras that have set new standards time and time again.

Olympus racing involvement reached new heights when all three drivers on the podium at the French Grand Prix were Olympus backed. World champion elect Mario Andretti won from Lotus team-mate Ronnie Peterson and McLarens James Hunt

OLYMPUS

1935

1952

1956

1959

1966

1968

1973

1978

1985

1990

1991

1993

1999

WE'LL SHOW YOU...

Michelin entered F1 in 1977 and revolutionised the sport by bringing radial racing tyres onto the circuit. Watch out for a new breed of radials on the starting grid when the 2001 season begins. It'll be as if we were never out of it.

www.michelin.co.uk

MICHELIN

WE'LL SHOW YOU THE LOGO

CHAPTER EIGHT: 1979–82
THE TURBO WARS

THE FIRST turbocharged Renault V6 took to the tracks at the 1977 British Grand Prix. It was not taken seriously. Most people regarded turbocharging as an unnecessarily complex means of exploiting a rule which had remained on the F1 statute book for more than a decade simply because nobody had bothered to delete it.

Jean-Pierre Jabouille struggled round at the back of the field in this dumpy new French contender before dropping out ignominiously in an expensive-looking cloud of smoke. Yet the turbos would not go away. Although two years would pass before Renault posted the first victory of this latest forced-induction era, the 1977 British Grand Prix represented a turning-point for the sport after which there would be no going back.

This 'equivalency' formula would eventually cause a great deal of debate and consternation. In truth, as many F1 engine designers would later point out, it was virtually impossible to accurately frame such comparisons between the performance of naturally aspirated and forced-induction engines.

Between 1948 and '51 the F1 rules were governed by regulations which provided for 1.5-litre supercharged or 4.5-litre non-supercharged engines. In reality, such notional equivalency was just plucked from the sky. There was no totally reliable method of predicting which would produce the most power, let alone which equation of relative cylinder capacity would provide some semblance of parity between the two types of engine.

So it was with the 1.5-litre supercharged/3-litre naturally aspirated rules introduced in 1966. In any event, there would turn out to be no shortage of 3-litre F1 engines. In particular, the advent of the Ford-financed Cosworth DFV V8 in 1967 would transform the entire commercial and sporting landscape of the F1 business.

This reliable, compact and efficient off-the-shelf F1 engine would usher in the era of Everyman Grand Prix racing. It was the ultimate irony that the engine which enabled F1 to thrive and expand for well over a decade should eventually be eclipsed by those developed under rules which the DFV had originally been seen to make totally redundant.

One of the most vocal critics of the turbo in F1 was Keith Duckworth, the man behind the Cosworth Ford DFV. In the late 1970s or early 1980s, if you wanted a really brisk argument in the pit lane, the easiest means of securing it was to ask Keith what he thought about the new generation of turbos.

Duckworth reckoned, quite rightly in theory, that this arbitrary equivalency formula made no sense whatsoever. What he advocated was a fuel-flow formula which would, in his view, encourage truly innovative engineering.

'When the rules were written back in 1963, only the word "supercharged" was used and "turbocharging" was

not mentioned at all,' Duckworth told Graham Robson, the author of *Cosworth, the Search for Power* (Patrick Stephens Limited, 1990).

'In a supercharged engine you can affect the weight of charge getting into the cylinder, albeit at the cost of taking work off the engine to drive the compressor. Then you only have the stroke of the piston to do the expansion work, which brings its own limits.

'On the other hand, a turbocharger is an air compressor driven by a turbine and the turbine itself is an expansion motor. Therefore a turbocharger not only allows you to "fiddle the books" but it allows you an unlimited expansion capacity as well. It means that the effective capacity of a turbocharged engine has an entirely different meaning to that of a supercharged engine.'

The F1 turbo era began inauspiciously with that tentative Renault V6 outing at Silverstone, but by 1982/83 it was certainly into top gear with engines from Ferrari, BMW, Honda, TAG-Porsche, Alfa Romeo and Hart joining those of the French car maker which had started the trend. At its absolute zenith this chapter of Grand Prix racing history spawned some of the most spectacular and powerful F1 cars of all time, power outputs brushing the 1000 bhp mark – even in race trim – on some occasions in 1986.

Thereafter a progressive reduction in turbo boost pressure over the next two seasons produced a gentle tactical retreat from the world of forced-induction Grand Prix cars. The final race of the turbocharged era was won by Alain Prost's McLaren MP4/4-Honda at Adelaide at the end of the 1988 season.

There could hardly have been a more appropriate combination of driver, chassis and engine to claim that distinction, bringing the curtain down on an era which, short though it may have been, was rich in technical variety and memorable motor racing.

The first seeds of the turbocharged F1 engine had been sown in the early 1970s, although perhaps not intentionally. Renault began its serious contemporary motor racing involvement in low-key fashion, starting with a 2-litre, four-cam V6 built round an iron cylinder block for the then-prestigious European 2-litre Sports Car Championship.

This engine was developed for use in the equally high-profile European F2 Championship and powered the Elf 2 single-seater driven by Jean-Pierre Jabouille to victory in that series in 1976. Jabouille would later play a key role in the history of Renault's F1 involvement, and would score the company's first victory in the 1979 French Grand Prix at Dijon.

At this stage in the story the French car maker's main priority was to develop a machine powered by a turbocharged version of the V6 capable of winning the Le Mans 24-hour sports car classic. That was duly achieved in 1978 when Jean-Pierre Jaussaud and Didier Pironi won

1979
May: Elton John is the first western rock star to perform in the USSR.
May: Margaret Thatcher becomes Britain's first female Prime Minister, after the Conservative Party wins the General Election.
June: John Wayne, US actor, dies.
August: Lord Mountbatten is killed when his holiday boat is destroyed by an IRA bomb.

1980
April: Alfred Hitchcock, British film director, dies.
July: Bjorn Borg wins the Wimbledon men's singles tennis championship for the fifth time.
November: Ronald Reagan defeats Jimmy Carter to become President of the United States.
December: John Lennon is shot dead by a deranged fan outside his Manhattan apartment.

the famous event, after which Renault swung its full attention and effort behind its fledgling F1 programme, which, by then, had been running for almost a year.

A reduction in the stroke of the 2-litre V6 had brought the engine down to 1.5 litres, but it quickly became obvious that there were serious shortcomings to be surmounted. From the driver's standpoint, the most obvious was 'turbo lag', which meant that there was a delay between the driver opening the throttle and the power chiming in. This would provide a major headache for pretty well all the turbo F1 teams over the next few years.

The concept of turbocharging was originally applied by the aviation industry as a method of sustaining intake manifold pressure at altitude on piston-engined aircraft. At higher altitudes the rate at which air can be introduced into a combustion chamber to mix with incoming fuel is obviously reduced by the lower barometric pressure.

At sea level, air density is 1 bar – around 14 pounds per square inch. But at 3000 feet, the density of the air drops to 0.85 bar. Thus a piston-engined aircraft progressively loses performance the higher it flies, in the same way that a car engine loses performance when it is being operated at high altitude.

The great advantage of turbocharging over supercharging is that the former consumes little in the way of power simply to drive itself. In contrast to a gear-driven supercharger, which would need up to 70 bhp just to drive it, the turbocharger simply produces back pressure in the exhaust manifold against which pistons have to fight on the exhaust stroke.

STRAWS IN THE WIND DURING 1979

Although Jody Scheckter won the 1979 World Championship for Ferrari, a combination of Michelin radial rubber and bullet-proof reliability contributed more to his success than the qualities of the 312T4 chassis.

More significant by far that year was the emergence of the Williams team and the near-collapse of both Lotus and McLaren. Frank Williams, the son of a Second World War bomber pilot, was motor racing's original self-made man. Throughout the 1960s he'd lived on his wits as he abandoned his own career as a budding F3 racer and concentrated on wheeler-dealing in second-hand racing cars.

In those days, the Williams team was a tiny operation with little more than fifty people working out of a small factory on a trading estate alongside the railway lines in Didcot, a far cry from its swish headquarters today at Grove, near Wantage, with its cathedral-like entrance hall, 30 acres of grounds and a workforce in excess of 250.

Williams himself has come a long way since he sought employment as a Campbell's Soup salesman in the mid-1960s to raise sufficient money to race his Austin A35. He eventually graduated to international Formula 3, financing his racing by selling spares to fellow-competitors on a nomadic basis at minor-league European events, but finally gave up driving in 1966 to support the career of his close friend, brewery heir Piers Courage.

Demonstrating considerable financial ingenuity, Williams eventually raised sufficient cash to go Grand Prix racing in 1969 with a private Brabham-Ford driven by Courage. Second places in the Monaco and US Grands Prix were a tremendous boost to their reputations and, as we have seen, the following year they continued together using an Italian-built de Tomaso chassis.

Sadly, Williams was to have his first taste of personal tragedy when the debonair Courage was killed when the de Tomaso crashed and caught fire in the Dutch Grand Prix at Zandvoort. Compounding his grief, the disaster left Williams virtually bankrupt but, not for the first time in his career, he picked himself up and relaunched his assault on the F1 Big Time.

In 1976, Williams decided to sell up, having received a financial offer he could not refuse from Austro-Canadian oil magnate Walter Wolf. Yet, although handsomely paid, Frank quickly found himself uncomfortable with his role as right-hand man to his new employer. In 1977, he decided to start from scratch running a private March and established Williams GP Engineering.

To design the team's own cars, he took on Patrick Head, then no more than a promising young engineer. The two men met in a London hotel where Williams asked, 'Are you prepared to work twenty-four hours a day to achieve motor racing success?' Head's response took him aback.

'No,' he replied. 'Because anybody who has to do that must be very badly organised.' Head got the job and, two years later, penned the superb Williams FW07, which rewrote the parameters of Grand Prix car design at a stroke.

The Williams FW07 would develop the ground effect concept pioneered by Lotus to fresh levels of performance, its chassis being considerably stiffer than that of the Lotus 79, which fell off the front-running pace in 1979. It did not make its race debut until the fifth round of the title chase, but Jones and his team-mate, Clay Regazzoni, quickly indicated that it was a highly promising proposition. For the British Grand Prix, Jones would be the man to beat.

After an initial skirmish with Jabouille's Renault turbo, Jones stormed off into the distance, only to be sidelined by a cracked water pump. That let Regazzoni through to achieve the historic distinction of the Williams team's first win.

Jones won four more races for the team that season to end up third in the World Championship on 40 points net, trailing new champion Scheckter (51 points net) and Gilles Villeneuve (47 net).

'Undoubtedly when we did the FW07 a great deal of the basic thinking centred on what Lotus had done with the 79,' said Head. 'Although, to be honest, from the outset I really didn't fully understand the function of ground effect, and it became very clear at the end of 1978 that we needed to get more time working in a wind tunnel.

'In fact, the entire aerodynamic design of the car was based on a single week's work in the Imperial College wind tunnel – in what amounted to the first wind tunnel work I'd ever done in my life.

'One notable area we made a significant improvement on was the front wing set-up, because the Lotus 79 had huge nose wings on it which damaged the airflow to the side pods. We twigged very early on that a ground-effect design would really be better without front wings, which is why we had tiny little neutral-profile trim tabs on FW07 from the start and it even raced on a few occasions without any front wings at all.'

Now Williams and Head were on their way. In 1980, the updated FW07B, still equipped with full sliding skirts, emerged as the car of the year and carried Alan Jones to the World Championship. It is no coincidence that

Williams now had its own wind tunnel and had recruited a specialist aerodynamicist, the highly respected Frank Dernie, during 1979, factors that helped them sustain their performance edge into the following year.

Jones was joined in the team by former Brabham, Ferrari and Lotus driver Carlos Reutemann, who won the Monaco Grand Prix and finished third in the final point standings. Jones won five of the season's 14 Grands Prix and deservedly took the title after a head-to-head battle with the young Brazilian, Nelson Piquet, who had emerged as a world-class contender at the wheel of the Gordon Murray-designed Brabham BT49-Ford at the end of the previous year.

Brabham owner Bernie Ecclestone had decided to ditch the unreliable new Alfa Romeo V12 engines which had been developed for 1979 in order to facilitate a ground-effect chassis design. Niki Lauda thought the new engines were awful and their inconsistent performance through the summer of '79 contributed to his decision to retire from the cockpit.

The Alfa 1260 was a 60-degree, 78.5 x 51.55 mm V12 developing an impressive 525 bhp at 12,300 rpm. It didn't work largely because its oil scavenging was inadequate and, at its worst, was horrifyingly unreliable. Add to that the fact that the detailed specification of the V12s varied from unit to unit and the whole exercise left the Brabham team in a pretty alarming situation. The switch to Cosworth Ford DFVs in time for the '79 Canadian Grand Prix came too late to retain Niki's interest and he walked away from F1 midway through the first practice session in Montreal.

THE EMERGENCE OF McLAREN INTERNATIONAL

Late in 1979, Formula 2 team owner Ron Dennis made contact with former Chaparral Champ car designer John Barnard, who had been recommended to him by the Williams team's Chief Designer, Patrick Head.

Barnard, who had served his motor racing apprenticeship at Lola, the Huntingdon-based manufacturer of production racing cars, assumed Dennis was looking for somebody to design and build a Formula 2 car for him. Only when they met did Barnard fully appreciate that Dennis had F1 ambitions – a happy meeting of minds, as things turned out, for John had some exciting plans of his own on that particular front.

The British engineer believed that it would be possible to manufacture an extremely light and very strong chassis from carbon fibre, then regarded as a highly esoteric material, the use of which had previously been confined to the aerospace industry.

As Dennis worked meticulously to calculate what sort of budget would be needed to launch an F1 team of his own, developments elsewhere gave a well-timed fillip to his efforts. The McLaren team's deteriorating form since James Hunt had won the World Championship in 1976 had naturally been a matter of some concern to Marlboro, its title sponsor.

As a result, Marlboro engineered an amalgamation of the team and Dennis's Project 4 organisation, which had gained considerable success in the second-division formulae. Under the terms of the merger, which was announced in September 1980, McLaren chief Teddy Mayer's 85 per cent stake in the original Team McLaren became 45 per cent of the new company, McLaren International, which sustained his position as the largest single shareholder. Yet it was the energy of Dennis and his Project 4 partner, Creighton Brown, which began to transform the team's image.

On the engineering front, Dennis and Barnard successfully concluded a deal with the US Hercules aerospace company for the supply of the carbon-fibre composite panels which would be bonded together to form the chassis of the radical new McLaren MP4. Smooth and sleek, with beautifully fitted body panels and finished with great attention to detail, the MP4 may only have had a Cosworth Ford DFV in its engine bay, but it was a major contribution to the process of raising the team's game.

Alain Prost had partnered John Watson during the final year of the old Team McLaren regime in 1980, but the young Frenchman switched to Renault at the end of the season as he was deeply concerned about the number of chassis breakages sustained by the old M29, which had replaced the unsuccessful M28 in the middle of the 1979 season.

Prost's abrupt departure from the team gave Watson the chance to restore his tarnished reputation; he was joined in the line-up for '81 by the erratic Andrea de Cesaris, who was, to be frank, a bit of a liability and only earned his drives through his close relationship with Marlboro. Happily, everything went to plan with Watson scoring the revamped team's first win at Silverstone after René Arnoux's Renault had wilted with engine trouble. Five years had passed since John had scored his sole previous F1 victory for the American Penske team in the 1976 Austrian Grand Prix and this latest success had come not a moment too soon.

For 1982, Dennis would hit the headlines by persuading Niki Lauda to come out of a retirement which had lasted two and a half years and, while McLaren would continue with Cosworth Ford DFVs for the moment, the management began to lay plans for the team's own turbocharged engine. Dennis was ambitious and Barnard totally uncompromising when it came to engineering the cars, so it was unlikely that either of them would be satisfied with any of the existing turbos already on the Grand Prix scene.

Left: Didier Pironi drove with spine-tingling commitment for Ligier in 1980, earning himself a move to Ferrari for '81.

Below: Carlos Reutemann won at Monaco for Williams in 1980, having joined the team as number two to Alan Jones.

Bottom: Where it all started: the 1.5-litre Renault V6 which triggered F1's turbo era.

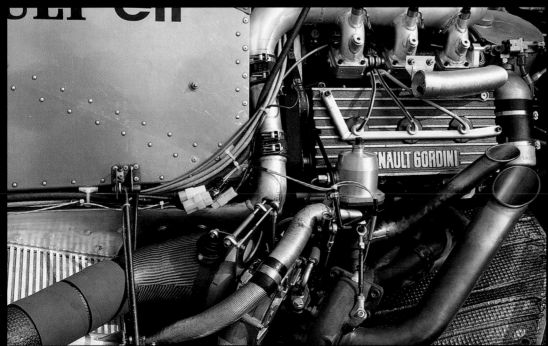

Photos: Paul-Henri Cahier

LOTUS LOSES BATTLE AGAINST FISA

LAT Photographic

AFTER THE Lotus 79 and its successor, the aerodynamically complex type 80, failed to sustain a competitive F1 pace in 1979 Colin Chapman's research and development department began to lay plans to redress the situation.

The way in which aerodynamic loadings had increased dramatically with the second generation of ground-effect machines preoccupied their thoughts and they turned to examining ways in which the aerodynamic forces could be isolated from the chassis itself.

Lotus's answer was the type 86, which was originally tested at the end of 1980 during the last season of the sliding skirt rules. Wind tunnel testing had convinced Chapman's engineers that, instead of having separate sliding skirts moving up and down relative to the bodywork, it would be better to spring-mount the body structure on the wheel uprights, thereby transmitting the aerodynamic loadings directly to the suspension and tyres, while at the same time incorporating a conventionally sprung chassis riding free within the movable aerodynamic body.

This concept would at one and the same time stabilise the under-car aerodynamics and insulate the driver from the physical battering caused by the ultra-stiff suspension. Unfortunately FISA got wind of what was happening and issued a 'rule clarification' making the point that any part of the car influencing its aerodynamic performance must be rigidly secured to the entirely sprung part of the car 'and must remain immobile in relation to the sprung part of the car'.

In Chapman's view this attitude was at odds with the two-year rule stability which was an essential element of the Concorde Agreement he had helped draft and then signed. He pressed on to produce a fixed-skirt version of the concept built round a carbon-fibre/Kevlar monocoque and dubbed the type 88. Unfortunately a succession of protests and unfavourable edicts from the governing body guaranteed the downfall of the 'twin chassis' Lotus before it ever raced.

For Chapman, this was a huge blow which completely undermined his basic belief that F1 should be about innovative engineering that pushed at the outer limits of technical boundaries. By this time, of course, the Lotus boss was deeply involved in developing the ill-starred De Lorean road car and his concentration on F1 seriously wavered after the Lotus 88 débâcle.

Nevertheless, Chapman would live to see Lotus win again when Elio de Angelis triumphed in the 1982 Austrian Grand Prix in the Cosworth-engined type 91. In December of that year, beleaguered by business worries which threatened to overwhelm the company he had founded, he died of a sudden heart attack.

THE BATTLE TO CONTROL FORMULA 1

Between 1979 and '83 the most important aspect of Grand Prix motor racing had precious little to do with the action taking place out on the circuit. It was the battle for the commercial heart of Formula 1 which really attracted the attention of the media, a high-profile contest with subtle undertones which was fought out between Bernie Ecclestone, on behalf of the F1 teams, and the sport's governing body.

During the 1970s, the Formula 1 Constructors' Association (FOCA) had become a powerful and influential grouping under Ecclestone's presidency. Its rise to prominence might have been ignored for the most part by the sport's administrators, the Commission Sportive Internationale (CSI), which later changed its title to the Fédération Internationale du Sport Automobile (FISA), but if, during that period, you were a race organiser then the only person you had to speak to was Ecclestone.

The Brabham proprietor organised the financial arrangements for the races on behalf of the team owners. Organisers did not pay out on a published prize scale; they handed the whole amount over to FOCA, which then distributed it among its members in accordance with a complex formula.

Some insiders believed matters had almost got to the point where FISA was effectively being bypassed by the commercially astute Ecclestone. For legal, administrative and historical reasons it certainly sanctioned the races, but its authority had been progressively diluted by the time volatile Frenchman Jean-Marie Balestre was elected FISA President at the end of 1978. From the very start of his tenure, sparks flew.

At a stroke, FOCA's unimpeded push towards overall F1 dominance appeared to have been checked. Balestre was an eccentric extrovert who seemed to like nothing better than playing the role of Napoleon. But he was no fool and no pushover.

Born in 1920, Balestre had enjoyed a colourful and action-packed career. He served in the French Resistance during the war and carried out covert activities against the German forces occupying his country. When, in the late 1970s, photographs began to circulate of Balestre apparently wearing a German uniform, he took unsuccessful legal action to prevent their publication.

He explained that he had been a double agent who had been ordered to infiltrate the enemy, and insisted that he was once arrested by the Gestapo, tortured and condemned to death. Only the Allied invasion had saved him.

During the post-war years he helped set up an important Paris-based publishing group and founded the FFSA (Fédération Française du Sport Automobile) in 1952, at a time when a handful of regional race-organising clubs dominated the administration of French motor sport.

In his new role as FISA President Balestre played hardball from the start. At the first race of the 1979 season, John Watson's McLaren M28 tangled with Jody Scheckter's Ferrari 312T3 and caused the race to be flagged to a halt. Watson suspects that Balestre's robust intervention may have been behind the stewards' decision to penalise him with a draconian fine.

In 1980, apparently with an eye to improving safety by reducing the lap speeds of F1 cars, Balestre announced that sliding aerodynamic side skirts would be banned

Bernard Cahier

from the start of the following season. This decision put FOCA on red alert. The organisation's members were predominantly the British-based specialist F1 teams who relied on their technical ingenuity in chassis design to get the best out of Cosworth Ford DFV engine performance.

They now suspected that Balestre was attempting to undermine their competitive edge at a time when both Renault and Ferrari were developing 1.5-litre turbocharged machines which, while they clearly had powerful engines, were seriously lacking when it came to chassis technology.

FERRARI JOINS THE TURBO BRIGADE

The first turbo Ferrari 126CK was a case in point. It may have been equipped with a powerful engine, but when it made its public debut in practice for the 1980 Italian Grand Prix at Imola its chassis looked crude and basic.

Its construction followed long-established Ferrari practice with a multi-tubular spaceframe overlaid with stressed alloy panelling. Rocker arm suspension activated inboard coil-spring/dampers all round and power was transmitted through a transverse gearbox, as on its successful T-series predecessors, but the whole package was a touch makeshift and unsophisticated.

For this new generation of Ferrari F1 cars a 120-degree, 81 x 48.4 mm, 1496.43 cc V6 engine had been produced. The four-cam unit featured its inlet camshafts on the outside and exhaust camshafts on the inside of the vee, enabling short exhaust pipes from each bank of cylinders to feed into the turbines and compressors, which were mounted just behind the large central fuel cell.

Power output from the Ferrari V6 was claimed to be in the region of 540 bhp, initially around 60 bhp more than the outmoded flat-12. Ferrari spent much of the winter of 1980/81 refining the performance of the KKK-turbocharged V6 engine, but Mauro Forghieri and his colleagues also took the opportunity to investigate a different system of forced induction which had been developed by the Swiss Brown-Boveri organisation.

This system, known as the 'Comprex', was a directly driven supercharger with the exhaust gases providing the pressure waves to compress incoming air as it entered the inlet manifold. Unlike the exhaust-driven turbochargers, the Comprex system seemed to have no throttle lag while the turbine/compressor units came up to speed once the throttles were opened.

Tests during the off-season indicated that this new system had genuine potential. Drivers Gilles Villeneuve and Didier Pironi – who had replaced Jody Scheckter on the South African's retirement from racing at the end of 1980 – quickly reported that the immediate throttle response from the Comprex system certainly seemed an improvement. But there were some distinct problems to be overcome and it was eventually shelved.

The 1981 season yielded Ferrari two Grand Prix victories with the 126CK, as this first rough and ready turbocar was designated. Both were scored by Gilles Villeneuve, one through sheer driving brilliance in Monaco, the other by shrewd tactics and total consistency at the head of a jinking queue of cars during the Spanish Grand Prix at Jarama.

Yet the Ferrari 126CK was far from the integrated design which would be needed to remain competitive in the years to come. The rival McLaren team had introduced its carbon-fibre composite chassis soon after the start of the 1981 season and, while the safety bonuses accruing from such developments were considerable, the rigidity offered by such construction techniques was absolutely crucial when it came to retaining the torsional strength of chassis. This would become an increasingly important factor for designers to take into account as the new generation of turbocharged engines increased their power output in leaps and bounds over the next few seasons.

In fact, by the start of the 1981 season there were no fewer than four turbocharged F1 engines poised to do

Photos: Paul-Henri Cahier

Opposite: Elio de Angelis in the controversial Lotus 88 in the pit lane at Silverstone prior to its being banned from the 1981 British Grand Prix.

Opposite, bottom: De Angelis wins the '82 Austrian Grand Prix by a length from Keke Rosberg's Williams FW08.

Above: A man with a mission: high-profile FISA President Jean-Marie Balestre.

Left: Gilles Villeneuve worked miracles in the turbocharged Ferrari 126CK, winning the 1981 Monaco and Spanish Grands Prix very much against the odds.

Below: Bruno Giacomelli in the turbo V8 Alfa 182T in 1982. It was fast on occasion, but far from reliable.

battle. However, while the Hart 415T joined the fray at the first race in Europe, BMW's four-cylinder production-based unit would not be seen in competitive action until the following year. The trusty Renault EF1 was now producing around 540 bhp at 11,500 rpm. The Ferrari 126CK had been developed to offer around 20 bhp more than its French counterpart, but in time the BMW M12/13 would come to be regarded as perhaps the most powerful of all these forced-induction engines.

A ROCKY PATH TO F1 CONSENSUS

It was perhaps ironic that Nelson Piquet should drive to his first World Championship in 1981 at the wheel of the Ecclestone-owned Brabham BT49. By this time Ecclestone left the day-to-day running of the Brabham team to his trusted lieutenants, most notably Chief Designer Gordon Murray, while he tried to deal with the contentious issues arising from the battle with FISA.

The first major confrontation had come the previous season. Balestre had started the year by threatening that any driver who failed to attend the pre-race briefing would be fined. Some of the FOCA teams attempted to encourage their men not to go, apparently anxious that they should not be seen to be bossed about by what was often perceived as a weak governing body.

Suddenly, a crisis arose. At Monaco and Zolder several drivers did not appear and Balestre said that the culprits would be suspended. FOCA accused FISA of being confrontational and demanded that the fines be rescinded.

At the time, these individual scuffles seemed suffi-ciently serious to be taken at face value. Yet it was the sub-text to the disputes, several of which erupted over different seemingly separate issues over a period of three seasons, which was, one realises with hindsight, much more important.

Ecclestone had shrewdly recognised the potential for growth of televised sports and was determined that he and the teams should have their share of a goose which seemed set to continue to lay golden eggs into the distant future. Bernie was right on target and would become one of the richest men in Britain as a result of that perspicacity.

The preliminary skirmish between FOCA and FISA came to a head over a sanctioning dispute at the 1980 Spanish Grand Prix. In the end, the race went ahead, but Ferrari, Renault and Alfa Romeo did not participate. They all had commercial interests in the motor industry and could not risk alienating FISA – and therefore its parent, the FIA – by competing in what was, to all intents and purposes, a pirate event.

Alan Jones won the race for Williams, but the result was not allowed to count for the World Championship. The same thing happened at the following year's South African Grand Prix. FOCA had made plans to combat the sliding skirt ban by taunting FISA with threats of a breakaway World Championship organised by the 'World Federation of Motor Sports', which would run its series for cars still using these aerodynamic appendages.

In fact, the World Federation of Motor Sports never existed and its rather grand-looking statutes, circulated in a document at the time, were cooked up by Ecclestone's legal adviser and collaborator, Max Mosley, of whom

Paul-Henri Cahier

Photos: Paul-Henri Cahier

Left: Bernie Ecclestone (right) with Sante Ghedini (left), racing manager of the Brabham team's title sponsor, Parmalat.

Below: Ligier soldiered on with non-turbo power into 1982 using the shrill-sounding – and sometimes very effective – Matra V12, a descendant of the engine which had made its Formula 1 debut some 14 years earlier.

Left: Skirts and rear diffuser on the 1982 Ligier JS19. All this would be swept away, for the moment at least, by the new flat-bottom rules the following year.

1981

February: British football breaks with tradition as league games are played on a Sunday for the first time.
March: The inaugural London Marathon is held, with 7055 runners taking part.
May: Bob Marley, Jamaican reggae singer, dies of cancer at the age of 36.
July: Prince Charles and Lady Diana Spencer are married in St Paul's Cathedral.

Nelson Piquet's Brabham BT49C overtakes Carlos Reutemann's Williams FW07C during the rain-soaked '81 Canadian GP in Montreal.

motor racing in general and F1 in particular would hear a great deal more in his future role as President of the FIA.

FOCA lost this second confrontation with FISA. Running on rag-tag used tyres, the F1 teams managed to produce some semblance of a motor race at Kyalami to open the 1981 season. But, again, Carlos Reutemann's victory in a Williams was not permitted to stand.

Eventually, just prior to the Long Beach Grand Prix, FISA and FOCA reached a *rapprochement* with the signing of the Concorde Agreement, a wide-ranging document which laid out the procedures whereby regulations could be changed and, while acknowledging FISA's role as the sporting power, effectively left financial control in the hands of the constructors.

Thus the 1981 season continued without sliding skirts and the whole World Championship programme was blighted by the need to build ridiculously complicated suspension systems which would enable the competing cars to conform with a 6 cm ground clearance rule when they were checked in the pits – while still running as close to the ground as possible while out on the circuit.

Brabham's Gordon Murray and his colleague, David North, came up with the best way round the rule. They devised a system of soft air springs which the aerodynamic load compressed as speed built up, dropping the team's BT49C contender down to a ground effect stance. As the speed dropped away again when the car arrived in the pit lane, so it rose on its suspension to clear the 6 cm requirement.

The system worked brilliantly at Buenos Aires, where Piquet ran away with the Argentine Grand Prix, the third

race of the title chase, and the rest of the field erupted in fury. Rivals objected on the basis that the Brabhams were running flexible skirts – not sliding skirts – and, in the view of the Williams team, for one, this was not legal.

Murray simply shrugged the protests aside, accusing his rivals of being bad losers, but then FISA issued a rule clarification on the subject and the whole issue of the complex Brabham suspension system became irrelevant when several of the cars arrived for the Belgian Grand Prix fitted with suspension-lowering switches in the cockpit. The FISA officials figuratively threw up their hands in horror but took no action and that was effectively the end of that.

Eventually everything settled down and the 1981 World Championship was clinched by an exhausted Piquet in the final race of the season in sweltering conditions in Las Vegas. Nelson struggled home fifth after his arch-rival for the title, Reutemann, faded to an inexplicable eighth after starting from a dazzling pole position.

Carlos relinquished the title with such astonishing docility that Piquet was simply amazed. 'He braked early to let me pass when I came up behind him,' he said. 'He made it so easy for me, I couldn't believe it.'

The quiet Argentinian was surely one of the most outstanding F1 drivers never to win a World Championship. Yet he was a complex character. After the 1981 British Grand Prix, ensconced in a comfortable points lead, he bet the author of this volume that he would not win the title. Two races into the 1982 season he abruptly decided to retire, a couple of months before the Falklands conflict erupted in the South Atlantic.

Bernard Cahier

Paul-Henri Cahier

BATTENING DOWN THE HATCHES FOR RENEWED STRIFE

As Ferrari and Renault gradually began to get into the competitive swing of things with their turbocharged F1 cars, so the British-based teams, aligned with FOCA, began to worry that they might be hard pressed to win many races in the foreseeable future.

Most of these teams relied on Cosworth customer power but, with the rival turbos nudging their way towards 580 bhp, going into battle with a 480 bhp naturally aspirated V8 was calculated to cause more than a few problems. And so the British teams sat down and worked out a clever ruse by which they could redress the balance of power. Quite literally.

For many years it had been the accepted practice to top up oil and water levels before cars were submitted for post-race scrutineering, thereby bringing them back up to the regulation minimum weight by replenishing these liquids to 'normal' levels. Now the Cosworth-engined teams were thinking along the same lines, but to subtly different effect.

Lotus, Brabham, McLaren and the others all decided to fit their cars with reservoirs to carry water for brake-cooling purposes. These were filled up at the start of the race and, claimed the teams, the water was then used to cool air entering the brake ducts, with the result that it was all consumed by the end of the event. Then the containers were refilled, and when the cars were scrutineered they would make the minimum weight limit as required.

However, many people suspected that the entire contents of the water containers were dumped at the first corner. A cynical view, perhaps. In fact, the truth was even more convoluted. In many cases – some would say most – the water bottles were never filled in the first place. Therefore the Cosworth-engined runners were effectively competing against the turbos to a separate – much lower – minimum weight limit. Or, to put it bluntly, they were running *beneath* the minimum weight limit in an effort to make up for their lack of horsepower.

This issue was first highlighted at the 1981 Monaco Grand Prix, where Piquet's Brabham BT49C qualified on pole position just ahead of the mercurial Gilles Villeneuve's Ferrari 126CK, a much heavier machine altogether with its full fuel load.

The vexed question of underweight racing cars was now firmly in the spotlight. Everybody in the pit lane tended to pick their words with care, but Ligier driver Jacques Laffite grasped the nettle in an interview carried by the French sporting newspaper, *L'Equipe*.

'Piquet has two cars, one ultra-light, which he uses in practice, and then his race car which is to normal weight,' he claimed. 'A regular Brabham is already on the weight limit. Good for them. But the practice car has carbon-fibre brake discs which save 12 kilos, and I'm told that the car also has a tiny fuel tank, much lighter than the normal one.

'The car should be weighed as soon as Piquet stops, before the mechanics can touch it. But no, no one will do anything, because it's a Brabham, owned by Ecclestone. Nobody can touch him. Everybody is frightened of him.'

Yet, as we shall see later on, Brabham was not alone in pursuing this strategy.

Niki Lauda's McLaren MP4B won two Grands Prix during the 1982 season.

MORE TROUBLE WITH
THE SCALES OF JUSTICE

The issue of cars running under the weight limit bubbled along through 1981 and then erupted again at the 1982 Brazilian Grand Prix. But this time it almost triggered another terminal split between FOCA and FISA.

Nelson Piquet's Brabham BT49D won the race ahead of Keke Rosberg's Williams FW07C, with Alain Prost's Renault turbo RE30B finishing third. During the course of the race, Piquet's featherweight Brabham had hustled Gilles Villeneuve, driving the heavier and less wieldy Ferrari turbo, into an error and the Canadian had spun off the circuit into a barrier.

However, the stewards of the Rio race were having none of the FOCA teams' subterfuge. They disqualified Piquet and Rosberg, thereby handing the race to Prost's Renault. The Brabham and Williams teams appealed, but a Court of Appeal convened by FISA upheld the disqualification. In turn, the FOCA teams claimed that this disqualification constituted a change in the rules. For its part, the governing body retorted that, far from being a change in the rules, it was merely a clarification.

Of course, nobody really expected the FOCA-aligned teams to take this lying down. Yet FOCA dramatically over-played its hand with a stubborn display of trades union-style muscle when it came to the San Marino Grand Prix at Imola. *En masse*, the FOCA teams boycotted the event, with the result that it was contested only by Ferrari, Renault, Osella, Toleman, ATS (unrelated to the earlier entrant of that name) and the renegade Tyrrell team, which, despite its alignment with FOCA, found itself obliged to take part at the insistence of its Italian sponsors.

In what was seen at the time as an effort to placate his furious FOCA colleagues, during the course of the San Marino GP weekend Tyrrell fired the first volley in the next major argument, namely a formal protest against all turbocharged cars competing at this event on the basis that their engines included turbines and, since turbines were banned by the F1 regulations, these were effectively illegal secondary power units.

The race was won by Didier Pironi's Ferrari 126C2 after the Frenchman had tricked his team-mate, Gilles Villeneuve, on the final lap. Pironi effectively gained his success against team orders and, 13 days later, Gilles was killed practising for the Belgian Grand Prix at Zolder. It was the start of a nightmare season for Ferrari which would see Pironi's career ended by horrendous leg injuries sustained during practice for the German Grand Prix.

It was also the season which effectively saw the FOCA teams cut and run into the turbo enclave. At the end of the day, they were in the racing business and winning races meant you had to go faster than the opposition. And, in 1982, that meant having a turbocharged F1 engine.

Opposite: Gilles Villeneuve, Little Big Man.

Below: Gilles on the last lap of his life at Zolder, '82, in the Ferrari 126C2.

Paul-Henri Cahier

CHAPTER NINE: 1982–87
IF YOU CAN'T BEAT THEM . . .

B Y THE SUMMER of 1982 the Formula 1 scene was starting to settle down again. Renault's turbo-cars were getting seriously into their stride and the Ferrari 126C2s, much more sophisticated machines than their immediate predecessors with chassis built round 'folded up' Nomex honeycomb/aluminium sandwich sheeting, were also becoming very competitive, although the Italian team's season had been sadly punctuated by the accidents to Gilles Villeneuve and Didier Pironi.

Meanwhile, Bernie Ecclestone had very shrewdly been hedging his bets as far as Brabham was concerned. The team had tested a BMW four-cylinder turbocharged engine as long ago as the '81 British Grand Prix, where Nelson Piquet appeared in the BT50 prototype during practice, but the unit was not raced until the start of the following year.

From the outset, the BMW board took the view that, for promotional reasons, it was extremely important that any Grand Prix involvement should be seen to rely upon a production-based engine. Chief Designer Paul Rosche was able to draw on considerable technical data from the 2.1-litre turbocharged 320 saloons which the US end of the McLaren operation had been running in the IMSA category across North America. In 1980 he was there-fore able to take the first steps to develop the BMW M12/13 F1 engine, which was based on the BMW 2002's four-cylinder block.

It did not take long for the BMW Motorsport engi-neers to discover that the standard production blocks performed at their optimum when aged. Two- or three-year-old blocks from cars which had covered as much as 100,000 kilometres on the road had less inherent stress in their structure than newer examples. However, apart from the machining away of around 5 kg of superfluous metal such as stiffening ribs and water channels on the inlet side, the blocks remained fundamentally unmodified from the basic production examples.

The twin-overhead-camshaft, four-valves-per-cylinder engines, which were initially supplied to the Brabham team on an exclusive basis, had a bore and stroke of 89.2 x 60 mm for a capacity of 1499 cc. The steel crankshaft ran in five main bearings and short, forged-alloy Mahle pistons with very rugged titanium connecting rods were employed to withstand the much higher loads to which the units were subjected.

Fitted with a single KKK turbocharger and employing a 6.7:1 compression ratio, the engine's initial output was quoted as 557 bhp at 9500 rpm, although it would even-tually achieve almost twice that figure in high-boost quali-fying form during the course of its F1 competition career.

Of course, after the 1981 season had been punctuated by arguments about the rules and technical controver-sies, it was ironic that 1982 should kick off with a major row involving the drivers.

Niki Lauda, returning to F1 to drive for McLaren, pro-vided the catalyst for this unfortunate confrontation. While examining the paperwork which accompanied his FISA superlicence prior to the start of the season, he suddenly realised that the governing body had issued the licence in conjunction with a specific team. It was not, if you like, a 'stand alone' licence issued individually to the Austrian.

The drivers quickly concluded that FISA and the team owners had conspired to establish a restrictive cartel, leaving them as nothing more than pawns in a big-budget chess game. They threatened a strike unless things were changed and, partly at least, carried out their threat by missing first practice for the South African Grand Prix at Kyalami.

Eventually the strike was broken by an apparent com-promise, which did not prevent FISA from imposing fines on those who had transgressed. It was an unsatisfactory episode which did not reflect well on the drivers, but the significance of which was largely swamped by wider issues engulfing the sport at that time – most notably the 'water bottle' scam.

Meanwhile, on the technical front one of the biggest problems facing the F1 teams was to resolve the prob-lem of lazy throttle response.

Renault's answer to the problem had been to squirt a jet of fuel into the turbo, which ensured that the turbines kept spinning when the driver was off the throttle.

Ferrari chose to tackle the same problem by linking the compressor manifold to the exhaust manifold by means of a valve which, when the throttles closed, opened to pass compressed air into the turbines. Once the driver went back on to the throttle, this valve closed and stopped combustion taking place within the turbines.

This was developed into a highly efficient system, although secondary problems arose in terms of higher wear on the turbine blades and bearings. As a conse-quence, the system was revised for 1982 with modifica-tions to the turbines, compressors and boost control valves.

Ferrari also sought to address the question of increas-ing combustion chamber temperatures with the help of a key development from the team's fuel supplier, Agip. Following a principle which was used to cool jet engines, the Agip fuel technicians developed a highly complex sys-tem whereby a globule of water could be encapsulated within a globule of petrol, lowering the temperature of the fuel as it entered the combustion chamber. At the point of combustion, the water turned to steam, 'explod-ing' the surrounding petrol in a process which offered improved atomisation and better mixture control within the combustion chamber.

Meanwhile the Brabham BT50-BMW had scored its first victory in the '82 Canadian Grand Prix at Montreal with Nelson Piquet at the wheel, a performance made

1982
June: Argentina's surrender brings an end to the war in the Falkland Islands.
June: The first son of the Prince and Princess of Wales, William, is born.
November: A fourth television channel is launched in the UK, called Channel 4.

1983
October: US forces invade Grenada following the murder of Prime Minister Maurice Bishop.
October: 299 US and French peacekeepers are killed when their Beirut barracks are devastated in suicide bomb attacks.
November: American cruise missiles are deployed in the UK at Greenham Common.

1984
September: The second son of the Prince and Princess of Wales, Harry, is born.
October: Indian Prime Minister Indira Gandhi is assassinated by her Sikh bodyguards in New Delhi.
October: Four people are killed when an IRA bomb rips through the Grand Hotel in Brighton during the Conservative Party conference.

Opposite: The BMW M12/13 four-cylinder production-based turbo F1 engine was possibly the most potent power unit ever used in a Grand Prix car.

Right: John Watson with the naturally aspirated McLaren MP4B-Cosworth at speed at Monza during the 1982 Italian Grand Prix.

Below: Keke Rosberg took the '82 World Championship with just a single race win to his credit.

Above right: Didier Pironi drove the Ferrari 126C2 to a flawless victory in the '82 Dutch Grand Prix at Zandvoort.

Right: At the Circuit Paul Ricard, venue for the 1982 French Grand Prix, it was impossible for Keke Rosberg to overcome the handicap of his Williams FW08's power deficit compared with the turbos, but at tighter tracks he more than held his own.

Paul-Henri Cahier

Star's return. Mario Andretti rejoined the Ferrari team for the 1982 Italian Grand Prix at Monza in place of the injured Didier Pironi and took pole position with the 126C2, finishing third in the race.

easier, perhaps, by the fact that the race start had been postponed to the late afternoon following a tragic fatal accident at the first start.

Yet again the Ferrari team would be at the centre of the disaster. Pironi stalled his pole-position 126C2 and, as the pack scattered to avoid him, F1 novice Riccardo Paletti slammed his Osella straight into the back of the stationary red car. Although he was removed to hospital promptly by helicopter, Paletti died soon afterwards from multiple injuries.

As the ambient temperature dropped dramatically in the late afternoon, so the charge temperature to the BMW's turbo engine dropped sympathetically. Nelson had no trouble keeping ahead of his team-mate, Riccardo Patrese, in the Cosworth DFV-engined BT49D.

Brabham also re-introduced the concept of mid-race refuelling, Chief Designer Gordon Murray working out that this was the quickest theoretical means of covering a race distance. It certainly made sense. The Brabhams needed to run as light as possible for as many laps as possible, given that they required a massive 47 gallons to see themselves through a Grand Prix distance – 11 gallons more than a corresponding Cosworth-engined machine.

Murray and his colleagues judged that starting the Brabham-BMWs on soft tyres and a half fuel load would enable them to stop, refuel and still be in front at the end of the race.

They first tried the strategy in the British Grand Prix at Brands Hatch but, ten laps into the race, Piquet had only opened a three-second advantage over Niki Lauda's McLaren-Cosworth DFV, which would eventually win when the Brazilian's engine failed.

Later, in the Austrian Grand Prix, Patrese would retain the lead during one of these highly publicised stops, only to suffer an engine failure shortly afterwards. The Brabham-BMWs would certainly sustain a reputation for being fast and fragile.

ROSBERG GETS THE JOB DONE

Through all this controversy, mechanical mayhem and off-track politicking, the feisty, extrovert Keke Rosberg picked his way through other people's debris to take the 1982 World Championship at the wheel of the naturally aspirated Williams FW08.

Rosberg, who had joined Williams only at the start of the '82 season following Alan Jones's retirement from F1, drove his heart out from start to finish. Although he won only a single Grand Prix, it was certainly an unusual year in that no other driver won more than two races.

'Sure, it was frustrating not to have a turbo,' said Keke, 'but there was no point in complaining about it. Anyway, I think I proved that a Cosworth car could be competitive on all but the fastest circuits when I put FW08 on pole for the British Grand Prix at Brands Hatch.'

Despite this, Keke's opposite-lock style would drive Williams Technical Director Patrick Head to despair. 'I've told him that, if he could only tidy up his driving style, he would be even quicker than he is,' said Patrick. Rosberg just puffed on a cigarette and replied that his style seemed to work pretty well, thanks very much.

There was also one occasion when Frank Williams – who hated Keke's smoking and made him leave the team motorhome when he wanted a drag – made the mistake of suggesting that Rosberg's occasional first-lap 'moments' could be attributed to a certain lack of physical fitness.

'That's bullshit,' replied the indignant Finn. 'We were starting the races with low tyre pressures so that they came up to precisely the correct pressure when they warmed up. It was necessary to manhandle the car on the opening lap because it was extremely twitchy until the tyres warmed up.'

At the end of the year, although Ferrari clinched the Constructors' Championship with 74 points to McLaren's

69, Rosberg squeezed home to win the drivers' title with 44 points to the 39 each of John Watson and Didier Pironi.

It's worth reflecting that seldom has a contemporary World Championship been won with fewer points than Rosberg amassed in 1982. To put it in perspective, Rosberg clinched the title with two fewer points than Mika Häkkinen squandered through a combination of driver and McLaren team error in 1999 up to the Italian Grand Prix alone. Ironically, by then, Rosberg was Häkkinen's business manager . . .

NEW UNDERBODY RULES PUT DESIGNER IN A FLAT SPIN

Ground effect aerodynamics were swept away for the 1983 season when FISA decreed that all cars should have flat bottoms from the start of the year. More welcome was the news that there was to be stability of engine regulations through to the end of 1985, plus a reduction in minimum weight to 540 kg and, from the start of 1984, a cut in fuel tankage from 250 to 220 litres.

Most immediately affected by this was Gordon Murray. Outsiders believed he had an inside line, via Ecclestone, to the FISA decision-making process. Yet he and his employer had remained confident that there would be no changes to the rules affecting under-car aerodynamics for 1983.

Encouraged by the obvious potential of the in-race refuelling strategy, Murray had decided to take this concept a step further for '83 with a 'half tank' chassis, dubbed the BT51, complete with a radical new transmission which was designed to get the best out of ground effect aerodynamics. Suddenly, on 3 November 1982, Murray realised that the new car would have to be scrapped.

And so he started again. Brabham had to produce a totally new car to the latest flat-bottom rules and it had to be ready for the Brazilian Grand Prix on 13 March. That was the deadline and there was absolutely no question of missing it.

More to the point, there was no realistic prospect of re-working the outdated BT50-BMW into some sort of stop-gap machine conforming to the new regulations. In anticipation of the BT51, Murray had requested that BMW alter the routing of the exhaust pipes and turbo-charger specifically to fit the new car. There was no way in which these modified engines could be installed into the back of the BT50.

The BT52 was duly readied in time for its race debut. It was a distinctively different machine which owed virtually nothing to the long line of Murray-designed Brabhams stretching back to 1973. The new car had no side pods and the chassis looked dramatically slim as a result.

Piquet started the 1983 campaign as he meant to go

Paul-Henri Cahier

on, storming to victory in the Brazilian Grand Prix at Rio, and kept the BT52 pretty well in play for the rest of the season. In-race refuelling would remain an integral component in F1 race strategy throughout the year, although it would be banned for 1984, and the Brabham mechanics came to be regarded as possibly the most accomplished of all in this respect.

Yet Renault's Alain Prost would give Piquet a good run for his money. He won the French Grand Prix and also scored maximum points in Belgium, Britain and Austria. The introduction of Ferrari's new carbon-fibre composite 126C3 at Silverstone helped keep Maranello in contention, with René Arnoux adding victories in Germany and Holland to his earlier win in Canada, but although the Italian team would retain its Constructors' Championship crown the main issue of the drivers' title came down to a battle between Prost and Piquet.

Put simply, Renault took its eye off the ball and Nelson's Brabham-BMW began to pick up the pace over the last four races of the season. The French team's failure to grasp the seriousness of the situation could be judged by the fact that they romanced a plane load of journalists to Kyalami for the final championship round in the confident expectation that Prost would clinch the title.

It was incredibly naïve. Piquet, who had won the two previous races at Monza and Brands Hatch, ran at a blistering pace in the early stages, easing back to finish third behind team-mate Riccardo Patrese and the Alfa Romeo 183T of Andrea de Cesaris only after Prost had succumbed to engine failure.

However, much controversy surrounded the specification of the fuel sample which was taken from Piquet's car. On the face of it, this exceeded the octane limits laid down by the rules, but nobody seemed to want to do anything about it. The results stood and the whole issue was forgotten.

WILLIAMS FORGES HONDA PARTNERSHIP

Honda had been away from Formula 1 for a full 14 seasons by the time the tiny UK-based Spirit team began experimenting with the 1.5-litre Honda RA163-E V6 turbocharged engine at the start of the 1983 season.

The Japanese company wanted to compete in F1 at the highest possible level, but started on a characteristically cautious note in partnership with Spirit, with whom it had already operated in F2. However, behind the scenes, Honda had taken a long-term strategic decision of even greater significance. In the early months of 1983, the Japanese company forged a long-term deal with Frank Williams.

At a time when John Barnard was precisely laying down the guidelines for the new TAG turbo, Williams Technical Director Patrick Head could have been forgiven a twinge of envy when the first lumpy, untidy 80-degree V6 Honda engine arrived in a crate at the team's Didcot factory. The package also contained two turbochargers, but little else. It was down to Williams to evolve a means of installing the engine into a chassis, to say nothing of finalising such ancillaries as radiators and general plumbing for the turbo and exhaust systems.

Head and his aerodynamicist, Frank Dernie, produced what amounted to a development chassis for the first Honda V6, the Williams FW09, which was still constructed round an aluminium honeycomb chassis; Williams would not make the move to carbon-fibre composite chassis until 1985. The FW09 made its race debut in the 1983 South African GP.

McLAREN KEEP TAGS ON THE OPPOSITION

No such engineering compromises would be accepted by the McLaren directors in their efforts to ensure that

Grand alliance: Frank Williams (right) and his long-time collaborator, friend and business partner, Patrick Head.

Right: John Watson, runner-up in the 1982 Drivers' World Championship with two wins that year.

Far right: Brabham design genius Gordon Murray, possibly the most innovative thinker in F1 since Colin Chapman.

Wild-eyed expressions from Jacques Laffite (below right) and René Arnoux (in Ferrari cockpit, bottom).

Below far right: Tyrrell driver Michele Alboreto has heard it all before.

the team had the best turbocharged F1 engine in the business available by the end of the 1983 season.

Ron Dennis approached this challenge in a methodical fashion. Having discussed the matter in detail with John Barnard, he decided that there were too many limitations involved in using any of the existing turbocharged F1 engines. With the Renault there was a lack of exclusivity, with the BMW installational problems and so on. Consequently Dennis approached Porsche, who had considerable accumulated experience of turbocharging sports car engines stretching back through the previous decade.

When Dennis arrived on their doorstep, the Porsche management may have been bracing themselves for the usual enquiry as to whether they would be interested in supplying F1 engines for the McLaren team. They were not. But the question Dennis asked them was very different.

He approached Porsche as a potential customer, asking whether they would be prepared to make a state-of-the-art turbocharged F1 engine with McLaren funding the project. Barnard would have the final say in its configuration: 'Too many engine designers give absolutely no thought to how it is going to be installed in a chassis,' he noted.

'They get it running on a test bed and then wonder why the chassis designer isn't interested. With the Porsche project, I had the final say.'

Meanwhile, Dennis pulled out all the stops and persuaded Techniques d'Avant Garde, a long-established international trading company founded by the Franco-Lebanese Ojjeh family, to back the project. Mansour Ojjeh was already an enthusiastic supporter of F1 as a Williams team sponsor, but the relationship with Dennis and McLaren would become far more wide-ranging. Today McLaren International is part of the TAG McLaren

Group, a high-technology empire which has expanded widely beyond the pure motor racing orbit.

With the funding secure, Barnard was in a position to lay down his specific design requirements to Hans Metzger, the leader of the Porsche design team. He wanted an aluminium-alloy V6 configured with a vee angle no wider than 90 degrees, with all the pumps and other ancillaries positioned at the head of the engine and room for upswept exhaust pipes which would enable it to be fitted into an ideal ground-effect concept.

'I would not compromise,' said Barnard. 'We had to have the right turbos. I made them pull in bolt heads which extended outside the overall prescribed profile of the engine, re-engineer various casings and so on. The work went back and forth between us.'

The end result had a bore and stroke of 82 × 47.3 mm, giving a capacity of 1499 cc. Initially Porsche claimed a power output of 600 bhp, at least 75 bhp more than the best available Cosworth DFY V8 (a derivative of the legendary DFV) at the time of the TAG turbo's debut in 1983. A single KKK turbocharger was piped into the exhaust manifolding on each cylinder bank and the engine used a Bosch electronic management system.

Much of the early development work of the TAG turbo was carried out by John Watson and Niki Lauda at Porsche's Weissach test circuit with prototype engines installed in 956 sports-racing cars. Early problems included throttle lag and oil breathing shortcomings, but these were eventually ironed out. Barnard was aghast when those changes to the FIA technical regulations in the autumn of 1982 effectively ruled out many of the benefits of his carefully crafted engine configuration intended for a ground-effect chassis. But there were other considerations.

The last of 155 Grand Prix wins for the Cosworth DFV and its DFY derivative. Michele Alboreto's Benetton-liveried Tyrrell 011 heads for victory in the 1983 Detroit Grand Prix with Eddie Cheever's Renault in hot pursuit.

SENNA WIN MIGHT HAVE HELPED PROST TO '84 TITLE

IRONICALLY, if Ayrton Senna had won the 1984 Monaco Grand Prix in the Toleman TG184-Hart, Alain Prost might well have ended up with that year's World Championship.

To understand the logic of this contention one must go back to 1981, when Toleman first decided to make the jump into F1 after winning the previous year's European F2 Championship with the Toleman TG280, which was powered by a 2-litre engine built by Brian Hart's small specialist company.

Toleman's ambitious Managing Director, Alex Hawkridge, persuaded Hart to develop his own 1.5-litre four-cylinder turbocharged engine on an exclusive basis. This started the team out on a long road strewn with technical pitfalls as Hart and his engineers effectively taught themselves all about F1 turbo technology.

By 1983, the lead Toleman TG183B-Hart driven by Derek Warwick had steadily developed into a competitive proposition. The Englishman scored the team's first World Championship points with a fourth place in the Dutch GP at Zandvoort, followed by a sixth at Monza, fifth at the Grand Prix of Europe at Brands Hatch and another fourth in the final race of the season, the South African GP at Kyalami.

Even so, Warwick had decided to leave Toleman and sign for Renault, leaving the way open for one of the most exciting drivers of all time to make his debut on the F1 World Championship stage.

'Late in 1983 we were testing at Silverstone when Alex arrived in the Toleman helicopter accompanied by a young man with remarkably intense eyes who had been blowing everybody off in F3,' recalled Brian Hart.

'Alex said, "This is Ayrton Senna, our new driver for next year – 1984." I was very excited, as I'd been to a couple of F3 races where he and [Martin] Brundle had been battling it out.

'Clearly the guy was unusually talented. But this was absolutely typical of Alex; who else could have pulled off something like this? Senna had tested for Williams, tested for McLaren, but Alex managed to persuade him that he should come to join the Toleman team.

'By the start of the 1984 season [Toleman designer] Rory [Byrne] had really got a handle on the flat-bottomed aerodynamics with the new TG184, but the real story of that year was Ayrton. What an incredible bloke, as well as being an unbelievably quick, motivated and complete racing driver.

'He rang me up in the winter. "This is Ayrton," he said. "As you know, Alex has signed me. I want to know all about the engine, what boost we're going to use, how I should drive it."

'I thought, "Hang on, you haven't even driven it yet." But this approach was absolutely characteristic of his determination to understand every detail of the car he would race.'

The highlights of the season came at Monaco, where Ayrton was only narrowly beaten into second place by Prost's McLaren as the race was flagged to a premature halt on a near-flooded track, and Estoril, where Ayrton took the Toleman TG184-Hart to a brilliant third place behind a Prost–Lauda McLaren 1–2.

'Despite Senna crossing the line ahead of Prost, Clerk of the Course Jacky Ickx stopped the race so the order on the lap before gave victory to Prost,' remembers Hawkridge. 'My enthusiasm for F1 never recovered from that cruel blow. Brian deserved that win, as did the team.'

Paradoxically, if Senna had won and the race run to its prescribed distance, it would have been better for Prost. As it was, Alain scored 4.5 points for a half-distance win. Second place in a full-distance race would have netted him six points. In those circumstances he might well have gone on to win the World Championship by a single point. Rather than lose it by half a point.

McLAREN-TAGS SET THE AGENDA

At the start of the 1984 season Niki Lauda suddenly found himself presented with an unexpected challenge. Instead of continuing to be paired with John Watson, a man whose qualities he knew well, he was joined in the McLaren squad by Alain Prost, who had been dropped by the Renault team after the World Championship débâcle of 1983.

Prost later admitted that he was signed by Dennis for a song, but that he was happy to agree to the contract if it meant he could put the whole Renault episode behind him. Lauda now found himself up against a very fast and ambitious new partner. There would be plenty of hard work ahead.

The new McLaren MP4/2-TAGs proved to be the class of the field in 1984. They were fast and reliable and handled well, all these qualities backed up by first-class standards of preparation on the part of McLaren International. In addition, the TAG V6s were adequately frugal when it came to fuel consumption, a major consideration in view of the ban on in-race refuelling and the reduction in maximum fuel capacity to 220 litres.

At the end of the day Prost won seven races and Lauda five, but Niki took the championship by the wafer-thin margin of half a point. Between them they thus won 12 of the season's 16 races, the only interlopers being Ferrari new boy Michele Alboreto, who triumphed in the Belgian Grand Prix at Zolder after the McLarens had suffered engine failures caused by fuel specification problems, Nelson Piquet, whose Brabham BT53 was victorious in Montreal and Detroit, and Keke Rosberg, who took the Williams FW09 – a veritable bucking bronco – to a memorable win in the one-off Dallas Grand Prix under the sweltering summer Texas sun.

Opposite, top: Niki Lauda clinches the 1984 World Championship with second place behind McLaren team-mate Alain Prost in the Portuguese Grand Prix at Estoril.

Opposite, bottom: A youthful Ayrton Senna holds Lauda's arm aloft in triumph on the podium after the Austrian's victory in the 1984 British Grand Prix. Senna finished in third place with the Toleman-Hart.

Above: Blue-eyed boy. Lost in thought, Lauda gazes from his helmet.

Overleaf: Prost and Lauda await the arrival of the rest of the field after stopping their McLarens on the grid in readiness for a restart when the 1984 British Grand Prix was red-flagged to allow an abandoned car to be removed.

Photos: Paul-Henri Cahier

Paul-Henri Cahier

WILLIAMS JOINS
THE TURBO FRONT LINE

The 1985 season brought two developments of considerable significance for the Williams-Honda team: British driver Nigel Mansell was signed up to partner Keke Rosberg and Patrick Head's engineering department produced its first carbon-fibre composite monocoque.

Williams was late in following the prevailing trend to carbon-fibre composite chassis construction, just as it had been late on to the turbo bandwagon. This reflected a degree of inbred caution on the part of Head, who wanted to be certain that Williams could remain on top of the engineering aspects of such developments when the decision was finally taken to make such a crucial change of direction.

'There were also aspects of the behaviour of certain carbon fibre/honeycomb materials which I wasn't terribly impressed about,' he explained.

'In addition, we had experienced two massive shunts with FW06 and FW07 monocoques – at Watkins Glen in 1978 when Alan Jones's car broke a hub shaft, and at Silverstone during testing in 1980 when Carlos Reutemann went straight into the vertical sleepers on the outside of Copse Corner – and had been extremely impressed with the way our aluminium monocoques had withstood the impacts.

'I had also always attempted to take a practical approach towards the cost involved in producing an F1 car, and I think in those days we were talking in terms of a cost increase of around 100 per cent between an aluminium and a carbon-fibre chassis.

'At that time I had a tendency to say, "Well, this may be a little bit nicer, but it will cost ten times as much, so we won't do it." I had always tried to keep costs down to a reasonable level and was quite shocked when we had some carbon-fibre panels made for experimental purposes and, when I got the quote, it seemed absolutely astronomic.

'I think that made me a little bit wary about dealing with a sub-contractor from that point onwards, and I decided we would accumulate all the expertise in-house before embarking on a major carbon-fibre chassis development programme.'

A total of nine moulded carbon-fibre composite Williams FW10 chassis were built during the course of the season. Rosberg would win at Detroit and Adelaide, sandwiching the first two victories of Mansell's F1 career at Brands Hatch (the Grand Prix of Europe) and Kyalami.

In the early part of the year the FW10s were powered by modified '84 D-spec Honda engines, but the revised E-spec arrived in time for Montreal, while a new six-speed transmission was used to handle the reputed 1000/1250 bhp qualifying capability offered by the Japanese V6s.

At the end of the 1985 season, Rosberg would move to McLaren. He'd been cautious about having Mansell in the Williams team, having heard rumours that he was difficult to get on with, and by the time he found that his misgivings had been exaggerated he was committed to making the change.

To replace him, Frank Williams did a deal with Nelson Piquet for a reputed $3 million, wooing the Brazilian away from the Bernie Ecclestone-owned Brabham team which many had believed was his spiritual home.

Opposite, top: Meltdown. Frustration for Elio de Angelis as his Lotus-Renault expires, 1984.

Opposite, bottom: The turbo engines produced blistering performance, but keeping temperatures in check presented designers with a considerable challenge.

Above: Keke Rosberg about to stub out his cigarette and smoke them off with a 160 mph-average lap to take pole at the 1985 British Grand Prix.

Above: After a generally disappointing season with the elegantly liveried Brabham BT54-BMW in 1985, Nelson Piquet decided it was time to move on.

Right: Even the belated advent of turbo power in '85 was not sufficient to allow Tyrrell's Martin Brundle to do justice to his obvious ability.

Opposite: Cars trailing plumes of dense white smoke were a regular feature of F1 in the mid-Eighties. Jonathan Palmer's Zakspeed suffers a turbo failure during practice for the '85 Belgian Grand Prix, which was subsequently postponed until later in the season due to problems with the track surface.

Below: McLaren design chief John Barnard's uncompromising approach paid dividends when the TAG-engined MP4/2 claimed three successive drivers' titles between 1984 and '86.

Bottom: Derek Warwick's two seasons with Renault proved largely unproductive and he found himself out in the cold when the French company closed its works team at the end of 1985.

Right: Alain Prost dives down through Paddock Hill Bend at Brands Hatch during the 1985 European Grand Prix. Fourth place was enough to give the Frenchman his first World Championship.

Paul Ricard when his Ford Sierra rental car crashed into a field. The team's Public Affairs Manager, Peter Windsor, was a passenger in the car and emerged unhurt, but Frank sustained very serious back injuries which left him a tetraplegic and confined to a wheelchair to this day.

In 1985, the Williams-Hondas had flexed their muscles, but the McLaren-TAGs had still had the upper hand. Prost was a model of consistency, adding victories in Brazil, Monaco, Britain, Austria and Italy to his mounting tally and posting six other podium finishes. Despite losing another win at Imola when his car was found to be underweight, he clinched his first World Championship with two races remaining, while Lauda rounded off his distinguished career with a fine victory in Holland.

In 1986, however, it was significantly different. The Williams-Hondas took the initiative and would hold it through two glorious, Constructors' Championship-winning seasons.

The smaller fuel cell of the FW11 enabled Williams to follow the trend of laying their drivers back into a semi-reclined driving position. The chassis was slightly longer than that of the FW10 as was its F-spec Honda RA163-E engine. The Williams-Hondas could run consistently fast in race trim with the drivers instructed to adjust their turbo boost across four possible settings controlled from the cockpit.

According to Patrick Head, position one was a fuel-conservation mode, two and three race boosts at a higher or lower level and position four a 50/60 bhp burst of 'overtaking boost' which could be used sparingly for very short periods. In practice, Mansell and Piquet usually juggled the settings between two and three during the course of a race. It says everything about the relative power/fuel efficiency of the Honda and TAG engines that Prost's McLaren finished the 1986 British Grand Prix at Brands Hatch in third place – but lapped by the victorious Mansell and Piquet.

With the help of fuel supplier Mobil's chemists, Honda was now pursuing the same route as that followed by Wintershall on BMW's behalf a couple of years earlier, opting for high-density aromatic 'hydrocarbon' fuels. A significant step towards Honda's increase in race power output to over 900 bhp could be attributed to this development path, which helped the injection system to atomise its fuel more completely, ensuring that nothing was wasted in the combustion chamber.

Meanwhile, Mansell developed into a natural winner. In 1986 he triumphed in the Belgian, Canadian, French, British and Portuguese Grands Prix, losing his grasp on the World Championship only when a rear tyre burst at 200 mph on the back straight in the final race at Adelaide when it seemed as though he had it in the bag. Mansell would have to wait another six years before being crowned World Champion.

Mansell's misfortune should have handed the title to Piquet, but Nelson was called in for a precautionary tyre change. Ironically, he had no problems, but now had to settle for second in the race behind Prost in the McLaren-TAG. The Frenchman thus became the first title holder since Jack Brabham in 1960 to retain his crown with 72 points net to Mansell's 70 (net) and Piquet's 69. However, this was a season in which the all-conquering McLaren International squad experienced a major internal shift of emphasis, with Chief Designer John Barnard leaving the organisation he had helped establish more than five years earlier.

Above: The agony and the ecstasy. Nigel Mansell makes no secret of the cost of victory after winning the 1986 British Grand Prix for Williams.

Opposite: Nelson Piquet relaxes in the pit garage at Rio, '86. A pair of his Williams team-mate's overalls hang on the wall behind the Brazilian.

Photos: Paul-Henri Cahier

For 1986 fuel capacity was restricted to 195 litres, prompting Head to produce yet another brand-new turbocar, the FW11, which would come to be regarded as the definitive Williams-Honda and would last through to the end of the 1987 season. The FW11 design represented a turning-point in the progress of the Williams team's design and manufacturing capability. Thanks to the benefits of a costly computer-aided design/manufacturing system, the new Williams set fresh standards of detailed finish and fit throughout the car.

Unfortunately, Frank Williams would not be at the pit wall for the 1986 season. A couple of weeks prior to the Brazilian Grand Prix, the team principal was driving back to Nice airport after the final off-season test session at

NELSON PIQUET: BRAIN BAFFLES BRAVADO

NELSON PIQUET was the sort of driver who relished going on to the Grand Prix starting grid secure in the knowledge that he secretly harboured a technical advantage which might give him a crucial performance edge over his rivals.

In that respect, the Brazilian driver, who was born in Rio on 17 August 1952, was one of the most cerebral of World Champions. During testing, for example, he would always be working away developing the best car set-up for the race rather than aiming for the out-and-out fastest lap time he could manage.

Like his compatriot, Ayrton Senna, Piquet would win three World Championships during a Grand Prix career which spanned 204 races from 1978 to '91. His father had been keen for him to develop his talent for tennis, packing him off to California during his teenage years for a programme of intensive coaching. Yet the attraction of karts, cars and motor cycles exerted an overwhelming pull on the young Brazilian and would ultimately shape his personal ambitions.

Piquet initially made his mark in the Brazilian national Formula Super Vee series before setting out for Europe, where he finished third in the 1977 European Formula 3 Championship. The following year he switched to the British F3 scene, winning no fewer than 13 races and clinching the BP Championship.

He made his F1 debut in the 1978 German Grand Prix at Hockenheim at the wheel of an Ensign, drove a private McLaren M23 in the Austrian, Dutch and Italian races and then joined the works Brabham-Alfa team alongside Niki Lauda and John Watson for the final Grand Prix of the year in Montreal.

In 1979, Piquet replaced Watson as Lauda's team-mate in the Bernie Ecclestone-owned Brabham squad. The team struggled with Alfa Romeo V12 engines for much of the season before Bernie decided that they were really getting nowhere. He took the decision to switch to Cosworth Ford V8 power and the new Brabham BT49 certainly proved competitive from the outset.

At virtually the same moment, Nelson found himself unexpectedly propelled into the role of team leader when Lauda decided, abruptly and with immediate effect, to retire midway through first practice for the '79 Canadian Grand Prix. Thereafter, Nelson would – unconsciously, perhaps – mould the Brabham team around him. He got on well with Chief Designer Gordon Murray and all the mechanics, being very much one of the boys. His first Grand Prix victory came in Long Beach in 1980 and he followed it up with further wins in the Dutch and Italian Grands Prix. He finished second in the World Championship, losing out to Williams driver Alan Jones in the final race of the season.

The following year Piquet duly bagged his first title, edging out an over-wrought Carlos Reutemann in a torrid finale beneath the scorching Nevada sun in Las Vegas. In 1982 the Brabham squad then switched from Ford V8 to BMW turbo power, heralding a mechanically troubled year and only a single win for Piquet. Yet his shrewd commitment to the Brabham-BMW development programme would certainly reap its rewards in 1983 when Nelson snatched his second World Championship after a down-to-the-wire

confrontation with Alain Prost and the factory Renault team.

This peak of achievement was followed by two relatively bleak seasons and, frustrated by Brabham's fruitless switch to Pirelli rubber in 1985 allied to Ecclestone's reluctance to pay him what he believed was his market value, Piquet stunned the F1 world by deciding on a change of team for 1986. Bernie might not have been willing to hike his pay from $1.1 million to $3 million, but Frank Williams certainly was. Thus it came about that Nelson switched to the Williams-Honda squad alongside Nigel Mansell.

Piquet relished the performance edge offered by the Williams-Hondas in 1986 and '87, but was less impressed with Mansell's unwillingness to fulfil a supporting role. Nelson believed he had been promised number one status, but in fact his contract stipulated equal treatment and priority access to the spare car. Nothing more.

In 1986, both Piquet and Mansell were pipped by McLaren rival Alain Prost in the battle for the championship, a state of affairs which left the Brazilian driver feeling particularly irked. His tactical and strategic approach would duly pay off with a third world title in 1987, but he was no happier with the Williams way of operating and moved to Lotus in 1988 – taking the Honda engine contract with him.

Unfortunately the Lotus 100T proved no match for the dominant McLaren-Hondas of Alain Prost and Ayrton Senna. In 1989 Lotus lost its Honda engine supply and Piquet suddenly found himself slumping to the role of a midfield runner, forced to use uncompetitive Judd V8s.

Another change of team was needed. In 1990 and '91 he switched to Benetton, winning three more races and benefiting from a bonus system which paid him $100,000 per championship point scored. He recorded his final win in the 1991 Canadian Grand Prix, after which his front-line racing career came to a painful end when he crashed heavily during practice for the 1992 Indianapolis 500, sustaining extensive foot injuries from which he happily made a full recovery.

Gerhard Berger sets the pace in the early stages of the 1986 Italian Grand Prix at Monza with the Benetton B186-BMW he

of Grand Prix racing increasingly onerous and the team faced that season without a tyre supply contract. It eventually bought the tiny Spirit organisation's tyre contract and recruited Benetton as a major sponsor, but at the end of the year the Italian clothing company bought the team, lock, stock and barrel.

Despite the impressive pace of the Williams-Hondas in 1986, it had been only a few races into the season before Piquet began to get very irritated over his status within the team. He firmly believed that he'd been guaranteed full number one status and that Mansell should play second fiddle. This misunderstanding, if you like, eventually caused a breach between Nelson and Williams at the end of 1987.

'What Nelson thought he was being guaranteed was a repeat of the Reutemann fiasco of 1981 when we controlled — or tried to control — the second driver,' said Williams, recalling the way the Argentinian, who had been recruited as number two to Alan Jones, disobeyed team orders and won that year's Brazilian Grand Prix ahead of his team-mate.

'What in fact had been discussed was that, in a classic case of one driver leading the championship and needing every bit of support, then we would control his team-mate.

'But he was not given unconditional priority over the second driver. We took the view that if they were both in the running for the World Championship they would have to fight it out between them.'

Elsewhere on the F1 landscape Renault's works team had shown dwindling form since Prost's departure at the end of 1983. Derek Warwick and Patrick Tambay took over the driving duties for the next two seasons, but neither managed to score a single victory as the machinery was never quite up to the job.

With the impressive young Brazilian, Ayrton Senna, moving to Lotus from Toleman at the start of 1985, it was clear that Renault would in fact be better served by its prime customer, Lotus having used Renault turbo power with steadily increasing success since 1983, and the factory team withdrew from F1 at the end of the season. In '86 Senna, who had won in Portugal and Belgium the previous year, posted eight pole positions, although he took maximum points only twice during the course of the season. One of these victories was a sensationally well-judged, split-second win over Nigel Mansell's Williams FW11 in the Spanish Grand Prix at Jerez by what was officially the closest winning margin in F1 history.

For 1986 Renault Sport's Chief Engineer, Bernard Dudot, produced the first pneumatically activated valve-gear system for the French V6. The saving in mass and weight enabled the engine's rev limit to be increased initially from 11,000 to 12,000 rpm, but later to over 13,000 rpm, which would hand Senna around 900 bhp in race trim.

For qualifying purposes, Lotus would use the EF15-spec Renault V6 with water injection and its turbo wastegates blanked off, the engine surviving concentrated bursts of 5-bar over-boost to catapult Ayrton to the front of the grid on so many occasions.

With sparks cascading from its undertray as it scraped the ground to gain the maximum possible downforce, and

The 1986 season was also marked by the final victory for the four-cylinder BMW turbocharged engine, which powered Gerhard Berger to a good win in Mexico City, where his Pirelli tyres enabled him to enjoy a non-stop

Left: Ayrton Senna with the Lotus 98T-Renault, winning at Detroit, 1986.

Below: Sparks fly from the skid plates of this mixed bag at Spa. Jacques Laffite's Ligier-Renault leads Thierry Boutsen's Arrows-BMW, Alan Jones's Lola-Ford and Michele Alboreto's Ferrari in the '86 Belgian Grand Prix.

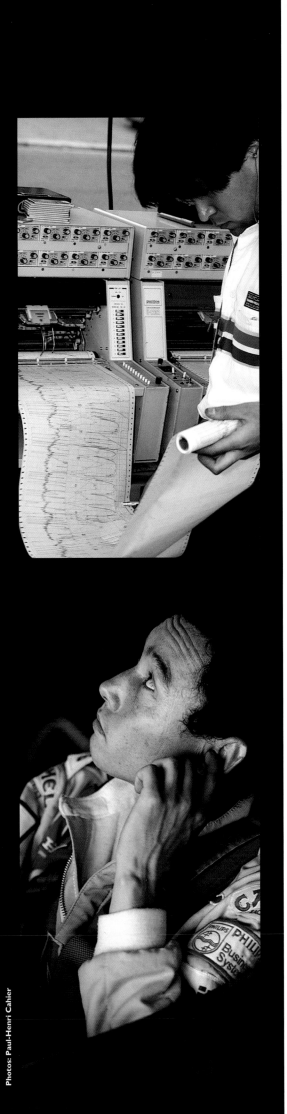

PIQUET TAKES
THIRD WORLD CHAMPIONSHIP

Nelson Piquet liked nothing more than working away with his engineers to develop a technical edge over his rivals and the Brazilian driver had to pull every ounce of strategic know-how out of the bag to win the 1987 World Championship.

Armed with the revised Williams FW11B, Piquet knew his biggest opposition would come from his team-mate, Nigel Mansell. It seemed as though the Englishman had the early advantage, winning the San Marino Grand Prix at Imola with relative ease after Piquet had been side-lined on medical advice after crashing heavily during practice due to a tyre failure.

Mansell won again in the French Grand Prix at Paul Ricard, following that up with a dynamic chase through the field at Silverstone to pass Nelson after a brilliant double-bluff manoeuvre going into Stowe Corner on the penultimate lap.

This was Mansell at his absolute best, wringing the last drop of speed from a dominant racing car in front of his adoring home crowd. Those who took in the shell-shocked expression on Piquet's face at the post-race press conference were in no way surprised when he announced he would be switching to Lotus the following year.

Yet this was not the end of the matter. Piquet bounced back with wins at Hockenheim and Budapest, took second to Mansell in Austria, then won the Italian Grand Prix at Monza through sheer cleverness.

Williams was developing its own 'reactive' suspension system – what might be described as a simplified version of the computer-controlled 'active' system being used by Ayrton Senna in the rival Honda-engined Lotus 99T – and Nelson reckoned it would give him an advantage at Monza. Honda was now supplying its very powerful V6 turbo engines to Lotus since Renault had withdrawn from all engine supply contracts at the end of the previous year.

Unhappy experiences with the prototype Lotus active system in its early years had left Mansell feeling rather cool towards such accessories so, while the Englishman opted for the standard car, Nelson took the gamble. Piquet was pretty sure what he was about. The week before, he had completed a race distance at Imola over a minute faster than Mansell's winning average three months earlier.

In the end, Piquet won the World Championship because Mansell crashed out in practice at Suzuka and missed the last two races. Even so, he had finished with Williams.

'I didn't come into this team to compete with another driver,' he said. 'I had a contract as number one driver and they screwed up the whole thing. Technically they were the best team I worked with, but I didn't join them to apply my experience to setting up cars for a team-mate who then made it difficult for me to win races.'

FERRARI BACK INTO
THE WINNER'S CIRCLE

Meanwhile, Ferrari had been struggling to get back into the winner's circle last occupied for the team by Michele Alboreto at the 1985 German Grand Prix at the rebuilt Nürburgring.

Enzo Ferrari had personally sanctioned the dramatic

1985

March: Mikhail Gorbachev becomes leader of the Soviet Union.
March: A system of genetic fingerprinting, using DNA, is discovered.
July: The Live Aid concert, staged for the benefit of Ethiopia's famine victims, takes place in London's Wembley Stadium.

1986

January: The space shuttle *Challenger* explodes in mid-air 90 seconds after lift-off, killing the crew of seven.
April: A reactor at the Chernobyl nuclear power station explodes, causing a large surrounding area to have dangerously high radiation levels.
June: Argentina win the football World Cup again, beating West Germany 3–1 in Mexico City, with Diego Maradona being Argentina's driving force.
July: Prince Andrew and Sarah Ferguson are married in London.

1987

March: The *Herald of Free Enterprise* capsizes off Zeebrugge, Belgium, killing about 100 people.
June: Fred Astaire, US actor and dancer, dies.
October: Southern England is devastated by the worst hurricanes recorded this century.
November: 34 people are killed when rubbish underneath an escalator catches fire at King's Cross underground station in London.

Opposite: Nelson Piquet and Nigel Mansell line up side by side in their Williams FW11B-Hondas in the Paul Ricard pit lane in readiness for practice, 1987.

Above left: A Honda technician examines a computer print-out in the pits. Sophisticated technology played an increasingly important role in F1 as the Eighties unfolded.

Left: Satoru Nakajima became the first Japanese driver to compete full-time in Grand Prix racing when his Honda connections helped him to a seat with Lotus in 1987.

Below: Feverish activity in the Ferrari garage with spare engines and gearbox sub-assemblies being fettled for action.

steps planned to shake the whole organisation back into some semblance of order. After John Barnard left his post as Chief Designer with McLaren in the summer of 1986, the elderly patriarch gave the British engineer the green light to establish his own Ferrari design studio in the UK.

In his new role as Technical Director of the Ferrari team, one of Barnard's main priorities was the development of a brand-new car for the 3.5-litre naturally aspirated regulations which would come into force at the start of 1989. As far as the future of the 1.5-litre turbocharged project was concerned, he had arrived a little late in the day to have much of an impact on the F1/87, which was the handiwork of engineer Gustav Brunner.

In 1987 the performance of the cars was further capped by a restriction of turbo boost pressure to 4 bar in conjunction with a fuel capacity maximum of 195 litres. For the new season Ferrari discarded its long-serving 120-degree V6 and replaced it instead with a 90-degree (Tipo 033) unit transmitting its power through a longitudinal gearbox.

The new engine was eclipsed by the front-line Honda opposition, but then that was a fate shared with just about every other F1 powerplant in 1987. What worsened Ferrari's plight, however, was the mechanical unreliability displayed by the new V6.

Barnard found himself spending too much time fiddling about with the 1987 car when he should have been toiling away on the new 3.5-litre project. Coincidentally, Michele Alboreto became vastly disillusioned over the manner in which Barnard, in his opinion, was trying to operate like 'a brain surgeon attempting a complicated operation over the telephone' from his base in England.

This confrontation between the wilful Italian driver and the single-minded British designer came to a head at Hockenheim over the German Grand Prix weekend. Thanks to Ferrari's inclination towards believing everything – anything – its senior management read in the media, Alboreto's remarks to *L'Equipe*, the French sporting newspaper, resulted in Barnard being hauled over to Germany for what amounted to a time-wasting trial by press.

Despite all these distractions, by the end of the season Ferrari was beginning to get itself under control again. Gerhard Berger – signed from Benetton at the start of the season – would have won the Portuguese GP at Estoril had he not spun off under pressure from Prost's McLaren. But the Austrian made up for this with a superb victory in the revived Japanese GP at Suzuka, a race from which Alboreto also emerged with considerable credit after climbing through to fourth place after his clutch had gone solid at the start, causing him to stall the car and then get away last after a push-start.

Ferrari's first win in almost two and a half years brought to an end the team's longest spell in F1 without a race victory. Berger immediately repeated this with a similarly impressive win in the Australian GP at Adelaide, Alboreto taking second after Ayrton Senna's Lotus-Honda, the original runner-up, was disqualified for a rule infringement relating to extra brake-cooling ducts which had been fitted especially for this race.

The McLaren-TAGs reached their sell-by date in 1987, but Prost scored three more race wins to take his career total to 28 victories. At last, Jackie Stewart's record of 27 wins, which had stood since 1973, had been broken.

Paul-Henri Cahier

Photos: Paul-Henri Cahier

Left: Ford's Cosworth-built turbo V6 was ditched after the '87 season. A major error of judgement, perhaps?

Below: Thierry Boutsen in the promising Benetton B187-Ford, Spa-Francorchamps, 1987.

HONDA
team of dreams

50
Years of Honda

THE YEAR is 1948. In Maranello, Italy, Enzo Ferrari is preparing for the debut of his first Grand Prix cars. Ferdinand Porsche is putting the finishing touches to the prototype of his new sports car, and in England Colin Chapman has just started work on his second trials machine. Thousands of miles away, another motoring visionary is beginning his own remarkable story.

Soichiro Honda was born on November 17, 1906, the eldest son of a village blacksmith. At the age of eight, a chance sighting of a Model T Ford on a dusty country road near his home fired Soichiro's imagination. He was determined to work with cars when he left school.

An apprenticeship at a Tokyo garage followed, where an understanding boss encouraged the young man's interest in racing cars. Soichiro built his own car using an old 8-litre Curtiss aircraft engine, and he raced with considerable success until almost losing his life in an accident in the All-Japan Speed Rally of 1936.

His passion for speed and remarkable engineering ability went hand in hand with a sharp business acumen. In 1936 he founded Tokai Seiki Heavy Industry, supplying Toyota and the Nakajima Aircraft company until an earthquake all but destroyed the factory in January 1945.

Defeat in the Second World War brought about a profound crisis in Japan. In a time of grave economic difficulty and social upheaval, the country needed hard-working and dynamic men of vision. Soichiro Honda had his part to play in the process of recovery: he would put Japan back on wheels.

The Honda Motor Company was set up in September 1948. While Ferrari, Porsche and Chapman pursued their own destinies on the roads and tracks of Europe, Soichiro Honda set out to make his country mobile again. Early Hondas were little more than bicycles with crude engines attached, but post-war Japan was hungry for any form of transport, not matter how unsophisticated. The Model D of 1949 was the company's first real motorcycle, but it was the 'Dream E-type' of 1951 which cemented Honda's reputation for durability and technical excellence. The new four-stroke machine set records for speed and for levels of production. Within ten years, Honda's production efficiency and advanced technology had put all but four of its domestic rivals out of business.

Fast forward to 1964. In Japan, Hondas continue to reign supreme on two wheels, and since 1954 Soichiro's machines have been winning bike races the world over. But memories of that Model T all those years ago and the races behind the wheel of his own aero-engined monster still linger in Soichiro's memory. The love of cars, and of racing cars in particular, burns undimmed. Honda's first road car, the S500 convertible, is rolling off the production lines, and the first Honda Formula 1 car is lining up on the starting grid.

The fearsome Nürburgring in Germany was no place for team and driver to make their debut. The inexperienced American racer, Ronnie Bucknum, hustled the under-developed RA271 round the 'Ring in eleventh place until crashing out four laps from the finish. The next race, the Italian Grand Prix at Monza, offered some encouragement. Bucknum ran as high as fifth before the Honda's engine over-heated. The American lasted 50 laps before retirement beckoned again at the US Grand Prix at Watkins Glen.

Three starts, three retirements. Not the stuff of which racing legends are made. But Honda's experience in motorcycle racing showed that success could not be expected over night. After all, this was the very pinnacle of motor racing. To

Far left: The brilliant Ayrton Senna, who won 32 Grands Prix and 3 world championships in Honda-engined cars.

Near left: Mr Honda with RA270F prototype F1 car.

Bottom: Honda's first Grand Prix challenger, the RA271, makes its debut in the hands of Ronnie Bucknum at the 1964 German Grand Prix.

break into the sport's elite would take time, money and determination.

What was the Grand Prix world to make of this upstart moped-maker and its little V12 racer? Certainly, the early outings in Formula 1 did not suggest that, one day, Honda-engined racers would humble Ferrari. The potential, however, was there to be seen. Honda's reputation on two wheels showed the established European teams that the Japanese company could make engines to match or beat the best in the world. The transversely-mounted 60-degree V12, with its four valves per cylinder, roller-bearing crank and 12,000-rpm rev ceiling, was a radical design, pushing out some 220 bhp. With better reliability, and a more experienced driver, RA271 could really have given the racing establishment something to think about.

Undeterred, Honda were back in 1965. The luckless Bucknum was joined by new Number One driver, Richie Ginther. As test driver for Ferrari and BRM, Ginther knew how to develop and set up a race-winning car. His sensitivity and ability to describe the minutiae of a car's behaviour were precisely the kind of qualities Honda's race engineers needed from a driver. Consistent and capable, Ginther would help them to develop a truly competitive machine.

The RA272 was not a radical departure from the '64 car. Rather, it built upon its strengths while seeking to iron out its weaknesses. Power increased still further, with 230 bhp developed at 12,000 rpm, making Honda's compact V12 the most powerful engine of the 1.5-litre era. If RA271 had failed to achieve much, here was a car with the potential to show the world the way home.

The season began in disappointing fashion. Ginther qualified poorly in Monaco and retired on the first lap. Matters improved at the Belgian Grand Prix at Spa, where Ginther finished sixth. The French Grand Prix brought more disappointment, both Hondas retiring short of the che-quered flag. Better times were just around the corner.

Ginther started from the front row at Silverstone, and briefly held the lead before being sidelined with engine problems. The supremely powerful Honda was ideally suited to Silverstone's long straights. Ginther led again at the Dutch Grand Prix among the dunes of

Zandvoort, before dropping back to finish sixth.

The team lost form over the next few races, missing the German Grand Prix altogether before retiring at Monza and finishing seventh and two laps down at Watkins Glen. After the highs of the British and Dutch Grands Prix, it seemed that the momentum of RA272's develop-ment had been lost.

The teams assembled for the last Grand Prix of the 1.5-litre era in Mexico City. The 7,000-ft altitude starved engines of oxygen, but the super-efficient Honda V12 coped admirably.

Ginther took the lead from the second row and was never headed. In spite of constant pressure from fellow American Dan Gurney in a Brabham-Climax, Ginther crossed the line to win by three seconds. History had been made. This was not only Honda's first Grand Prix win, it was the first ever victory by a Japanese marque. Ferrari, Porsche and Lotus had all been left trailing in the Honda's wake. Soichiro Honda had achieved a dream.

Victory at Mexico City should have been the springboard for great things, but RA272's greatest race was also its last. Honda would need a com-pletely new engine and chassis for the new 3-litre Formula 1 of 1966.

The next three seasons were to prove frustrating. The new 3-litre engine was potent but overweight, and RA273 rarely looked competi-tive. The RA300 of 1967 was as beautiful as it was powerful but suf-fered from the same weight problem as its predecessor. Matching the mighty Honda engine to a Lola chas-sis brought some success, with 1964 World Champion John Surtees tak-ing victory at Monza in one of the most thrilling races of the decade. Beating Ferrari on its home ground was satisfying, but fundamental prob-lems remained.

The radical air-cooled RA302 of 1968 failed to turn around Honda's fortunes, and when Frenchman Louis Schlesser was killed at Rouen, the team lost heart. Honda withdrew from F1 at the end of 1968.

In a short space of time, Honda had achieved much. The company had won races, and created the most powerful and technically advanced engines of the day. But the final step, from race winner to cham-pion, had proven difficult. For Honda, Grand Prix racing was to

Far left: Richie Ginther takes Honda's first historic win at Mexico City in 1965.

Bottom left: Monza 1967. In a thrilling finish John Surtees' Honda just beats Jack Brabham to the chequered flag.

50

Years of Honda

Far right: Keke Rosberg wins the US Grand Prix at Dallas for Williams-Honda in 1984.

Bottom far right: Nigel Mansell came agonisingly close to winning the championship in a Williams-Honda in 1986.

Right: Nelson Piquet was World Champion in 1987 driving the Williams-Honda.

Below: Stefan Johansson in the Spirit Honda in 1983. It was the Japanese company's first involvement in Formula 1 since the late 1960s.

remain unfinished business for nearly two decades.

Dominance on the track would have to wait. Building up the road car business came first. The S500/600 sports car had evolved into the S800, with an engine that revved to 8,000 rpm and put out 70 bhp from just 791 cc. Technologically, the S800 was light years ahead of its antiquated British opposition.

But it was the Civic of 1972 that really established Honda as a big motor industry player. Its neat front-engined, front-wheel drive packaging gave fine road manners and a roomy interior, wile Honda's pioneering of Compound Vortex Controlled Combustion gave exceptionally low emissions. In Europe and the USA, the Civic sold by the shipload.

The Accord saloon and Prelude coupé continued Honda's remarkable expansion. Sales continued to rise as the company teamed up with British Leyland and opened a new factory in Marysville, Ohio, USA.

The race for commercial success was being won. But the urge to race for real was still strong. Soichiro had stepped down from the company presidency in 1973, but his successors recognised the tremendous value of Grand Prix racing, both as an image builder and as a proving ground for Honda's technical brilliance. The return to Formula 1 was inevitable.

Honda was back on track for the British Grand Prix of 1983. In truth, the Honda Spirit car, driven by Stefan Johansson, was a toe in the water in preparation for a more serious effort the following year. The car competed in six Grands Prix that year without conspicuous success,

but the experience gained was invaluable.

From 1984 to 1987 Honda competed in partnership with the Williams team. The first season was not an easy one. Formula 1 had altered beyond all recognition from the sport of the '60s. Sponsorship, ground effect, downforce and turbo engines had all changed the face of Grand Prix racing, and Honda's early efforts with its 1.5-litre turbocharged V6 demonstrated the difficulty of combining competitive power with reliability. In spite of the problems, it was not long before Honda was winning again, with Keke Rosberg taking victory in the ninth race of the season, the US Grand Prix in Dallas.

For 1985, both Williams and Honda made great progress. Nigel Mansell now partnered Rosberg, and the pair enjoyed a tremendous run of late-season success. The V6 turbo unit had been thoroughly redesigned, and although problems persisted in the first half of the season, when the Williams-Honda hit form the results were spectacular. Rosberg and Mansell won two races apiece and ended the year on a high. The achievements of the '60s had already been eclipsed. Could Honda go one step further, and challenge for the championship?

The Williams-Honda was the class of the field in each of the following two seasons. Mansell was now partnered by Brazilian Nelson Piquet, and if their off-track relationship was spiky at best, it certainly produced some spectacular racing. Mansell won five races and Piquet four, comfortably winning the 1986 constructors' championship. The drivers' crown eluded Mansell by just two

50 Years of Honda

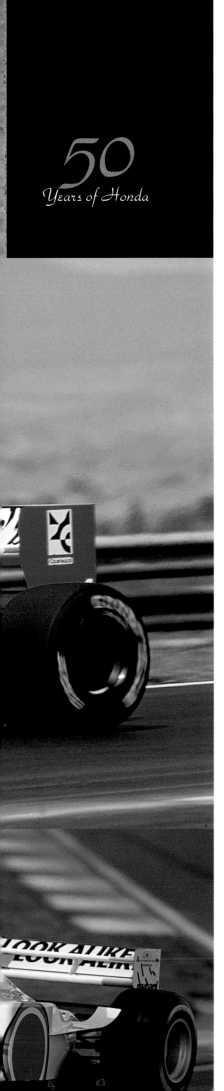

50 Years of Honda

points after a spectacular tyre blow-out in the final race of the season.

In 1987 Honda was even more dominant, now supplying both Williams and Lotus. With the Honda's turbo V6 now providing a balance of power and reliability which was the envy of the field, Honda-powered cars took 11 victories from 16 races, two for Ayrton Senna, three for Nelson Piquet, and six for Nigel Mansell. The drivers' championship for Piquet was the icing on the cake, with Honda powering its way to a second consecutive constructors' championship.

Already, Honda had little more to prove. In four years, the company had won 25 Grands Prix, and comprehensively beaten the world's finest teams. Just as at Mexico City in 1965, the great European marques had been left trailing. Incredibly, better still was to come.

In 1988 Williams was replaced with a new partner: McLaren. The season that followed was unprecedented, and its like will probably never be seen again. With the best car, the best engine, and the best drivers, McLaren-Hondas won 15 of 16 races. Senna won eight times and took the first of his three drivers' titles, with team-mate Prost finishing second with seven wins. With a scarcely believable 199 points, the constructors' cup went to a Honda-powered team yet again.

Honda had proven itself undisputed master of the turbo era. If rivals hoped the change to the 3.5-litre naturally-aspirated formula in 1989 would slow the company down, they were to be bitterly disappointed. Ferrari, Renault and Lamborghini had all fallen behind schedule in the development of their non-turbo powerplants, and struggled to be ready for the first race of the new season. It is a testimony to the depth of Honda's commitment to Grand Prix racing that their V10 engine was race-ready as early as October 1988.

The superiority of the McLaren-Honda was almost as crushing as it had been the year before, ten victories giving Honda its fourth consecutive constructors' championship. It was Prost's turn to take the title, after a controversial collision with Senna in the Japanese Grand Prix at Suzuka. Honda's V10 powered Senna to the title once again in 1990, while a new V12 unit brought another championship in 1991.

At the end of 1992, Honda withdrew from F1 racing, job done. From the dreams of a young blacksmith's son had grown a world-beater. The company which once attached two-stroke engines to bicycles had become manufacturer of some of the best-engineered and technologically advanced cars on the road, and an undisputed Grand Prix great. The achievements in Formula 1 speak for themselves. From 1984 to 1992, Honda-powered cars entered 144 Grands Prix, and won 69 of them. In the same period, Ferrari won just 15 times.

Honda returns to the Formula 1 arena in 2000 with the newest team on the grid, British American Racing, and the arrival of the legendary Honda power, in the form of the all-new RA000E 3-litre V10 engine, could help the team to recover from a difficult maiden season.

But in its third era of participation, Honda will concern itself not simply with the supply of engines to BAR. A full-time Honda team of chassis engineers will be based at BAR's Brackley headquarters and a further 50 people are involved in the chassis development programme at Honda Research and Development in Tochigi, Japan.

After a seven-year absence from the pinnacle of world motor sport, a successful Grand Prix history is clearly not enough to ensure automatic success in the Formula 1 of today. With its reputation for innovation, reliability and engineering excellence, however, Honda will once again become a major player in the Grand Prix elite.

Watch out, Formula 1. Honda hasn't finished yet.

Far left: Suzuka, 1989, Senna and Prost collide at the hairpin and the championship is decided in favour of the Frenchman.

Near left: Gerhard Berger raced for McLaren between 1990 and 1992, scoring three victories for the Honda powered cars.

Centre left: Ayrton Senna in 1992, the final year of Honda's partnership with McLaren.

Bottom right: Honda's return in 2000 in partnership with British American Racing.

Bottom far left: Honda's stunning new S2000 sportscar.

BRINGING RACE TECHNOLOGY TO THE ROAD

'Racing improves the breed' may be the oldest cliché in the book, but it's a basic rule of thumb for Honda. The same passionate commitment to quality and high-tech performance shown on the racetrack applies to every Honda car.

Throughout the great Grand Prix successes of the '80s and early '90s, Honda regularly moved its engineers between the racing campaign and the production line in order to infuse the whole company with racing know-how.

The fabulous NSX is the obvious example. Ayrton Senna had a hand in the development of the only supercar that was as easy to drive as a supermini.

But you don't need the thick end of £70,000 to enjoy the benefits of Honda's racing experience. The Civic, Prelude and Accord ranges and the new S2000 sports car are powered by engines as advanced and efficient as those of any track car. The company's VTEC powerplants combine the best of all worlds: tractable and economical at low speeds, yet lively and powerful at high revs.

Whichever Honda you choose, race-bred engineering comes as standard.

Right: McLaren Managing Director Ron Dennis talks earnestly with Honda President Nobuhiko Kawamoto.

Below: Wheel to wheel. The McLaren MP4/4s of Alain Prost and Ayrton Senna scramble into the first corner ahead of the pack at the start of the 1988 Portuguese Grand Prix. Seconds earlier, Senna believed that Prost had squeezed him dangerously to the outside of the corner.

SENNA VERSUS PROST

A new era is about to dawn as Ayrton Senna and McLaren are paired together for the first time at the opening race of the 1988 season.

McLAREN-HONDA achieved a stranglehold on Formula 1 during the final season of turbo competition and the early years of the 3.5-litre formula, but the bitter rivalry between Ayrton Senna and Alain Prost ensured that interest in Grand Prix racing had never been greater.

Squeezed out of McLaren by the Brazilian, Prost waged a fierce but ultimately unsuccessful battle to retain the crown after switching to Ferrari in 1990 and eventually captured his fourth title following a move to Williams-Renault in 1993.

Meanwhile there had been a spectacular advance in the use of high technology, fuelled by the cash available from major sponsors and the motor industry, with the result that computer-controlled driver aids were now usurping the role of the driver.

After three seasons with Lotus, Senna had decided to move on for 1988. The young Brazilian had forged a unique collaborative bond with Honda and the Japanese car maker was keen to continue working with him. That meant that he would either have to go to Williams, to replace the '87 World Champion, Nelson Piquet, or move to McLaren – which had clinched a deal to use Honda power in place of its previous TAG V6s.

This was a classic case of F1 musical chairs and even the most casual observer could work out that three into two would leave somebody dejected on the sidelines. In the event, it was Williams who lost the Honda engines – despite the fact that they had a firm contract through to the end of 1988.

McLAREN-HONDAS DOMINATE FINAL TURBO SEASON

Williams was told it could keep its engines as long as it agreed to have Japanese driver Satoru Nakajima in the second car. Frank Williams and Patrick Head were not interested and chose to go it alone with naturally aspirated Judd V8s in what was to be a transitional season between the turbo and new non-turbo eras. Piquet's popularity with Honda ensured that Lotus retained its engine deal when the Brazilian moved there from Williams. McLaren, of course, won on all fronts.

The 1988 season would see two different types of car compete in the FIA Formula 1 World Championship, both qualifying equally for points in both the drivers' and constructors' title battles. On the one hand, a team could opt to run under the 3.5-litre naturally aspirated rules to a 500 kg minimum weight limit, a formula which would become obligatory the following season. On the other, it could opt for a final fling with the 1.5-litre turbos. Many people believed they hadn't got a chance, restricted as they were by a 2.5-bar boost limitation, a 150-litre fuel capacity maximum and a 540 kg minimum weight limit.

One such individual was FISA President Jean-Marie Balestre, who, speaking at a meeting at Estoril in late 1986 to announce this interim season, made a remark which matched anything a professional politician could have produced in its capacity for being wide of the mark.

'I promise you, gentlemen, in 1988, no way for the turbos,' said Balestre. He would have been correct in that

Below: The all-conquering
'88 Honda V6 twin turbo.

Right: Ferrari's 1988 turbo
won the Italian Grand Prix.

Below right: The Judd V8
which powered Nigel
Mansell's Williams FW12.

Photos: Paul-Henri Cahier

prediction had it not been for the McLaren-Hondas. They won 15 out of the season's 16 races. If they hadn't been there, the laurels would have been pretty evenly spread between naturally aspirated and turbocharged machinery. But they were.

Ironically, there was one team which might have challenged McLaren had it made subtly different arrangements for its 1988 engine-supply deal.

At the start of 1987 the Benetton team had decided to switch from BMW to Ford power, taking over supplies of the Cosworth-built 120-degree V6 turbo which had been used by the Haas Lola team the previous season. Although not the most obviously powerful of the turbo generation, its wide cylinder angle enabled it to be packaged extremely tightly within the B187 chassis, which made for a notably effective aerodynamic profile.

Additional development progress was made with the Ford turbo throughout the 1987 season, during which Italy's Teo Fabi had been joined in the driver line-up by Thierry Boutsen, the popular Belgian replacing Gerhard Berger, who had gone off to Ferrari. Boutsen and Fabi both made it to lower placings on the rostrum during the course of the season, finishing eighth and ninth in the drivers' championship and helping the team to earn 28 points – and fifth place – in the constructors' contest.

It is a matter of debate just how close the Ford V6 turbo came to winning its first Grand Prix in a Benetton. Nobody will ever know, because its development was brought to an abrupt halt – in Ford's view – by the latest change in the F1 engine regulations. The days of the turbo had suddenly become numbered and naturally aspirated engines, this time of 3.5 litres capacity, which had been re-admitted to F1 in 1987, would be the only permitted power source from 1989 onwards.

Ford decided to concentrate its resources on developing the new naturally aspirated Cosworth DFR and it was this engine that was supplied to Benetton in 1988, although hindsight now suggests that they would have done better to have stuck with the turbo, even under the restrictive new regulations.

Had Benetton used the Ford turbo in 1988 it is quite possible that Honda would not have enjoyed the performance advantage which helped the McLaren team to dominate the World Championship.

Of course, in 1988 McLaren didn't go into battle with just the benefit of Honda engines. By recruiting Senna to drive alongside Prost, they had also assembled one of the very strongest driver line-ups ever seen in F1. However, the rivalry between the two men developed to an uncomfortable level of intensity: they were too different, yet too similar, at one and the same moment.

Prost eventually came to believe that his position in the team was being undermined, but Senna simply regarded his own confrontational stance as a pragmatic means whereby he could stamp his identity on the McLaren team as a whole.

In the run-up to the new partnership with Honda, the McLaren team also reorganised its technical department. Former Brabham Chief Designer Gordon Murray was recruited to handle the management and administration

Below: Ayrton Senna heads to victory in the '88 Hungarian Grand Prix. Alain Prost took second place to give McLaren its seventh 1–2 finish in the first ten races of the season.

ALAIN PROST combined mental astuteness and considerable speed with an economy of physical effort behind the wheel. He ran hard and fast, but like Niki Lauda – his teenage hero – he let the car do as much of the work as possible.

Prost always performed when it really mattered. Within three laps of the start of his first F1 test at Paul Ricard in late 1979 he was right on the pace and McLaren team manager Teddy Mayer was rummaging through his briefcase, looking for a draft contract and a pen.

First time round, he stayed just a single year at McLaren. It would unfortunately be 1981 before McLaren International, a revised and revamped company motivated and shaped by the ambitious Ron Dennis, began to play a significant role on the Grand Prix scene. By then Prost was committed to a three-year deal with the Renault works team.

In 1983 Alain came close to the World Championship, but it slipped from his grasp in the closing races of the year as rivals BMW raised the engine development stakes and provided Nelson Piquet's works Brabham with more power. Renault failed to respond to this obvious challenge and lost the title at the last Grand Prix, in South Africa.

Made the fall-guy for this failure, Prost returned to McLaren in 1984, prepared to take peanuts from Ron Dennis as long as it got him away from Renault. He and his McLaren-TAG team-mate, Niki Lauda, carved up that season between them. Prost won seven races, Lauda five. Yet it was Niki who took the championship by the slender margin of half a point.

Prost had arrived at McLaren with nine Grand Prix victories under his belt. He finished '84 with 16 to his credit and added another five in 1985, when he finally became France's first World Champion. He would retain the title in 1986, although he needed a bit of bad luck to strike at the more powerful rival Williams-Hondas of Nigel Mansell and Nelson Piquet to do so. In the event, Alain dodged through to win the championship at the last race of the year.

By 1987 the McLaren-TAG was past its best. Even so, Alain's third win that season was his 28th, making him the most successful Grand Prix driver to date – eclipsing Jackie Stewart's record of 27 wins which had endured since 1973. To this day, Prost's position at the head of the all-time winner's list has never been challenged, his final tally standing at 51 victories.

The 1988 season witnessed another critical sea-change at McLaren. The team signed a long-term deal to use Honda engines and Ayrton Senna joined Prost to produce the most formidable line-up on the contemporary Grand Prix scene. Suddenly Alain found himself in exactly the same situation as that in which he had put Niki Lauda, back in 1984.

At the end of the season Senna won the World Championship with eight wins to Prost's seven. The two drivers continued together in 1989, only for their personal relationship to fall apart after Senna apparently reneged on a no-overtaking agreement on the opening lap at Imola. Tensions between the two men increased and Prost decided to leave at the end of the season and join Nigel Mansell at Ferrari. But not before he'd clinched his third title following a controversial collision between the two McLaren drivers in the Japanese Grand Prix.

Sadly, Prost's initially successful partnership with Maranello became seriously unravelled in 1991. Mansell had left the team at the end of the previous season and Prost found it difficult to work with team manager Cesare Fiorio. The team had a poor year and this, combined with some intemperate remarks to the media, resulted in Prost being dismissed with one race still to run.

Prost sat out the following season but he still wanted to race. Renault and Elf, his old partners, were keen to get him back behind the wheel of a front-running car and in 1993 he was signed up to drive a Williams-Renault.

He rounded off what was to be his final season in Formula 1 with victories in the South African, San Marino, Spanish, Canadian, French, British and German Grands Prix. His new team-mate, Damon Hill, certainly put him under pressure, but Alain inevitably seemed capable of pulling a little extra out of the bag every time he looked seriously challenged.

Prost retired largely because he didn't want to be paired with Senna again in 1994. The two men even discussed it by telephone, Ayrton urging Alain that, this time, it might well work out. Alain thought otherwise.

It clearly gave Alain considerable satisfaction that he and Senna seemed to be approaching a personal *rapprochement* on the day prior to Ayrton's fatal accident at Imola in the 1994 San Marino Grand Prix. It was as if they had both suddenly realised the truth of the previous ten years. Each had been feeding off the other to sustain his competitive instinct and passion behind the wheel.

Paul-Henri Cahier

side of the design process, leaving Steve Nichols free to become Project Leader of the design team which would produce the 1988 challenger, the MP4/4.

From a structural standpoint, the carbon-fibre composite chassis of the latest McLaren was subject to fresh design requirements. Under revised safety regulations applicable from the start of 1988, the foot pedals had to be drawn back by 20 cm from their previous position in order to get the driver's feet behind the front wheel centre-line.

However, this was compensated for by the shorter centre section required to accommodate the 150-litre fuel cell, resulting in a modest overall 4 cm increase on the wheelbase of the 1987 chassis. More than ever, in 1988 the McLaren hallmark was attention to minute detail, but the engine was perhaps the key factor in the team's success, although they also had the advantage of Prost and Senna in the driving seats and a much better chassis than the similarly powered Lotus 100T driven by Piquet and Nakajima.

Honda's new 'XE2' and 'XE3' twin-turbo V6s offered better economy or enhanced top-end performance respectively, depending on the circuit requirements. Honda attempted to improve their turbo response by the use of ceramic turbine wheels and opted for a 79 × 50.8 mm bore and stroke in conjunction with a 9.4:1 compression ratio and near-flat-headed pistons which made a major contribution to the sought-after fuel efficiency.

The engines incorporated a new small-diameter clutch which, in turn, enabled the Japanese company to build its engine lower, dropping the crankshaft centre-line a full 28 mm from its 1987 level. McLaren matched this development by producing a three-axis gearbox which raised the drive line sufficiently to facilitate the use of an upswept aerodynamic rear undertray, in addition to reducing potentially wearing driveshaft angularity.

Honda's engine management system was refined to fresh levels of efficiency on this latest V6, air intake temperatures being of absolutely paramount importance to its efficient functioning. The temperature of the air flowing into the engine was regulated to as close to 40°C as possible by the opening of the intercooler's bypass valve at the appropriate moment. In addition, there was a temperature control system which utilised a heat exchanger fed by water from the cooling system, the flow through which was controlled by a solenoid valve.

The amount of fuel remaining in the McLaren's tanks at any point in a race was calculated by computer and displayed to the driver throughout the event, enabling Senna and Prost to select the correct balance of boost pressure, intake air temperature, fuel temperature and air/fuel mix during the course of the race. Even in conditions of marginal fuel consumption, this latest Honda RA163-E variant produced around 630 bhp – still about 40 bhp more than the best of the naturally aspirated cars.

During that remarkable final season of turbo competition, Ayrton Senna won eight races, Alain Prost seven. The World Championship battle went right down to the penultimate race of the season, Senna finally clinching the title with a decisive victory over the Frenchman in the Japanese Grand Prix at Suzuka.

McLaren boss Ron Dennis has had great drivers before and since, but there has never been anything that has even come close to the high-tension static which positively crackled between the ascetic Brazilian and his *dégagé* French colleague.

When Senna arrived in the McLaren enclave at the start of 1988, Ron Dennis might have believed he was a good team man, yet the reality was that he was anything but that. Senna, a charismatic combination of towering ego, presence and talent, simply dominated every F1 team for which he drove.

Prost had been McLaren's baby, the sitting tenant ever since the start of 1984. During that first season with the revamped team, the Frenchman had shown a thing or two to Niki Lauda about dodging through gaps in traffic. Four years later the driving boot was very firmly on the other foot.

By 1988, Prost had become the seasoned campaigner, unwilling to put everything on the line for a *kamikaze* qualifying lap, risking all going for gaps which might close before you got to them. But the Frenchman judged that he would be able to match Senna on racecraft and tactics, if not on sheer qualifying speed.

It proved to be a quite electrifying season and, although it passed more or less without untoward incident, the

In the bag. Senna's expression on the victory podium at Imola, 1989, seems to reflect an inner knowledge that he has now got the psychological upper hand over McLaren team-mate Prost.

Above: Nigel Mansell scored the most brilliantly opportunistic victory of his F1 career at the Hungaroring in 1989 at the wheel of the Ferrari 640.

Right: Alessandro Nannini with the Benetton B189-Ford. The popular Italian inherited a lucky win in the 1989 Japanese Grand Prix when Senna was disqualified.

relationship between the two drivers was certainly far from personally harmonious. Whereas Prost favoured a calm and sympathetic team environment, Senna simply thrived on tension and confrontation as a means of heightening his competitive edge.

Alain found the whole experience extremely stressful, but Ayrton clearly revelled in every minute of it.

By the time they arrived at the 1988 Portuguese Grand Prix, Prost was beginning to fight back after Senna had won four straight races through July and August. And it was at Estoril that things very nearly became physical between the two McLaren drivers.

Senna got it into his head that Prost had squeezed him out towards the left-hand kerb as they sprinted to the first corner, although a quick glance at the TV tapes revealed that the Frenchman – as you'd expect – had done nothing out of the ordinary. Never mind, Ayrton led from the second start, the race having been stopped due to a startline shunt among the tail-enders, only for Alain to come swooping out of his slipstream at 170 mph as they came past the pits at the end of the opening lap.

Amazingly, Senna then lunged to the right and tried to pincer his so-called team-mate against the pit wall, but Prost kept his foot hard on the throttle and forced his way through, even though pit signalling boards had to be hastily withdrawn for fear of actually hitting the roll-over bar on the Frenchman's car.

Make no mistake about it, this was crassly dangerous driving on Senna's part. Yet neither the stewards nor the McLaren management, for some reason cowed by the sheer force of Senna's character, opted to make any intervention.

After winning the race Prost tore Senna off a strip behind the closed doors of the team's motorhome. 'I hadn't appreciated you were prepared to die to win the World Championship,' he told the startled Brazilian. Later he added to a friend: 'If he wants the title that badly, he can have it.'

Senna duly won the championship that year and the two men stayed together as McLaren team-mates in 1989. Yet if a fragile peace had existed between them in '88, now it was torn asunder after what Prost regarded as Senna's brazen duplicity.

SENNA AND PROST AT EACH OTHER'S THROATS

For the 1989 San Marino Grand Prix at Imola, Prost suggested to Senna a first-lap no-passing pact: whichever of them made the best start in their 3.5-litre Honda RA109E V10-engined McLaren MP4/5s should lead through the uphill left-hander at Tosa, after which they would be free to race unfettered. Ayrton agreed.

At the start Senna got away first, but the race was stopped after only four laps following a huge accident to Gerhard Berger's Ferrari, from which the Austrian driver was lucky to emerge with only superficial injuries.

After a delay, the race was duly restarted. This time Prost got the jump on the Brazilian, but Senna slipstreamed past him on the run down to Tosa in apparent breach of their private agreement. The blue touch paper had well and truly been ignited.

Prost confronted Senna and again gave him a dressing-down. He was not, he told him, a man whose word could be relied on. Ron Dennis was understandably keen to nip this confrontation in the bud and engineered a

meeting between the two men during a test at Pembrey the following week.

Senna was persuaded to apologise, fighting back tears of frustration as he did so. But the relationship was long gone. Before Monaco, the next race on the calendar, Prost gave an interview to *L'Equipe* in which he said: 'At a level of technical discussion, I shall not close the door completely, but for the rest I no longer wish to have any business with him. I appreciate honesty and he is not honest.'

The ultimate embarrassment for McLaren came later that year when the two drivers, once again locked in a fierce struggle for the World Championship as the season neared its climax, collided while battling for the lead of the Japanese Grand Prix. Prost, who had removed the tail strip from his car's rear wing only moments before the parade lap in the interests of straightline speed, led from the start and seemed to have the edge. But Ayrton produced a superhuman lap to haul up on to his tail as they approached the tight chicane before the start/finish straight with only six of the race's 53 laps to go.

It had to happen. Senna braked incredibly late, two wheels shaving the grass on the inside. But Prost wasn't having it. As Ayrton kept coming, the Frenchman – who had by now had enough of his intimidation – closed the door. The two cars skidded to an interlocked halt in the middle of the track.

Prost hopped out and walked away. Senna beckoned for the marshals to help restart his car and accelerated back into the race through the chicane. He was later disqualified, McLaren made an unsuccessful appeal and the whole episode degenerated into a morass of bitterness and recrimination. Prost would be World Champion as a result.

Twelve months later, with Alain now driving for Ferrari, Senna would exact his revenge by ramming him deliberately off the road at 130 mph on the first corner of the race. The FIA stewards did nothing, nor again did the McLaren management. It was one of motor racing's most outrageous scandals, made all the more pathetic by the idiotic apologies offered for Senna's behaviour by many leading lights within the sport who should have known better.

Less than four years later, on the eve of Senna's death at Imola, the two men seemed to have achieved a genuine *rapprochement*. Prost, by now retired, had returned as a television commentator. For Ayrton, it was as if the penny had dropped, as if he'd suddenly realised just how much of his motivation behind the wheel had come from trying to beat the little Frenchman with the crooked nose when they were rivals on the track.

Throughout this enthralling period it was almost as if every other driver was pushed to the sidelines in some sort of supporting role. Even Nigel Mansell, who left Williams after a frustrating 1988 season struggling with the 3.5-litre Judd V8 engine, had to wait until the sunset years of the McLaren-Honda alliance before he could get a serious look-in.

Mansell joined Ferrari in 1989 and celebrated his arrival with a fortuitous win in the Brazilian Grand Prix at Rio, armed with the John Barnard-designed Ferrari 640 complete with its 3.5-litre naturally aspirated V12 engine and electro-hydraulic automatic gearchange. That season he would also win superbly in Hungary, where he beat Senna's McLaren MP4/5 into second place after a great fight, and Berger would add another victory in Portugal in September, but shortly afterwards it was announced that Barnard would be leaving the team.

Above: Alain Prost in the Ferrari 641 kicks up showers of sparks from his skidplates at Spa-Francorchamps, 1990.

Opposite: A tense-looking Prost (left) sits with Mansell and Senna at the media conference following the 1990 Portuguese Grand Prix at Estoril.

PROST AND MANSELL IN 1990 CONFLICT

Prost won the 1989 World Championship with 76 points (net) to Senna's 60, while Riccardo Patrese wound up third on 40 points during the first year of the nascent Williams-Renault partnership using the French company's 3.5-litre V10 which had been quietly developed behind the scenes ever since the 1.5-litre turbo project had been shelved at the end of 1986.

Having tired of the tensions involved in being Senna's team-mate, Prost decided to switch to the Ferrari team in 1990 to partner Mansell, while Berger moved in the other direction to take on what was to prove very much a number two seat in the McLaren-Honda squad.

Prost and Mansell proved to be a volatile pairing, particularly as everything seemed to go the Frenchman's way during the first half of the season. By the time they arrived at Silverstone for the British Grand Prix, Prost had already won three races and would bag his fourth on Nigel's home soil when the Englishman's gearbox went haywire after he had qualified superbly on pole position and led commandingly in the early stages. In a knee-jerk response to his disappointment, Mansell

announced that he would retire from racing at the end of the year.

Thereafter, everything went wrong for Mansell. He retired an only lightly damaged car at Hockenheim, hurt his wrist in a silly collision with Berger's McLaren in Hungary and then trailed round in midfield after being forced to take the spare car following a first-corner shunt which saw the Belgian GP red-flagged at the end of the opening lap.

What happened next was that Ferrari negotiated for Jean Alesi to replace Mansell in 1991. Once that was tied up, Nigel announced that he had changed his mind about retirement – largely under overwhelming pressure from his adoring fans – and signed for Williams. Prost, meanwhile, found his position in the Ferrari team undermined when Mansell, in his view at least, ganged up with Senna to thwart his efforts in the Portuguese GP at Estoril.

At the start, Mansell's pole-position Ferrari 641 veered across in front of Prost, allowing Senna to take an immediate lead. Ayrton eventually finished second behind Nigel, with Alain third.

'Ferrari doesn't deserve to be World Champion,' said the furious Prost after climbing from the cockpit. 'It is a team without directive and without strategy trying to win

against a well-structured team like McLaren. Berger helped Senna to the maximum to win the race.'

A week later, Prost won the Spanish Grand Prix at Jerez, where Mansell played second fiddle to finish second. Then came the Japanese GP at Suzuka, where Alain's hopes of becoming the first Ferrari World Champion driver in 11 years were wiped out when Senna used his McLaren as a battering ram going into the first corner and wiped both cars out of the race.

'If everybody wants to drive in this way, then the sport is finished,' said Prost. He was right, of course. Fiat Vice-President Cesare Romiti best summed it up when he hinted that Ferrari might consider withdrawing from F1. 'We do not feel part of this world without rules,' he noted. Ferrari's Chairman, Piero Fusaro, also called upon FISA President Jean-Marie Balestre to legislate against such wayward driving tactics.

Either way, Ferrari's hopes of a World Championship had been wrecked. Senna took his second title with 78 points to Prost's 71 (net).

Alain went into the 1991 season with Alesi as his partner, but there were to be no more Grand Prix victories coming Ferrari's way. Prost also found himself increasingly at odds with the team and, in particular, the team manager, the politically minded Cesare Fiorio, who was ditched midway through the campaign. Yet it would not be enough.

As the season wore on, Prost came under attack by the influential Italian media, but he would not be intimidated. 'This is the last straw in a ridiculous sequence of events,' he said. 'I suppose it was the same for John Barnard when he was working here, but I never imagined the influence of the press would be so considerable.'

In the end, after a season in which Steve Nichols's latest updates of Barnard's original design – the 643 replacing the 642 at the French GP – failed to win a single race, Prost was fired before the final round of the title chase. His offence was to have described the 643 as 'a truck'. But his judgement was correct and the Ferrari management's stubbornness had now cost them the services of one of the very greatest Grand Prix drivers of all time.

1990
August: Iraq invades neighbouring Kuwait.
November: Roald Dahl, British author, dies.
November: Margaret Thatcher's 11-year reign as British Prime Minister ends. John Major takes over.

1991
February: A US-led coalition defeats Iraq in the Gulf War, ending its occupation of Kuwait.
March: Argentine football player Diego Maradona is banned for 15 months after testing positive for cocaine.
April: Around 100,000 people are killed when a cyclone hits Bangladesh.
August: Bob Beamon's 22-year-old long jump record is beaten. Mike Powell beats Beamon's distance of 8.9 metres by 5 centimetres.
August: Mikhail Gorbachev resigns as First Secretary of the Soviet Communist Party.

Photos: Paul-Henri Cahier

SENNA ON TECHNIQUE

Ayrton Senna put more mental firepower into his driving technique than possibly any other F1 competitor of his era. In the 1990/91 edition of AUTOCOURSE he graphically described to the late Denis Jenkinson just how much intensity and personal focus were required for his breathtaking pole-position lap at the 1988 Monaco Grand Prix at the wheel of the McLaren MP4/4-Honda.

'MONTE CARLO, 1988, qualifying . . . What happened was that we had race tyres, not qualifying tyres, so it was lap after lap, not just one lap. We had the turbo car. I went out, had a good lap, another lap. I was on pole, then the next lap with a bigger margin, and I was going more and more and more and more.

'I got to the stage when I was over two seconds faster than anybody, including my team-mate [Alain Prost], who was using the same car, same engine, everything. That was the direct comparison and over two seconds. It wasn't because he was going slow, but because I was going too fast.

'I felt at one point that the circuit was no longer really a circuit, just a tunnel of Armco. But in such a way that I suddenly realised that I was over the level that I considered . . . reasonable. There was no margin whatsoever, in anything.

'When I had that feeling I immediately lifted. I didn't have to, because I was still going. I immediately lifted. Then I felt that I was on a different level. I didn't fully understand that level and I still don't.

'I understand it a bit better, but I'm still far away from satisfying my own needs as to how it works in that [mental] band.

'So I backed off and came slowly into the pits. I said to myself, "Today that is special. Don't go out any more. You are vulnerable. For whatever reason, you are putting yourself in a situation where you are doing it more in a sub-conscious way."

'I could not really cope with that in a manner that I could find easy.'

Top: Thierry Boutsen's Williams fends off Senna's McLaren to win the 1990 Hungarian Grand Prix.

Above: New star rising. Jean Alesi displayed stupendous form for Tyrrell in 1990, racing Senna wheel-to-wheel in the Phoenix Grand Prix.

Opposite page: The combination of Senna, McLaren and the 3.5-litre naturally aspirated Honda V10 took the 1990 World Championship honours.

Left: Senna in conversation with one of his most committed fans, veteran journalist Denis Jenkinson.

Right: Eddie Jordan joined the ranks of the F1 team owners in 1991 and soon became embroiled in controversy.

Opposite: Determined to stay ahead of the opposition, Ron Dennis and Ayrton Senna check the practice times on a monitor perched on top of the Brazilian's McLaren.

Opposite, bottom: Riccardo Patrese took the Williams FW14-Renault to two wins in 1991 and finished third in the drivers' championship.

Below: The drivers prepare for the annual class photo at the season-opener at Phoenix, 1991. Back row (left to right): Riccardo Patrese, Aguri Suzuki, Bertrand Gachot, Gianni Morbidelli, Ivan Capelli, Mauricio Gugelmin, FISA President Jean-Marie Balestre and Ayrton Senna. Front row: Alain Prost, Jean Alesi, Nigel Mansell, Gerhard Berger and Emanuele Pirro.

MANSELL'S RETURN TO WILLIAMS PROVES WELL TIMED

By the end of 1990 Williams was poised to stage a major recovery as a winning force; as we have seen, in late summer the team had opened negotiations which would bring Nigel Mansell back into its fold.

Frank Williams suspected that his former driver might have made a hair-trigger decision to retire after his misfortunes with Ferrari and successfully coaxed him into changing his mind. With Renault raising the stakes with the latest version of its V10 engine, running to 14,000 rpm with its pneumatic valvegear, and a new chassis benefiting from aerodynamic input from new Chief Designer Adrian Newey, Mansell did not need much persuading.

Mansell duly signed and the Williams FW14 proved to be a highly competitive tool from the outset. Had mechanical problems not blighted the car early in the season, Nigel might have made an even more serious bid for the 1991 World Championship. But Ayrton Senna, his McLaren, the new MP4/6, now powered by Honda's RA121E V12 engine, won the first four races of the season to earn a worthwhile points cushion.

Despite this, Mansell won the French, British, German, Italian and Spanish Grands Prix in dominant style, carrying his bid for the championship all the way to the penultimate race at Suzuka, where Senna finally clinched the crown after the Williams driver ended up in a gravel trap.

The 1991 season also saw two very important developments which would have a profound effect on the F1 landscape in the longer term. Firstly, leading F3000 entrant and wheeler-dealer Eddie Jordan made the huge

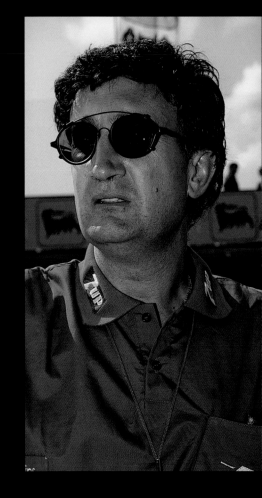

Right: Andrea de Cesaris earned his keep for Jordan during the British team's freshman year in 1991.

Below: Baby-faced Mika Häkkinen prepares for his first Grand Prix at Phoenix.

Bottom: Juan Manuel Fangio reappeared on the F1 scene in '91 to launch his autobiography.

Right: Mansell and Senna get serious during their thrilling wheel-to-wheel battle for the lead of the 1991 Spanish Grand Prix at Barcelona's Circuit de Catalunya.

Below: Sparks fly as Brazil's Mauricio Gugelmin guns his Ilmor-powered Leyton House CG911 through the tunnel at Monaco in 1991.

Photos: Paul-Henri Cahier

Right: Ayrton Senna takes an emotional first home F1 victory in the 1991 Brazilian Grand Prix.

Bottom (left to right): Gerhard Berger's three years at McLaren proved an instructive time for the popular Austrian; Williams Technical Director Patrick Head listens to Nigel Mansell's thoughts on the FW14; the start of a new order as Michael Schumacher has his first F1 outing for Jordan at Spa, 1991.

jump into F1 with the Gary Anderson-designed 191 challenger powered by leased Cosworth Ford HB V8 engines. Secondly, at the Belgian Grand Prix, Jordan made a car available for a promising young lad who qualified seventh at his first attempt, only for the clutch to fail almost at the start. His name was Michael Schumacher.

Benetton engineering boss Tom Walkinshaw had seen Schumacher racing the Mercedes sports cars against his own Jaguars and suspected that he was something really special. Now Walkinshaw had no doubts whatsoever.

He rightly judged that Benetton could offer Schumacher more than Jordan at this stage in his career. Ever since Flavio Briatore had been brought in to run the team in 1989, Benetton had made steady progress. His task was aided by the arrival of John Barnard as Technical Director and the team's continuing partnership with Ford, which supplied its 'works' operation with a succession of Cosworth-developed V8s, although Barnard had ironically left Benetton midway through the '91 season, shortly after his B191 design had scored its first victory in Canada.

The fortnight separating the Belgian and Italian Grands Prix saw frantic negotiations to get Schumacher out of his Jordan contract and into a Benetton. With Bernie Ecclestone taking a hand in the contractual debate, the deal was eventually done, leaving Jordan temporarily humiliated and vowing legal retribution.

Roberto Moreno was duly replaced in the Benetton squad, briefly taking over Schumacher's vacated Jordan, and Michael found himself lining up alongside Nelson Piquet, who was starting his 200th Grand Prix, at Monza. Some people felt that Piquet was past his best but, while the veteran Brazilian could perhaps no longer demonstrate the sort of form which had carried him to his three World Championship titles, his huge experience would prove enormously helpful to Schumacher.

At Monza, Michael started as he meant to go on, outrunning Piquet all weekend to finish fifth in the race, just over ten seconds ahead of the Brazilian. The rest of the 1991 season went quite smoothly for Schumacher, who finished sixth in Portugal and Spain but retired with a mechanical failure and a collision in the other two races.

Yet there was to be no stopping the Williams-Renaults in 1992. Fitted with state-of-the-art electronic driver aids

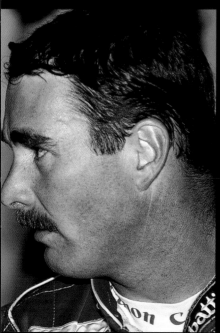

AYRTON SENNA: F1'S HOLY WARRIOR

PERHAPS UNIQUE in the intensity of his commitment to his chosen sport, Ayrton Senna ranks as one of the very greatest Grand Prix drivers of all time, not merely in the period covered by this volume. Dynamic and highly committed, even when he was a junior driver on the lower rungs of the racing ladder, Senna always showed himself to be bold and aggressive, whether in driving technique or in dealing with the top teams.

In 1983 McLaren offered to fund Senna's British Formula 3 Championship programme in exchange for an option on his services. Many youngsters in that position would have jumped at such an opportunity, but Ayrton declined politely. He told Ron Dennis that he would generate his own finance, and chart his own path through the motor racing maze.

Senna graduated to Formula 1 with Toleman after winning the 1983 F3 title, which ironically earned him a test drive with McLaren. Instantly the Toleman team was won over by the brilliant young Brazilian. At the wheel of their Hart turbo-engined TG184, Ayrton finished a superb second in Monaco and third – beaten only by the McLarens of Prost and Lauda – in Portugal.

Senna switched to Lotus the following year and scored his first Grand Prix victory in the second race of the season, held in pouring rain at Estoril. This spellbinding example of high-speed car control was followed by five more Lotus victories during his three seasons with the team, but it wasn't until he joined the McLaren-Honda squad at the start of 1988 that he really began to notch up the wins at a quite dramatic rate.

Few drivers in history have ever applied so much mental focus to the business of Formula 1. Ayrton was forever probing, exploring and analysing every means of gaining an edge. It took him little more than a season of intense psychological warfare to unseat Alain Prost from his position at McLaren, driving him into the arms of the rival Ferrari camp.

This highly confrontational attitude towards Prost, which developed during their second year together at McLaren and intensified thereafter, was seen by many as nothing more than a reflection of Senna's competitive spirit. It was not enough for Ayrton simply to succeed. He had to do so from a position of total dominance. Even if that meant crushing the morale of his opposition.

It was also the view of many colleagues that Senna lacked not only a sense of humour but also a degree of perspective. He almost exclusively reserved the former for his close friends who came from in or around his closeted family environment.

Yet perhaps the tensions which brewed up between Prost and Senna in 1988/89 were to some extent inevitable. Prost wanted to protect his position, Senna to undermine it. Prost had been central to all McLaren's success since 1984 and now he could see the balance of power shifting decisively in Senna's favour.

Senna was not a man who could accept defeat. This was graphically demonstrated when he deliberately pushed Prost's Ferrari off the circuit on the first corner of the 1990 Japanese Grand Prix after being frustrated in his attempt to move pole position to the other side of the track. This episode suggested that Senna's messianic zeal might extend to discarding considerations of his own personal safety, let alone that of anybody else on the circuit.

The difference between the two drivers was that Alain, in a car that he liked and was set up specially for him, was untouchable. Unbeatable. But Ayrton could drive anything, no matter how badly it was handling.

That was the case in his last, fateful race at Imola. The Williams FW16 was probably not a car which should have been on pole position at that stage in its development. It was on pole position because Ayrton was driving it. Michael Schumacher, whose Benetton was following Senna in the early stages, later said he could see that the Brazilian was having problems with his car. But Ayrton Senna was never a man to take it easy.

Senna on the limit during practice for the 1991 British Grand Prix at the wheel of the V12-powered McLaren MP4/6-Honda.

Paul-Henri Cahier

Nigel Mansell's Williams FW14B leads Ayrton Senna's McLaren MP4/7 into the first chicane at Monza at the start of the 1992 Italian Grand Prix.

such as traction control, active suspension and automatic gearchange, the Williams FW14B, powered by the even more powerful Renault RS4 engine, enabled Mansell to blitz his way to the World Championship with nine victories. He also started all but two of the 16 races from pole position. Senna and McLaren were defeated and Mansell had the title wrapped up by the Hungarian Grand Prix in the middle of August.

For McLaren, the 1992 season produced something of a humiliation. Although the new MP4/7 chassis was probably the most sophisticated and beautifully made McLaren had produced so far, Honda's latest V12 engine was certainly lagging behind in terms of power.

Unbeknown to those outside the team's senior management, Honda had advised McLaren chief Ron Dennis early in the season that they would not be continuing in F1 in 1993. As a result of this decision, the Japanese company slowed down its technical development and McLaren personnel were left to smile bravely, taking responsibility for disappointing performances in an effort to be politically tactful.

Over at Ferrari, meanwhile, Jean Alesi had yet to win his first race. It would be a long haul for the talented Frenchman, who had first come to prominence with Tyrrell in 1989 and then stunned the world with two storming second places to Senna's McLaren in the 1990 Phoenix and Monaco Grands Prix. After being tutored by his friend Prost in 1991, Alesi found himself forced into the Ferrari team leadership the following year and, partnered by Ivan Capelli, was unable to produce much in the way of hard results.

In the next race following Mansell's 1992 title clincher there was an almost symbolic endorsement of F1's new

order when Michael Schumacher returned to Spa-Francorchamps on the first anniversary of his debut outing in the Jordan. With the Benetton B192-Ford he now took his maiden victory in treacherously wet/dry conditions, winning by nearly 40 seconds from Mansell's Williams-Renault.

Mansell by this stage was a very rich man. In 1991 he had earned a reputed £4.6 million and he stayed on to win the title the following year for a slightly increased £5 million fee. For 1993, Williams's connections with Elf and Renault steered the team towards signing Alain Prost – who had sat out the '92 season – as Riccardo Patrese's replacement.

For his part, Mansell had serious doubts over whether this would work, feeling apprehensive about being paired with Prost after his experience at Ferrari in 1990. But a fee of £937,000 was agreed as additional compensation for his having to relinquish his absolute number one status. It looked as though a deal had been struck.

If Mansell had been able to sign the Williams deal early, all would have been well. However, Elf, whose profits had fallen by 23 per cent during the first six months of 1992, then had second thoughts about how much it wanted to spend on F1. Williams offered Mansell a substantially lower figure. He refused.

The matter came to a head at the 1992 Italian Grand Prix, where Nigel convened a press conference announcing that he would be quitting F1 at the end of the season. A last-minute intervention by a Williams emissary, who arrived with word from Frank that a deal could be reached, came too late. Mansell was already midway through his statement. The partnership had now passed beyond the point of no return.

NIGEL MANSELL: BRITAIN'S MOST SUCCESSFUL F1 DRIVER

BY THE TIME Nigel Mansell retired from racing, he was the most successful British Grand Prix driver ever with a total of 31 career victories, a record which places him fourth in the all-time winners' stakes behind Alain Prost, the late Ayrton Senna and Michael Schumacher.

Mansell fought his way up to Formula 1 with the same blend of absolute commitment and physical pugnacity he applied to the business of driving a racing car. Having cut his teeth in karting and established himself as a proven winner in Formula Ford, Mansell eventually got his F1 break when he was invited to test a Lotus 79 in the summer of 1979.

Colin Chapman was deeply impressed with the brash young man's tenacity and determination and gave him his F1 chance in the 1980 Austrian Grand Prix. It was typical of Mansell that he drove much of the race in acute discomfort from petrol burns caused by a fuel cell leaking its contents into the cockpit. He would not give up until the engine had expired.

Mansell was signed up as a regular Team Lotus driver alongside Elio de Angelis in 1981, but while Chapman's faith in his ability never wavered Nigel found himself robbed of a close friend and mentor when the Lotus founder died from a sudden heart attack in December 1982.

He remained with Lotus through to the end of 1984 but real success did not come his way until he moved to Williams the following year. He scored his first victory in the Grand Prix of Europe at Brands Hatch with the Williams FW10-Honda, after which the wins came cascading in his direction.

Another nine seasons would pass before Mansell, who had won the 1992 World Championship in a Williams FW14B-Renault, posted his final GP victory at the wheel of a Williams FW16 at Adelaide. In 1989 and '90 he had interrupted his stormy romance with Williams by spending two seasons driving for the Ferrari squad, during which the Italian fans nicknamed him 'Il Leone'.

Mansell was braver than Dick Tracy, more accident prone than John Prescott and more confrontational than Mike Tyson. Yet he seldom gave less than 100 per cent effort when he was behind the wheel and his presence would always guarantee a hysterical capacity crowd at Silverstone for the British Grand Prix.

Williams Technical Director Patrick Head recounts an anecdote which puts Mansell's character into context. 'I remember Nigel's race at Montreal in 1986,' he said.

'I told him to turn his boost down from 3.6 to 3.5, or whatever. He was in the lead, but needed to save fuel, so I got on the radio and said, "Change the boost to 3.5."

'There was a long silence, then he

Paul-Henri Cahier

came on the radio saying, "I don't want to turn the boost down, I'll be beaten."

'So I had to say to him, "Turn your effing boost down." There was no reaction and I got even angrier. "Turn your effing boost down and do what you're told!"

'So he did and the lap time went a second slower. But he was determined to show he was better than the situation. So the next lap he made up half a second and then another half-second on the

following lap, so that he was back doing the same times as before but with less turbo boost.

'Once he had the time back down, the radio clicked on. "Today's the day the teddy bears have their picnic" came over the airwaves. Nigel was singing "Teddy Bears' Picnic" while going round the circuit as he broke the lap record, lap after lap.

'He was just making the point that we were not going to screw him that way.'

'Il Leone'. Mansell with his wife, Rosanne, and two of their children during his two-year stint with Ferrari.

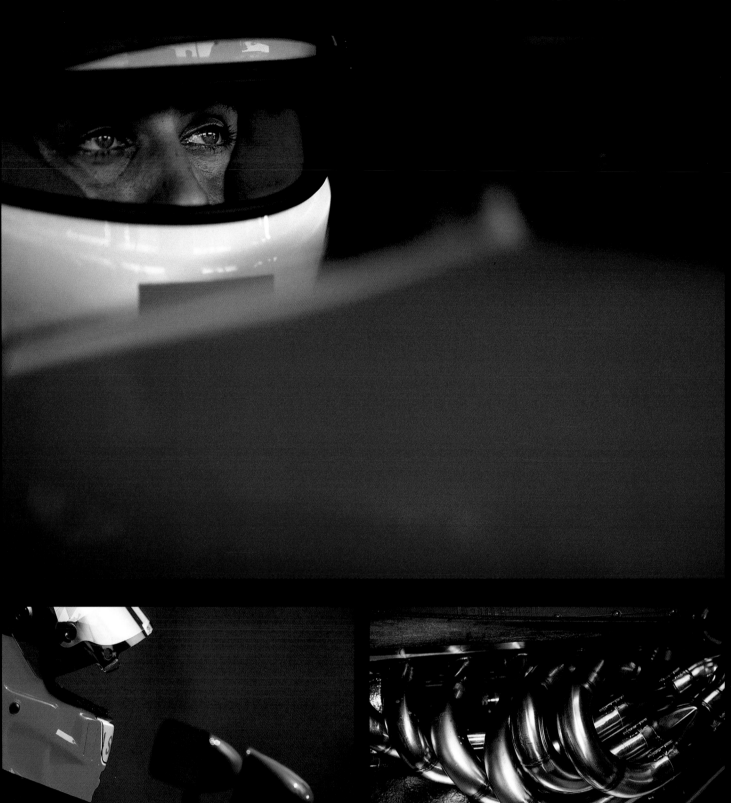
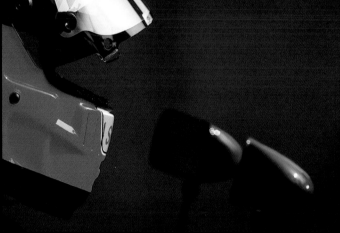

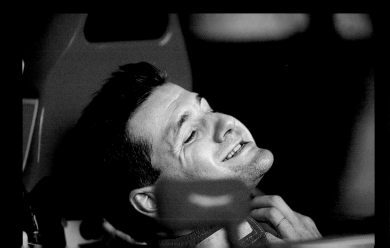

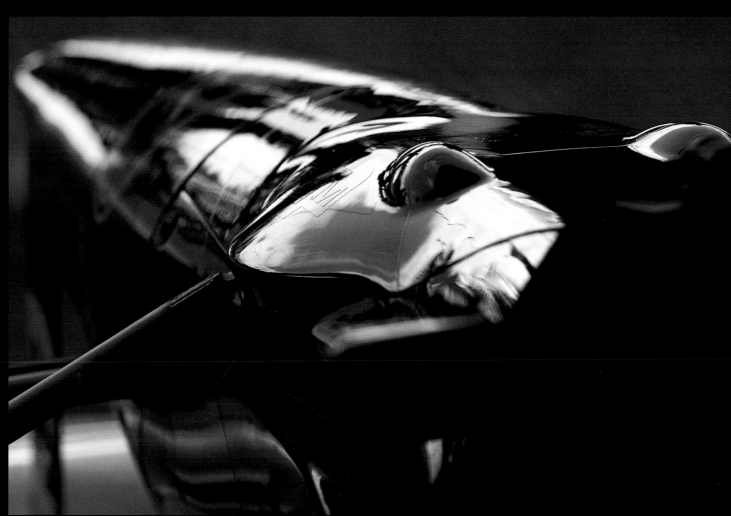

1992

April: Benny Hill, British comedian, dies.

August: The new Premier League is launched, replacing the First Division as the top football league in England.

November: The Democratic candidate, Bill Clinton, is elected President of the United States.

1993

February: Bobby Moore, England's captain in the 1966 World Cup final, dies.

February: At least seven people are killed when a bomb explodes in a car park underneath the World Trade Centre in New York.

April: The Grand National steeplechase, at Aintree racecourse in Liverpool, is abandoned after two false starts.

November: Schoolboys Robert Thompson and Jon Venables are convicted of the murder of two-year-old James Bulger, in Liverpool.

McLAREN FORCED TO TURN TO FORD

At the end of the 1992 season McLaren duly relinquished its partnership with Honda and had to cast around for an alternative source of engine supply.

While this task was not the work of a moment, Ron Dennis duly secured a supply of Renault engines by the expedient of agreeing to purchase the Ligier team, the idea being then to switch its powerful French V10s to the McLarens and find Ligier some new engines to use.

However, although Dennis obtained the agreement of Renault that they would run the engines on Shell fuel and lubricants for at least one season (an important consideration since Shell had been a major McLaren sponsor for many years), the idea was vetoed by Elf – Renault's long-established fuel partner – and that was that.

Instead, McLaren opted to become a customer for the Cosworth Ford HB V8 at a reputed cost of £6 million, an investment which would be supplemented by technical input from TAG Electronic Systems, a McLaren associate company specialising in the development of sophisticated automotive electronic systems.

The Ford V8 was installed in the brand-new McLaren MP4/8 chassis, which may have been giving away 50 bhp to the Williams FW15C-Renault but with Senna's genius behind the wheel managed to squeeze out no fewer than five wins during the course of 1993. These included his breathtaking victory in the one-off Grand Prix of Europe at Donington Park on Easter Monday where, in torrential rain, he saw off the Williams duo of Damon Hill and Prost to score what many people regarded as the best win of his career.

Yet Senna was not an easy man to live with in 1993. He was alternately frustrated and embittered that McLaren could not get its hands on the latest-specifica-

Paul-Henri Cahier

tion Ford HB engines, which were reserved for the rival Benetton squad as a central plank of its factory deal. Senna had also demanded a fee of $1 million per race and initially agreed to compete only on a race-by-race basis. In a classic piece of brinkmanship, he was partying in a São Paulo discothèque on the eve of first practice for the San Marino Grand Prix.

Only the overnight Alitalia flight to Rome, a private jet to Bologna, a helicopter to Imola and a motor cycle pillion ride eventually got him to the paddock minutes before the first timed session. Earlier, Ayrton had kept everybody guessing by testing a Penske Indy car in North America before deciding to remain in F1. If it frayed Ron Dennis's nerves, the McLaren boss never showed his frustration.

Prost, meanwhile, was having a frustrating time in his role as Williams team leader, but for different reasons. He had returned to the F1 firmament after his season

out of the cockpit in 1992 only to find himself propelled headlong into a confrontation with FISA President Max Mosley, who, in a dramatic change of roles, had replaced Jean-Marie Balestre in 1991.

They clashed over FISA's efforts to change the rules to make F1 more interesting. For 1993 the cars were slightly narrower (down from 215 to 200 cm) and rear wheel rim widths were reduced from 18 to 15 in., but during the course of the season it was decided that the costly computer-controlled driver aids would be stripped from the cars for 1994.

This obviously provoked squeals of indignation from teams such as Williams and McLaren, which had made great technical progress in these areas. In addition, the 1993 season also saw a prohibition of the use of the spare car in practice and qualifying and the introduction of limits on the number of laps permitted on both practice days.

On the face of it, these changes might have been

Ayrton Senna's McLaren about to overtake Alain Prost's Williams at the end of the opening lap of the 1993 European Grand Prix at Donington Park. Ayrton thereafter drove away into the distance to score what many regard as his finest victory.

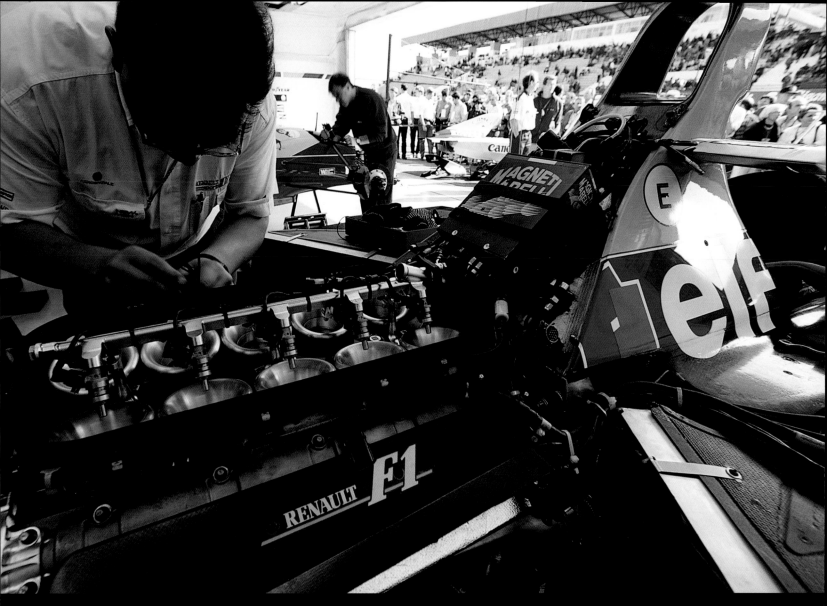

Above: An engineer at work on the dominant Renault V10.

Right: Prost's Williams FW15C is obscured by a rain-cover.

Below: Piping everywhere in the era of active suspension.

Far right: Frank Williams may have been confined to a wheelchair, but his passion for F1 remained undimmed.

made with a view to saving money, but there was certainly one man in the field who cursed them from the outset. This was Indy car star Michael Andretti, who had been recruited to drive the second McLaren alongside Senna. He never got into the swing of the Grand Prix business and was replaced by Mika Häkkinen, the team's young test driver, with three races of the year remaining.

Prost won seven of the first ten races and clinched the 1993 World Championship by taking second place to Schumacher's Benetton in the Portuguese Grand Prix at Estoril, where he had earlier announced he would be retiring for good at the end of the season. Senna went on to win the final two races of the year at Suzuka and Adelaide, thereby consolidating his second place in the championship on 73 points – 26 behind Prost's total.

Although Prost may have ended his F1 career feeling a little unwanted within the wider political situation surrounding Williams and Senna, Patrick Head remembers the Frenchman as one of the most outstanding performers in terms of mechanical sympathy.

'You could see with Alain that he was more concerned with looking after his tyres, rather than deliberately thinking about the fuel load,' he said, recalling the turbo era and its fuel-restriction rules.

'He would drive a quite conservative race for the first ten to twenty laps or so, because he did not see the point of using mega amounts of boost while he had 240 litres of fuel on board. If he really gave it the big power he would destroy the tyres.'

'When we were running Keke Rosberg and he was roaring off into the lead we would think, "No problem," when we checked that Prost was down around 15th place. But then the quick laps would start to come in from Prost and he would be on you like a rash, while Keke's tyres were going off. Prost's attitude was that he did not want to use a lot of fuel while he had to take it easy on the tyres. He would save the power and fuel until later.'

The second Williams was driven by the team's former test driver, Damon Hill, who had been promoted to fill the void created by Mansell's departure. The son of the late Graham Hill, Damon was as focused and single-minded as his father and had carried out excellent test and development work for the team over two seasons.

Hill got the job after Frank Williams had dithered for a while, first offering a deal to Häkkinen, then talking to Martin Brundle before deciding on a modest £200,000 retainer for Hill. Frank can be a shrewd negotiator, but after Damon had won the Hungarian, Belgian and Italian Grands Prix for the team it must have looked like the bargain of the age.

For the 1994 season, Senna decided to switch to Williams while McLaren, who clinched a deal to use the new Peugeot V10 F1 engine, relied on Häkkinen and Brundle. Ferrari would retain its established pairing of Gerhard Berger and Jean Alesi while Benetton and Ford braced themselves for a major push forward with Michael Schumacher.

Below: Former test driver Damon Hill and multiple World Champion Alain Prost enjoyed a splendid working relationship at Williams in 1993.

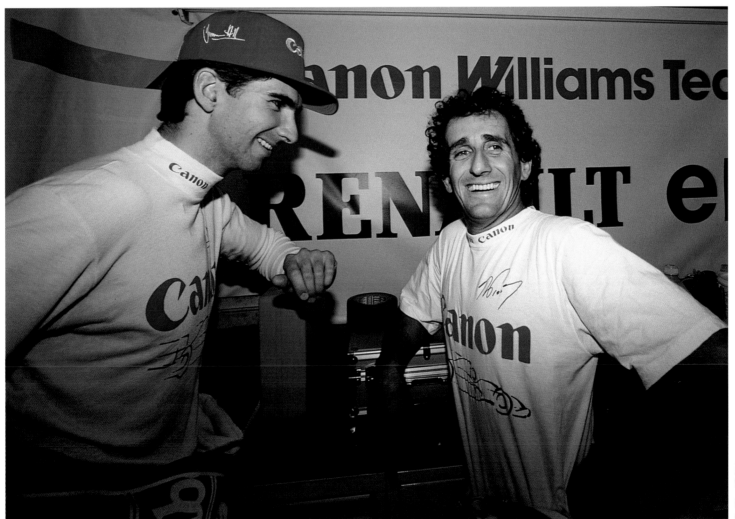

Paul-Henri Cahier

Below: Ayrton Senna on the grid at Imola before the start of the ill-fated 1994 San Marino Grand Prix.

Opposite, top: Senna starts his fateful last lap at Imola chased by Schumacher. He is seemingly on course to run over debris from Lehto's Benetton left on the track from the earlier startline shunt. This was later touted as a possible cause of the ensuing tragedy, although the subsequent investigation discounted this theory.

Opposite: In the aftermath of the tragedy modifications were made to a number of circuits including the emasculation of Spa's daunting Eau Rouge. Pole-position starter Rubens Barrichello in the Jordan is chased by Schumacher's Benetton and Alesi's Ferrari.

DOUBLE DISASTER AT IMOLA

Ayrton Senna struggled for the first two races of 1994 with the new Williams FW16, spinning off in front of his home crowd at Interlagos and then tangling with Mika Häkkinen's McLaren-Peugeot on the first corner of the Pacific Grand Prix at Japan's TI-Aida circuit.

In-race refuelling was part of the revised technical challenge facing the F1 teams from the start of the '94 season but, although Ayrton found himself slightly wrong-footed by the winning pace of Michael Schumacher's new Ford Zetec-R V8-engined Benetton B194 in those first two races, improvements to the Williams made him more confident about his prospects for the San Marino Grand Prix at Imola.

Yet this was to be the bleakest weekend F1 had known since the 1960 Belgian Grand Prix claimed the lives of British drivers Chris Bristow and Alan Stacey. During Saturday qualifying Austrian novice Roland Ratzenberger was killed when his Simtek-Ford crashed at 190 mph on the approach to the Tosa hairpin after the nose section of his car, loosened in an earlier off-track excursion, flew off at a crucial moment.

The 31-year-old from Salzburg was the first driver to be killed in an F1 car since the Italian, Elio de Angelis, died testing at Paul Ricard at the wheel of a Brabham BT55-BMW during the summer of 1986. Senna, in particular, felt deeply moved by the whole episode and discussed the possibility of not racing with the FIA Medical Delegate, the respected neuro-surgeon, Professor Sid Watkins.

On race day it seemed as though everything was coming unstitched. J.J. Lehto's Benetton stalled on the grid and was rammed from behind by Pedro Lamy's Lotus, scattering wreckage all over the start/finish line. Debris also flew into the grandstand and injured several spectators, thankfully none seriously.

The safety car – a new F1 development which mimicked the Indy car racing 'pace car' concept – was deployed to slow the field and to give the marshals a chance to clear up the mess. For three laps the field was kept down to cruising speed and the safety car then pulled off as Senna led the pack round to complete its fifth lap of the afternoon.

Despite his car bottoming out dramatically in a shower of sparks on the fast Tamburello left-hander after the pits,

Senna held on to lead from Schumacher by 0.6s at the end of lap six. Going into lap seven, the Brazilian's Williams FW16 suddenly twitched dramatically and slammed off the track into the retaining wall at Tamburello. The race was red-flagged to a halt while Senna was removed by helicopter to hospital in Bologna, where he died from massive head injuries a few hours later.

It was a shattering blow to the F1 community, but life had to go on and the restarted race was won by Schumacher's Benetton from Nicola Larini's Ferrari – the Italian subbing for the injured Jean Alesi – and Häkkinen's McLaren.

THE AFTERMATH OF THE ACCIDENT

The implications of the Senna accident were a matter of acute concern for the F1 community. But it would be two and a half years before the long-awaited trial of Frank Williams and five others on charges of 'culpable homicide' eventually took place in Bologna.

Williams himself and his co-defendants, Patrick Head, Williams Chief Designer Adrian Newey, FIA Race Director Roland Brunseyraede and Imola track officials Federico Bendenelli and Giorgio Poggi, were not present. Nor did the law require them to be so.

Yet it was clear that the prosecution seemed set on pressing home its contention that badly welded alterations to the steering column on Senna's Williams caused a pre-impact failure which sent car and driver into the retaining wall of the flat-out Tamburello left-hander at 193 mph.

The indications were that investigating magistrate Maurizio Passarini lent no credence to photographic evidence, published in the previous week's Sunday Times, showing Senna about to run over debris on the circuit.

However, there was evidence to consider that Senna may have pressed too hard on cold tyres after several laps running at much-reduced speed behind the safety car while debris from the startline collision was removed from the straight in front of the pits.

Senna had come to Imola vowing that 'the World Championship starts here', and was known to be suspicious that there was something not quite right about his key rival Schumacher's Benetton. It was subsequently established that this car had an illegal electronic 'launch control' system contained within its electronic software systems, but the FIA later accepted that it had not been used.

The implication was that Ayrton might have over-driven in the heat of the moment, his determination to get the better of Schumacher causing him to press too hard before his tyres were up to temperature. In this configuration, his car might have been particularly nervous to drive over the bumps on the Tamburello corner and this could have contributed to a rare error.

Interestingly, safety car driver Max Angelelli admitted that he was very worried that the breathless Opel used for the job was not quick enough. He said a Porsche Carrera RSR would have been more appropriate, and recalls Senna pulling level with him, beckoning him to speed up. 'I could see from his eyes that he was very angry,' said Angelelli.

More than another year would pass before the defendants were finally acquitted, but the controversy lingered on even as late as 1999 when rumours circulated that the prosecuting magistrate was considering lodging an appeal for a re-trial.

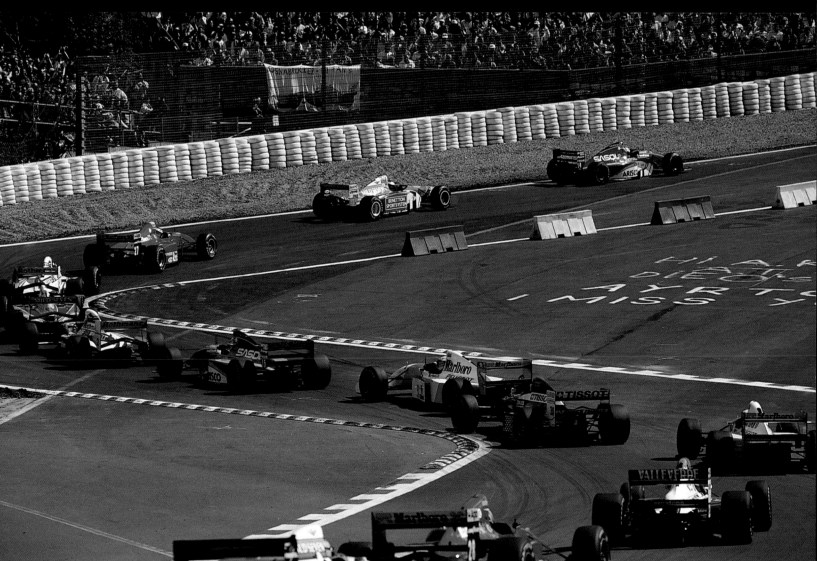

EXPERIENCE BREEDS EXCELLENCE

For more than half a century, AP Racing has been a world leader in competition components.

It is no coincidence that every Formula One championship since 1967 has been won using our equipment.

In every branch of motor sport, from Champcars to Club Rallying, in more than 100 countries around the world, you'll find AP Racing behind the winning teams.

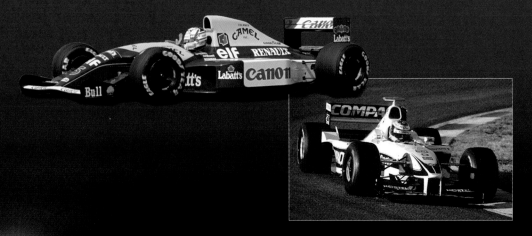

ap RACING

the SCIENCE of FRICTION

AP Racing, Wheler Road, Coventry, CV3 4LB, England. Tel +44 (0)24 7663 9595 Fax +44 (0)24 7663 9559
website: www.apracing.com   email: sales@apracing.co.uk

THE SCHUMACHER YEARS

AS THE DUST settled in the aftermath of Ayrton Senna's fatal accident and the sport began to grapple with its long-term consequences, one thing quickly became very clear. The baton had now passed to Michael Schumacher as the leading exponent of the F1 technique. Just as Jim Clark had taken over from Stirling Moss and Jackie Stewart had eventually inherited the mantle of his fellow-Scot, so Schumacher set the pace in 1994 and '95 at the wheel of his Benetton.

The start of the '94 season had seen Ford back Benetton's factory effort with the all-new 65-degree Zetec-R V8, which owed nothing in terms of shared parts to its immediate predecessor. It certainly benefited greatly, however, from the technical lessons learned from a shelved Ford V12 F1 programme, particularly in the areas of heat rejection, crankshaft configuration and the use of ceramics in the cylinder head design.

Sharing Cosworth's optimism was the Benetton design staff headed by Ross Brawn, Rory Byrne and Pat Symonds, whose new B194 chassis was a logical development of the previous year's machine which had won the '93 Portuguese GP.

Senna's death triggered an immediate programme of rule changes from the FIA, which had absorbed FISA, its sporting arm, the previous year, with Max Mosley becoming President of the parent organisation. Truncated diffusers and shortened front wing endplates were required with effect from the Spanish Grand Prix, and a reduction in engine size from 3.5 to 3 litres from the start of 1995 was also announced.

Over at Williams, Damon Hill found himself forced to shoulder the team leadership after the Brazilian's death, a task which he performed with admirable resilience. Hill won in Spain but it was clear that Williams's engine partner,

Below: Michael Schumacher applies a touch of opposite lock to the Ford Zetec-R V8-engined Benetton B194 which he drove to a controversial World Championship title in 1994.

Opposite: Damon Hill earned many admirers with the brave and dignified way he shouldered the burden of leading the Williams team following the death of Ayrton Senna.

Opposite, bottom: Test driver David Coulthard was brought in to partner Hill and immediately impressed with his mature and confident approach.

Below: FIA President Max Mosley introduced immediate safety changes in the wake of the fatal accidents to Senna and Ratzenberger.

Renault, felt it could give only qualified support for his new status as team leader. They pressured Williams to re-hire Nigel Mansell, who, having won the 1993 Indy car championship with a Newman/Haas team Lola-Ford, was now having a much less happy time in his second season in the US-based series.

Mansell was duly paid £900,000 for a one-off drive in the French Grand Prix and also secured agreement for a £2 million compensation fee if Williams did not wish to take up his services and confirm a £7 million deal for 1995. Mansell drove in a total of four races for Williams in 1994, ending the season with a comfortable victory in Australia.

When Mansell was not available, Hill was now partnered by the young Scot, David Coulthard, a Formula 3000 graduate who gained promotion from the role of test driver.

Schumacher began a run of domination which was dramatically frustrated by a major confrontation with the authorities following events at the British Grand Prix at Silverstone. On the final parade lap, Schumacher breached the rules by overtaking Hill's Williams. After a considerable delay, the German driver was shown a black flag together with his race number, indicating that he had been given a stop–go penalty for this transgression, but he enraged the governing body by staying out on the circuit while Benetton directors Flavio Briatore and Tom Walkinshaw argued at length with the stewards.

Michael eventually pulled into the pits to serve his penalty and finished the race in second place behind Hill, with Benetton incurring a fine of $25,000. However, at a

Hockenheim produced another problem for Benetton with the team's second driver, Jos Verstappen, lucky to escape all but uninjured after a refuelling conflagration during a routine pit stop. Schumacher retired with engine problems, allowing Gerhard Berger's Ferrari an easy win, but the Benetton ace bounced back in Hungary, beating Hill's Williams with an audacious three-stop strategy to the Englishman's two stops.

Benetton was fortunate to escape from the Hockenheim fuel fire without an additional penalty; the fuel rig used for Verstappen's car had a filter missing, illegally speeding up its flow rate. There were some ambiguities, however, which prevented the team from facing further sanction, but Michael's two-race suspension was upheld and he duly missed the Italian and Portuguese Grands Prix – having previously been disqualified from first place in Belgium after excessive wear was detected in the B194's under-car skid block when it was checked after the race.

Hill won all three of those races to vault into contention for the World Championship, although in reality this was a somewhat artificial situation in the sense that the various transgressions committed by Schumacher and his team had cost the German driver the chance of winning another 40 championship points from four races, when the Silverstone disqualification was added to the other setbacks.

Michael returned to the fray at Jerez, where he won the European Grand Prix, but was beaten into second place by Hill in the rain-soaked Japanese Grand Prix at Suzuka three weeks later. Schumacher then rounded off the season by clinching the 1994 World Championship in intensely controversial fashion by apparently ramming Hill out of the Australian Grand Prix in Adelaide.

Whether Schumacher made an innocent error, or took a pragmatic decision to take Hill out after he himself had inflicted potentially terminal damage on his Benetton by side-swiping a wall, has never been satisfactorily resolved. Suffice it to say that the 1994 season was one which the F1 fraternity was happy to put behind it.

It was not simply that Senna, one of the sport's greatest-ever exponents, had died in such tragic circumstances. The controversy surrounding the various Benetton issues had also contributed to an uncomfortable climate of suspicion which F1 found difficult to purge from its image.

The 1994 season also saw new Sporting Director Jean Todt getting into his stride at Ferrari, even though Berger's win at Hockenheim was as far as any Maranello revival went. At the opposite end of the scale, Lotus, whose fortunes had been administered by the tenacious and committed former Benetton team manager, Peter Collins, ever since 1991, finally dropped from the F1 stage for good after being overwhelmed by financial problems.

Thus ended a strand of F1 continuity which had endured ever since Graham Hill and Cliff Allison gave the Lotus 12s their debut at Monaco 36 years earlier.

Over at McLaren, the Peugeot V10s proved hideously unreliable, consuming fuel and lubricants in pretty well equal measure. Martin Brundle stormed home second to Schumacher at Monaco, leaving team owner Ron Dennis to make his memorable observation that 'second is just the first of the losers' when he found the Peugeot lads celebrating after the race.

It was an undeniably harsh judgement, but correct. The

special meeting of the FIA World Motor Sports Council he was subsequently disqualified from the results while Benetton's fine was increased to $500,000 as a punishment for their failure to obey the instructions of race officials. In addition, Schumacher was given a two-race ban, although the team lodged an appeal which at least allowed him to race in the German Grand Prix at Hockenheim a few days later.

Right: The start of something big. Mercedes-Benz joined forces with McLaren in 1995 but the partnership would go through a couple of difficult seasons before beginning to realise its huge potential in '97.

Below: Variants of the reliable, powerful and extremely driveable Renault V10 sat behind the World Champion driver in 1992, '93, '95, '96 and '97.

Photos: Paul-Henri Cahier

McLaren-Peugeot relationship was going nowhere. Similarly, Mercedes-Benz was becoming increasingly frustrated by its relationship with the Swiss Sauber team.

Eventually Mercedes motor sport manager Norbert Haug brokered a deal with Dennis to switch the German V10 engines to McLaren for 1995. As part of the deal, Dennis also arranged for Peugeot to move its engines to the Jordan team, replacing the promising Brian Hart V10s which they had used for the previous two seasons.

When Mercedes-Benz set out to dominate F1 racing in the 1990s, they turned to British technology to propel them to the top of the victory rostrum. Instead of building their own engines, the famous German car maker bought a stake in Ilmor Engineering, the specialist race engine builder established by Mario Illien and his partner, Paul Morgan, back in 1983.

Illien is a formal, reserved Swiss with a burning passion for racing engines. 'I always wanted to be involved with engines since I was a kid,' he said. 'It is, if you like, a childlike passion which has never left me. But the nature of this business, with all its pressures, is such that you simply have to be passionate about it. Otherwise you quite simply can't put in the hours which it requires.'

In 1979 Illien joined Cosworth, the makers of Ford's F1 engines, where he duly met Morgan. In 1983 they decided to go it alone in an audacious move to beat their former employers at their own game.

'When we left Cosworth, we considered carefully which racing category to tackle and concluded that taking on Cosworth's monopoly in US Indy car racing would make most sense,' said Illien.

With backing from legendary Indy car team owner Roger Penske, General Motors and, subsequently, Mercedes-Benz, Ilmor became firmly established as a leading race engine builder. Eventually, under the Mercedes banner, they made a concerted assault on Formula 1 with the Sauber team in 1994. But it soon became clear that Sauber was unlikely to develop into a fully competitive prospect.

RENAULT GOES WITH BENETTON

For the 1995 season Renault agreed to expand the supply of its works engines to include Benetton. Frank Williams and his colleagues were not happy about this, but knuckled down to concentrate on developing their new FW17 to the point where it was more competitive than the Benetton B195. On balance, the FW17 would end up with the performance edge. But Hill found himself increasingly outclassed by Schumacher.

For Damon, the off-season had been a time to sit and consider what was required to beat the German. You could tell that Hill was still smarting over the way in which the 1994 World Championship had been resolved, but he knew only too well that Schumacher regarded F1 racing as much as a mind game as anything else. So not only did Damon have to keep control on the track, capitalising on the Williams FW17's performance advantage for as long as possible while Benetton played catch-up, but he also had to avoid becoming embroiled in any psychological battle with his great rival.

In qualifying for the first Grand Prix of the season at Interlagos, Hill pipped Schumacher for pole, but the Williams and Benetton efforts in that event were thwarted by a discrepancy in their Elf fuel specifications. Schumacher led the race initially, but Hill vaulted ahead at the first refuelling stops, thereafter pulling away before spinning to a halt with broken rear suspension.

That left Schumacher an easy run to victory from Coulthard, the Scot having been signed for the high-profile Williams drive alongside Hill in preference to the high-priced Mansell, after which both were excluded – as expected – for the apparent fuel discrepancy. Both teams naturally appealed and the FIA International Court of Appeal duly reinstated them in the results, accepting that there were valid differences of opinion over whether or not the fuel discrepancy offered any performance benefit, although Benetton and Williams

Damon Hill and Benetton team chief Flavio Briatore stand drenched in champagne after the 1995 Monaco Grand Prix, in which the British driver finished second to Michael Schumacher (seen in the background).

1994
May: The Channel Tunnel is officially opened, linking Britain and France.
May: John Smith, leader of the British Labour Party, dies.
July: A Colombian footballer, Andres Escobar, is shot dead on returning home after his own-goal eliminated his country from the World Cup finals in the USA.

1995
January: Manchester United footballer Eric Cantona of France is disgraced when he launches a 'kung-fu' kick at a fan in the crowd after being sent off.
April: Dozens of people are killed when a government building in Oklahoma City is ripped apart by a huge bomb blast.
July: British athlete Jonathan Edwards sets a new triple jump world record of 17.98 metres.

Left: Jean Alesi took his only F1 win to date at the wheel of the Ferrari 412T2 in Montreal, 1995.

Below far left: Despite two wins, Johnny Herbert's '95 season at Benetton was not a particularly happy one.

Below left: Occasionally brilliant, frequently exasperating, Alesi failed to do justice to his great natural talent during his five turbulent seasons at Ferrari.

Bottom: The Hockenheim paddock at night: a private, exclusive world of mystery and excitement.

Opposite, top: Johnny Herbert scored an immensely popular win in the 1995 British Grand Prix after a controversial collision between his Benetton team-mate, Michael Schumacher, and Damon Hill.

Opposite: Schumacher underlined his status as the outstanding driver of his generation with a well-judged victory in the '95 Monaco Grand Prix in the Benetton-Renault.

Photos: Paul-Henri Cahier

279

Opposite: Damon Hill celebrates his richly deserved World Championship win with his old rival, Michael Schumacher, the second-placed finisher, on the podium at Suzuka, 1996.

Opposite, bottom: Damon had clinched the title in the best way possible, rounding off his Williams career with a dominant lights-to-flag victory.

were not allowed their Constructors' Championship points for first and second places.

Hill would then surge on to score wins in both the Argentine and San Marino Grands Prix, after which his title challenge progressively fell apart. Most notable among his slips were collisions with Schumacher's Benetton which eliminated the two contenders from the British and Italian Grands Prix, Benetton number two Johnny Herbert ducking through to take victory on both occasions.

Hill admittedly scored a good win in Hungary, which he optimistically described as a 'payback race', but it did not signal a major shift in his fortunes. In fact, as Schumacher stormed on to clinch his second World Championship Hill floundered increasingly, culminating in a truly awful performance at Suzuka for the Japanese Grand Prix, where he seemed to be spinning in all directions.

It was certainly a frustrating period for both Frank Williams and Patrick Head, neither of whom had ever been inclined to take a sympathetic stance towards any psychological problems experienced by their drivers. By mid-season they had already decided that Coulthard wasn't quite the ticket after his failure to beat Schumacher's Benetton in the German Grand Prix at Hockenheim, where Hill spun off at the start of the second lap.

The pleasant Scot, who had been grappling with tonsillitis for much of the season, would be replaced by that year's Indy car champion and Indy 500 winner, Jacques Villeneuve, the son of the famous Ferrari ace who had been killed at Zolder in 1982. Hill, who had signed his 1996 contract in August '95, was safe for one more year with the Williams team, but at Suzuka Williams and Head vowed to replace him at the end of the following season with German rising star Heinz-Harald Frentzen, who had made his F1 debut with Sauber in 1994.

It is difficult to understand why they needed to take that decision so early in the day. Hill dug deep into his personal resources and then stormed back into contention with a fine win in the '95 Australian Grand Prix in Adelaide, the final race of the season. It would set the scene for his performances in 1996.

MANSELL'S McLAREN INTERLUDE

In the McLaren camp, there had been pressure from Marlboro, the team's title sponsor, to secure the services of a top-line driver for the first year of the Mercedes partnership in 1995.

The only front-rank performer available was Nigel Mansell and the alliance turned out to be a fiasco. Some years before, Ron Dennis had offered the view that Mansell was the one driver he really would not want to have at McLaren, but now force of circumstance had thrown them together.

The 41-year-old veteran's taste for F1 success had been reawakened by those outings for Williams in 1994, but now he found that the new McLaren MP4/10-Mercedes was simply not up to scratch. Its engine had abrupt throttle response and power delivery, qualities which aggravated the poor balance of the chassis.

As if this wasn't enough, McLaren also had to expend many man-hours designing and building an enlarged monocoque to accommodate the British driver. Eventually Mansell drove only in the San Marino and Spanish Grands Prix, touring into the pits after a difficult

time wrestling with the car in the latter event before apparently throwing in the towel.

Before the next race of the season in Monaco, Dennis and Mansell agreed to dissolve their partnership. The disentangling of their contractual relations was at least conducted with a professional formality which impressed Dennis, even though he was happy to be released from the pressure created by such a demanding driver at a time when McLaren's product did not match up to Mansell's ambitions.

McLaren saw out 1995 with Mark Blundell partnering Mika Häkkinen and the team made steady progress with Mercedes, although the final race, the Australian Grand Prix in Adelaide, was blighted by a terrible practice accident in which Mika sustained quite serious head injuries. After some doubt as to how well he might recover, the Finn happily returned to robust health in time for the start of the 1996 season.

HILL WINS THE 1996 WORLD CHAMPIONSHIP

Damon Hill's remarkable resolve paid off in 1996. He began the year with victory in the Australian Grand Prix – now the opening race, and held in Melbourne – and fended off a season-long challenge from his increasingly confident new team-mate, Jacques Villeneuve, to take the World Championship.

With the Canadian moving in at Williams, Coulthard duly took up a pre-arranged vacancy in the McLaren-Mercedes squad, replacing fellow-Briton Mark Blundell, himself an ex-Williams test driver. Meanwhile Villeneuve was to enjoy more than 10,000 kilometres of pre-season testing with his new team. Seldom, if ever, had there been a better-prepared F1 newcomer.

Villeneuve would win four races during his maiden season. An irreverent non-comformist, he brought a refreshingly open-minded approach to F1. He was a racer through and through, cowed by none of his rivals, and a man who firmly believed that one racing car was pretty much like another, whether F1, Indy car or whatever.

He scored his first F1 victory in only the fourth race of the season, winning the European Grand Prix at the new Nürburgring in a split-second finish ahead of Michael Schumacher, the German twice World Champion having switched from Benetton to Ferrari. Quite clearly, Hill now faced his most dangerous opposition from within the ranks of his own team.

Hill had started the season noting that every driver since 1990 who had won the opening race had gone on to take that year's World Championship. 'It is a tradition I intend to continue,' he said after scoring a rather fortuitous victory in the first race of the season after Villeneuve had been slowed by fluctuating oil pressure.

He was as good as his word, although if there was a tinge of disappointment attaching to his title bid it was probably when a rare Renault engine failure prevented him from winning the Monaco Grand Prix, an event in which his late father, Graham, had triumphed no fewer than six times.

The realisation that his contract would not be renewed, and that he was effectively being replaced by Frentzen – despite claims to the contrary – was quite a blow for Hill. But Damon shrugged aside the disappointment as best he could, sat back and relished his role as F1's first second-generation World Champion driver.

Right: One of the world's most eminent neuro-surgeons, Professor Sid Watkins has played a key role in the provision of ever-improving emergency facilities at circuits across the world over the past 20 years.

Below: Gerhard Berger, the easy-going Austrian who marked his last season in F1 with a fine win at Hockenheim, '97.

Bottom: Eyes on the prize: F1 new boy Jacques Villeneuve.

Photos: Paul-Henri Cahier

Left: Time for reflection. A member of the Jordan team makes the most of a quiet interlude during another hectic race weekend.

Below: Under interrogation. The news-hungry media lay siege to Damon Hill at Suzuka, '96.

Opposite: Jacques Villeneuve took the 1997 World Championship for Williams in only his second season in F1.

Opposite, bottom: Rubens Barrichello scored a sensational second place for the fledgling Stewart team in the rain at Monaco in '97.

1996

June: Playing on home soil, England reach the semi-finals of the Euro '96 football tournament, but lose to the eventual champions, Germany, on penalties.

July: 230 people are killed when a TWA jet explodes in mid-air near New York.

August: The Prince and Princess of Wales are divorced, less than three months after the Duke and Duchess of York.

1997

January: Tony Bullimore survives after spending five days trapped underneath his capsized boat while competing in a round-the-world yacht race.

May: The Labour Party sweeps to victory in the British general election, with Tony Blair becoming Prime Minister.

August: Diana, Princess of Wales, is killed in a car crash in a Paris underpass. Her companion, Dodi Fayed, and the chauffeur, Henri Paul, also die.

The 1997 season duly delivered more of the same, with Williams still decisively on top and clinching another Constructors' Championship. Jacques Villeneuve took the drivers' crown, while Michael Schumacher was left to repent at leisure the dubious piece of driving which beached his own title hopes in a Jerez gravel trap.

Technically Schumacher was the best driver, even though Villeneuve's talent developed apace during the course of the season. Michael's victorious performances in the rain at Monaco and Spa were absolutely from the top drawer. He also had luck on his side when he won in Canada and the assistance of a compliant team-mate at Suzuka, where Eddie Irvine balked the opposition while Michael made good his escape.

Of course, over at Williams no such preferential treatment was on the menu. Not that Villeneuve needed much help from Frentzen, even though the German newcomer produced a fine victory in the San Marino Grand Prix at Imola.

For his part, Hill was lured by a £5 million retainer into driving for the Arrows team – now under the control of Tom Walkinshaw – in 1997. With the team using Yamaha V10 engines, it was always going to be a long shot, but the prospect of running on Bridgestone tyres during the Japanese company's first season of F1 involvement looked like a reasonable gamble. In the event, Hill was unable to provide the motivation which Walkinshaw believed was the team's due from such a highly paid driver and, apart from a strong run to second place in Hungary, pretty well wasted his time.

Meanwhile, McLaren-Mercedes was busy assembling a serious World Championship challenge. In the autumn of 1996 Williams's highly respected Chief Designer, Adrian Newey, effectively suspended himself on full pay after indicating that he wanted to leave the team he had worked for since 1990.

Newey's reputation as one of the sport's top aerodynamicists had been confirmed by the succession of excellent Williams-Renault designs from 1992 through to 1996. He disagreed with Frank Williams and Patrick Head over the decision to ditch Damon Hill, but also wanted more influence in the company as a whole.

It might have been possible to salvage Newey's relationship with Williams had he been offered a shareholding in the company. Eventually, after protracted negotiations over the issue of an early termination of his contract, Newey joined the McLaren-Mercedes squad as Technical Director in the summer of 1997.

STEWART ARRIVES ON THE SCENE

After Benetton switched to Renault power at the end of 1994, Ford turned its attention to an alliance with the Swiss constructor, Sauber. This endured for two seasons, but even before the end of 1995 it was becoming doubtful whether Sauber would develop into a front-line team and plans were laid for a totally new F1 operation run by Jackie Stewart and his son, Paul.

This was finally confirmed at the start of 1996 and the first Stewart SF1-Ford, designed by Alan Jenkins and powered by the latest Ford Zetec-R V10 engine, took to the tracks the following year, driven by Rubens Barrichello and F3 graduate Jan Magnussen.

It proved to be a difficult first season for the fledgling F1 team, highlighted by a magnificent second place for

Barrichello in Monaco in the pouring rain. On too many other occasions the Ford V10 failed spectacularly and the sight of Stewart SF1s parked at the side of various circuits was a regular feature of Grand Prix racing in 1997.

By the end of the season, Ford's top brass freely admitted that they had become tired of being labelled half-hearted in their commitment to F1 and indicated their seriousness of purpose by unveiling a totally new Zetec-R V10 engine, built by their long-time partners, Cosworth Engineering.

If anything, 1998 was slightly worse than Stewart's maiden season, the team scoring a measly five points – one fewer than they had managed with Barrichello's second place in Monaco the previous year. In the middle of 1998 Magnussen was replaced by Jos Verstappen and there followed a major shake-up for 1999. Ford produced the excellent CR-1 V10, which immediately propelled the Stewart SF3 into the role of regular top-six contender, with Johnny Herbert scoring the team's first victory in the Grand Prix of Europe at the Nürburgring.

In the summer of 1999 the Stewarts sold the team to Ford for an estimated $95 million. Barely four months later, in one of the most audacious pieces of rebranding yet seen in motor racing's most senior category, its new owners announced at the Frankfurt Motor Show that the cars would race under the Jaguar Racing banner from the start of the 2000 season.

'Jaguar has a long and distinguished record in motor sport,' said Dr Wolfgang Reitzle, Chairman of Jaguar. 'We have won Le Mans seven times and we have twice been Sports Car World Champions. We have also won the Monte Carlo Rally as well as countless other events. The next logical move is F1.

'The move into F1 will undoubtedly benefit Jaguar technologically. It will also clearly promote a wider recognition of the Jaguar brand as we significantly expand our product range over the next few years.'

Ford – which had purchased Jaguar ten years earlier – also confirmed that Eddie Irvine, who at that point shared the lead at the head of the World Championship points table, would quit Ferrari to become number one driver from the start of 2000.

The emergence of Jaguar as an F1 contender was highly significant on two counts. Firstly, it revived the sporting pedigree of a company whose links with front-line motor sport stretch back to the immediate post-war years. Secondly, it served as another major endorsement of Grand Prix racing's commercial pulling power among the world's major car makers.

At a time when tobacco sponsorship in Grand Prix racing was being scaled down prior to a complete ban from 2006 onwards, Jaguar chose to go head-to-head with Mercedes, who had recently arranged an option to purchase a 40 per cent holding in McLaren, and BMW, the Williams team's engine supplier from the start of 2000, in a battle which could end with more major car makers owning many of the top Grand Prix teams.

Commented Neil Ressler, Ford Motor Company's Vice-President and Chief Technical Officer: 'The need to solve problems quickly breeds a nimble and innovative culture which we will be able to transfer to the road car development programmes. I regard the technology transfer as one of the biggest single benefits of Jaguar's decision to enter F1.'

Engines for the team would continue to be designed, developed and built by Cosworth Racing, which was

Below: Ferrari Sporting Director Jean Todt congratulates Michael Schumacher on his victory in the 1996 Belgian Grand Prix, the second of his three wins that season.

acquired by Ford in 1998. Trevor Crisp, Jaguar's Group Chief Engineer for Powertrain Engineering, was named to head up the F1 engine development programme.

FERRARI CLIMBS BACK INTO CONTENTION

As we have seen, at the end of 1995 Michael Schumacher confirmed that he would be leaving Benetton to join the Ferrari team the following season. Maranello was really getting its corporate shoulder behind Jean Todt's efforts to achieve an F1 revival and recruiting Schumacher was another key element in that rebuilding process.

Michael would be joined in the team by Ulsterman Eddie Irvine, who had spent the previous two seasons with the Jordan team, learning the ropes alongside Rubens Barrichello. By this stage John Barnard was back in charge of the engineering department at Ferrari, again being allowed to establish a UK-based design studio to carry out the crucial research and development programmes.

Schumacher found the new V10-powered Ferrari F310 promising, if not an unqualified success, from the start of

the 1996 season. 'We are pretty much on schedule,' he commented, 'and I really want to take the first two or three races more as testing [sessions] rather than go for race results.'

As things transpired, Michael retired from his first Ferrari race with brake problems. That left Irvine to come home third to wet the new Maranello baby's head on his first run for the Prancing Horse.

In the early races of the year the new F310 struggled. Transmission problems meant that the previous car's rear end had to be used for a couple of races and the atmosphere in the team was not helped when Ferrari President Luca di Montezemolo made some observations about the car which were construed as being critical of Barnard's efforts.

Montezemolo carefully reserved praise for the engine department, even though there was evidence that the new 3-litre V10 was still around 30 bhp down on the previous year's V12. 'It depends how you measure it,' observed Barnard. 'Whether you take the readings from the dynamometer or calculate what it's producing when it is installed in the car.'

Montezemolo added: 'Last year we took a very important decision to make a V10-cylinder engine. This was to have a better power unit not only from the viewpoint of performance, but also economy, heat dissipation and ease of installation.

'I think we have made good progress with this engine at a time when the engine in F1 is definitely important, but less than before. I think that is demonstrated [by the way] that Benetton and Williams, which both use the same engine, were almost two seconds apart in qualifying here at the Nürburgring.

'For 1996 we at Ferrari were also obliged to do a brand-new car. My approach is that I generally prefer an evolutionary approach, but with the switch to the V10-cylinder engine its dimensions were very different from the V12 and we were obliged to make a totally new car from a clean sheet.

'To be honest, I expected altogether a more competitive car, I will admit. But on the other hand, I know that it was necessary to pay a big price, particularly in the first half of the season, because we have everything new – even the fuel. The drivers, the chassis, the engine and the gearbox.

'We know that our engine is making very steady progress, but the first priority was to make the engine reliable. Now, after the first three races, we are involved in a deep investigation of the chassis in conjunction with John Barnard, because the interpretation of the rules for driver protection [introduced for 1996] theoretically leaves us with the possibility of having to think of a new chassis. But I sincerely hope not, both from financial and timing reasons. In the meantime we will concentrate on working on the car, which is obviously very late indeed.'

For his part, Barnard remarked: 'To be honest, I'm a bit fed up with this pantomime – and I'm looking forward to some serious Shakespearian theatre at some time in the future. It's the usual situation: we're [Ferrari Design & Development] here as a scapegoat and the moment something goes wrong they start popping off at us. I can only assume that there is tremendous pressure from Turin.'

Later that season Barnard would finally tire of what he regarded as the endless politicking of the Ferrari team. He left and his place was taken by former Benetton designers Ross Brawn and Rory Byrne, who, unlike their predecessor, were happy to relocate to Italy.

Left: Schumacher earned the devotion of the *tifosi* with a glorious victory for Ferrari at Monza in 1996.

Below: Schumacher's Ferrari F310B is no more than a red blur as the German negotiates the harbour front at Monaco in 1997 on his way to his third win in the street-circuit classic in four years.

MICHAEL SCHUMACHER: CHAMPION OF CHAMPIONS

IT IS A GRAPHIC reminder of the millions of pounds involved in contemporary Grand Prix motor racing that when Michael Schumacher traded up to a sleek Challenger private jet in 1998 his manager, Willi Weber, purchased the smaller used Cessna Citation plane which the Ferrari ace was discarding.

It is a story which raises the prospect of the F1 manager now being rich enough to need his own manager. Yet if Weber, a sleek-suited, immaculately coiffed Stuttgart-based entrepreneur, can afford his own wings, then he has certainly earned the privilege. Take Schumacher's genius at the wheel out of the equation and it is 56-year-old Weber who has almost single-handedly been responsible for the German driver's rise to fame and fortune.

At home in Germany, Michael rode through much of the 1990s on a tidal wave of popular support which probably transcended any similarly public displays of adulation towards fellow-German sporting legends such as Boris Becker and Jürgen Klinsmann.

By the time an accident at Silverstone interrupted his 1999 season the 31-year-old Ferrari driver had amassed no fewer than 35 Grand Prix victories. That put him six away from Ayrton Senna's tally of 41 and a more challenging 16 away from Alain Prost's all-time record. Even so, it would be a brave man indeed to bet against him passing both these distinguished milestones before he finally calls it a day.

There is something compellingly attractive about the 'little boy lost' demeanour of this lad from the wrong side of the tracks who has made the Big Time. Michael's father was a bricklayer; his mother ran the hamburger stand at the little go-kart track at Kerpen where the future champion first cut his competitive teeth as a boy.

He may seem slightly surly and uninterested when faced with one of the obligatory press conferences which take place daily at each Grand Prix for a number of selected celebrities. He ducks questions, replies with sweeping and anodyne generalities and generally manages to look slightly morose.

On his own, Schumacher is better value. Like the late Ayrton Senna, he weighs his replies carefully behind a mask of slightly distant formality. But as Eddie Irvine, his Ferrari team-mate over four seasons to 1999, said, 'Michael is always pretty intense. There is nothing light-hearted about Grand Prix racing for him. He is there to win and nothing else.'

It was in 1989 that Weber recruited the young Michael Schumacher to drive for his own F3 team and the two men have never looked back, getting richer than their wildest dreams together. Schumacher's third place in that year's German F3 championship put him on the map.

Thanks to these performances, Weber was able to negotiate a deal for him to join the Mercedes-Benz sports car racing team, where he, Karl Wendlinger and Heinz-Harald Frentzen were shrewdly promoted as Germany's new generation of future racing stars.

Schumacher trusts Weber's judgement completely. 'If they have a new sponsor or a contract, Willi will do all the negotiations,' says a Schumacher camp

insider. 'If the terms seem to Willi's liking, he will then present them to Michael.

'This is a serious partnership; they are business colleagues and close friends. Willi knows that his main priority is to take all the worries off Michael's shoulders. It is very important that he has his mind free for what he does best, the racing.'

Such division of labour clearly works well. Schumacher earns about $30 million annually from his latest Ferrari contract, which lasts through to the end of 2002. At the same time Weber's assiduous dealings have helped his driver collect around $125 million from retainers and marketing agreements since joining the team in 1996. Less Weber's commission, of course, which is put at around 20 per cent.

Ironically, it seems that Schumacher may never drive a Mercedes-engined car in Formula 1. At a Mercedes shareholders' meeting in the summer of 1998, board director Jürgen Schrempp emphasised that the car company wanted Mika Häkkinen and David Coulthard to continue driving the McLarens which are powered by its engines.

Mercedes insiders hint that Schumacher carries with him a little too much controversial baggage: the collision with Damon Hill which resolved the 1994 World Championship and the incident with Jacques Villeneuve at Jerez in '97, for example. By contrast, Ferrari wants the very best driver available and is prepared to put up with everything to keep him.

Under such circumstances, it is quite understandable that Ferrari are prepared to accept Michael's requirement that they sign an acquiescent number two driver who is prepared to play second fiddle. However, Eddie Irvine had grown tired of that role by the middle of the 1999 season and decided to switch to the new Jaguar F1 operation as team leader for the new millennium. Rubens Barrichello willingly took over his position.

In days gone by, of course, the F1 team owners called the shots. Enzo Ferrari bestrode the Grand Prix world like an irascible automotive colossus, paying his star drivers a few hundred dollars a month and invariably heightening the tension between them by failing to nominate a team leader.

In the era of Michael Schumacher, the best driver in the world dictates the terms at Ferrari. He knows just how

difficult it really is to win a World Championship and does not intend to let the interests of his team-mate get in the way of his own towering ambition.

Schumacher burst on to the Grand Prix scene in the summer of 1991 when he was invited to test at Silverstone for the Jordan team, coincidentally later the employers of his younger brother, Ralf.

'It was instantly clear that Michael was very special,' said Eddie Jordan. 'We tested him on the South Circuit at Silverstone, which in those days was a fairly hair-raising place. Within a few laps he was braking 15 metres later for the kink before the pits than anybody else who had previously driven the car and we were signalling him that he should come in, because we thought he was going too quickly too soon.

'But Michael knew what he was doing. Within five minutes we were convinced that he was pretty special.'

Ken Tyrrell recognised the same sort of natural talent in Schumacher that he had seen in Jackie Stewart more than thirty years ago. 'It is that terrific ability to put in a fantastically quick first lap at the start of a race,' he said.

'Stewart was exactly the same, easily the best of his generation. Now Schumacher, but we all want to see Michael challenged, otherwise he could run away with all the championships.'

Michael's first Ferrari victory came in the pouring rain at Barcelona in 1996. He followed that up with two equally fine wins at Spa and Monza, but the Ferrari didn't consistently come on to the pace until the second half of the year. It was too late to mount a title challenge, but the omens were certainly promising for 1997.

Luca di Montezemolo, Ferrari's high-

profile President, made it the team's priority to win more races in 1997 than it had the previous year. Michael duly delivered, almost doubling the tally to five. But then came the vital fumble at Jerez which handed Villeneuve the World Championship and left Michael facing more criticism and doubt.

Even the controversy at Jerez, where he rammed his Ferrari into the side of Villeneuve's overtaking Williams in an effort to settle the outcome of the World Championship by what was universally condemned as a 'professional foul', failed materially to dent his popularity.

There were short-term criticisms, but Schumacher quickly regained his status in the eyes of the fans. The so-called punishment of being disqualified from second place in the World Championship brought with it an obligation for him to help with a European road safety campaign backed by motor racing's governing body, the FIA. The exercise was deftly turned into something of a PR triumph for the Ferrari driver.

Surely 1998 had to be the year in which the World Championship was Ferrari's. Six wins were firmly under Michael's belt by the time he lined up on pole position at Suzuka and it was even money as to whether he would finally get the job done.

Then, at the first restart, he stalled the engine. It was an episode which served as a reminder that even the greatest drivers are still human. He was consigned to the back of the grid and eventually retired with a punctured tyre, leaving Mika Häkkinen to win both race and championship.

Yet again, Michael had proved that he possesses a dazzling talent, an almost

magical touch, behind the wheel. Yet, like the late Ayrton Senna, whose mantle he has now assumed, he can display a tendency towards arrogance and intolerance of others. When he bundled Heinz-Harald Frentzen's Williams off the road at Montreal, he could scarcely bring himself to make a grudging apology. After hitting the back of David Coulthard's McLaren in the rain at Spa, he completely lost control of his temper. Yet the driving genius still transcended his weak and vulnerable points.

Then, in 1999, Schumacher suffered the biggest setback of his career so far. On the opening lap of the British Grand Prix at Silverstone he crashed under braking for Stowe Corner and slammed into the tyre barrier. Having already won the San Marino and Monaco Grands Prix in splendid style, the German driver now had to recover from a broken right leg and accept that his title hopes were at an end for another year.

Michael himself offers the most straightforward explanation of his own success. In his view, he has a mental margin, not needing to use all his brain power in the heat of Grand Prix battle. Obviously he has all the outstanding balance, co-ordination and natural talent which are needed to be a top driver, but he is not a man who lies awake trying to analyse why he exerts such superiority over his frustrated rivals.

'Look, the ability I have is a natural thing,' he explained. 'I don't work at it, and I don't have to make big preparations before I get into the car.

'I just do up the straps, start the engine, let in the clutch – and do what I do.' His rivals must certainly find themselves wishing it was all so blindingly straightforward for them.

Paul-Henri Cahier

Mika Häkkinen leads McLaren team-mate David Coulthard and eventual winner Jacques Villeneuve at the start of the 1997 Luxembourg Grand Prix at the Nürburgring. Meanwhile Ralf Schumacher (far right) is about to inflict terminal damage on his elder brother's Ferrari.

VILLENEUVE DENIES FERRARI THE TITLE

Many F1 insiders would have wholeheartedly approved had Ferrari been able to celebrate its 50th anniversary by securing either the 1997 Drivers' or Constructors' World Championship. As things transpired, throughout that season the team was not a sufficiently consistent scorer to fend off Williams in the battle for the constructors' title, and a down-to-the-wire shoot-out between Maranello's team leader, Michael Schumacher, and Jacques Villeneuve ended in tears with the German vilified in the European media for trying to ram the Williams driver out of the final race of the season, the European Grand Prix at Jerez.

This strategy backfired dramatically on Schumacher, although the FIA World Motor Sports Council took a lenient view of his alleged malfeasance. Despite expectations of draconian fines, possible race suspensions or even a points penalty that would see him start the following season with a negative points total, FIA President Max Mosley announced that the German would be stripped of his second place in the World Championship and required to carry out some road safety campaign work on an FIA/European Union initiative in 1998.

Many F1 insiders regarded this as little more than a slap on the wrist, but Mosley explained it was intended as a deterrent aimed at anybody who had a mind to transgress the rules in the future.

'It sends a message to all drivers at all levels of the sport that, if you do something you shouldn't do, when the championship is at issue, you will be excluded from that championship,' he said. 'You cannot possibly gain anything by engaging in an illegitimate act.'

At the start of the season Ferrari President Luca di Montezemolo had said that it was the team's ambition to improve on its 1996 record of three wins. Schumacher had obliged with five victories, so from that standpoint it was a case of 'Mission Accomplished'. Perhaps the biggest sin of which Michael had been guilty was to have raised Maranello's expectations so high that when the final disappointment arrived the sense of anti-climax and pain was even more acutely felt.

It was therefore left to Jacques Villeneuve in the Williams FW19-Renault to win the World Championship in only his second season of F1 driving. The 26-year-old former Indy car champion survived a wobbly mid-season slump to bounce back and take the title against the odds. Even exclusion from the Japanese Grand Prix, a somewhat harsh if admittedly self-induced penalty for a trifling offence, failed to ruffle his calm, despite the fact that he went into the final race one point behind title favourite Schumacher.

If Villeneuve's outspoken personality was hailed by some as a welcome breath of fresh air, the fact remains that the French-Canadian driver was the latest beneficiary of the Williams team's technical excellence. Like Nigel Mansell, Alain Prost and Damon Hill before him, Villeneuve was the throttle jockey who profited, assuring

the British team of its ninth Constructors' Championship in only 17 years. It was a remarkable, not to mention all-time record, achievement.

There were other achievements worth noting in 1997. The McLaren-Mercedes alliance scored its first three wins, returning Ron Dennis's team to the top step of the rostrum for the first time in its post-Ayrton Senna era.

Giancarlo Fisichella, Jarno Trulli and Alexander Wurz all signalled that there was another generation of F1 hopefuls waiting in the wings, while Damon Hill was left to go into 1998 as Grand Prix racing's Senior Citizen following the retirement of the ever-popular Gerhard Berger, who, having won brilliantly for Benetton at Hockenheim, rounded off his distinguished career with a hard-fought fourth place at Jerez, less than two seconds behind Mika Häkkinen's victorious McLaren.

McLAREN AND FERRARI HEAD-TO-HEAD IN '98

The rule makers again sought to put a brake on F1 lap speeds in 1998, introducing a new breed of narrow-track car running on grooved tyres. The move was effective as far as it went, although much of the on-paper speed reduction was cancelled out by the intensity of the tyre war between Bridgestone and Goodyear. It was clear, however, that, had these changes not been brought in, lap speeds would have spiralled dangerously out of control.

The popularity of Grand Prix racing remained remarkable, with Bernie Ecclestone pursuing plans for the sport to be in pole position for the forthcoming digital television revolution, although his monopoly on F1 television rights continued to attract the questioning – and certainly very protracted – scrutiny of EU Competition Commissioner Karel van Miert.

The 1998 season was good for Ecclestone and the

Below: All smiles at the 1997 European Grand Prix at Jerez. Jacques Villeneuve (centre) is the new World Champion, Mika Häkkinen has just recorded his first Grand Prix win and David Coulthard looks happy – well, quite happy – with his second place.

Paul-Henri Cahier

No pain.

No glory.

▶ West McLaren Mercedes and Mika Hakkinen, Formula 1 world champions 1998 and 1999.

Mercedes-Benz

competing teams because a new Concorde Agreement was finally approved, signed, sealed and delivered. Frank Williams and Ron Dennis had stood out against signing in 1997 because they considered the other competing teams had failed to understand precisely what intellectual property rights they were signing away.

Eventually a new deal was formalised which provided for between $9 and $23 million in annual television revenue for the 11 competing teams – with provision for a 12th in anticipation of Honda entering with its own factory team at the start of 2000. However, this never actually came to pass.

Meanwhile the McLaren design team reckoned it had expended more than 12,000 man-hours over the winter of 1997/98 attempting to claw back aerodynamic downforce lost to the new regulations. The new MP4/13 also had a completely revised Mercedes-Benz FO110G V10 engine which weighed in at around five per cent lighter than its immediate predecessor.

McLaren had gambled on leaving the build programme for the new car as late as possible, Adrian Newey and his technical group reasoning that the team's serious development work for the new regulations had not really started until his arrival in August 1997. 'Williams and the others had been hard at it since February or March,' he said enigmatically, 'so we had a steep learning ramp to climb.'

McLaren also switched to Bridgestone tyres for 1998, deciding that, as Goodyear had indicated its intention to withdraw from F1 at the end of the season, it made sense to be among the advanced guard developing a relationship with what was set to become Grand Prix racing's sole tyre supplier.

Newey conceded that the change had cost the team a crucial extra week or so in terms of finalising the car's detailed suspension geometry, but this was judged well worth the effort. 'The harder you use those tyres, the faster you go,' reported Mika Häkkinen. 'You can slide the car a lot and the rubber will sustain its grip. At last I can drive the car in the way I have always wanted to.'

Once the season began the MP4/13 was quite simply the class of the field, even after its asymmetric braking system was removed voluntarily by the team prior to the Brazilian GP after a protest initiated by Ferrari. The car proved versatile, quick and generally moderately reliable. The Merc V10s were less so, crucial engine failures at Monaco and Monza sidelining Coulthard, who suffered another retirement when the throttle mechanism fell apart at Montreal. A counterfeit gearbox bearing also found its way into the McLaren supply chain to cause Häkkinen's retirement at Imola.

The lowest point of the year for the team came in the Belgian Grand Prix at Spa-Francorchamps, with Häkkinen being eliminated in a collision at La Source on the opening lap and Coulthard having his rear wing ripped off when Michael Schumacher's Ferrari F300 slammed into the back of him in torrential rain later in the race while lapping the Scot.

Schumacher three-wheeled back to the pits after his right-front wheel was torn off in the impact and had to be restrained from assaulting Coulthard as the two men

Below: David Coulthard scored an impressive win for the McLaren-Mercedes team in the 1998 San Marino Grand Prix at Imola.

Paul-Henri Cahier

Opposite: The return of the Silver Arrows. The contoured engine cover of the 1997 McLaren MP4/12-Mercedes is lent additional elegance by the evocative new livery adopted by the team that season.

Opposite, bottom: The Ford Zetec-R V10 engine which powered the Stewarts in 1998.

Left: A hallowed name returned to F1 when Alain Prost acquired the Ligier team prior to the start of the '97 season.

Below: Ralf Schumacher surrounded by a sea of yellow in the cockpit of his Jordan. The young German was quick but erratic during his maiden season in F1 in 1997.

FINNISH FIRST

FINLANDIA
VODKA

West McLaren Mercedes
FORMULA ONE WORLD CHAMPIONS 1999
ASSOCIATE PARTNER

RON DENNIS: PLAYING THE LONG GAME

McLAREN INTERNATIONAL founder Ron Dennis had a pretty clear idea of how he wanted his business to develop from the moment he left his job as Chief Mechanic on the Brabham F1 team at the end of 1970 to start up on his own.

In 1971 Dennis and colleague Neil Trundle set up their own Formula 2 team and this provided a crucial springboard for Dennis's long-term ambitions. High standards of preparation and turn-out were absolutely central to the Rondel Racing credo and set the tone for everything which was to follow throughout Dennis's business career in motor racing.

He frankly admits that he even put the idea of getting married consciously on hold until he was firmly established as a successful businessman and team owner, even if the fact that he now has a young family in his early fifties makes him a little nervous and uneasy.

Dennis took effective control of the ailing McLaren F1 team in 1980 and revived its fortunes to brilliant effect, World Championship titles following in 1984, '85, '86, '88, '89, '90 and '91. There was then a dramatic performance slump from which the team successfully emerged in 1997, in partnership with engine supplier Mercedes-Benz, and further World Championships were added to the tally in 1998 and '99.

'I have a belief that everything is important in life and everything is important when you are trying to achieve high levels of success in any business – certainly in Formula 1,' says Dennis.

'I believe that at all times you should have the best – or at least try to have the best. This is not simply about money, it is mainly about commitment. We try to instil it into the very fibre of everyone's approach to their work for the team.'

It is this basic attitude which underpins every aspect of his whole operation. Not only the racing team, but also the new technology centre which he plans to build near the current factory near Woking, where he intends to continue producing high-quality cars for many years to come.

'Winning is not just about winning on the circuit, it is also about winning off the circuit,' he explains. 'Consequently, when people pass less-than-favourable remarks about the things that we do, most of the time those remarks broadly reflect the fact that they recognise that we have higher standards than they have achieved.'

Dennis is particularly adept at lateral thinking and projects a shrewd understanding of Grand Prix racing which extends beyond the simple, obvious scenario of cars running round a circuit. Unlike many of his contemporaries in the ranks of F1 team owners, he also understands that success in F1 may involve playing what he habitually describes as 'the long game'.

In essence that means investing in improvements in the McLaren team's design and manufacturing infrastructure. In brief, there is no short-cut to success. It involves sustained hard work and self-belief which can be made more frustrating by the inherent complexity of the Grand Prix machine.

'When you look at many sports, you realise that the role the equipment plays in the overall equation is very small,' he explains. 'By contrast, a Grand Prix car is one of the most complex pieces of equipment you could ever place in the hands of a sportsman. That is what sets motor racing apart, and why it is so enormously difficult to win a Grand Prix.

'We have very much a desire to win as many races as possible. The simple fact is that you win Grands Prix and World Championships not by considering the next race, or even the race after that, but you do it by means of what you plan for the future.

'Our approach with Mercedes is many years into the future, to try and give our respective engineering groups the very best facilities for them to contribute to us winning races. To make it possible, you have to have everybody around you with the same long-term vision. We are trying to develop a long-term strategy to win consistently, both for McLaren and for Mercedes, both of whom have a distinguished heritage.'

Left: Looking ahead: McLaren chief Ron Dennis.

Below: The team's long-term partnerships with major sponsors have been a crucial factor in its enduring success.

Photos: Paul-Henri Cahier

squared up to each other in a fury. Meanwhile, Michael's misfortune handed the lead to Damon Hill, the Englishman having moved from Arrows to the Jordan team at the start of the season.

Jordan had spent three years using Peugeot's promising V10, but had made the switch to Mugen-Honda power at the start of 1998. Initially the Gary Anderson-designed Jordan 198 had proved very troublesome to set up. To see Hill just scraping home ahead of a Minardi, lapped by Häkkinen's winning McLaren, in Monaco that season was to see a team on the verge of a major crisis.

Thereafter a fine effort reversed Jordan's fortunes during the second half of the year and Hill surged home the winner at Spa, a few yards ahead of his team-mate, Ralf Schumacher, the younger brother of the Ferrari ace, who was fast making a reputation for himself as one of the most outstanding F1 rising stars of the decade.

Ferrari, meanwhile, was having a storming season and it was really beginning to look as though the Italian team's consistency and reliability would finally pay off with a World Championship.

The F300 was a logical evolution of the previous year's F310B, although Ferrari Technical Director Ross Brawn admitted that under the new regulations basic elements in the design, such as the centre of gravity, were even more critical. The cockpit on the new car had been moved back slightly by about 10 cm to facilitate the use of shorter side pods while still conforming to the more exacting lateral impact tests introduced for 1998 and lowering the centre of gravity, a change also assisted by a slightly wider fuel tank and lower engine position.

Ferrari also switched to a longitudinal gearbox to transmit the power from its outstandingly reliable V10 developed by Paolo Martinelli's engine group. Rory Byrne remained as Chief Designer, working closely with Brawn.

Maranello was playing for high stakes. The team's Sporting Director, Jean Todt, opened the year by saying that anything less than winning the World Championship simply wasn't acceptable. The Frenchman had been in charge of Ferrari's F1 fortunes since the summer of 1993 and now, five years down the road, the level of expectancy was running on over-boost.

From the start of the season it seemed as though Ferrari had been wrong-footed in the biggest possible way by the McLaren-Mercedes-Bridgestone alliance. Goodyear had been slow off the mark developing tyres for the new grooved regulations and their new wider front cover – which would prove crucial in boosting Ferrari's fortunes – was also later than hoped for, but Akron was worried that it did not have a rear cover which matched it.

Once Goodyear got into the swing of the season, Ferrari could exploit its mechanical reliability to great advantage. Schumacher's win in Buenos Aires was followed by second place at Imola and third in Spain. Then came Monaco and one of the season's biggest disappointments. Michael qualified fourth and finished down in tenth place after a collision with Alexander Wurz's Benetton.

Monaco was followed by three more decisive wins at Montreal, Magny-Cours and Silverstone. All were controversial. In Canada Schumacher pushed off Heinz-Harald

Opposite: Michael Schumacher heads for victory in the 1998 Italian Grand Prix. The Ferrari ace scored six wins that season but his virtuosity behind the wheel was not sufficient to cancel out the performance advantage enjoyed by McLaren.

Below: Victory at last. A joyful moment for Eddie Jordan at Spa-Francorchamps in '98 after his team's first Grand Prix win. Drivers Damon Hill and Ralf Schumacher share out the Moët in time-honoured fashion.

Below: Michael Schumacher wearing a redesigned helmet at the 1998 Japanese Grand Prix at Suzuka. His challenge for that year's World Championship was effectively ended when he stalled his pole-position Ferrari and was sent to the back of the grid.

Frentzen's Williams as he rejoined the track after a pit stop, carelessly but possibly not deliberately, while in France McLaren was left crying 'foul' after an aborted start gave Michael a second chance following a poor getaway from the grid first time round. Second time he made no mistake and won easily while Irvine fended off the McLarens in the opening phase of the race.

Silverstone saw Häkkinen give the German a rare wet-weather driving lesson, but the Ferrari driver emerged triumphant after Mika spun, although his victory was inevitably overshadowed by the controversy surrounding the ten-second stop–go penalty which Michael took *after* passing the chequered flag to win the race. This may have been technically correct to the letter of the rule book, but it allowed an absurd anomaly to enter the pages of history.

By this stage in the year Ferrari was coming under close scrutiny from McLaren, who believed their rivals were using some sort of asymmetric braking system, similar to that which the Mercedes-backed team had removed from their cars in Brazil following objections from Ferrari.

This was in addition to suspicions that Ferrari was using an engine mapping system which effectively duplicated the effects of the now-banned traction control devices, although this was less of an issue since most teams in the F1 field were attempting to develop this technology behind the scenes.

Unquestionably Hungary was Schumacher's finest race of the season, a combination of fine pit-wall strategy and Michael's committed genius at the wheel ensuring that McLaren went down to an embarrassing defeat. Then came Spa and Schumacher's crucial stumble: over-wound and over-wrought at the sight of Coulthard's McLaren ahead of him in a ball of spray, he made a momentary misjudgement. It could have cost him the title.

Monza brought with it a slice of good fortune with the faster McLarens hitting trouble, allowing Schumacher and Irvine to post a 1–2 for Maranello. But at the Nürburgring, Ferrari found its Goodyear tyre choice insufficiently soft for the job. 'It was a bit of a contrast to 1997 when we dreaded hot races,' Brawn reflected. 'This year's compounds have generally been very good in high temperatures, but we were too hard at the Nürburgring and couldn't get the grip.'

Eddie Irvine had second places in France and Italy, plus his first-ever front-row qualifying position at the Nürburgring, as consolation for the fact that he had yet to win a Grand Prix.

'I suppose being Michael's team-mate is good in a way, because you are measuring yourself against the very best,' he admitted. 'You are always aiming to climb Mount Everest every day you get into the car, whereas if there was somebody else in the other car, it would just be a gentle stroll up the Alps, wouldn't it?

'If you are running the team, everything goes your way. If you say something which is ignored because somebody in the team is more powerful – as Michael is here at Ferrari – then it's not good for your pysche. Michael is a bit of a phenomenon, isn't he? It's a pisser, but it's true!'

The confrontation between Häkkinen and Schumacher reached its climax at the final race of the season, the Japanese Grand Prix at Suzuka, where Michael qualified on pole ahead of his rival.

A tingling sense of anticipation could almost be felt through the track surface itself as Häkkinen's sleek grey and silver McLaren-Mercedes took up its place alongside Schumacher's brilliant red Ferrari on the front row of the grid. Round the parade lap they went, pausing in their positions to await the starting signal, only for the whole procedure to be aborted after Jarno Trulli's Prost-Peugeot stalled down in 14th place.

The rules require that anybody who stalls and causes a restart should be put to the back of the grid. So off they went on their second parade lap.

Back on the grid, Schumacher pulled for first gear, the car lurched forward and stalled. 'The engine stalled because the clutch did not free itself and I don't know why,' he later explained, 'All the work this weekend was then wasted as I had to start from the back.' It was later concluded that the problem had been caused by overheating hydraulics, which affected the way in which the clutch mechanism engaged.

With the start aborted again, the scarlet Ferrari had to go to the back of the grid for the second restart. That allowed Häkkinen a clear run through to a decisive race win and the World Championship title with 100 points, 14 more than Schumacher, who fought back through the field only for a rear tyre to explode and cause his retirement. McLaren number two David Coulthard finished a distant third overall on 56 points.

Left: Three years after an accident in Australia that could have ended his career, Mika Häkkinen became the 1998 World Champion.

Below: Häkkinen just squeezes into the first corner at Monaco ahead of team-mate David Coulthard. The Finn won dominantly but Coulthard retired with engine failure.

TOBACCO WARS FUND F1 EXPANSION

IT WAS AT the start of the 1968 season that Colin Chapman's Team Lotus rewrote the F1 sponsorship book by accepting funding from the Player's tobacco company, at a stroke replacing his cars' distinctive green and yellow livery with the gaudy red, white and gold of the Gold Leaf cigarette brand.

At the time this was regarded as imaginative and up-to-the-minute promotion in tune with the mood of the day. This tone continued well into the 1970s, when Lotus carried the distinctive black and gold livery of the JPS brand.

At the height of the JPS sponsorship programme, with Lotus enjoying great success, the cigarette company adopted an extremely lofty attitude towards those scribes who still referred to the cars as 'Lotus-Fords'. Its argument was that they were officially entered in the World Championship as 'John Player Specials'. Needless so say, this did not wash. Not for long, anyway.

In 1972 the giant Philip Morris organisation was persuaded to sponsor the fading BRM team under its Marlboro brand. The sponsorship lasted for just two seasons before Marlboro switched to McLaren, a partnership which would endure for 23 seasons.

It was Marlboro's marketing managers who really showed how to make sponsorship effective, and in the process the sport as a whole became dramatically dependent on its money. Not only was the company active at the highest level in Formula 1, but it also sponsored junior

formulae in an effort to bring on F1 drivers of the future, notably the British Formula 3 Championship, which spawned such talents as Ayrton Senna, Martin Brundle and Johnny Herbert.

In 1984 Marlboro made a huge commercial leap by gaining space on the side of the Ferrari F1 cars, even though the company founder, Enzo Ferrari, had been critical of tobacco sponsorship's arrival in F1 more than a decade earlier.

Initially the Marlboro/Ferrari deal was excused on the basis that the sponsor simply contributed to driver retainers – and no more – but since Enzo Ferrari's death in 1988 Marlboro backing for the famous Italian team has become the biggest single sponsorship deal in Grand Prix racing, worth in excess of £35 million annually.

Yet the role of the tobacco companies as Grand Prix motor racing's most prolific paymasters came under gradual threat from as early as 1983, when Britain followed Germany's example and banned competing teams from carrying sponsorship identification on their cars and transporters.

Yet it was a measure of the success of subliminal advertising that the substitution of 'McLaren' for 'Marlboro' on the red and white McLarens and, more recently, of 'Racing' for 'Rothmans' on the Williams-Renaults was scarcely noticed by a large proportion of race fans. And, more particularly, of television viewers.

Up until the late 1990s tobacco companies involved in F1 sponsorship

remained cautiously relaxed about any further restrictions, feeling that they had to a large degree pre-empted the planned government legislation by their voluntary restrictions.

However, by the start of the 1999 season things were changing. Ironically, F1's newest team, British American Racing, almost unwittingly played a crucial role in helping the FIA prove to the European Union that it was not giving the tobacco companies an easy ride.

British American Racing, whose number one driver was 1997 World Champion Jacques Villeneuve, ran into a head-on confrontation with the FIA and its President, Max Mosley, over the issue of dual branding.

BAR's intention of running one of its cars in red and white Lucky Strike livery and the other in dark-blue 555 identification was not acceptable under the current F1 rules which require both a team's cars to be fielded in substantially the same livery.

Despite an agreed arbitration hearing which went against BAR, Craig Pollock, the team's Managing Director, went one step further and lodged an official complaint with EU Competition Commissioner Karel van Miert over what he regarded as the FIA's anti-competitive stance. This was a breach of the Concorde Agreement and BAR was summoned to appear before the FIA's World Council five days after the Australian Grand Prix.

The matter was resolved without

further sanction, but there was much more to this than simply the issue of an ambitious newcomer rocking the F1 boat. For some time the FIA had been keen to be seen to be responsive to the anti-tobacco lobby, while at the same time orchestrating a well-ordered retreat from reliance on the industry's funds in order to comply with the European Union's requirement that the sport should dispense with tobacco sponsorship from 2006. Pollock's attempt to bring two brands on to the Grand Prix stage for the price of one had given Mosley an opportunity to take a tough line.

'We feel their attempt to run two tobacco sponsors is going too far,' said Mosley. 'Several governments make concessions and allow teams to run with tobacco advertising, but one mustn't overdo it.'

However, with a firm line now drawn in the sand for the end of F1 tobacco sponsorship, it soon became clear that both the cigarette companies and motor racing's governing body had become alert to the important issues involved.

A shift of emphasis in terms of F1 funding was clearly looming on the distant horizon. Increased involvement from major motor manufacturers quickly signalled the path ahead. By the end of 1999 Ford had purchased Stewart Grand Prix, Mercedes-Benz had taken a $250 million 40 per cent stake in the TAG McLaren Group and BMW had forged a commercial partnership in addition to a five-year engine-supply deal with Williams.

Paul-Henri Cahier

JORDAN IN THE ASCENDANT

The 1999 season promised more of the same with McLaren-Mercedes and Ferrari the most obvious contenders, although Benetton, Williams and the new British American Racing team all held out high hopes for progress with the Renault-derived Supertec V10 engines which had been raced by Williams and Benetton under the Mecachrome label in 1998.

With Goodyear now retired from the F1 scene, the FIA still went ahead with another speed-reducing rule change, requiring that front tyres be deprived of more grip through the addition of a fourth circumferential groove. Most of the drivers were soon up in arms over these changes, which many insisted made the cars absolutely impossible to drive. Yet despite some processional races early in the season, the 1999 World Championship contest would turn out to be an electrifying affair, full of unexpected drama.

Aiming for a second straight season of domination, McLaren produced the superbly engineered new MP4/14, which was powered by an even lighter 72-degree Mercedes FO110H V10 developing an estimated 785 bhp at 16,700 rpm from the start of the season. With extra weight trimmed off the entire chassis/engine package, the new car offered even more scope for the strategic placement of ballast.

Mika Häkkinen and David Coulthard used the new cars from the start of the season despite some serious consideration being given to running uprated MP4/13s at the first race if the new car did not prove quick enough in testing.

Ranged against the McLarens at the front of the field were the new Ferrari F399s, these being evolutionary versions of the 1998 car, but now equipped with seven-speed longitudinal gearboxes to make the most of the 780 bhp at 17,000 rpm offered by the type 048 V10 developed by Paolo Martinelli's engine department. Michael Schumacher was poised to start his fourth season with the team partnered by the dutiful Eddie Irvine, whose contract still required him to give the German driver priority in his bid to win the Italian team's first Drivers' World Championship for twenty years.

Over at Williams, Ralf Schumacher and former CART champion Alex Zanardi formed a new driver line-up, replacing Jacques Villeneuve and Heinz-Harald Frentzen, who had moved to British American Racing and Jordan respectively.

Jordan, meanwhile, started the season in an upbeat mood after very promising tests with the new Mike Gascoyne-developed 199 chassis, which was powered by a further uprated Mugen Honda MF301HD engine pumping out a reputed 765 bhp. Damon Hill continued as team leader, with Frentzen – ironically the man who had displaced him at Williams in 1997 – alongside him.

The McLarens seemed set to dominate the first race in Australia but technical problems sidelined both Häkkinen and Coulthard, leaving Irvine's Ferrari to beat Frentzen's Jordan in a race that also saw Schumacher's Ferrari beset by gearchange problems which caused him to finish out of the points.

Häkkinen managed to get McLaren's score off the ground with a win at Interlagos, but the first signs of the Constructors' Champions' potential vulnerability came at Imola, where Mika inexplicably crashed while leading the San Marino Grand Prix and Coulthard simply couldn't get on terms with Schumacher's winning Ferrari.

Johnny Herbert, Jackie Stewart and Rubens Barrichello celebrate Stewart Grand Prix's maiden F1 victory at the Nürburgring in 1999.

Opposite: British American Racing was obliged to run the cars of Jacques Villeneuve (pictured) and team-mate Ricardo Zonta in the same combined livery in 1999 after plans to use two different colour schemes were blocked by the sport's governing body.

Opposite: Heinz-Harald Frentzen really shone during 1999 at the wheel of the Jordan-Mugen Honda, notching up two wins for the Silverstone-based team.

Below: Eddie Irvine locks a wheel as he attempts to hold off Mika Häkkinen's McLaren in the 1999 European Grand Prix at the Nürburgring. Picking up the Ferrari banner after Michael Schumacher's Silverstone accident, Irvine mounted a surprise championship challenge but fell short at the last round at Suzuka.

Michael backed this up with a superb win in Monaco, soundly beating Häkkinen into third place behind Irvine, but the Finn bounced back to head a McLaren 1–2 in Spain and then the tables were turned in Canada, where the German driver crashed heavily while leading and the McLaren team leader took the win.

Unpredictable wet/dry conditions, allied to a shrewd Jordan refuelling strategy, helped Frentzen to victory in the French Grand Prix at Magny-Cours, but then the title chase took on a whole new complexion when Schumacher crashed heavily on the opening lap of the British Grand Prix at Silverstone, sustaining a broken right leg.

With Häkkinen's McLaren being prudently withdrawn from the battle after shedding its left-rear wheel, the number two drivers picked up the gauntlet to produce a close-fought battle all the way to the chequered flag, Coulthard just winning from Irvine.

Coulthard's McLaren had the performance edge over Irvine's Ferrari and the Scot drove with great restraint and self-discipline to conserve his machinery, edging away from Irvine in the closing stages when he realised the race was all but won.

On a day inevitably clouded by the sombre sight of Ferrari's brilliant team leader clattering away to hospital in a medical helicopter, Coulthard's win represented a crucial moment of restoration for the easy-going 28-year-old, who had last tasted victory in the 1998 San Marino Grand Prix.

Schumacher's nightmare began in the first few yards of the race when the advantage of his front-row starting position immediately slipped away as Häkkinen and

Coulthard surged their McLarens into first and second places. As if to add insult to injury, Irvine's Ferrari swept majestically round the outside of the German ace going into Copse, pushing him back to fourth place.

Down through the luridly quick ess-bend at Becketts, Schumacher came hard at Irvine and he slipstreamed on to his tail as the two Ferraris accelerated up to 185 mph on the Hangar Straight. Irvine glanced in his mirror and dutifully allowed just enough room for Schumacher to have free passage down the inside into the tricky Stowe right-hander, which tightens up on itself as it leads round into the Vale.

Suddenly things went wrong. Instead of cutting a gentle arc to the right, Michael locked up his front brakes. From then on everything was lost. The Ferrari skidded on to the gravel trap – which did virtually nothing in terms of reducing his speed – and slammed head on into the retaining tyre wall.

The horrifying impact ripped off the front end of the Ferrari monocoque. Schumacher caught his breath and began to lift himself from the shattered F399. After a moment's effort, he slumped back into the cockpit as marshals swarmed round the car.

He had sustained a double fracture below his right knee and would have to wait for the ambulance to arrive before being released from the wreckage and taken off to the circuit medical centre, jauntily waving to his fans from the stretcher.

'I had to touch the brakes to avoid David [Coulthard] going into Becketts on the first lap and it's possible that Michael may have touched me and damaged his front

Paul-Henri Cahier

Paul-Henri Cahier

Opposite: Bernie Ecclestone has been instrumental in the total transformation of Grand Prix racing during the last three decades.

Photo: Paul-Henri Cahier

1998

May: India and Pakistan detonate nuclear devices.

May: US singer and film star Frank Sinatra dies at the age of 82 in Los Angeles.

July: France win the football World Cup for the first time, beating Brazil 3–0 in the final.

October: Mick Doohan wins the 500 cc motor cycle World Championship for the fifth time in succession.

October: John Glenn, the first American to orbit the Earth in 1962, returns to space aboard the shuttle *Discovery*.

1999

May: Manchester United win unprecedented treble of European Cup, Premiership and FA Cup.

June: Prince Edward and Sophie Rhys Jones are married in Westminster Abbey, London.

June: Yugoslavia ends repression in Kosovo after sustained air attacks by NATO forces.

August: Thousands lose their lives in a massive earthquake in Turkey.

wing,' said Irvine. 'All I know is that he came flying past me all locked up. I think he just outbraked himself.'

On the face of it, this seemed the logical view. Schumacher had been frustrated by the handling of his car during the race morning warm-up and made a quick-fix change to the set-up in an effort to improve things. He was then jumped into Copse by Irvine and, in his anxiety to stay in touch with the McLarens, might just have been willing to take one risk too many as he slammed into Stowe.

In fact, having examined all the technical data at their disposal, the Ferrari team concluded that a rear brake malfunction had caused the accident.

The incident was also an endorsement of the overall high safety standards which have come to be taken for granted over the past few years and have been encouraged by both the F1 constructors and the FIA. When one considers that many drivers in the 1990s regularly walked away uninjured from the sort of impacts which tore apart Jochen Rindt's Lotus 72 during the Austrian's fatal accident at Monza in 1970, it is a graphic illustration of how effectively technology has been applied to making Grand Prix racing a safer and more secure professional sport.

Meanwhile, back at Silverstone, Ralf Schumacher's Williams finished third after vaulting ahead of Frentzen's Jordan while Damon Hill, who had by now decided that he would retire from racing at the end of the season, took fifth at the chequered flag. Jordan was ever-present and increasingly in touch at the front of the field.

Häkkinen's misfortunes now multiplied dramatically. He was pushed off on the opening lap of the Austrian Grand Prix after an over-ambitious passing move by Coulthard on the second corner. As if this wasn't bad enough, Irvine dodged through to win after the McLaren team failed to keep Coulthard sufficiently well briefed about the Ferrari's progress. Häkkinen recovered to finish third.

At Hockenheim, a 200 mph rear tyre failure sent Häkkinen sailing into a tyre barrier and left Irvine to saunter home for his second win in as many weeks ahead of Schumacher stand-in Mika Salo. Häkkinen regained his composure to win from Coulthard in Hungary, but then the positions were reversed at Spa, where the Scot notched up his second win of the season in the Belgian Grand Prix after an unruly first-corner barging match between the two McLaren drivers.

By this time the apparent lack of team orders discriminating between the two McLaren-Mercedes drivers was the subject of intense media scrutiny. In an effort to appear even handed – understandably so, perhaps, since both Häkkinen and Coulthard had signed identical contracts in this respect – the management wanted to give them both a fair chance.

Even so, while they might have been forgiven for discounting Irvine's chances after his surprise midsummer victories in Austria and Germany, they seemed to ignore Frentzen in the ever-improving Jordan, who was coming up on the rails as a strong outsider.

When Häkkinen then inexplicably threw away victory in the Italian Grand Prix at Monza with a spin while leading, Frentzen dodged through to take the win and moved into third place in the World Championship, two points ahead of Coulthard and just ten points – a single win – behind the dead-heated Häkkinen and Irvine.

However, McLaren boss Ron Dennis was not about to be bullied by the media into changing the nature of his contractual relations with the team's drivers. In his view,

his policy had served McLaren pretty well for more than a decade and he was anxious to play fair with the men he employed behind the wheel.

'During the course of the season we work strenuously to treat both our drivers evenly and ensure that they are both equally favoured in terms of chances to win the World Championship,' he insisted.

'Having said that, when we are seeking to close down the championship from a threat by another team, it is only logical to help the driver who has the best mathematical chance of doing so. This is entirely different from deciding at the start of the season that one driver is a number one and will be specifically favoured over the number two irrespective of the status of the World Championship.'

Nevertheless, Häkkinen's slip at Monza gave a timely boost to Irvine's title chances. The Ferrari driver could only finish a disappointed sixth on his team's home turf, unhappy with the F399's fast-circuit performance on this occasion, but he and Häkkinen were now level on 60 points with three races left to run. 'We got out of jail today,' said Irvine thankfully.

This really was turning into the World Championship nobody seemed to want to win. The European Grand Prix at the Nürburgring followed, where Johnny Herbert gave the Stewart-Ford squad a memorable maiden victory, the veteran British driver calling his tyre stops to perfection in tricky wet/dry/wet conditions.

McLaren and Ferrari again bombed out. Häkkinen was called in for a premature first tyre change and eventually scraped home in fifth while Coulthard crashed out of the lead, a slip which finally wiped out his hopes of the title. Mika now led by two points with two races to run.

The penultimate event of the season was the inaugural Malaysian Grand Prix at Kuala Lumpur's magnificent new government-funded Sepang circuit. After endless pre-race uncertainty, Michael Schumacher made a brilliant return to the cockpit, qualifying on pole position and driving a defensive, tactical race into second place behind Irvine.

This proved a hugely controversial episode, for not only did Schumacher ruthlessly balk Häkkinen, keeping the frustrated McLaren driver bottled up in third place all the way to the flag, but both Ferraris were then excluded from the results at post-race scrutineering after their aerodynamic side deflectors ('bargeboards') were found to have infringed the permitted dimensions.

On the face of it, this now handed Häkkinen his second straight World Championship, but Ferrari quite naturally lodged an appeal against the disqualification. The following Saturday the FIA Court of Appeal, in a highly controversial and questionable interpretation of the technical rules, reversed that exclusion and reinstated Irvine and Schumacher in first and second places.

Häkkinen now had it all to do at the Japanese Grand Prix, going into the final event of the season four points behind Irvine. But the Finn regained his composure quite brilliantly to dominate the race, winning from Schumacher and Irvine to retain his championship crown by two points.

By way of consolation, Ferrari clinched the constructors' title for the first time in 16 years, which many people regarded as a fair division of the season's spoils. In reality, of course, it was a case of McLaren losing the constructors' crown rather than Ferrari winning it, but it was all grist to the mill for the news-hungry media, setting up the prospect of yet another enthralling struggle for supremacy at the start of the new millennium.

THE RISE OF BERNIE ECCLESTONE

IT HAS TAKEN Bernie Ecclestone less than 30 years to come from running a used-car dealership in a south London suburb to his present position as arguably the richest man in Britain, reputedly worth well in excess of £1500 million. He has reached this spectacular level of business success by having the foresight to understand and exploit the television coverage potential offered by Grand Prix motor racing.

Now officially Vice-President, Promotional Affairs of the FIA, he is the most powerful man in world motor racing. Some people would claim he is even the most powerful man in world sport. A compact, trim 69-year-old, he knows everybody and everything that goes on within F1, operating his empire at the race tracks in Europe from a discreet silver-grey motorhome in the paddock.

By any standards Ecclestone is a fascinating character. On the one hand he can be a ruthless negotiator, deploying a brain power and intellect which few can rival in any business sphere. On the other, he can be one of the boys when among those on the inside of motor racing whom he has known for a long time. He will get richer still if digital television coverage in Europe really takes off over the next few years, standing poised to reap the benefits of a £40 million investment in a 'portable' television studio which is transported round the world simply to handle the digital coverage.

His F1 Administration organisation, together with FOCA Communications, now employs such a large number of people that he has purchased a BAe146 60-seater jet airliner to transport those required to the European races.

So where did all this start? Bernie was born in 1930, the son of a trawler captain from Suffolk. His interest in motor racing stretches back to the immediate post-war years when he raced a motor cycle on the grass track at Brands Hatch while only a teenager.

Later he would become an active and enthusiastic car racer, first at the wheel of a Formula 3 Cooper, later with a Cooper-Bristol single-seater and a Cooper-Jaguar sports car. In 1958 he made an unsuccessful attempt to qualify a Connaught for the Monaco Grand Prix, by which time he was managing the interests of the British driver, Stuart Lewis-Evans, who was driving in the Vanwall team alongside Stirling Moss and Tony Brooks.

After Lewis-Evans sadly suffered what were to prove fatal burns when he crashed in the 1958 Moroccan Grand Prix, Bernie dropped from the racing scene to concentrate on his business interests. When he reappeared eight years later, he was acting as the business manager of Jochen Rindt, who was to be killed at Monza practising for the 1970 Italian Grand Prix at the wheel of a Lotus 72.

Bernie was a close friend of Rindt – Jochen's daughter Natascha, now 31, today works for his television coverage

operation – and the Austrian driver's death deeply affected him. He had been his partner in Jochen Rindt Racing, the semi-works Lotus Formula 2 team, and continued running those cars briefly through the winter of 1970/71.

However, Bernie, who had made a success of the motor cycle and car sales business as well as some shrewd and timely property dealings, by now had bigger ambitions. He was to purchase the Brabham Formula 1 team from its co-founder, Ron Tauranac, and when he took control at the start of 1972 his foot was on the bottom step of a ladder which would eventually carry him to multi-millionaire status.

Distinguished motor cycle champion John Surtees recalls being taken by his father to buy motor cycle parts from Bernie's family home in the early post-war years, the future Brabham boss apparently operating out of his mother's kitchen at the time. Although Bernie actually trained as a chemist, his true talents proved to be as a dealer and the world of commerce was destined to take him a long way from his modest beginnings in life.

By 1979 it was clear that Ecclestone and the FOCA-aligned teams were in a strong position to stake a claim to a larger share of the television income which, on the face of it, accrued to the sport's governing body, FISA. Yet it was Bernie's tireless efforts which had generated all this income for the sport and, quite rightly, FOCA felt it was worth a larger slice of the cake.

For their part, the governing body did not like what they saw. Ecclestone and FOCA, they reasoned, were having too much in the way of commercial influence. The whole affair was exacerbated in 1979 when the newly elected FISA President, Jean-Marie Balestre, decided to take on FOCA, determined to retrieve for FISA the notional concept of 'sporting power'.

Ecclestone now led his FOCA-aligned teams into a battle over the fundamental matter of who controlled motor racing. It was a turbulent period in the sport's history, with races being boycotted and

others taking place outside the official World Championship.

Yet Bernie continued to be the most influential man in the F1 pit lane. FOCA and FISA eventually reached an accommodation which was enshrined in the Concorde Agreement, a complex protocol of rules and regulations which was originally framed to control the way in which the sport was administered from the technical, financial and sporting viewpoints.

A significant long-term consequence of the FOCA/FISA wars, as they became known, was the emergence of Ecclestone's legal adviser, Max Mosley, as one of the most influential personalities behind the scenes.

As F1 became more popular throughout the 1980s, and Ecclestone grew progressively richer, so Mosley laid the foundations of his own personal challenge for power on the international motorsporting scene. In 1991, after a carefully judged campaign, Mosley defeated Balestre for the FISA Presidency. Two years later he was elected President of the FIA, the sporting body being absorbed by its parent organisation shortly afterwards. The FIA would eventually devolve the right to exploit the commercial aspects of the F1 World Championship to Ecclestone's companies, which would make him even richer in the longer term.

The Concorde Agreement was renewed several times, but by 1997 three teams – Williams, McLaren and Tyrrell – stood out against signing a new deal simply because they felt that Ecclestone's business organisation was taking too big a slice of the commercial cake.

As things stood in the summer of 1997, those teams which had signed the Concorde Agreement – Ferrari, Benetton, Jordan, Sauber, Minardi, Arrows and Prost – enjoyed a seven-way split of a fixed percentage of the gross television revenue. This money is payable whether or not the Commercial Rights Holder – in this case Ecclestone – makes a profit on the overall operation of the various television

coverage contracts through his FOCA TV organisation and associated subsidiaries.

Williams, Tyrrell and McLaren, meanwhile, held out for better terms but, after more than 60 revised drafts, a new 1998 Concorde Agreement was finally signed by the existing seven participants, the three dissenters and newcomers Stewart and British American Racing (which had bought out Tyrrell's place in the F1 game).

Meanwhile, Bernie became ever richer. In the year to March 1996 he drew Britain's largest pay packet of £54.9 million. He also hit the headlines in 1997 when it was revealed that he had made a payment of £1 million to the Labour Party, which won that year's general election. That finished Bernie's efforts to retain a low profile and he was subjected to a barrage of media interest.

Not that he should worry. Since 1989 he is judged to have earned £142 million in salary and dividends from his various companies. If digital television takes off, he and his family trusts could be another £750 million richer.

The growth of his fortune was accelerated in May 1999, when Ecclestone defied the big-business sceptics in the City by launching his long-awaited bond issue secured against Grand Prix racing's future revenues.

At a stroke Bernie added £875 million to the value of a family trust established for his wife, Slavica, and their daughters, Tamara and Petra. The bond issue, originally announced the previous September, had been dogged by seemingly endless speculation that joint managers Morgan Stanley Dean Witter and Westdeutsche Landesbank were having trouble attracting investors.

However, the banks involved were regarding the whole affair as something of a triumph when the launch was achieved. 'We look forward to the future stock-market flotation of this exciting business,' said Bernie. 'We can now build on the relationships we have established with the investment community.'

In February 2000 Ecclestone then pulled off the sale of the century by clinching a deal to sell 37.5 per cent of his F1 business to Hellman & Friedman, a San Francisco-based private equity firm, after Morgan Grenfell Private Equity decided against taking up its option to buy that share.

Morgan Grenfell had previously paid £234 million for a 12.5 per cent stake in Slec – the Ecclestone F1 holding company whose name is an abbreviation of that of Slavica Ecclestone, Bernie's wife – but said it could not raise sufficient additional investors to take a share in its proposed further investment. The Ecclestone trust had had an agreement with Hellman & Friedman since January to buy the stake if Morgan Grenfell failed to do so.

The sale valued Slec at £1.7 billion and leaves the Ecclestone trust as the biggest shareholder with a 50 per cent stake in the equity. By any standards, it was quite a deal.

350 Grand Prix Wins
Another Champion performance

The European Grand Prix, Nurburgring, 26th September 1999. History in the making. Stewart-Ford scores its first Grand Prix win. Johnny Herbert, his third. Ford, a remarkable 175th. And Champion - an astonishing 350th. No other spark plug has achieved so much in world motorsport. No other has won 21 F1 World Championships. And no other puts so much world-beating expertise into the spark plugs you fit in your car.

CHAMPION ®

Performance Driven

THE FINAL WORD:
GRAND PRIX RACING IN THE NEW MILLENNIUM

THE FUTURE of the FIA Formula 1 World Championship looks firm and secure as the competing teams stand poised to start the first season of the new millennium.

In his role as Formula 1 commercial rights holder, Bernie Ecclestone's efforts in expanding the sport's television coverage have been absolutely central to the explosion of interest in F1 racing, which now produces simply massive income for drivers, team owners and, in particular, for Ecclestone himself.

Across the 16-race series, taking into account race broadcasts, additional programmes and news coverage, the World Championship attracts almost 300 million viewers per race across 160 countries. Good value, even for a title sponsor paying top dollar to a front-line team.

Yet the budgets required by the leading teams to maintain their competitiveness are simply huge. Over the past 20 years Grand Prix racing has probably benefited more than any other single sport from the enormous revenues available from cigarette sponsorship – in 1999

British American Tobacco committed to an investment of around £250 million over five years to take a stake in British American Racing, the newest and most ambitious F1 team in the business.

In this respect, British American Tobacco was ahead of the game. The sponsorship benefits which accrue from Grand Prix racing are clearly defined. Yet BAT was one of the very first investors to discern the commercial advantages of having a stake in a competing team. Within months of their decision to take a share in British American Racing, their example was being followed by several major multi-national companies and financial institutions.

The new team was the brainchild of Craig Pollock, who had originally become involved in the sport as Jacques Villeneuve's business manager. It was Tom Moser, Head of Global Sponsorships at British American Tobacco, who took the decision to throw the giant tobacco group's commercial support behind Pollock's ambitions. Moser had been impressed from the first time

Below: British American Racing was seldom out of the media spotlight during its first season in Formula 1 in 1999 even though the team did not achieve the results it had hoped for.

Opposite: The involvement of major car manufacturers in Formula 1 continues to expand, with Honda forging a potentially formidable partnership with British American Racing.

Opposite, bottom: The Jaguar name comes to Formula 1 for the first time in 2000 following Ford's decision to rebrand the Stewart team.

Below: BMW is returning to the Grand Prix scene to take on its main commercial rivals in alliance with the hugely successful Williams squad.

they met with the way in which Pollock had steered and cared for Villeneuve's career.

However, it was Pollock's 'clean sheet' approach that turned out to be the element of the proposed F1 partnership which most intrigued British American Tobacco. For its part, BAT had carried out a huge amount of research into brand awareness. It probed in considerable detail precisely what made Formula 1 tick and how the images of its various competing teams might affect the individual brands within its control. It was a painstaking and meticulous process.

In the end, British American Tobacco concluded that the most advantageous route would be to back the outsider. With the Reynard group becoming technology partners with both Pollock and BAT, the new team would be founded on a secure three-pronged base.

'British American Tobacco had now merged with Rothmans and we had 80,000 employees in over 180 countries,' explained Moser. 'The F1 programme was one thing that offered a very strong unity of purpose, something that all the employees around the world could believe in and support at a time of changing strategies, different brands and so on. It was one thing that we could all rally behind and support.'

The future expansion of Grand Prix racing will have secure commercial foundations with the guaranteed participation of the 11 teams who are signatories of the 1998 Concorde Agreement, the complex protocol which lays down the means by which the regulations and commercial dimensions of the sport are administered. In 2001 it is expected that this will expand to 12 teams with the arrival of Toyota on the F1 championship stage.

Of course, the Grand Prix teams' budgets are progressively smaller the further down the grid one travels. While Ferrari has an annual budget of some £85 million, the most modestly financed team – the Italian Minardi squad – exists on a 'survival' budget of around £10 million. Under the terms of the 1998 Concorde Agreement, it derives about two-thirds of its overall financing (£6 million) from television income. Ferrari, which receives about £16 million annually from television, gains a lesser proportion of its finance from this source.

For those fortunate teams who have engine-supply contracts, this effectively saves more than £10 million annually. In 1997 Williams won its ninth Constructors' Championship using Renault V10s supplied free of charge on a works-supported basis. In 1998 and 1999 the team used the same engines, but was charged £13 million in lease fees. This was a temporary arrangement designed to fill the gap until the new BMW F1 engine – together with an investment by the German company of about £20 million – became available to the British team on an exclusive basis in 2000.

Yet £13 million cannot buy the best F1 engine performance, as has been emphasised by the Williams team's recent travails. Mercedes-Benz is believed to have invested around £40 million annually for the past five seasons developing its V10 to help the McLaren-Mercedes squad achieve its current position as the prime World Championship contender.

Most leading teams are extremely profitable but there is no clear indication whether the wealth and stratospheric income of Grand Prix motor racing as a whole will eventually lead to a stock exchange flotation of Bernie Ecclestone's F1 Holdings empire. Ecclestone has traditionally been a secretive businessman and may eventually decide that he is not prepared to have his business acumen laid open to the sort of scrutiny which goes hand-in-hand with a share flotation.

Many of Ecclestone's hopes for the future expansion of F1's popularity are based on the possibilities afforded by pay-to-view digital channels which will offer much-enhanced picture quality and variety to the viewer. With this in mind, he has already invested £40 million in a remarkable air-conditioned mobile digital television production studio which has been shipped from race to race across the world since the start of the 1997 season.

However, it remains to be seen whether digital coverage takes off in the way Ecclestone anticipates. There are sceptics who believe that most viewers want their TV coverage packaged and delivered to their screens as a rounded, cohesive product rather than having to dart around with a hand control, making decisions on whether to have a cockpit-eye view from Jean Alesi's car, for example, or watch the refuelling process. The jury is still out on this matter, but its successful resolution is absolutely crucial to the way in which F1's television finances develop over the next few years.

It may also be crucial in guaranteeing the future income of Grand Prix racing's top drivers. Michael Schumacher's status as the best driver in the F1 business, allied to the global television coverage his Marlboro- and Dekra-bedecked image offered those two key sponsors, gave him an income of £16 million from his racing activities in 1999.

At the end of the season it was announced that he would be benefiting from an additional sponsorship of £5 million over three years after the German asset management company, DVAG, replaced Dekra as the personal sponsor identified on the baseball cap he wears when out of the cockpit. Add to that another £10 million from merchandising and the German ace, still only 31, could be earning a million pounds for every year of his life during the 2000 F1 season.

However, the signs are very encouraging as regards the involvement of major car manufacturers at the highest level of the sport. For example, the fact that Honda has decided to re-enter Grand Prix racing in 2000 as a

BMW

Opposite: Jacques Villeneuve's BAR running in unbranded livery at the 1999 Belgian Grand Prix at Spa-Francorchamps as a result of a ban on tobacco advertising. It has been suggested that mounting restrictions could lead to a reduction in the number of F1 races held in Europe.

Below: Not satisfied with its recent domination of Formula 1 in partnership with McLaren, Mercedes reinforces its marketing message by supplying the safety car which joins the track to slow the cars in the event of an interruption to the racing.

major technical and commercial partner of British American Racing bodes well for the future. It emphasises that the world's leading car makers have considerable confidence about the continuing merit of the F1 arena as an ideal spotlight under which to put their engineering prowess on very public display.

In that respect, Honda is lining up firmly with companies such as BMW, which, as mentioned above, begins its partnership with Williams in 2000; Mercedes-Benz, currently relishing its productive relationship with McLaren and committed to taking a 40 per cent stake in the TAG McLaren Group, which owns the team; and Ford, delighted with its reputed £60 million purchase of the Stewart team, which it has rebranded under the Jaguar Racing banner for the new season.

'The involvement of major car makers in F1 has come as a result of market research,' says TAG McLaren Group Managing Director Ron Dennis.

'Cars are becoming more and more legislated. Bumper heights, A-frame angles, driver safety criteria, headlight position, everything. The end result is becoming more and more similar. If you painted a lot of cars one colour and took the badges off, you'd be surprised how difficult it was to recognise the makes.

'Manufacturers, therefore, are looking for any means to achieve product differentiation. If you win in F1 it is black and white. It signifies advanced technical competence. In my opinion it is a completely logical step for Ford. The volume markets are very much influenced by the public's perception of the brand as a whole.'

Jackie Stewart, however, thinks it was the arrival of

Mercedes-Benz, Dennis's current partner but a much lower volume manufacturer, which really rang the bell.

'I think timing is everything,' Stewart says. 'There are commercial benefits from a sport clearly at the sharpest edge of technology. They have always been there. Today, though, the consumer is more studious about his or her choice of vehicle. What you are trying to do is influence that choice by making a statement. Formula 1 is glamorous, colourful and exciting and that is what most people want to see from a vehicle they buy. And there has never been a time when the lifestyle of F1 has been so highly profiled or recognised. The sport simply cannot be ignored by the agency people or the marketing and sales directors buried in the bureaucracy of the world's largest companies.

'For me, what really attracted everybody's attention was Mercedes-Benz coming in when they were extremely vulnerable to being beaten by, let's say, marques of lesser esteem. And when they came in they were not competitive, either with Sauber or, in the beginning, with McLaren.'

Mercedes has admitted that its involvement was clearly designed to generate a more youthful consumer for the brand.

'They knew precisely what they were doing,' Stewart agrees. 'Take the S-Class. The age group buying that car were pretty much in God's waiting room. Mercedes knew it was a very small volume manufacturer in reality, less than a million a year. Ford almost makes more Focuses than that.

'But they also knew they were not only having a good E-Class car but also an M-Class and an A-Class. Formula 1,

Paul-Henri Cahier

Below: The futuristic main grandstand at Sepang towers over a Formula I car during practice for the inaugural Malaysian Grand Prix in 1999. The magnificent new circuit set a standard which some of the more traditional F1 venues will find difficult to match.

with its technical excellence, appeals to a younger-generation market. Suddenly the logic of coming in was not about the Silver Arrows of the Fifties or Thirties, it was about reaching those people.'

As far as the growth of the FIA Formula I World Championship is concerned over the first decade of the new century, a more widely diverse selection of racing venues can be expected to expand the sport's appeal to fresh areas of the world.

The inaugural Malaysian Grand Prix on Kuala Lumpur's splendid Sepang circuit was a case in point and it will be followed in 2000 by the spectacularly redeveloped Indianapolis track which will host the first United States Grand Prix since the street race in Phoenix, Arizona, back in 1990.

Further afield, China must be a logical stopping place for the F1 World Championship in the future and competition from ambitious emerging nations who see a Grand Prix as a prestigious means of putting their country on the international map, where events will benefit

from considerable governmental support, will obviously place huge pressure on some of the European races which have to stand or fall on their own independent commercial capabilities. Whether this will result in a thinning-out of 'traditional' European Grands Prix may to some extent depend on what view the European Union takes towards continued tobacco advertising over the next few years.

Ironically, the element of the F1 equation which is least likely to change in the short term is the racing itself. The current F1 technical and sporting regulations, whether relating to chassis or engine technology, or even to the format of the races themselves, have evolved over many years and are unlikely to be changed in the foreseeable future.

However, the efforts to make Grand Prix racing more secure for participants and spectators alike will be unremitting. The end result should be a sport which is not only closer fought and more spectacular, but much safer as well.

LAT Photographic

Goldline– the Race Leaders – Bearing up to the millennium!

Goldline have been producing high quality bearings for motor sport, aerospace and high precision industrial applications for 27 years.

All of our products are manufactured to a standard, but with cost-effectiveness strongly borne in mind, which is why so many teams and drivers have won on Goldline bearings over the years, and why this number continues to grow.

Goldline produce different ranges of bearings to meet different requirements across the whole spectrum of the motor sport, automotive, aerospace and transport industries. If you have a bearing need, we can fulfil it. Goldline will prove that Formula 1 know-how and real cost-effectiveness are not mutually exclusive!

Nowadays, Goldline is not so much a supplier to top line motor sport, but more a technical partner – in the truest sense – working with teams and manufacturers to solve motor sport bearing problems to satisfy specific needs.

We will work with you to fulfil your specific requirements.

This is why we are the Race Leaders.

Goldline F1 drop-link bearing

Ceramic/Cronidur 30 ®

Goldline F1 suspension bearings

AMPEP X1/AISI440C/AMS5643

Goldline F1 wheel bearings

Ceramic/Cronidur 30 ®

Goldline F1 push-clutch bearings
Ceramic/Cronidur 30 ®

Goldline F1 pull-clutch bearing
Ceramic/Cronidur 30 ®

Goldline Bearings Ltd
Stafford Park 17, Telford TF3 3DG. Tel: (01952) 292401 Fax: (01952) 292403

MICHELIN'S RETURN

50 YEARS OF FORMULA ONE MARK ANOTHER SIGNIFICANT MILESTONE

AFTER MANY years of speculation and rumour in the press, Michelin has confirmed it will bring its formidable tyre technology back to F1 racing in 2001. It was in 1977 that Michelin first made its impact with the kind of innovation that alters the nature of a sport forever and for the better. That great leap forward was witnessed at the British Grand Prix in Silverstone when Renault took to the starting grid in mid-season. The bright yellow 1.5-litre V6 turbocharged car was equipped with what was to prove the most radical development since the invention of the pneumatic tyre – the radial! Not only did its use quickly come to dominate racing, it has become the norm for all cars on the road today. Between 1978 and 1984, Michelin-equipped teams won no fewer than 59 Grand Prix races – eleven more than the tyre giant's nearest rival.

Formula 1, of course, is not everyday use. It is at the forefront of automotive technology, a fact not lost on Michelin. As a world-wide group, Michelin has remained in touch with developments within the sport over the past decades and has also provided the podium with the vast majority of winners in world rallying and touring car racing for a quarter of a century and more.

In parallel with preparations for next year's return to Formula 1 with BMW-Williams and Toyota, Michelin is this year looking for overall victory in a long list of world-class motor racing, building on outstanding results achieved in 1999.

After the win in the Daytona 24 Hours by Dodge-Michelin (Wendlinger, Dupuy and Beretta) in February this year, the next challenge is the Le Mans 24-Hours where, in partnership with Audi, Panoz and Chrysler, the target is a seventh outright victory in this endurance classic since 1989. Michelin will be looking to follow up its triumph of last summer, not only in the overall classification (BMW-Michelin with Winkelhock, Dalmas and Martini) but also in the GTS category (Chrysler-Michelin with Beretta, Wendlinger and Dupuy). Another important win for Michelin was the Team Viper Oreca victory in the FIA-GT Championship.

Michelin's extensive experience at Le Mans over the years has contributed a great deal to tyre development and, working hand in hand with vehicle manufacturers, continues to pay dividends. The company achieved success in 1999 in disciplines totally new to it. For example, the Prototype Manufacturers' title in the newly created American Le Mans Series went to none other than the team of Panoz-Michelin. In 2000, Michelin returns to defend its crown in this new Series, which promises to grow in importance in the years to come.

Among the clearest illustrations of Michelin's ability to tackle a new discipline from scratch and win first time out was in the 1999 Japanese GT Championship. The Teams' Title went to the partnership of Team TOM'S Toyotas and Michelin. There was even a grand slam to celebrate: victory, pole position and fastest race lap in the final round. Michelin is back in Japan this season in a bid to repeat last year's success with TOM'S Toyotas.

Michelin's commitment to motor sports reflects its philosophy of developing technology in the heat of competition as well as in the cool of the research laboratory.

Above: Michelin and Brabham-BMW combined to help Nelson Piquet win the 1983 World Championship. Michelin returns to Formula 1 in 2001 with Williams-BMW.

SPECIAL FEATURE

MICHELIN

The more we progress, the further you go.

World Champion Drivers

1950	Giuseppe Farina	Alfa Romeo
1951	Juan Manuel Fangio	Alfa Romeo
1952	Alberto Ascari	Ferrari
1953	Alberto Ascari	Ferrari
1954	Juan Manuel Fangio	Maserati/Mercedes-Benz
1955	Juan Manuel Fangio	Mercedes-Benz
1956	Juan Manuel Fangio	Ferrari
1957	Juan Manuel Fangio	Maserati
1958	Mike Hawthorn	Ferrari
1959	Jack Brabham	Cooper-Climax
1960	Jack Brabham	Cooper-Climax
1961	Phil Hill	Ferrari
1962	Graham Hill	BRM
1963	Jim Clark	Lotus-Climax
1964	John Surtees	Ferrari
1965	Jim Clark	Lotus-Climax
1966	Jack Brabham	Brabham-Repco
1967	Denny Hulme	Brabham-Repco
1968	Graham Hill	Lotus-Ford Cosworth
1969	Jackie Stewart	Matra-Ford Cosworth
1970	Jochen Rindt	Lotus-Ford Cosworth
1971	Jackie Stewart	Tyrrell-Ford Cosworth
1972	Emerson Fittipaldi	Lotus-Ford Cosworth
1973	Jackie Stewart	Tyrrell-Ford Cosworth
1974	Emerson Fittipaldi	McLaren-Ford Cosworth
1975	Niki Lauda	Ferrari
1976	James Hunt	McLaren-Ford Cosworth
1977	Niki Lauda	Ferrari
1978	Mario Andretti	Lotus-Ford Cosworth
1979	Jody Scheckter	Ferrari
1980	Alan Jones	Williams-Ford Cosworth
1981	Nelson Piquet	Brabham-Ford Cosworth
1982	Keke Rosberg	Williams-Ford Cosworth
1983	Nelson Piquet	Brabham-BMW
1984	Niki Lauda	McLaren-TAG
1985	Alain Prost	McLaren-TAG
1986	Alain Prost	McLaren-TAG
1987	Nelson Piquet	Williams-Honda
1988	Ayrton Senna	McLaren-Honda
1989	Alain Prost	McLaren-Honda
1990	Ayrton Senna	McLaren-Honda
1991	Ayrton Senna	McLaren-Honda
1992	Nigel Mansell	Williams-Renault
1993	Alain Prost	Williams-Renault
1994	Michael Schumacher	Benetton-Ford
1995	Michael Schumacher	Benetton-Renault
1996	Damon Hill	Williams-Renault
1997	Jacques Villeneuve	Williams-Renault
1998	Mika Häkkinen	McLaren-Mercedes-Benz
1999	Mika Häkkinen	McLaren-Mercedes-Benz

Constructors' Champions

1958	Vanwall
1959	Cooper-Climax
1960	Cooper-Climax
1961	Ferrari
1962	BRM
1963	Lotus-Climax
1964	Ferrari
1965	Lotus-Climax
1966	Brabham-Repco
1967	Brabham-Repco
1968	Lotus-Ford Cosworth
1969	Matra-Ford Cosworth
1970	Lotus-Ford Cosworth
1971	Tyrrell-Ford Cosworth
1972	Lotus-Ford Cosworth
1973	Lotus-Ford Cosworth
1974	McLaren-Ford Cosworth
1975	Ferrari
1976	Ferrari
1977	Ferrari
1978	Lotus-Ford Cosworth
1979	Ferrari
1980	Williams-Ford Cosworth
1981	Williams-Ford Cosworth
1982	Ferrari
1983	Ferrari
1984	McLaren-TAG
1985	McLaren-TAG
1986	Williams-Honda
1987	Williams-Honda
1988	McLaren-Honda
1989	McLaren-Honda
1990	McLaren-Honda
1991	McLaren-Honda
1992	Williams-Renault
1993	Williams-Renault
1994	Williams-Renault
1995	Benetton-Renault
1996	Williams-Renault
1997	Williams-Renault
1998	McLaren-Mercedes-Benz
1999	Ferrari

GRAND PRIX RESULTS
1950-99
Compiled by David Hayhoe

1952

Position	Driver	Car	Switzerland	Belgium	France	Britain	Germany	Netherlands	Italy	Points total	
1	Alberto Ascari	Ferrari	–	p1	p1	1	p1	p1	p1	36	(17.5)
2	Giuseppe Farina	Ferrari	pr	2	2	p6	2	2	4	24	(3)
3	Piero Taruffi	Ferrari	1	r	3	2	4	–	7	22	
4	Rudi Fischer	Ferrari	2	–	11=	13	3	–	r	10	
	Mike Hawthorn	Cooper-Bristol	–	4	r	3	–	4	nc	10	
6	Robert Manzon	Gordini	r	3	4	r	r	5	14	9	
7	Luigi Villoresi	Ferrari	–	–	–	–	–	3	3	8	
8	Froilán González	Maserati	–	–	–	–	–	–	2	6.5	
9	Jean Behra	Gordini	3	r	7	–	5	r	r	6	
10	Ken Wharton	Frazer Nash-Bristol	4	r	–	–	–	r	–	3	
		Cooper-Bristol	–	–	–	–	–	–	9		
	Dennis Poore	Connaught	–	–	–	4	–	–	12	3	
12	Alan Brown	Cooper-Bristol	5	6	–	22	–	–	15	2	
	Paul Frère	HWM	–	5	–	–	r	–	–	2	
		Simca Gordini	–	–	–	–	–	r	–		
	Maurice Trintignant	Ferrari	ns	–	–	–	–	–	–	2	
		Gordini	–	–	5	r	r	6	r		
	Eric Thompson	Connaught	–	–	–	5	–	–	–	2	
	Felice Bonetto	Maserati	–	–	–	dq	–	5	2		

1950

Position	Driver	Car	Britain	Monaco	Switzerland	Belgium	France	Italy	Points total
1	Giuseppe Farina	Alfa Romeo	p1	r	1	p4	7r	1	30
2	Juan Manuel Fangio	Alfa Romeo	r	p1	pr	1	p1	pr	27
3	Luigi Fagioli	Alfa Romeo	2	r	2	2	2	3	24 (4)
4	Louis Rosier	Talbot Lago	5	r	3	3	6=	4	13
5	Alberto Ascari	Ferrari	–	2	r	5	–	2=	11
6	B. Bira	Maserati	r	5	4	–	–	r	5
7	Reg Parnell	Alfa Romeo	3	–	–	–	–	–	4
		Maserati	–	–	–	–	r	–	
	Louis Chiron	Maserati	r	3	9	–	r	r	4
	Peter Whitehead	Ferrari	–	ns	–	–	3	7	4
10	Yves Giraud-Cabantous	Talbot Lago	4	–	r	r	8	–	3
	Raymond Sommer †	Ferrari	–	4	r	–	–	–	3
		Talbot Lago	–	–	–	r	r	r	
	Robert Manzon	Simca Gordini	–	r	–	–	4	r	3
	Dorino Serafini	Ferrari	–	–	–	–	–	2=	3
	Philippe Étancelin	Talbot Lago	8	r	r	r	5=	5	3
15	Felice Bonetto	Maserati Milano	–	–	5	–	r	–	2
		Milano-Maserati	–	–	–	–	–	ns	
16	Eugène Chaboud	Talbot Lago	–	–	–	r	5=	–	1

1951

Position	Driver	Car	Switzerland	Belgium	France	Britain	Germany	Italy	Spain	Points total
1	Juan Manuel Fangio	Alfa Romeo	p1	p9	p1=	2	2	pr	1	31 (6)
2	Alberto Ascari	Ferrari	6	2	2=	r	p1	1	p4	25 (3)
3	Froilán González	Talbot Lago	r	–	–	–	–	–	–	24 (3)
		Ferrari	–	–	2=	p1	3	2	2	
4	Giuseppe Farina	Alfa Romeo	3	1	5	r	r	3=	3	19 (3)
5	Luigi Villoresi	Ferrari	r	3	3	3	4	4	r	15 (3)
6	Piero Taruffi	Ferrari	2	r	–	–	5	5	r	10
7	Felice Bonetto	Alfa Romeo	–	–	–	4	r	3=	5	7
8	Reg Parnell	Thinwall Ferrari	–	–	4	–	–	–	–	5
		BRM	–	–	–	5	–	ns	–	
9	Luigi Fagioli	Alfa Romeo	–	–	1=	–	–	–	–	4
10	Consalvo Sanesi	Alfa Romeo	4	r	10	6	–	–	–	3
	Louis Rosier	Talbot Lago	9	4	r	10	8	7	7	3
12	Emmanuel de Graffenried	Alfa Romeo	5	–	–	–	–	r	6	2
		Maserati	–	–	r	–	r	–	–	
	Yves Giraud-Cabantous	Talbot Lago	r	5	7	–	r	8	r	2

1953

Position	Driver	Car	Argentina	Netherlands	Belgium	France	Britain	Germany	Switzerland	Italy	Points total
1	Alberto Ascari	Ferrari	p1	p1	1	p4	p1	p8=	1	pr	34.5(12.5)
2	Juan Manuel Fangio	Maserati	r	r	pr	2	2	2	p4=	1	27.5 (1.5)
3	Giuseppe Farina	Ferrari	r	2	r	5	3	1	2	2	26 (6)
4	Mike Hawthorn	Ferrari	4	4	6	1	5	3	3	4	19 (8)
5	Luigi Villoresi	Ferrari	2	r	2	6	r	8=	6	3	17
6	Froilán González	Maserati	3	3=	3	r	4	–	r	r	13.5 (1)
7	Emmanuel de Graffenried	Maserati	–	5	4	7	r	5	r	r	7
8	Felice Bonetto †	Maserati	r	3=	–	r	6	4	4=	r	6.5
9	Onofré Marimón	Maserati	–	–	3	9	r	r	r	4	4
	Maurice Trintignant	Gordini	7=	6	5	r	r	r	r	5	4
11	Oscar Gálvez	Maserati	5	–	–	–	–	–	–	–	2
	Hermann Lang	Maserati	–	–	–	–	–	–	5	–	2

1954

Position	Driver	Car	Argentina	Belgium	France	Britain	Germany	Switzerland	Italy	Spain	Points total
1	Juan Manuel Fangio	Maserati	1	p1	–	–	–	–	–	–	42 (15.14)
		Mercedes-Benz	–	–	p1	p4	p1	1	p1	3	
2	Froilán González	Ferrari	3	4=	r	1	2=	p2	3=	–	25.14(1.5)
3	Mike Hawthorn	Ferrari	dq	4=	r	2	2=	r	2	1	24.64
4	Maurice Trintignant	Ferrari	4	2	r	5	3	r	5	r	17
5	Karl Kling	Mercedes-Benz	–	–	2	7	4	r	r	5	12
6	Hans Herrmann	Mercedes-Benz	–	–	r	–	r	3	4	r	8
7	Giuseppe Farina	Ferrari	p2	r	–	–	–	–	r	–	6
	Luigi Musso	Maserati	ns	–	–	–	–	–	r	2	6
	Roberto Mières	Maserati	r	r	r	6	r	4	r	4	6
10	Stirling Moss	Maserati	–	3	–	r	r	r	10	r	4.14
	Onofré Marimón †	Maserati	r	r	3	ns	–	–	–	–	4.14
12	Robert Manzon	Ferrari	–	–	3	r	9	ns	r	r	4
	Sergio Mantovani	Maserati	–	7	ns	–	5	5	9	r	4
14	B. Bira	Maserati	7	6	4	r	r	–	–	9	3
15	Elie Bayol	Gordini	5	–	–	–	–	–	–	–	2
	André Pilette	Gordini	–	5	–	9	r	–	–	r	2
	Luigi Villoresi	Maserati	–	–	5	r	ns	–	r	–	2
		Lancia	–	–	–	–	–	–	–	r	
	Umberto Maglioli	Ferrari	9	–	–	–	7	3=	–	–	2
19	Alberto Ascari	Maserati	–	–	r	r	–	–	–	–	1.14
		Ferrari	–	–	–	–	–	r	–	–	
		Lancia	–	–	–	–	–	–	–	pr	
20	Jean Behra	Gordini	dq	r	6	r	10	r	r	r	0.14

KEY

=	shared
dq	disqualified
ew	entry withdrawn
exc	excluded
nc	not classified
npq	non-pre-qualified
nq	non-qualified
ns	non-started
p	pole position
r	retired
†	driver died during the year

It was common practice in the 1950s for drivers to share a car. In these situations, a driver's best result in the race is shown in the tables.

Points shown in brackets are those scored but not counted towards the final World Championship total.

1955

Position	Driver	Car	Argentina	Monaco	Belgium	Netherlands	Britain	Italy	Points total
1	Juan Manuel Fangio	Mercedes-Benz	1	pr	1	p1	2	p1	40 (1)
2	Stirling Moss	Mercedes-Benz	4=	9	2	2	p1	r	23
3	Eugenio Castellotti	Lancia	r	2	pr	–	–	–	12
		Ferrari	–	–	–	5	6=	3	
4	Maurice Trintignant	Ferrari	2=	1	6	r	r	8	11.33
5	Giuseppe Farina	Ferrari	2=	4	3	–	–	–	10.33
		Lancia	–	–	–	–	–	ns	
6	Piero Taruffi	Ferrari	–	8=	–	–	–	–	9
		Mercedes-Benz	–	–	–	–	4	2	
7	Roberto Mières	Maserati	5	r	5=	4	r	7	7
8	Luigi Musso	Maserati	7=	r	7	3	5	r	6
	Jean Behra	Maserati	6=	3=	5=	6	r	4	6
10	Karl Kling	Mercedes-Benz	4=	–	r	r	3	r	5
11	Paul Frère	Ferrari	–	8=	4	–	–	–	3
12	Froilán González	Ferrari	p2=	–	–	–	–	–	2
	Cesare Perdisa	Maserati	–	3=	8	–	–	–	2
	Luigi Villoresi	Lancia	r	5	–	–	–	ns	2
	Carlos Menditéguy	Maserati	r	–	–	–	–	5	2
16	Umberto Maglioli	Ferrari	3=	–	–	–	–	6	1.33
17	Hans Herrmann	Mercedes-Benz	4=	ns	–	–	–	–	1

1956

Position	Driver	Car	Argentina	Monaco	Belgium	France	Britain	Germany	Italy	Points total
1	Juan Manuel Fangio	Lancia Ferrari	p1=	p2=	pr	p4	1	p1	p2=	30 (3)
2	Stirling Moss	Maserati	r	1	3=	5=	pr	2	1	27 (1)
3	Peter Collins	Ferrari	r	–	–	–	–	–	–	25
		Lancia Ferrari	–	2=	1	1	2=	r	2=	
4	Jean Behra	Maserati	2	3	7	3	3	3	r	22
5	Eugenio Castellotti	Lancia Ferrari	r	4=	r	2	10=	r	8=	7.5
6	Paul Frère	Lancia Ferrari	–	–	2	–	–	–	–	6
	Chico Godia	Maserati	–	–	r	7	8	4	4	6
8	Jack Fairman	Connaught	–	–	–	–	4	–	5	5
9	Mike Hawthorn	Maserati	3	–	ns	–	–	–	–	4
		BRM	–	ns	–	–	r	–	–	
		Vanwall	–	–	–	10=	–	–	–	
	Luigi Musso	Lancia Ferrari	1=	r	–	–	–	r	r	4
	Ron Flockhart	BRM	–	–	–	–	r	–	–	4
		Connaught	–	–	–	–	–	–	3	
12	Harry Schell	Vanwall	–	r	4	10=	r	–	r	3
		Maserati	–	–	–	–	–	r	–	
	Alfonso de Portago	Lancia Ferrari	–	–	–	r	2=	r	r	3
	Cesare Perdisa	Maserati	–	7	3=	5=	7	ns	–	3
15	Olivier Gendebien	Ferrari-Lancia	5	–	–	–	–	–	–	2
		Lancia Ferrari	–	–	–	r	–	–	–	
	Nano da Silva Ramos	Gordini	–	5	–	8	r	–	r	2
	Luigi Villoresi	Maserati	–	–	5	r	6	r	r	2
	Horace Gould	Maserati	–	8	r	–	5	r	–	2
	Louis Rosier †	Maserati	–	r	8	6	r	5	–	2
20	Gerino Gerini	Maserati	4=	–	–	–	–	–	10	1.5
	Chico Landi	Maserati	4=	–	–	–	–	–	10	1.5

1957

Position	Driver	Car	Argentina	Monaco	France	Britain	Germany	Pescara	Italy	Points total
1	Juan Manuel Fangio	Maserati	1	p1	p1	r	p1	p2	2	40 (6)
2	Stirling Moss	Maserati	p8	–	–	–	–	–	–	25
		Vanwall	–	r	p1=	5	1	1		
3	Luigi Musso	Lancia Ferrari	r	–	2	2	4	r	8	16
4	Mike Hawthorn	Lancia Ferrari	r	7=	4	3	2	–	6	13
5	Tony Brooks	Vanwall	–	2	–	1=	9	r	7	11
6	Masten Gregory	Maserati	–	3	–	–	8	4	4	10
7	Jean Behra	Maserati	2	–	5	r	6	r	r	8
	Peter Collins	Lancia Ferrari	6=	r	3	4=	3	–	r	8
	Harry Schell	Maserati	4	r	6	r	7	3	5=	8
10	Stuart Lewis-Evans	Connaught	–	4	–	–	–	–	–	5
		Vanwall	–	–	r	7	r	5	pr	
	Maurice Trintignant	Lancia Ferrari	–	5	r	4=	–	–	–	5
12	Carlos Menditéguy	Maserati	3	–	r	–	–	–	–	4
	Wolfgang von Trips	Lancia Ferrari	6=	7=	–	–	–	–	3	4
14	Roy Salvadori	BRM	–	nq	–	–	–	–	–	2
		Vanwall	–	–	r	–	–	–	–	
		Cooper-Climax	–	–	–	5	r	r	–	
15	Froilán González	Lancia Ferrari	5=	–	–	–	–	–	–	1
	Alfonso de Portago †	Lancia Ferrari	5=	–	–	–	–	–	–	1
	Giorgio Scarlatti	Maserati	–	r	–	10	6	5=	–	1

1958

Position	Driver	Car	Argentina	Monaco	Netherlands	Belgium	France	Britain	Germany	Portugal	Italy	Morocco	Points total
1	Mike Hawthorn	Ferrari	3	r	5	p2	p1	2	pr	2	2	p2	42 (7)
2	Stirling Moss	Cooper-Climax	1	–	–	–	–	–	–	–	–	–	41
		Vanwall	–	r	1	r	2	pr	r	p1	pr	1	
3	Tony Brooks	Vanwall	–	pr	r	1	r	7	1	r	1	r	24
4	Roy Salvadori	Cooper-Climax	–	r	4	8	11	3	2	9	5	7	15
5	Peter Collins †	Ferrari	r	3	r	r	5	1	r	–	–	–	14
6	Harry Schell	Maserati	6	–	–	–	–	–	–	–	–	–	14
		BRM	–	5	2	5	r	5	r	6	r	5	
7	Maurice Trintignant	Cooper-Climax	–	1	9	–	8	3	8	r	r		12
		Maserati	–	–	7	–	–	–	–	–	–	–	
		BRM	–	–	–	r	–	–	–	–	–	–	
	Luigi Musso †	Ferrari	2	2	7	r	r	–	–	–	–	–	12
9	Stuart Lewis-Evans †	Vanwall	–	r	pr	3	r	4	–	3	r	r	11
10	Phil Hill	Maserati	–	–	–	7	–	–	–	–	–	–	9
		Ferrari	–	–	–	–	–	–	9	–	3	3	
	Jean Behra	Maserati	5	–	–	–	–	–	–	–	–	–	9
		BRM	–	r	3	r	r	r	4	r	r		
	Wolfgang von Trips	Ferrari	–	–	–	3	4	5	r	–	9		9
13	Juan Manuel Fangio	Maserati	p4	–	–	4	–	–	–	–	–	–	7
14	Jack Brabham	Cooper-Climax	–	4	8	r	6	6	r	7	r	11	3
15	Cliff Allison	Lotus-Climax	–	6	6	4	r	r	10	–	7	10	3
		Maserati	–	–	–	–	–	–	–	r	–	–	
	Jo Bonnier	Maserati	–	r	10	9	8	r	r	r	–	–	3
		BRM	–	–	–	–	–	–	–	–	r	4	

Masten Gregory and Carroll Shelby shared a Maserati in Italy where they finished fourth. Consequently they were ineligible for points.

1959

Position	Driver	Car	Monaco	Netherlands	France	Britain	Germany	Portugal	Italy	USA	Points total
1	Jack Brabham	Cooper-Climax	1	2	3	p1	r	r	3	4	31 (3)
2	Tony Brooks	Ferrari	2	r	p1	–	p1	9	r	3	27
		Vanwall	–	–	–	r	–	–	–	–	
3	Stirling Moss	Cooper-Climax	pr	r	–	–	r	p1	p1	pr	25.5
		BRM	–	–	dq	2	–	–	–	–	
4	Phil Hill	Ferrari	4	6	2	–	3	r	2	r	20
5	Maurice Trintignant	Cooper-Climax	3	8	11	5	4	4	9	2	19
6	Bruce McLaren	Cooper-Climax	5	–	5	3	r	r	r	1	16.5
7	Dan Gurney	Ferrari	–	–	r	–	2	3	4	–	13
8	Jo Bonnier	BRM	r	p1	r	r	5	r	8	–	10
	Masten Gregory	Cooper-Climax	r	3	r	7	r	2	–	–	10
10	Innes Ireland	Lotus-Climax	–	4	r	ns	r	r	r	5	5
	Harry Schell	BRM	r	r	7	4	7r	5	7	r	5
12	Olivier Gendebien	Ferrari	–	–	4	–	–	6	–		3
13	Jean Behra †	Ferrari	r	5	–	–	–	–	–	–	2
		Behra Porsche	–	–	–	ns	–	–	–	–	
	Cliff Allison	Ferrari	r	9	–	–	r	–	5	r	2

1960

Position	Driver	Car	Argentina	Monaco	Netherlands	Belgium	France	Britain	Portugal	Italy	USA	Points total
1	Jack Brabham	Cooper-Climax	r	dq	1	p1	p1	p1	1	–	4	43
2	Bruce McLaren	Cooper-Climax	1	2	r	2	3	4	2	–	3	34 (3)
3	Stirling Moss	Cooper-Climax	p3=	–	–	–	–	–	–	–	–	19
		Lotus-Climax	–	p1	p4	ns	–	dq	–	p1		
4	Innes Ireland	Lotus-Climax	6	9	2	r	7	3	6	–		18
5	Phil Hill	Ferrari	8	3	r	4	12r	7	r	p1	–	16
		Cooper-Climax	–	–	–	–	–	–	–	–	6	
6	Olivier Gendebien	Cooper-Climax	–	–	–	3	2	9	7	–	12	10
	Wolfgang von Trips	Ferrari	5	8r	5	r	11r	6	4	5	–	10
		Cooper-Maserati	–	–	–	–	–	–	–	9		
8	Richie Ginther	Ferrari	–	6	6	–	–	–	2	–		8
		Scarab	–	–	–	ns	–	–	–	–		
	Jim Clark	Lotus-Climax	–	–	r	5	5	16	3	–	16	8
10	Tony Brooks	Cooper-Climax	–	4	r	r	5	5	r			7
		Vanwall	–	–	–	r	–	–	–	–		
11	Cliff Allison	Ferrari	2	nq	–	–	–	–	–			6
	John Surtees	Lotus-Climax	–	r	–	–	2	pr	r			6
13	Graham Hill	BRM	r	7r	3	r	r	r	r	r		4
	Willy Mairesse	Ferrari	–	–	r	r	–	3	–			4
	Jo Bonnier	BRM	7	5	r	r	r	r	r	5		4
16	Carlos Menditéguy	Cooper-Maserati	4	–	–	–	–	–	–			3
	Henry Taylor	Cooper-Climax	–	7	–	4	8	ns	–	14		3
	Giulio Cabianca	Cooper-Castellotti	–	–	–	–	–	4	–			3
19	Lucien Bianchi	Cooper-Climax	–	6	r	r	–					1
	Ron Flockhart	Lotus-Climax	–	6	–	–	–					1
		Cooper-Climax	–	–	–	–	–					
	Hans Herrmann	Porsche	–	–	6	–						1

Stirling Moss shared the Cooper with Maurice Trintignant in Argentina and so both were ineligible for points.

1961

Position	Driver	Car	Monaco	Netherlands	Belgium	France	Britain	Germany	Italy	USA	Points total
1	Phil Hill	Ferrari	3	p2	p1	p9	p2	p3	1	–	34 (4)
2	Wolfgang von Trips †	Ferrari	4r	1	2	r	1	2	pr		33
3	Stirling Moss	Lotus-Climax	p1	4	8	r	r	1	r	r	21
		Ferguson-Climax	–	–	–	dq=	–	–	–	–	
	Dan Gurney	Porsche	5	10	6	2	7	7	2	2	21
5	Richie Ginther	Ferrari	2	5	3	15r	3	8	r	–	16
6	Innes Ireland	Lotus-Climax	ns	–	r	4	10	r	r	1	12
7	Jim Clark	Lotus-Climax	10	3	12	3	r	4	r	7	11
	Bruce McLaren	Cooper-Climax	6	12	r	5	8	6	3	4	11
9	Giancarlo Baghetti	Ferrari	–	–	1	r	–	r	r		9
10	Tony Brooks	BRM-Climax	13r	9	13	r	9	r	5	3	6
11	Jack Brabham	Cooper-Climax	r	6	r	r	4	r	r	pr	4
	John Surtees	Cooper-Climax	11r	7	5	r	r	5	r	r	4
13	Olivier Gendebien	Emeryson-Maserati	nq	–	–	–	–	–	–	–	3
		Ferrari	–	–	4	–	–	–	–	–	
		Lotus-Climax	–	–	–	–	–	–	11=		
	Jack Lewis	Cooper-Climax	–	9	r	r	9	4	–		3
	Jo Bonnier	Porsche	12r	11	7	7	5	r	r	6	3
	Graham Hill	BRM-Climax	r	8	r	6	r	r	r	5	3
17	Roy Salvadori	Cooper-Climax	–	–	8	6	10	6	r	2	

1962

Position	Driver	Car	Netherlands	Monaco	Belgium	France	Britain	Germany	Italy	USA	South Africa	Points total
1	Graham Hill	BRM	1	6r	p2	9r	4	1	1	2	1	42 (10)
2	Jim Clark	Lotus-Climax	9	pr	1	pr	p1	4	pr	p1	pr	30
3	Bruce McLaren	Cooper-Climax	r	r	4	3	5	3	3	2		27 (5)
4	John Surtees	Lola-Climax	pr	4	5	5	2	2	r	r	r	19
5	Dan Gurney	Porsche	r	r	–	1	9	p3	13r	5	–	15
		Lotus-BRM	–	–	ns	–	–	–	–	–	–	
6	Phil Hill	Ferrari	3	2	3	–	r	r	11	–	–	14
		Porsche	–	–	–	–	–	–	–	ns	–	
7	Tony Maggs	Cooper-Climax	5	r	r	2	6	9	7	7	3	13
8	Richie Ginther	BRM	r	r	r	3	13	8	2	r	7	10
9	Jack Brabham	Lotus-Climax	r	8r	6	r	5	–	–	–	–	9
		Brabham-Climax	–	–	–	–	–	r	–	4	4	
10	Trevor Taylor	Lotus-Climax	2	r	r	8	8	r	r	12	r	6
11	Giancarlo Baghetti	Ferrari	4	–	r	–	–	10	5	–	–	5
12	Lorenzo Bandini	Ferrari	–	3	–	–	r	–	8	–	–	4
	Ricardo Rodriguez †	Ferrari	r	ns	4	–	–	6	14r	–	–	4
14	Willy Mairesse	Ferrari	–	7r	r	–	–	r	4	–	–	3
	Jo Bonnier	Porsche	7	5	–	10r	r	7	6	13	–	3
16	Innes Ireland	Lotus-Climax	r	r	r	r	16	r	r	8	5	2
	Carel Godin de Beaufort	Porsche	6	nq	7	6	14	13	10	r	11r	2
18	Masten Gregory	Lotus-Climax	r	–	–	–	–	7	–	–	–	1
		Lotus-BRM	–	nq	r	r	–	–	12	6	–	
	Neville Lederle	Lotus-Climax	–	–	–	–	–	–	–	–	6	1

1963

Position	Driver	Car	Monaco	Belgium	Netherlands	France	Britain	Germany	Italy	USA	Mexico	South Africa	Points total
1	Jim Clark	Lotus-Climax	p8r	1	p1	p1	p1	p2	1	3	p1	p1	54 (19)
2	Graham Hill	BRM	1	pr	r	3	3	r	16r	p1	4	3	29
	Richie Ginther	BRM	2	4	5	r	4	3	2	2	3	r	29 (5)
4	John Surtees	Ferrari	4	r	3	r	2	1	pr	9r	dq	r	22
5	Dan Gurney	Brabham-Climax	r	3	2	5	r	14r	r	6	2		19
6	Bruce McLaren	Cooper-Climax	3	2	r	12r	r	r	3	11r	r	4	17
7	Jack Brabham	Lotus-Climax	–	–	–	–	–	–	–	–	–		14
		Brabham-Climax	–	–	r	4	7	5	4	2	13r		
8	Tony Maggs	Cooper-Climax	5	7r	r	2	9	r	6	r	r	9	9
9	Innes Ireland	Lotus-BRM	r	–	–	–	–	r	–	–	–		6
		BRP-BRM	–	r	4	9	dq	–	4r	–	–		
	Lorenzo Bandini	BRM	–	–	–	10	5	r	–	–	–		6
		Ferrari	–	–	–	–	–	–	r	5	r	5	
	Jo Bonnier	Cooper-Climax	7	5	11	r	r	6	7	8	5	6	6
12	Gerhard Mitter	Porsche	–	–	r	–	–	4	–	–	–		3
	Jim Hall	Lotus-BRM	r	8	11	6	5	8	10r	8	–		3
14	Carel Godin de Beaufort	Porsche	–	6	9	–	10	r	nq	6	10	10	2
15	Trevor Taylor	Lotus-Climax	6	r	10	13r	dq	8	–	r	r	8	1
	Ludovico Scarfiotti	Ferrari	–	–	6	ns	–	–	–	–	–		1
	Jo Siffert	Lotus-BRM	r	r	7	6	r	9r	r	r	9	–	1

Graham Hill was awarded no points for his third place in France, because he was push-started on the grid.

1964

Position	Driver	Car	Monaco	Netherlands	Belgium	France	Britain	Germany	Austria	Italy	USA	Mexico	Points total
1	John Surtees	Ferrari	r	2	r	r	3	p1	r	p1	2	2	40
2	Graham Hill	BRM	1	4	5r	2	2	2	pr	r	1	11	39 (2)
3	Jim Clark	Lotus-Climax	p4r	1	1	pr	p1	r	r	r p7r=	p5r		32
4	Lorenzo Bandini	Ferrari	10r	r	9	5	3	3	2	4	r		23
	Richie Ginther	BRM	2	11	4	5	8	7	2	4	4	8	23
6	Dan Gurney	Brabham-Climax	r	pr	p6r	1	13	10	r	10	r	1	19
7	Bruce McLaren	Cooper-Climax	r	7	2	6	r	r	r	2	r	7	13
8	Peter Arundell	Lotus-Climax	3	3	9	3	–	–	–	–	–	–	11
	Jack Brabham	Brabham-Climax	r	r	3	3	4	12r	9	14r	r	r	11
10	Jo Siffert	Lotus-BRM	8	–	–	–	–	–	–	–	–		7
		Brabham-BRM	–	13	r	r	11	4	r	7	3	r	
11	Bob Anderson	Brabham-Climax	7r	6	ns	12	7	r	3	11	–	–	5
12	Tony Maggs	BRM	–	ns	ns	r	6	4	–	–	–		4
	Mike Spence	Lotus-Climax	–	–	–	–	9	8	r	6	7r=	4	4
	Innes Ireland	Lotus-BRM	ns	–	–	–	–	–	–	–	–		4
		BRP-BRM	–	10	r	10	–	5	5	r	12		
15	Jo Bonnier	Cooper-Climax	5	–	–	–	–	–	–	–	–		3
		Brabham-BRM	–	9	r	r	r	r	–	–	–		
		Brabham-Climax	–	–	–	–	–	–	6	12	r	r	
16	Chris Amon	Lotus-BRM	nq	5	r	10	r	11r	–	–	–		2
		Lotus-Climax	–	–	–	–	–	–	r	–	–		
	Maurice Trintignant	BRM	r	–	–	11	nq	5r	–	r	–		2
	Walt Hansgen	Lotus-Climax	–	–	–	–	–	–	–	5	–		2
19	Mike Hailwood	Lotus-BRM	6	12r	r	–	8	r	8	8r	r		1
	Phil Hill	Cooper-Climax	9r	8	r	7	6	r	r	–	r	9r	1
	Trevor Taylor	BRP-BRM	r	–	7	r	r	–	r	nq	6	r	1
	Pedro Rodriguez	Ferrari	–	–	–	–	–	–	–	–	–	6	1

1965

Position	Driver	Car	South Africa	Monaco	Belgium	France	Britain	Netherlands	Germany	Italy	USA	Mexico	Points total
1	Jim Clark	Lotus-Climax	p1	–	1	p1	p1	1	p1	p10r	r	pr	54
2	Graham Hill	BRM	3	p1	p5	5	2	p4	2	2	p1	r	40 (7)
3	Jackie Stewart	BRM	6	3	2	2	5	2	r	1	r	r	33 (1)
4	Dan Gurney	Brabham-Climax	r	–	10	r	6	3	3	3	2	2	25
5	John Surtees	Ferrari	2	4r	r	3	3	7	r	r	–	r	17
6	Lorenzo Bandini	Ferrari	15r	2	9	8r	r	9	6	4	4	8	13
7	Richie Ginther	Honda	–	r	6	r	r	6	–	14r	7	1	11
8	Mike Spence	Lotus-Climax	4	–	7	7	4	8	r	11r	r	3	10
	Bruce McLaren	Cooper-Climax	5	5	3	r	10	r	r	5	r	r	10
10	Jack Brabham	Brabham-Climax	8	r	4	–	ns	–	5	–	3	r	9
11	Denny Hulme	Brabham-Climax	–	8	–	4	r	5	r	r	–	5	5
	Jo Siffert	Brabham-BRM	7	6	8	6	9	13	r	r	11	4	5
13	Jochen Rindt	Cooper-Climax	r	nq	11	r	14r	r	4	8	6	r	4
14	Pedro Rodriguez	Ferrari	–	–	–	–	–	–	–	–	5	7	2
	Ronnie Bucknum	Honda	–	–	–	–	–	–	r	13	5		2
	Dickie Attwood	Lotus-BRM	–	r	14r	–	13	12	r	6	10	6	2

1966

Position	Driver	Car	Monaco	Belgium	France	Britain	Netherlands	Germany	Italy	USA	Mexico	Points total
1	Jack Brabham	Brabham-Repco	r	4	1	p1	p1	1	r	pr	2	42 (3)
2	John Surtees	Ferrari	r	p1	–	–	–	–	–	–	–	28
		Cooper-Maserati	–	–	r	r	r	2	r	3	p1	
3	Jochen Rindt	Cooper-Maserati	r	2	4	5	r	3	4	2	r	22 (2)
4	Denny Hulme	Brabham-Climax	r	r	–	–	–	–	–	–	–	18
		Brabham-Repco	–	–	3	2	r	r	3	r	3	
5	Graham Hill	BRM	3	r	r	3	2	4	r	r	r	17
6	Jim Clark	Lotus-Climax	pr	r	ns	4	3	pr	–	–	–	16
		Lotus-BRM	–	–	–	–	–	–	r	1	r	
7	Jackie Stewart	BRM	1	r	–	r	4	5	r	r	r	14
8	Mike Parkes	Ferrari	–	–	2	–	–	r	p2	–	–	12
	Lorenzo Bandini	Ferrari	2	3	pnc	–	6	6	r	r	–	12
10	Ludovico Scarfiotti	Ferrari	–	–	–	–	–	–	1	–	–	9
11	Richie Ginther	Cooper-Maserati	r	5	–	–	–	–	–	–	–	5
		Honda	–	–	–	–	–	–	r	nc	4	
12	Dan Gurney	Eagle-Climax	–	nc	5	r	r	7	–	–	5	4
		Eagle-Weslake	–	–	–	–	–	–	–	r	–	
	Mike Spence	Lotus-BRM	r	r	r	r	5	r	5	r	ns	4
14	Bob Bondurant	BRM	4	r	9	r	7	–	–	–		3
		Eagle-Climax	–	–	–	–	–	–	dq	–	–	
		Eagle-Weslake	–	–	–	–	–	–	–	r	–	
	Jo Siffert	Brabham-BRM	r	r	–	–	–	–	–	–	–	3
		Cooper-Maserati	–	r	r	nc	r	r	r	4	r	
	Bruce McLaren	McLaren-Ford	r	–	–	–	–	–	5	r		3
		McLaren-Serenissima	–	ns	–	6	ns	–	–	–	–	
17	John Taylor †	Brabham-BRM	–	–	6	8	8	r	–	–	–	1
	Bob Anderson	Brabham-Climax	r	–	7	nc	r	r	6	–	–	1
	Peter Arundell	Lotus-BRM	–	ns	r	r	12	8r	r	–	7	1
		Lotus-Climax	–	–	–	–	–	–	–	6	–	
	Jo Bonnier	Cooper-Maserati	nc	r	–	7	r	r	nc	6	r	1
		Brabham-Climax	–	–	nc	–	–	–	–	–	–	

1967

Position	Driver	Car	South Africa	Monaco	Netherlands	Belgium	France	Britain	Germany	Canada	Italy	USA	Mexico	Points total
1	Denny Hulme	Brabham-Repco	4	1	3	r	2	2	1	2	r	3	3	51
2	Jack Brabham	Brabham-Repco	p6	pr	2	r	1	4	2	1	2	5	2	46 (2)
3	Jim Clark	Lotus-BRM	r	–	–	–	–	–	–	–	–	–	–	41
		Lotus-Climax	–	r	–	–	–	–	–	–	–	–	–	
		Lotus-Ford Cosworth	–	–	1	p6	r	p1	pr	pr	p3	1	p1	
4	John Surtees	Honda	3	r	r	r	–	6	4	–	1	r	4	20
	Chris Amon	Ferrari	–	3	4	3	r	3	3	6	7	r	9	20
6	Pedro Rodriguez	Cooper-Maserati	1	5	r	9r	6	5	11	–	–	–	6	15
	Graham Hill	Lotus-BRM	r	2	–	–	–	–	–	–	–	–	–	15
		Lotus-Ford Cosworth	–	–	pr	r	pr	r	r	4	r	p2	r	
8	Dan Gurney	Eagle-Climax	r	–	–	–	–	–	–	–	–	–	–	13
		Eagle-Weslake	–	r	r	1	r	r	r	3	r	r	r	
9	Jackie Stewart	BRM	r	r	r	2	3	r	r	r	r	r	r	10
10	Mike Spence	BRM	r	6	8	5	r	r	r	5	5	r	5	9
11	John Love	Cooper-Climax	2	–	–	–	–	–	–	–	–	–	–	6
	Jochen Rindt	Cooper-Maserati	r	r	r	4	r	r	r	r	4	r	–	6
	Jo Siffert	Cooper-Maserati	r	r	10	7	4	r	r	ns	r	4	12r	6
14	Bruce McLaren	McLaren-BRM	–	4	r	–	–	–	–	7	r	r	r	3
		Eagle-Weslake	–	–	–	–	r	r	r	–	–	–	–	
	Jo Bonnier	Cooper-Maserati	r	–	–	r	–	r	6	8	r	6	10	3
16	Bob Anderson †	Brabham-Climax	5	nq	9	8	r	r	–	–	–	–	–	2
	Mike Parkes	Ferrari	–	–	5	r	–	–	–	–	–	–	–	2
	Chris Irwin	Lotus-BRM	–	–	7	–	–	–	–	–	–	–	–	2
		BRM	–	–	–	r	5	7	9	r	r	r	r	
19	Ludovico Scarfiotti	Ferrari	–	–	6	nc	–	–	–	–	–	–	–	1
		Eagle-Weslake	–	–	–	–	–	–	–	–	r	–	–	
	Guy Ligier	Cooper-Maserati	–	–	–	10	nc	–	–	–	–	–	–	1
		Brabham-Repco	–	–	–	–	–	10	8	–	r	r	11	
	Jacky Ickx	Matra-Ford Cosworth	–	–	–	–	–	–	r	–	–	–	–	1
		Cooper-Maserati	–	–	–	–	–	–	–	–	6	r	–	

1968

Position	Driver	Car	South Africa	Spain	Monaco	Belgium	Netherlands	France	Britain	Germany	Italy	Canada	USA	Mexico	Points total
1	Graham Hill	Lotus-Ford Cosworth	2	1	p1	r	9r	r	pr	2	r	4	2	1	48
2	Jackie Stewart	Matra-Ford Cosworth	r	–	–	4	1	3	6	1	r	6	1	7	36
3	Denny Hulme	McLaren-BRM	5	–	–	–	–	–	–	–	–	–	–	–	33
		McLaren-Ford Cosworth	–	2	5	r	r	5	4	7	1	1	r	r	
4	Jacky Ickx	Ferrari	r	r	–	3	4	1	3	p4	3	ns	–	r	27
5	Bruce McLaren	McLaren-Ford Cosworth	–	r	r	1	r	8	7	13	r	2	6	2	22
6	Pedro Rodriguez	BRM	r	r	r	2	3	nc	r	6	r	3	r	4	18
7	Jo Siffert	Cooper-Maserati	7	–	–	–	–	–	–	–	–	–	–	–	12
		Lotus-Ford Cosworth	–	r	r	7r	r	11	1	r	r	r	5	p6	
	John Surtees	Honda	8	r	r	r	r	2	5	r	pr	r	3	r	12
9	Jean-Pierre Beltoise	Matra-Ford Cosworth	6	5	–	–	–	–	–	–	–	–	–	–	11
		Matra	–	–	r	8	2	9	r	r	5	r	r	r	
10	Chris Amon	Ferrari	4	pr	–	pr	p6	10	2	r	r	r	r	r	10
11	Jim Clark †	Lotus-Ford Cosworth	p1	–	–	–	–	–	–	–	–	–	–	–	9
12	Jochen Rindt	Brabham-Repco	3	r	r	r	r	pr	r	3	r	pr	r	r	8
13	Dickie Attwood	BRM	–	–	2	r	7	7	r	14	–	–	–	–	6
	Johnny Servoz-Gavin	Matra-Ford Cosworth	–	–	r	–	–	–	–	–	2	r	–	11r	6
		Cooper-BRM	–	–	–	–	–	r	–	–	–	–	–	–	
	Jackie Oliver	Lotus-Ford Cosworth	–	–	r	5r	nc	ns	r	11	r	r	ns	3	6
	Ludovico Scarfiotti †	Cooper-Maserati	r	–	–	–	–	–	–	–	–	–	–	–	6
		Cooper-BRM	–	4	4	–	–	–	–	–	–	–	–	–	
17	Lucien Bianchi	Cooper-BRM	–	–	3	6	r	–	–	r	–	nc	r	r	5
	Vic Elford	Cooper-BRM	–	–	–	–	–	4	r	r	r	5	r	8	5
19	Brian Redman	Cooper-Maserati	r	–	–	–	–	–	–	–	–	–	–	–	4
		Cooper-BRM	–	3	–	r	–	–	–	–	–	–	–	–	
	Piers Courage	BRM	–	r	r	r	r	6	8	8	4	r	r	r	4
21	Dan Gurney	Eagle-Weslake	r	–	r	–	–	–	r	9	r	r	4	r	3
		Brabham-Repco	–	–	–	–	r	–	–	–	–	–	–	–	
	Jo Bonnier	Cooper-Maserati	r	–	–	–	–	–	–	–	–	–	–	–	3
		McLaren-BRM	–	–	nq	r	8	–	r	–	6	r	r	–	
		Honda	–	–	–	–	–	–	–	–	–	–	–	5	
23	Silvio Moser	Brabham-Repco	–	–	nq	–	5	–	nc	ns	nq	–	–	–	2
	Jack Brabham	Brabham-Repco	r	ns	r	r	r	r	r	5	r	r	r	10r	2

Mario Andretti (Lotus-Ford Cosworth) started from pole position in the USA. He scored no points during the season.

1969

Position	Driver	Car	South Africa	Spain	Monaco	Netherlands	France	Britain	Germany	Italy	Canada	USA	Mexico	Points total
1	Jackie Stewart	Matra-Ford Cosworth	1	1	pr	1	p1	1	2	1	r	r	4	63
2	Jacky Ickx	Brabham-Ford Cosworth	r	6r	r	5	3	2	p1	10r	p1	r	2	37
3	Bruce McLaren	McLaren-Ford Cosworth	5	2	5	r	4	3	3	4	5	ns	r	26
4	Jochen Rindt	Lotus-Ford Cosworth	r	pr	–	pr	r	p4	r	p2	3	p1	r	22
5	Jean-Pierre Beltoise	Matra-Ford Cosworth	6	3	r	8	2	9	12r	3	4	r	5	21
6	Denny Hulme	McLaren-Ford Cosworth	3	4	6	4	8	r	r	7	r	r	1	20
7	Graham Hill	Lotus-Ford Cosworth	2	r	1	7	6	7	4	9r	r	r	–	19
8	Piers Courage	Brabham-Ford Cosworth	–	r	2	r	r	5	r	5	r	2	10	16
9	Jo Siffert	Lotus-Ford Cosworth	4	r	3	2	9	8	11r	8r	r	r	r	15
10	Jack Brabham	Brabham-Ford Cosworth	pr	r	r	6	–	–	–	r	2	4	p3	14
11	John Surtees	BRM	r	5	r	9	–	r	ns	nc	r	3	r	6
12	Chris Amon	Ferrari	r	r	r	3	r	r	–	–	–	–	–	4
13	Dickie Attwood	Lotus-Ford Cosworth	–	–	4	–	–	–	–	–	–	–	–	3
		Brabham-Ford Cosworth	–	–	–	–	–	–	6	–	–	–	–	
	Vic Elford	Cooper-Maserati	–	–	7	–	–	–	–	–	–	–	–	3
		McLaren-Ford Cosworth	–	–	–	10	5	6	–	–	–	–	–	
	Pedro Rodriguez	BRM	r	r	r	–	–	–	–	–	–	–	–	3
		Ferrari	–	–	–	–	–	r	–	6	r	5	7	
16	Johnny Servoz-Gavin	Matra-Ford Cosworth	–	–	–	–	–	–	r	–	6	nc	8	1
	Silvio Moser	Brabham-Ford Cosworth	–	–	r	r	7	–	–	r	r	6	11r	1
	Jackie Oliver	BRM	7	r	r	r	–	r	r	r	r	r	6	1

1970

Position	Driver	Car	South Africa	Spain	Monaco	Belgium	Netherlands	France	Britain	Germany	Austria	Italy	Canada	USA	Mexico	Points total
1	Jochen Rindt †	Lotus-Ford Cosworth	13r	r	1	r	p1	1	p1	1	pr	ns	–	–	–	45
2	Jacky Ickx	Ferrari	r	r	r	8	3	pr	r	p2	1	pr	1	p4	1	40
3	Clay Regazzoni	Ferrari	–	–	–	–	4	–	4	r	2	1	2	13	p2	33
4	Denny Hulme	McLaren-Ford Cosworth	2	r	4	–	–	4	3	3	r	4	r	7	3	27
5	Jack Brabham	Brabham-Ford Cosworth	1	pr	2	r	11	3	2	r	13	r	r	10	r	25
	Jackie Stewart	March-Ford Cosworth	p3	1	pr	pr	2	9	r	r	r	2	–	–	–	25
		Tyrrell-Ford Cosworth	–	–	–	–	–	–	–	–	–	–	pr	r	r	
7	Pedro Rodriguez	BRM	9	r	6	1	10	r	r	r	4	r	4	2	6	23
	Chris Amon	March-Ford Cosworth	r	r	r	2	r	2	5	r	8	7	3	5	4	23
9	Jean-Pierre Beltoise	Matra Simca	4	r	r	3	5	13r	r	r	6	3	8	r	5	16
10	Emerson Fittipaldi	Lotus-Ford Cosworth	–	–	–	–	–	–	8	4	15	ns	–	1	r	12
11	Rolf Stommelen	Brabham-Ford Cosworth	r	r	nq	5	nq	7	ns	5	3	5	r	12	r	10
12	Henri Pescarolo	Matra Simca	7	r	3	6r	8	5	r	6	14	r	7	8	9	8
13	Graham Hill	Lotus-Ford Cosworth	6	4	5	r	nc	10	6	r	–	ns	nc	r	r	7
14	Bruce McLaren †	McLaren-Ford Cosworth	r	2	r	–	–	–	–	–	–	–	–	–	–	6
15	Mario Andretti	March-Ford Cosworth	r	3	–	–	–	–	r	r	r	–	–	–	–	4
	Reine Wisell	Lotus-Ford Cosworth	–	–	–	–	–	–	–	–	–	–	–	3	nc	4
17	Ignazio Giunti	Ferrari	–	–	–	4	–	14	–	–	7	r	–	–	–	3
	John Surtees	McLaren-Ford Cosworth	r	r	r	–	6	–	–	–	–	–	–	–	–	3
		Surtees-Ford Cosworth	–	–	–	–	–	–	r	9r	r	r	5	r	8	
19	John Miles	Lotus-Ford Cosworth	5	nq	nq	r	7	8	r	r	r	ns	–	–	–	2
	Johnny Servoz-Gavin	March-Ford Cosworth	r	5	nq	–	–	–	–	–	–	–	–	–	–	2
	Jackie Oliver	BRM	r	r	r	r	r	r	r	r	5	r	nc	r	7	2
22	Dan Gurney	McLaren-Ford Cosworth	–	–	–	–	r	6	r	–	–	–	–	–	–	1
	François Cevert	March-Ford Cosworth	–	–	–	–	r	11	7	7	r	6	9	r	r	1
	Peter Gethin	McLaren-Ford Cosworth	–	–	–	–	r	–	–	r	10	nc	6	14	r	1
	Derek Bell	Brabham-Ford Cosworth	–	–	–	r	–	–	–	–	–	–	–	–	–	1
		Surtees-Ford Cosworth	–	–	–	–	–	–	–	–	–	–	–	6	–	

1971

Position	Driver	Car	South Africa	Spain	Monaco	Netherlands	France	Britain	Germany	Austria	Italy	Canada	USA	Points total
1	Jackie Stewart	Tyrrell-Ford Cosworth	p2	1	p1	11	p1	1	p1	r	r	p1	p5	62
2	Ronnie Peterson	March-Ford Cosworth	10	r	2	4	–	2	5	8	2	2	3	33
		March-Alfa Romeo	–	–	–	–	r	–	–	–	–	–	–	
3	François Cevert	Tyrrell-Ford Cosworth	r	7	r	r	2	10	2	r	3	6	1	26
4	Jacky Ickx	Ferrari	8	p2	3	p1	r	r	r	r	r	8	r	19
	Jo Siffert †	BRM	r	r	r	6	4	9	r	p1	9	9	2	19
6	Emerson Fittipaldi	Lotus-Ford Cosworth	r	r	5	–	3	3	r	2	–	7	nc	16
		Lotus-Pratt & Whitney	–	–	–	–	–	–	–	–	8	–	–	
7	Clay Regazzoni	Ferrari	3	r	r	3	r	pr	3	r	r	r	6	13
8	Mario Andretti	Ferrari	1	r	nq	r	–	–	4	–	–	13	ns	12
9	Peter Gethin	McLaren-Ford Cosworth	r	8	r	nc	9	r	r	–	–	–	–	9
		BRM	–	–	–	–	–	–	–	10	1	14	9	
	Pedro Rodriguez †	BRM	r	4	9	2	r	–	–	–	–	–	–	9
	Chris Amon	Matra Simca	5	3	r	r	5	r	r	–	p6	10	12	9
	Reine Wisell	Lotus-Ford Cosworth	4	nc	r	dq	6	–	8	4	–	5	r	9
		Lotus-Pratt & Whitney	–	–	–	–	–	nc	–	–	–	–	–	
	Denny Hulme	McLaren-Ford Cosworth	6	5	4	12	r	r	r	r	–	4	r	9
14	Tim Schenken	Brabham-Ford Cosworth	–	9	10	r	12r	12r	6	3	r	r	r	5
	Howden Ganley	BRM	r	10	nq	7	10	8	r	r	5	ns	4	5
16	Mark Donohue	McLaren-Ford Cosworth	–	–	–	–	–	–	–	–	–	3	ns	4
	Henri Pescarolo	March-Ford Cosworth	11	r	8	nc	r	4	r	6	r	ns	r	4
18	Mike Hailwood	Surtees-Ford Cosworth	–	–	–	–	–	–	–	–	4	–	15r	3
	John Surtees	Surtees-Ford Cosworth	r	11	7	5	8	6	7	r	r	11	17	3
	Rolf Stommelen	Surtees-Ford Cosworth	12	r	6	dq	11	5	10	7	ns	r	–	3
21	Graham Hill	Brabham-Ford Cosworth	9	r	r	10	r	r	9	5	r	r	7	2
22	Jean-Pierre Beltoise	Matra Simca	–	6	r	9	7	7	–	–	–	r	8	1

1972

Position	Driver	Car	Argentina	South Africa	Spain	Monaco	Belgium	France	Britain	Germany	Austria	Italy	Canada	USA	Points total
1	Emerson Fittipaldi	JPS Lotus-Ford Cosworth	r	2	1	p3	p1	2	1	r	p1	1	11	r	61
2	Jackie Stewart	Tyrrell-Ford Cosworth	1	pr	r	4	–	1	2	11r	7	r	1	p1	45
3	Denny Hulme	McLaren-Ford Cosworth	2	1	r	15	3	7	5	r	2	3	3	3	39
4	Jacky Ickx	Ferrari	3	8	p2	2	r	11	pr	p1	r	pr	12	18r	27
5	Peter Revson	McLaren-Ford Cosworth	r	3	5	–	7	–	3	–	3	4	p2	18r	23
6	François Cevert	Tyrrell-Ford Cosworth	r	9	r	nc	2	4	r	10	9	r	r	2	15
	Clay Regazzoni	Ferrari	4	12	3	r	r	–	–	2	r	r	5	8	15
8	Mike Hailwood	Surtees-Ford Cosworth	–	r	r	r	4	6	r	r	4	2	–	17r	13
9	Ronnie Peterson	March-Ford Cosworth	6	5	r	11	9	5	7r	3	12	9	dq	4	12
	Chris Amon	Matra Simca	r	15	r	6	6	p3	4	15	5	r	6	15	12
11	Jean-Pierre Beltoise	BRM	–	r	r	1	r	15	11	9	8	8	r	r	9
12	Mario Andretti	Ferrari	r	4	r	–	–	–	–	–	–	7	–	6	4
	Howden Ganley	BRM	9	nc	r	r	8	ns	–	4	6	11	10	r	4
	Brian Redman	McLaren-Ford Cosworth	–	–	–	5	–	9	–	5	–	–	–	–	4
		BRM	–	–	–	–	–	–	–	–	–	–	–	r	
	Graham Hill	Brabham-Ford Cosworth	r	6	10	12	r	10	r	6	r	5	8	11	4
16	Andrea de Adamich	Surtees-Ford Cosworth	r	nc	4	7	r	14	r	13	14	r	r	r	3
	Carlos Reutemann	Brabham-Ford Cosworth	p7	r	–	–	13	12	8	r	r	r	4	r	3
	Carlos Pace	March-Ford Cosworth	–	17	6	17	5	r	r	nc	nc	r	9r	r	3
19	Tim Schenken	Surtees-Ford Cosworth	5	r	8	r	r	17	r	14	11	r	7	r	2
20	Arturo Merzario	Ferrari	–	–	–	–	–	–	6	12	–	–	–	–	1
	Peter Gethin	BRM	r	nc	r	dq	r	ns	r	–	13	6	r	r	1

1973

Position	Driver	Car	Argentina	Brazil	South Africa	Spain	Belgium	Monaco	Sweden	France	Britain	Netherlands	Germany	Austria	Italy	Canada	USA	Points total
1	Jackie Stewart	Tyrrell-Ford Cosworth	3	2	1	r	1	p1	5	p4	10	1	p1	2	4	5	ns	71
2	Emerson Fittipaldi	JPS Lotus-Ford Cosworth	1	1	3	1	3	2	12r	r	r	r	6	p11r	2	2	6	55
3	Ronnie Peterson	JPS Lotus-Ford Cosworth	r	pr	11	pr	pr	3	p2	1	p2	p11r	r	1	p1	pr	p1	52
4	François Cevert †	Tyrrell-Ford Cosworth	2	10	nc	2	2	4	3	2	5	2	2	r	5	r	ns	47
5	Peter Revson	McLaren-Ford Cosworth	8	r	2	4	r	5	7	–	1	4	9	r	3	1	5	38
6	Denny Hulme	McLaren-Ford Cosworth	5	3	p5	6	7	6	1	8	3	r	12	8	15	13	4	26
7	Carlos Reutemann	Brabham-Ford Cosworth	r	11	7	r	r	r	4	3	6	r	r	4	6	8	3	16
8	James Hunt	March-Ford Cosworth	–	–	–	–	–	9r	–	6	4	3	–	r	ns	7	2	14
9	Jacky Ickx	Ferrari	4	5	r	12	r	r	6	5	8	–	–	–	8	–	–	12
		McLaren-Ford Cosworth	–	–	–	–	–	–	–	–	–	–	–	3	–	–	–	
		Iso Marlboro-Ford Cosworth	–	–	–	–	–	–	–	–	–	–	–	–	–	–	7	
10	Jean-Pierre Beltoise	BRM	r	r	r	5	r	r	r	11	r	5	r	5	13	4	9	9
11	Carlos Pace	Surtees-Ford Cosworth	r	r	r	r	8	r	10	13	r	7	4	3	r	18r	r	7
12	Arturo Merzario	Ferrari	9	4	4	–	–	r	–	7	–	–	–	7	r	15	16	6
13	George Follmer	Shadow-Ford Cosworth	–	–	6	3	r	ns	14	r	r	10	r	r	10	17	14	5
14	Jackie Oliver	Shadow-Ford Cosworth	–	–	r	r	r	10	r	r	r	r	8	r	11	3	15	4
15	Andrea de Adamich	Surtees-Ford Cosworth	–	–	8	–	–	–	–	–	–	–	–	–	–	–	–	3
		Brabham-Ford Cosworth	–	–	–	r	4	7	–	r	r	–	–	–	–	–	–	
	Wilson Fittipaldi	Brabham-Ford Cosworth	6	r	r	10	r	11r	r	16r	r	r	5	r	r	11	nc	3
17	Niki Lauda	BRM	r	8	r	r	r	13	9	12	r	r	ns	r	r	r	r	2
	Clay Regazzoni	BRM	p7	6	r	9	10r	r	9	12	7	8	r	6	r	–	8	2
19	Chris Amon	Tecno	–	–	–	–	6	r	–	–	r	r	–	ns	–	–	–	1
		Tyrrell-Ford Cosworth	–	–	–	–	–	–	–	–	–	–	–	–	–	10	ns	
	Gijs van Lennep	Iso Marlboro-Ford Cosworth	–	–	–	–	–	–	–	–	–	6	–	9	r	–	–	1
	Howden Ganley	Iso Marlboro-Ford Cosworth	nc	7	10	r	r	r	11	14	9	9	ns	nc	nc	6	12	1

1974

Position	Driver	Car	Argentina	Brazil	South Africa	Spain	Belgium	Monaco	Sweden	Netherlands	France	Britain	Germany	Austria	Italy	Canada	USA	Points total
1	Emerson Fittipaldi	McLaren-Ford Cosworth	10	p1	7	3	1	5	4	3	r	2	r	r	2	p1	4	55
2	Clay Regazzoni	Ferrari	3	2	r	2	p4	4	r	2	3	4	1	5	r	2	11	52
3	Jody Scheckter	Tyrrell-Ford Cosworth	r	13	8	5	3	2	1	5	4	1	2	r	3	r	r	45
4	Niki Lauda	Ferrari	2	r	p16r	p1	2	pr	r	p1	p2	p5	pr	pr	pr	r	r	38
5	Ronnie Peterson	JPS Lotus-Ford Cosworth	p13	6	r	r	r	1	r	8	1	10	4	r	1	3	r	35
6	Carlos Reutemann	Brabham-Ford Cosworth	7r	7	1	r	r	r	r	12	r	6	3	1	r	9	p1	32
7	Denny Hulme	McLaren-Ford Cosworth	1	12	9	6	6	r	r	r	6	7	r/dq	2	6	6	r	20
8	James Hunt	March-Ford Cosworth	r	9	–	–	–	–	–	–	–	–	–	–	–	–	–	15
		Hesketh-Ford Cosworth	–	–	r	10	r	r	3	r	r	r	r	3	r	4	3	
9	Patrick Depailler	Tyrrell-Ford Cosworth	6	8	4	8	r	9	p2	6	8	r	r	r	11	5	6	14
10	Jacky Ickx	JPS Lotus-Ford Cosworth	r	3	r	r	r	r	r	11	5	3	5	r	r	13	r	12
	Mike Hailwood	McLaren-Ford Cosworth	4	5	3	9	7	r	r	4	7	r	15r	–	–	–	–	12
12	Carlos Pace	Surtees-Ford Cosworth	r	4	11	13	r	r	r	–	–	–	–	r	5	8	2	11
		Brabham-Ford Cosworth	–	–	–	–	–	–	–	–	nq	9	12	r	5	8	2	
13	Jean-Pierre Beltoise	BRM	5	10	2	r	5	r	r	r	10	12	r	r	r	nc	nq	10
14	Jean-Pierre Jarier	Shadow-Ford Cosworth	r	r	–	nc	13	3	5	r	12	r	8	8	r	r	10	6
	John Watson	Brabham-Ford Cosworth	12	r	r	11	11	6	11	7	16	11	r	4	7	r	5	6
16	Hans-Joachim Stuck	March-Ford Cosworth	r	r	5	4	r	r	–	r	nq	r	7	11r	r	r	nq	5
17	Arturo Merzario	Iso Marlboro-Ford Cosworth	r	r	6	r	r	r	ns	r	9	r	r	r	4	r	r	4
18	Graham Hill	Lola-Ford Cosworth	r	11	12	r	8	7	6	r	13	13	9	12	8	14	8	1
	Tom Pryce	Token-Ford Cosworth	–	–	–	–	r	–	–	–	–	–	–	–	–	–	–	1
		Shadow-Ford Cosworth	–	–	–	–	–	–	–	r	r	8	6	r	10	r	nc	
	Vittorio Brambilla	March-Ford Cosworth	–	–	10	ns	9	r	10r	10	11	r	13	6	r	nq	r	1

1975

Position	Driver	Car	Argentina	Brazil	South Africa	Spain	Monaco	Belgium	Sweden	Netherlands	France	Britain	Germany	Austria	Italy	USA	Points total
1	Niki Lauda	Ferrari	6	5	5	pr	p1	p1	1	p2	p1	8	p3	p6	p3	p1	64.5
2	Emerson Fittipaldi	McLaren-Ford Cosworth	1	2	nc	ns	2	7	8	r	4	1	r	9	2	2	45
3	Carlos Reutemann	Brabham-Ford Cosworth	3	8	2	3	9	3	2	4	14	r	1	14	4	r	37
4	James Hunt	Hesketh-Ford Cosworth	2	6	r	r	r	r	r	1	2	4r	r	2	5	4	33
5	Clay Regazzoni	Ferrari	4	4	16r	nc	r	5	3	3	r	13	r	7	1	r	25
6	Carlos Pace	Brabham-Ford Cosworth	r	1	p4	r	3	8	r	5	r	2r	r	r	r	r	24
7	Jody Scheckter	Tyrrell-Ford Cosworth	11	r	1	r	7	2	7	16r	9	3r	r	8	8	6	20
	Jochen Mass	McLaren-Ford Cosworth	14	3	6	1	6	r	r	r	3	7r	r	4	r	3	20
9	Patrick Depailler	Tyrrell-Ford Cosworth	5	r	3	r	5	4	12	9	6	9r	9	11	7	r	12
10	Tom Pryce	Shadow-Ford Cosworth	12r	r	9	r	r	6	r	6	r	pr	4	3	6	nc	8
11	Vittorio Brambilla	March-Ford Cosworth	9	r	r	5	r	r	pr	r	r	6	r	1	r	7	6.5
12	Jacques Laffite	Williams-Ford Cosworth	r	11	nc	–	nq	r	–	r	11	r	2	r	r	ns	6
	Ronnie Peterson	JPS Lotus-Ford Cosworth	r	15	10	r	4	r	9	15r	10	r	r	5	r	5	6
14	Mario Andretti	Parnelli-Ford Cosworth	r	7	17r	r	r	–	4	–	5	12	10r	r	r	r	5
15	Mark Donohue †	Penske-Ford Cosworth	7	r	8	r	r	11	5	8	r	–	–	–	–	–	4
		March-Ford Cosworth	–	–	–	–	–	–	–	–	–	5r	ns	–	–	–	
16	Jacky Ickx	JPS Lotus-Ford Cosworth	8	9	12	2	8	r	15	r	r	–	–	–	–	–	3
17	Alan Jones	Hesketh-Ford Cosworth	–	–	–	r	r	r	11	–	–	–	–	–	–	–	2
		Hill-Ford Cosworth	–	–	–	–	–	–	–	13	16	10	5	–	–	–	
18	Jean-Pierre Jarier	Shadow-Ford Cosworth	pns	pr	r	4	r	r	r	r	8	14r	r	–	–	r	1.5
		Shadow-Matra	–	–	–	–	–	–	–	–	–	–	–	r	r	–	
19	Tony Brise †	Williams-Ford Cosworth	–	–	–	7	–	–	–	–	–	–	–	–	–	–	1
		Hill-Ford Cosworth	–	–	–	–	–	r	6	7	7	15r	r	15	r	r	
	Gijs van Lennep	Ensign-Ford Cosworth	–	–	–	–	–	–	–	10	15	–	6	–	–	–	1
21	Lella Lombardi	March-Ford Cosworth	–	–	r	6	nq	r	r	14	18	r	7	17	r	–	0.5
		Williams-Ford Cosworth	–	–	–	–	–	–	–	–	–	–	–	–	–	ns	

Half points were awarded in Spain and Austria where the races were stopped early.

1976

Position	Driver	Car	Brazil	South Africa	USA West	Spain	Belgium	Monaco	Sweden	France	Britain	Germany	Austria	Netherlands	Italy	Canada	USA East	Japan	Points total
1	James Hunt	McLaren-Ford Cosworth	pr	p2	r	p1	r	r	5	p1	dq	p1	p4	1	r	p1	p1	3	69
2	Niki Lauda	Ferrari	1	1	2	2	p1	p1	3	r	p1	r	–	–	4	8	3	r	68
3	Jody Scheckter	Tyrrell-Ford Cosworth	5	4	r	r	4	2	p1	6	2	2	r	5	5	4	2	r	49
4	Patrick Depailler	Tyrrell-Ford Cosworth	2	9	3	r	r	3	2	2	r	r	r	7	6	2	r	2	39
5	Clay Regazzoni	Ferrari	7	r	p1	11	2	14r	6	r	r/dq	9	–	2	2	6	7	5	31
6	Mario Andretti	JPS Lotus-Ford Cosworth	r	–	–	r	r	–	r	5	r	12	5	3	r	3	r	p1	22
		Parnelli-Ford Cosworth	–	6	r	–	–	–	–	–	–	–	–	–	–	–	–	–	
7	John Watson	Penske-Ford Cosworth	r	5	nc	r	7	10	r	3	3	7	1	r	11	10	6	r	20
	Jacques Laffite	Ligier-Matra	r	r	4	12	3	12r	4	14	r/dq	r	2	r	p3	r	r	7	20
9	Jochen Mass	McLaren-Ford Cosworth	6	3	5	r	6	5	11	15	r	3	7	9	r	5	4	r	19
10	Gunnar Nilsson	JPS Lotus-Ford Cosworth	–	r	r	3	r	r	r	r	r	5	3	r	13	12	r	6	11
11	Ronnie Peterson	JPS Lotus-Ford Cosworth	r	–	–	–	–	–	–	–	–	–	–	–	–	–	–	–	10
		March-Ford Cosworth	–	r	10	r	r	r	7	19r	r	r	6	pr	1	9	r	r	
	Tom Pryce	Shadow-Ford Cosworth	3	7	r	8	10	7	9	8	4	8	r	4	8	11	r	r	10
13	Hans-Joachim Stuck	March-Ford Cosworth	4	12	r	r	r	4	r	7	r	r	r	r	r	r	5	r	8
14	Carlos Pace	Brabham-Alfa Romeo	10	r	9	6	r	9	8	4	8	4	r	r	r	7	r	r	7
	Alan Jones	Surtees-Ford Cosworth	–	–	nc	9	5	r	13	r	5	10	r	8	12	16	8	4	7
16	Carlos Reutemann	Brabham-Alfa Romeo	12r	r	r	4	r	r	r	11	r	r	r	r	–	–	–	–	3
		Ferrari	–	–	–	–	–	–	–	–	–	–	–	–	9	–	–	–	
	Emerson Fittipaldi	Copersucar-Ford Cosworth	13	17r	6	r	nq	6	r	r	6	13	r	r	15	r	9	r	3
18	Chris Amon	Ensign-Ford Cosworth	–	14	8	5	r	13	r	r	r	r	–	–	–	–	–	–	2
		Wolf Williams-Ford Cosworth	–	–	–	–	–	–	–	–	–	–	–	–	ns	–	–	–	
19	Rolf Stommelen	Brabham-Alfa Romeo	–	–	–	–	–	–	–	–	6	–	–	r	–	–	–	–	1
		Hesketh-Ford Cosworth	–	–	–	–	–	–	–	–	–	–	–	12	–	–	–	–	
	Vittorio Brambilla	March-Ford Cosworth	r	8	r	r	r	r	10	r	r	r	r	6	7	14	r	r	1

1977

Position	Driver	Car	Argentina	Brazil	South Africa	USA West	Spain	Monaco	Belgium	Sweden	France	Britain	Germany	Austria	Netherlands	Italy	USA East	Canada	Japan	Points total
1	Niki Lauda	Ferrari	r	3	1	p2	ns	2	2	r	5	2	1	p2	1	2	4	–	–	72
2	Jody Scheckter	Wolf-Ford Cosworth	1	r	2	3	3	1	r	r	r	r	p2	r	3	r	3	1	10	55
3	Mario Andretti	JPS Lotus-Ford Cosworth	5r	r	r	1	p1	5	pr	p6	p1	14r	r	r	pr	1	2	p9r	pr	47
4	Carlos Reutemann	Ferrari	3	1	8	r	2	3	r	3	6	15	4	4	6	r	6	r	2	42
5	James Hunt	McLaren-Ford Cosworth	pr	p2	p4	7	r	r	7	12	3	p1	r	r	r	pr	p1	r	1	40
6	Jochen Mass	McLaren-Ford Cosworth	r	r	5	r	4	4	r	2	9	4	r	6	r	4	r	3	r	25
7	Alan Jones	Shadow-Ford Cosworth	–	–	–	r	r	6	5	17	r	7	r	1	r	3	r	4	4	22
8	Gunnar Nilsson	JPS Lotus-Ford Cosworth	ns	5	12	8	5	r	1	19r	4	3	r	r	r	r	r	r	r	20
	Patrick Depailler	Tyrrell-Ford Cosworth	r	r	3	4	r	r	8	4	r	r	r	13	r	r	14	2	3	20
10	Jacques Laffite	Ligier-Matra	nc	r	r	9r	7	7	r	1	8	6	r	r	2	8	7	r	5r	18
11	Hans-Joachim Stuck	March-Ford Cosworth	–	–	r	–	–	–	–	–	–	–	–	–	–	–	–	–	–	12
		Brabham-Alfa Romeo	–	–	–	r	6	r	6	10	r	5	3	3	7	r	r	r	7	
12	Emerson Fittipaldi	Copersucar-Ford Cosworth	4	4	10	5	14	r	r	18	11	r	nq	11	4	nq	13	r	–	11
13	John Watson	Brabham-Alfa Romeo	r	r	6	dq	r	pr	r	5	2	r	r	8	r	r	12	r	r	9
14	Ronnie Peterson	Tyrrell-Ford Cosworth	r	r	r	r	8	r	3	r	12	r	9r	5	r	6	16	r	r	7
15	Carlos Pace †	Brabham-Alfa Romeo	2	r	13	–	–	–	–	–	–	–	–	–	–	–	–	–	–	6
	Vittorio Brambilla	Surtees-Ford Cosworth	7r	r	7	r	r	8	4	r	13	8	5	15	12r	r	19	6r	8	6
17	Patrick Tambay	Surtees-Ford Cosworth	–	–	–	–	–	–	–	nq	–	–	–	–	–	–	–	–	–	5
		Ensign-Ford Cosworth	–	–	–	–	–	–	–	–	r	–	6	r	5r	r	nq	5	r	
	Clay Regazzoni	Ensign-Ford Cosworth	6	r	9	r	r	nq	r	7	7	nq	r	r	r	5	5	r	r	5
19	Renzo Zorzi	Shadow-Ford Cosworth	r	6	r	r	r	–	–	–	–	–	–	–	–	–	–	–	–	1
	Jean-Pierre Jarier	Penske-Ford Cosworth	–	–	–	6	nq	11	11	8	r	9	r	14	r	r	–	–	–	1
		Shadow-Ford Cosworth	–	–	–	–	–	–	–	–	–	–	–	–	–	–	–	9	–	
		Ligier-Matra	–	–	–	–	–	–	–	–	–	–	–	–	–	–	–	–	r	
	Riccardo Patrese	Shadow-Ford Cosworth	–	–	–	–	–	9	r	–	r	r	10r	–	13	r	–	10r	6	1

1978

Position	Driver	Car	Argentina	Brazil	South Africa	USA West	Monaco	Belgium	Spain	Sweden	France	Britain	Germany	Austria	Netherlands	Italy	USA East	Canada	Points total
1	Mario Andretti	JPS Lotus-Ford Cosworth	p1	4	7	2	11	p1	p1	pr	1	r	p1	r	p1	p6	pr	10	64
2	Ronnie Peterson †	JPS Lotus-Ford Cosworth	5	pr	1	4	r	2	2	3	2	pr	r	p1	2	r	–	–	51
3	Carlos Reutemann	Ferrari	7	1	r	p1	p8	3	r	10	18	1	r	dq	7	3	1	3	48
4	Niki Lauda	Brabham-Alfa Romeo	2	3	pr	r	2	r	r	1	r	2	r	r	3	1	r	r	44
5	Patrick Depailler	Tyrrell-Ford Cosworth	3	r	2	3	1	r	r	r	r	4	r	2	r	11	r	5	34
6	John Watson	Brabham-Alfa Romeo	r	8	3	r	4	r	5	r	p4	3	7	7	4	2	r	r	25
7	Jody Scheckter	Wolf-Ford Cosworth	10	r	r	r	3	r	4	r	6	r	2	r	12	12	3	2	24
8	Jacques Laffite	Ligier-Matra	16r	9	5	5	r	5r	3	7	7	10	3	5	8	4	11	r	19
9	Gilles Villeneuve	Ferrari	8	r	r	r	r	4	10	9	12	r	8	3	6	7	r	1	17
	Emerson Fittipaldi	Copersucar-Ford Cosworth	9	2	r	8	9	r	r	6	r	r	4	4	5	8	5	r	17
11	Alan Jones	Williams-Ford Cosworth	r	11	4	7	r	10	8	r	5	r	r	r	r	13	2	9	11
	Riccardo Patrese	Arrows-Ford Cosworth	–	10	r	6	6	r	r	2	8	r	9	r	r	r	–	4	11
13	James Hunt	McLaren-Ford Cosworth	4	r	r	r	r	r	6	8	3	r	dq	r	10	r	7	r	8
	Patrick Tambay	McLaren-Ford Cosworth	6	r	r	12r	7	–	r	4	9	6	r	r	9	5	6	8	8
15	Didier Pironi	Tyrrell-Ford Cosworth	14	6	6	r	5	6	12	r	10	r	5	r	r	10	7	–	7
16	Clay Regazzoni	Shadow-Ford Cosworth	15	5	nq	10	nq	r	15r	5	r	r	nq	nc	nq	nc	14	nq	4
17	Jean-Pierre Jabouille	Renault	–	–	r	r	10	nc	13	r	r	r	r	r	r	r	4	12	3
18	Hans-Joachim Stuck	Shadow-Ford Cosworth	17	r	nq	ns	r	r	r	11	11	5	r	r	r	r	r	r	2
19	Hector Rebaque	Lotus-Ford Cosworth	nq	r	10	npq	npq	npq	r	12	nq	r	6	r	11	nq	r	nq	1
	Vittorio Brambilla	Surtees-Ford Cosworth	18	nq	12	r	nq	13r	7	r	17	9	r	6	dq	r	–	–	1
	Derek Daly	Hesketh-Ford Cosworth	–	–	–	npq	npq	nq	–	–	–	–	–	–	–	–	–	–	1
		Ensign-Ford Cosworth	–	–	–	–	–	–	–	–	nq	r	–	dq	r	10	8	6	

Jean-Pierre Jarier (JPS Lotus-Ford Cosworth) started from pole position in Canada. He scored no points during the season.

1979

Position	Driver	Car	Argentina	Brazil	South Africa	USA West	Spain	Belgium	Monaco	France	Britain	Germany	Austria	Netherlands	Italy	Canada	USA East	Points total
1	Jody Scheckter	Ferrari	r	6	2	2	4	1	p1	7	5	4	4	2	1	4	r	51 (9)
2	Gilles Villeneuve	Ferrari	12r	5	1	p1	7	7r	r	2	14r	8	2	r	2	2	1	47 (6)
3	Alan Jones	Williams-Ford Cosworth	9	r	r	3	r	r	r	4	pr	1	1	1	9	p1	pr	40 (3)
4	Jacques Laffite	Ligier-Ford Cosworth	p1	p1	r	r	pr	p2	r	8	r	3	3	3	r	r	r	36
5	Clay Regazzoni	Williams-Ford Cosworth	10	15	9	r	r	r	2	6	1	2	5	r	3	3	r	29 (3)
6	Patrick Depailler	Ligier-Ford Cosworth	4	2	r	5	1	r	5r	–	–	–	–	–	–	–	–	20 (2)
	Carlos Reutemann	Lotus-Ford Cosworth	2	3	5	r	2	4	3	13r	8	r	r	r	7	r	r	20 (5)
8	René Arnoux	Renault	r	r	r	ns	9	r	r	3	2	r	p6	pr	r	r	2	17
9	John Watson	McLaren-Ford Cosworth	3	8	r	r	r	6	4	11	4	5	9	r	r	6	6	15
10	Didier Pironi	Tyrrell-Ford Cosworth	r	4	r	dq	6	3	r	r	10	9	7	r	10	5	3	14
	Jean-Pierre Jarier	Tyrrell-Ford Cosworth	r	r	3	6	5	11	r	5	3	–	–	r	6	r	r	14
	Mario Andretti	Lotus-Ford Cosworth	5	r	4	4	3	r	r	r	r	r	r	r	5	10r	r	14
13	Jean-Pierre Jabouille	Renault	r	10	pr	ns	r	r	8	p1	r	pr	r	r	p14r	r	r	9
14	Niki Lauda	Brabham-Alfa Romeo	r	r	6	r	r	r	r	r	r	r	r	r	4	–	–	4
		Brabham-Ford Cosworth	–	–	–	–	–	–	–	–	–	–	–	–	–	ew	–	
15	Nelson Piquet	Brabham-Alfa Romeo	r	r	7	8	r	r	7r	r	r	12r	r	4	r	–	–	3
		Brabham-Ford Cosworth	–	–	–	–	–	–	–	–	–	–	–	–	–	r	8r	
	Elio de Angelis	Shadow-Ford Cosworth	7	12	r	7	r	r	nq	16	12	11	r	r	r	r	4	3
	Jacky Ickx	Ligier-Ford Cosworth	–	–	–	–	–	–	r	6	r	r	5	r	r	r	3
	Jochen Mass	Arrows-Ford Cosworth	8	7	12	9	8	r	6	15	r	6	r	6	r	nq	nq	3
19	Riccardo Patrese	Arrows-Ford Cosworth	ns	9	11	r	10	5	r	14	r	r	r	r	13r	r	r	2
	Hans-Joachim Stuck	ATS-Ford Cosworth	ns	r	r	dq	14	8	r	ns	nq	r	r	r	11	r	5	2
21	Emerson Fittipaldi	Copersucar-Ford Cosworth	6	11	13	r	11	9	r	r	r	r	r	r	8	8	7	1

1980

Position	Driver	Car	Argentina	Brazil	South Africa	USA West	Belgium	Monaco	France	Britain	Germany	Austria	Netherlands	Italy	Canada	USA East	Points total
1	Alan Jones	Williams-Ford Cosworth	p1	3	r	r	p2	r	1	1	p3	2	11	2	1	1	67 (4)
2	Nelson Piquet	Brabham-Ford Cosworth	2	r	4	p1	r	3	4	2	4	5	1	1	pr	r	54
3	Carlos Reutemann	Williams-Ford Cosworth	r	r	5	r	3	1	6	3	2	3	4	3	2	2	42 (7)
4	Jacques Laffite	Ligier-Ford Cosworth	r	r	2	r	11	2	p3	r	1	4	3	9	8r	5	34
5	Didier Pironi	Ligier-Ford Cosworth	r	4	3	6	1	pr	2	pr	r	r	r	6	3	3	32
6	René Arnoux	Renault	r	1	1	9	4	r	5	nc	r	p9	p2	p10	r	7	29
7	Elio de Angelis	Lotus-Ford Cosworth	r	2	r	r	10r	9r	r	r	16r	6	r	4	10	4	13
8	Jean-Pierre Jabouille	Renault	r	pr	pr	10	r	r	r	r	r	1	r	r	r	–	9
9	Riccardo Patrese	Arrows-Ford Cosworth	r	6	r	2	r	8	9	9	9	14	r	r	r	r	7
10	Keke Rosberg	Fittipaldi-Ford Cosworth	3	9	r	r	7	nq	r	nq	r	16	nq	5	9	10	6
	Derek Daly	Tyrrell-Ford Cosworth	4	14	r	8	9	r	11	4	10	r	r	r	r	r	6
	John Watson	McLaren-Ford Cosworth	r	11	11	4	nc	nq	7	8	r	r	r	r	4	nc	6
	Jean-Pierre Jarier	Tyrrell-Ford Cosworth	r	12	7	r	5	r	14	5	15	r	5	13r	7	nc	6
	Gilles Villeneuve	Ferrari	r	16r	r	r	6	5	8	r	6	8	7	r	5	r	6
15	Emerson Fittipaldi	Fittipaldi-Ford Cosworth	nc	15	8	3	r	6	13r	12	r	11	r	r	r	r	5
	Alain Prost	McLaren-Ford Cosworth	6	5	ns	–	r	r	r	6	11	7	6	7	r	ns	5
17	Jochen Mass	Arrows-Ford Cosworth	r	10	6	7	r	4	10	13	8	nq	ew	–	11	r	4
	Bruno Giacomelli	Alfa Romeo	5	13	r	r	r	r	r	r	5	r	r	r	r	pr	4
19	Jody Scheckter	Ferrari	r	r	r	5	8	r	12	10	13	13	9	8	nq	11	2
20	Hector Rebaque	Brabham-Ford Cosworth	–	–	–	–	–	–	–	7	r	10	r	r	6	r	1
	Mario Andretti	Lotus-Ford Cosworth	r	r	12	r	r	7	r	r	7	r	8r	r	r	6	1

1981

Position	Driver	Car	USA West	Brazil	Argentina	San Marino	Belgium	Monaco	Spain	France	Britain	Germany	Austria	Netherlands	Italy	Canada	Las Vegas	Points total
1	Nelson Piquet	Brabham-Ford Cosworth	3	p12	p1	1	r	pr	r	3	r	1	3	2	6r	p5	5	50
2	Carlos Reutemann	Williams-Ford Cosworth	2	1	2	3	p1	r	4	10	2	r	5	r	3	10	p8	49
3	Alan Jones	Williams-Ford Cosworth	1	2	4	12	r	2	7	17	r	11	4	3	2	r	1	46
4	Jacques Laffite	Talbot Ligier-Matra	r	6	r	r	2	3	p2	r	3	3	1	r	r	1	6	44
5	Alain Prost	Renault	r	r	3	r	r	r	r	1	r	p2	r	p1	1	r	2	43
6	John Watson	McLaren-Ford Cosworth	r	8	r	10	7	r	3	2	1	6	6	r	r	2	7	27
7	Gilles Villeneuve	Ferrari	r	r	r	p7	4	1	1	r	r	10	r	r	r	3	dq	25
8	Elio de Angelis	Lotus-Ford Cosworth	r	5	6	–	5	r	5	6	r	7	7	5	4	6	r	14
9	René Arnoux	Renault	8	r	5	8	nq	r	9	p4	p9r	13	p2	r	pr	r	r	11
	Hector Rebaque	Brabham-Ford Cosworth	r	r	r	4	r	nq	r	9	5	4	r	4	r	r	r	11
11	Riccardo Patrese	Arrows-Ford Cosworth	pr	3	7	2	r	r	r	14	10r	r	r	r	r	r	11	10
	Eddie Cheever	Tyrrell-Ford Cosworth	5	nc	r	r	6	5	nc	13	4	5	nq	r	r	12r	r	10
13	Didier Pironi	Ferrari	r	r	r	5	8	4	15	5	r	r	9	r	5	r	9	9
14	Nigel Mansell	Lotus-Ford Cosworth	r	11	r	–	3	r	6	7	nq	r	r	r	r	r	4	8
15	Bruno Giacomelli	Alfa Romeo	r	nc	10r	r	9	r	10	15	r	15	r	r	8	4	3	7
16	Marc Surer	Ensign-Ford Cosworth	r	4	r	9	11	6	–	–	–	–	–	–	–	–	–	4
		Theodore-Ford Cosworth	–	–	–	–	–	–	12	11r	14r	r	8	nq	9	r		
17	Mario Andretti	Alfa Romeo	4	r	8	r	10	r	8	8	r	9	r	r	r	7	r	3
18	Patrick Tambay	Theodore-Ford Cosworth	6	10	r	11	nq	7	13	–	–	–	–	–	–	–	–	1
		Talbot Ligier-Matra	–	–	–	–	–	–		r	r	r	r	r	r	r		
	Andrea de Cesaris	McLaren-Ford Cosworth	r	r	11	6	r	r	r	11	r	r	8	ns	7r	r	12	1
	Slim Borgudd	ATS-Ford Cosworth	–	–	–	13	nq	npq	nq	nq	6	r	r	10	r	r	nq	1
	Eliseo Salazar	March-Ford Cosworth	nq	nq	nq	r	nq	npq	–	–	–	–	–	–	–	–	–	1
		Ensign-Ford Cosworth	–	–	–	–	–		14	r	nq	nc	r	6	r	r	nc	

1982

Position	Driver	Car	South Africa	Brazil	USA West	San Marino	Belgium	Monaco	Detroit	Canada	Netherlands	Britain	France	Germany	Austria	Switzerland	Italy	Las Vegas	Points total
1	Keke Rosberg	Williams-Ford Cosworth	5	dq	2	–	2	r	4	r	3	pr	5	3	2	1	8	5	44
2	Didier Pironi	Ferrari	18	6	r	1	ns	2r	3	p9	1	2	3	pns	–	–	–	–	39
	John Watson	McLaren-Ford Cosworth	6	2	6	–	1	r	1	3	9	r	r	r	r	13	4	2	39
4	Alain Prost	Renault	1	p1	r	r	pr	7r	pnc	r	r	6	2	r	8r	p2	r	p4	34
5	Niki Lauda	McLaren-Ford Cosworth	4	r	1	–	dq	r	r	r	4	1	8	ns	5	3	r	r	30
6	René Arnoux	Renault	p3	r	r	pr	r	pr	10	r	pr	r	p1	2	r	16r	1	r	28
7	Patrick Tambay	Ferrari	–	–	–	–	–	–	–	–	8	3	4	1	4	ns	2	ns	25
	Michele Alboreto	Tyrrell-Ford Cosworth	7	4	4	3	r	10r	r	r	7	nc	6	4	r	7	5	1	25
9	Elio de Angelis	Lotus-Ford Cosworth	8	r	5	–	4	5	r	4	r	4	r	r	1	6	r	r	23
10	Riccardo Patrese	Brabham-BMW	r	–	–	–	r	–	–	–	15	r	r	r	r	5	r	r	21
		Brabham-Ford Cosworth	–	r	3	–	–	1	r	2	–	–	–	–	–	–	–	–	
11	Nelson Piquet	Brabham-BMW	r	–	–	–	5	r	nq	1	2	r	r	r	pr	4	r	r	20
		Brabham-Ford Cosworth	–	dq	–	–	–	–	–	–	–	–	–	–	–	–	–	–	
12	Eddie Cheever	Talbot Ligier-Matra	r	r	r	–	3	r	2	10r	nq	r	16	r	r	nc	6	3	15
13	Derek Daly	Theodore-Ford Cosworth	14	r	r	–	–	–	–	–	–	–	–	–	–	–	–	–	8
		Williams-Ford Cosworth	–	–	–	–	r	6r	5	7r	5	5	7	r	r	9	r	6	
14	Nigel Mansell	Lotus-Ford Cosworth	r	3	7	–	r	4	r	r	–	r	–	9	r	8	7	r	7
15	Carlos Reutemann	Williams-Ford Cosworth	2	r	–	–	–	–	–	–	–	–	–	–	–	–	–	–	6
	Gilles Villeneuve †	Ferrari	r	r	dq	2	ns	–	–	–	–	–	–	–	–	–	–	–	6
17	Andrea de Cesaris	Alfa Romeo	13	r	pr	r	r	3r	r	6r	r	r	r	r	r	10	10	9	5
	Jacques Laffite	Talbot Ligier-Matra	r	r	r	–	9	r	6	r	r	r	14	r	3	r	r	r	5
19	Mario Andretti	Williams-Ford Cosworth	–	–	r	–	–	–	–	–	–	–	–	–	–	–	–	–	4
		Ferrari	–	–	–	–	–	–	–	–	–	–	–	–	–	–	p3	r	
20	Jean-Pierre Jarier	Osella-Ford Cosworth	r	9	r	4	r	nq	r	r	14	r	r	r	nq	r	r	ns	3
	Marc Surer	Arrows-Ford Cosworth	–	–	–	–	7	9	8	5	10	r	13	6	r	15	r	7	3
22	Manfred Winkelhock	ATS-Ford Cosworth	10	5	r	dq	r	r	r	nq	12	nq	11	r	r	r	nq	nc	2
	Eliseo Salazar	ATS-Ford Cosworth	9	r	r	5	r	r	r	r	13	nq	r	r	nq	14	9	nq	2
	Bruno Giacomelli	Alfa Romeo	11	r	r	r	r	r	r	r	11	7	9	5	r	12	r	10	2
	Mauro Baldi	Arrows-Ford Cosworth	nq	10	nq	–	r	nq	r	8	6	9	r	r	6	nq	12	11	2
26	Chico Serra	Fittipaldi-Ford Cosworth	17	r	nq	–	6	npq	11	nq	r	r	nq	11	7	nq	11	nq	1

1983

Position	Driver	Car	Brazil	USA West	France	San Marino	Monaco	Belgium	Detroit	Canada	Britain	Germany	Austria	Netherlands	Italy	Europe	South Africa	Points total
1	Nelson Piquet	Brabham-BMW	1	r	2	r	2	4	4	r	2	13r	3	pr	1	1	3	59
2	Alain Prost	Renault	7	11	p1	2	p3	p1	8	5	1	4	1	r	r	2	r	57
3	René Arnoux	Ferrari	10	3	7	p3	r	r	pr	p1	p5	1	2	1	2	9	r	49
4	Patrick Tambay	Ferrari	5	pr	4	1	4	2	r	3	3	pr	pr	2	4	r	pr	40
5	Keke Rosberg	Williams-Ford Cosworth	pdq	r	5	4	1	5	2	4	11	10	8	r	11	r	–	27
		Williams-Honda	–	–	–	–	–	–	–	–	–	–	–	–	–	–	5	
6	John Watson	McLaren-Ford Cosworth	r	1	r	5	nq	r	3	6	9	5	9	3	–	–	–	22
		McLaren-TAG Porsche	–	–	–	–	–	–	–	–	–	–	–	–	r	r	dq	
	Eddie Cheever	Renault	r	13r	3	r	r	3	r	2	r	r	4	r	3	10	6	22
8	Andrea de Cesaris	Alfa Romeo	exc	r	12	r	r	r	r	r	8	2	r	r	r	4	2	15
9	Riccardo Patrese	Brabham-BMW	r	10r	r	13r	r	r	r	r	r	3	r	9	pr	7	1	13
10	Niki Lauda	McLaren-Ford Cosworth	3	2	r	r	nq	r	r	r	6	dq	6	–	–	–	–	12
		McLaren-TAG Porsche	–	–	–	–	–	–	–	–	–	–	–	–	r	r	11r	
11	Jacques Laffite	Williams-Ford Cosworth	4	4	6	7	r	6	5	r	12	6	r	r	nq	nq	–	11
		Williams-Honda	–	–	–	–	–	–	–	–	–	–	–	–	–	–	r	
12	Michele Alboreto	Tyrrell-Ford Cosworth	r	9	8	r	r	14	1	8	13	r	r	6	r	r	r	10
	Nigel Mansell	Lotus-Ford Cosworth	12	12	r	12r	r	r	6	r	–	–	–	–	–	–	–	10
		Lotus-Renault	–	–	–	–	–	–	–	–	4	r	5	r	8	3	nc	
14	Derek Warwick	Toleman-Hart	8	r	r	r	r	7	r	r	r	r	r	4	6	5	4	9
15	Marc Surer	Arrows-Ford Cosworth	6	5	10	6	r	11	11	r	17	7	r	8	10	r	8	4
16	Mauro Baldi	Alfa Romeo	r	r	r	10r	6	r	12	10	7	r	r	5	r	r	r	3
17	Danny Sullivan	Tyrrell-Ford Cosworth	11	8	r	r	5	12	r	dq	14	12	r	r	r	r	7	2
	Elio de Angelis	Lotus-Ford Cosworth	dq	–	–	–	–	–	–	–	–	–	–	–	–	–	–	2
		Lotus-Renault	–	r	r	r	r	9	r	r	r	4	r	r	5	pr	r	
19	Johnny Cecotto	Theodore-Ford Cosworth	14	6	11	r	npq	10	r	r	nq	11	nq	nq	12	–	–	1
	Bruno Giacomelli	Toleman-Hart	r	r	13r	r	nq	8	9	r	r	r	r	13	7	6	r	1

1984

Position	Driver	Car	Brazil	South Africa	Belgium	San Marino	France	Monaco	Canada	Detroit	Dallas	Britain	Germany	Austria	Netherlands	Italy	Europe	Portugal	Points total
1	Niki Lauda	McLaren-TAG Porsche	r	1	r	r	1	r	2	r	9r	1	2	1	2	1	4	2	72
2	Alain Prost	McLaren-TAG Porsche	1	2	r	1	7	p1	3	4	r	r	p1	r	p1	1	1	1	71.5
3	Elio de Angelis	Lotus-Renault	p3	7	5	3r	5	5	4	2	3	4	r	r	4	r	r	5	34
4	Michele Alboreto	Ferrari	r	11r	p1	r	r	6	r	r	r	5	r	3	r	2	2	4	30.5
5	Nelson Piquet	Brabham-BMW	r	pr	9r	pr	r	r	p1	p1	r	p7	r	p2	r	pr	p3	p6	29
6	René Arnoux	Ferrari	r	r	3	2	4	3	5	r	2	6	6	7	11r	r	5	9	27
7	Derek Warwick	Renault	r	3	2	4	r	r	r	r	r	2	3	r	r	r	11r	r	23
8	Keke Rosberg	Williams-Honda	2	r	4r	r	6	4	r	r	1	r	r	r	8r	r	r	r	20.5
9	Nigel Mansell	Lotus-Renault	r	r	r	r	3	r	6	r	p6r	r	4	r	3	r	r	r	13
	Ayrton Senna	Toleman-Hart	r	6	6	nq	r	2	7	r	r	3	r	r	r	–	r	3	13
11	Patrick Tambay	Renault	5r	r	7	r	p2	r	ew	r	r	8r	5	r	6	r	r	7	11
12	Teo Fabi	Brabham-BMW	r	r	r	r	9	–	–	3	–	r	r	4	5	r	r	–	9
13	Riccardo Patrese	Alfa Romeo	r	4	r	r	r	r	r	r	r	12r	r	10r	r	3	6	8	8
14	Jacques Laffite	Williams-Honda	r	r	r	r	8	8	r	5	4	r	r	r	r	r	r	14	5
	Thierry Boutsen	Arrows-Ford Cosworth	6	12	–	5	–	–	–	–	–	–	–	–	–	–	–	–	5
		Arrows-BMW	–	–	r	–	11	nq	r	r	r	r	r	r	5	10	9r	r	
16	Eddie Cheever	Alfa Romeo	4	r	r	7r	r	nq	11r	r	r	r	r	r	13r	9r	r	17	3
	Stefan Johansson	Tyrrell-Ford Cosworth	–	–	–	–	–	–	–	–	–	dq	dq	nq	dq	–	–	–	3
		Toleman-Hart	–	–	–	–	–	–	–	–	–	–	–	–	–	4	r	11	
	Andrea de Cesaris	Ligier-Renault	r	5	r	6r	10	r	r	r	r	10	7	r	r	r	7	12	3
19	Piercarlo Ghinzani	Osella-Alfa Romeo	r	ns	r	nq	12	7	r	r	5	9	r	r	r	7r	r	r	2
20	Marc Surer	Arrows-Ford Cosworth	7	9	8	–	r	nq	r	r	–	–	–	–	–	–	–	–	1
		Arrows-BMW	–	–	–	r	–	–	–	–	–	r	11	r	6	r	r	r	
21	Jo Gartner	Osella-Alfa Romeo	–	–	–	r	r	–	–	–	–	r	r	r	12	5	12r	16r	– (2)
	Gerhard Berger	ATS-BMW	–	–	–	–	–	–	–	–	–	–	–	12r	–	6	r	13	– (1)

Half points were awarded in Monaco where the race was stopped early. Jo Gartner and Gerhard Berger did not score points for the World Championship because their constructors had entered only one car for the season.
All points scored by Tyrrell were redistributed due to technical infringements.

1985

Position	Driver	Car	Brazil	Portugal	San Marino	Monaco	Canada	USA	France	Britain	Germany	Austria	Netherlands	Italy	Belgium	Europe	South Africa	Australia	Points total
1	Alain Prost	McLaren-TAG Porsche	1	r	dq	1	3	r	3	1	2	p1	2	1	p3	4	3	r	73 (3)
2	Michele Alboreto	Ferrari	p2	2	r	2	1	3	r	2	1	3	4	13r	r	r	r	r	53
3	Keke Rosberg	Williams-Honda	r	r	r	8	4	1	p2	pr	12r	r	r	r	4	3	2	1	40
4	Ayrton Senna	Lotus-Renault	r	p1	p7r	pr	16	pr	r	10r	r	2	3	p3	1	p2	r	pr	38
5	Elio de Angelis	Lotus-Renault	3	4	1	3	p5	5	5	nc	r	5	5	6	r	5	r	dq	33
6	Nigel Mansell	Williams-Honda	r	5	5	7	6	r	ns	r	6	r	6	11r	2	1	p1	r	31
7	Stefan Johansson	Tyrrell-Ford Cosworth	7	–	–	–	–	–	–	–	–	–	–	–	–	–	–	–	26
		Ferrari	–	8	6r	r	2	2	4	r	9	4	r	5r	r	r	4	5	
8	Nelson Piquet	Brabham-BMW	r	r	8r	r	r	6	1	4	r	r	p8	2	5	r	r	r	21
9	Jacques Laffite	Ligier-Renault	6	r	r	6	8	12	r	3	3	r	r	r	11r	r	–	2	16
10	Niki Lauda	McLaren-TAG Porsche	r	r	4	r	r	r	r	r	5	r	1	r	ns	–	r	r	14
11	Thierry Boutsen	Arrows-BMW	11	r	2	9	9	7	9	r	4	8	r	9	10r	6	6	r	11
	Patrick Tambay	Renault	5	3	3	r	7	r	6	r	r	10r	r	7	r	12	–	r	11
13	Marc Surer	Brabham-BMW	–	–	–	–	15	8	8	6	r	6	10r	4	8	r	r	r	5
	Derek Warwick	Renault	10	7	10	5	r	r	7	5	r	r	r	r	6	r	–	r	5
15	Philippe Streiff	Ligier-Renault	–	–	–	–	–	–	–	–	–	–	10	9	8	–	3	4	
		Tyrrell-Renault	–	–	–	–	–	–	–	–	–	–	–	–	–	r	–		
	Stefan Bellof †	Tyrrell-Ford Cosworth	–	6	r	nq	11	4	13	11	–	–	–	–	–	–	–		4
		Tyrrell-Renault	–	–	–	–	–	–	–	–	8	7r	r						
17	René Arnoux	Ferrari	4	–	–	–	–	–	–	–	–	–	–	–	–	–	–	–	3
	Andrea de Cesaris	Ligier-Renault	r	r	r	4	14	10	r	r	r	r	r	–	–	–	–	–	3
	Ivan Capelli	Tyrrell-Renault	–	–	–	–	–	–	–	–	–	–	–	–	–	r	–	4	3
	Gerhard Berger	Arrows-BMW	r	r	r	r	13	11	r	8	7	r	9	r	7	10	5	6	3

Teo Fabi (Toleman-Hart) started from pole position in Germany. He scored no points during the season.

1986

Position	Driver	Car	Brazil	Spain	San Marino	Monaco	Belgium	Canada	USA	France	Britain	Germany	Hungary	Austria	Italy	Portugal	Mexico	Australia	Points total
1	Alain Prost	McLaren-TAG Porsche	r	3	1	p1	6	2	3	2	3	6r	r	1	r/dq	2	2	1	72 (2)
2	Nigel Mansell	Williams-Honda	r	2	r	4	1	p1	5	1	1	3	3	r	2	1	5	pr	70 (2)
3	Nelson Piquet	Williams-Honda	1	r	2	7	pr	3	r	3	p2	1	1	r	1	3	4	2	69
4	Ayrton Senna	Lotus-Renault	p2	p1	pr	3	2	5	p1	pr	r	2	p2	r	r	p4r	p3	r	55
5	Stefan Johansson	Ferrari	r	r	4	10	3	r	r	r	r	11r	4	3	3	6	12r	3	23
6	Keke Rosberg	McLaren-TAG Porsche	r	4	5r	2	r	4	r	4	r	p5r	r	9r	4	r	r	r	22
7	Gerhard Berger	Benetton-BMW	6	6	3	r	10	r	r	r	r	10	r	7	5	r	1	r	17
8	Jacques Laffite	Ligier-Renault	3	r	r	6	5	7	2	6	r	–	–	–	–	–	–	–	14
	Michele Alboreto	Ferrari	r	r	10r	r	4	8	4	8	r	r	r	r	2	r	5	r	14
	René Arnoux	Ligier-Renault	4	r	r	5	r	6	r	5	4	4	r	10	r	7	15r	7	14
11	Martin Brundle	Tyrrell-Renault	5	r	8	r	r	9	r	10	5	r	6	r	10	r	11	4	8
12	Alan Jones	Lola-Hart	r	r	–	–	–	–	–	–	–	–	–	–	–	–	–	–	4
		Lola-Ford Cosworth	–	–	r	r	11r	10	r	r	r	9	r	4	6	r	r	r	
13	Philippe Streiff	Tyrrell-Renault	7	r	r	11	12	11	9	r	6	r	8	r	9	r	r	5r	3
	Johnny Dumfries	Lotus-Renault	9	r	r	nq	r	r	7	r	7	r	5	r	r	9	r	6	3
15	Teo Fabi	Benetton-BMW	10	5	r	r	7	r	r	r	r	r	r	pr	pr	8	r	10	2
	Patrick Tambay	Lola-Hart	r	8	r	–	–	–	–	–	–	–	–	–	–	–	–	–	2
		Lola-Ford Cosworth	–	–	–	r	r	ns	–	r	r	8	7	5	r	nc	r	nc	
	Riccardo Patrese	Brabham-BMW	r	r	6r	r	8	r	6	7	r	r	r	r	r	r	13r	r	2
18	Philippe Alliot	Ligier-Renault	–	–	–	–	–	–	–	–	r	9	r	r	r	r	6	8	1
	Christian Danner	Osella-Alfa Romeo	r	r	r	nq	r	r	–	–	–	–	–	–	–	–	–	–	1
		Arrows-BMW	–	–	–	–	–	–	r	11	r	r	r	6	8	11	9	r	

1987

Position	Driver	Car	Brazil	San Marino	Belgium	Monaco	USA	France	Britain	Germany	Hungary	Austria	Italy	Portugal	Spain	Mexico	Japan	Australia	Points total
1	Nelson Piquet	Williams-Honda	2	ns	r	2	2	2	p2	1	1	p2	p1	3	p4	2	15r	r	73 (3)
2	Nigel Mansell	Williams-Honda	p6	1	pr	pr	p5	p1	1	pr	p14r	1	3	r	1	p1	ns	–	61
3	Ayrton Senna	Lotus-Honda	r	p2	r	1	1	4	3	3	2	5	2	7	5	r	2	dq	57
4	Alain Prost	McLaren-TAG Porsche	1	r	1	9r	3	3	r	7r	3	6	15	1	2	r	7	r	46
5	Gerhard Berger	Ferrari	4	r	r	4	4	r	r	r	r	r	4	p2	r	r	p1	p1	36
6	Stefan Johansson	McLaren-TAG Porsche	3	4	2	r	7	8r	r	2	r	7	6	5	3	r	3	r	30
7	Michele Alboreto	Ferrari	8r	3	r	3	r	r	r	r	r	r	r	r	15r	r	4	2	17
8	Thierry Boutsen	Benetton-Ford Cosworth	5	r	r	r	r	r	7	r	4	4	5	14	16r	r	5	3	16
9	Teo Fabi	Benetton-Ford Cosworth	r	r	r	8	r	5r	6	r	r	3	7	4r	r	5	r	r	12
10	Eddie Cheever	Arrows-Megatron	r	r	4	r	6r	r	r	r	8	r	r	6	8r	4	9	r	8
11	Jonathan Palmer	Tyrrell-Ford Cosworth	10	r	r	5	11	7	8	5	7	14	14	10	r	7	8	4	7
	Satoru Nakajima	Lotus-Honda	7	6	5	10	r	nc	4	r	r	13	11	8	9	r	6	r	7
13	Riccardo Patrese	Brabham-BMW	r	9	r	r	9	r	r	r	5	r	r	r	13	3	11r	–	6
		Williams-Honda	–	–	–	–	–	–	–	–	–	–	–	–	–	–	–	9r	
14	Andrea de Cesaris	Brabham-BMW	r	r	3r	r	r	r	r	r	r	r	r	r	r	r	r	8r	4
	Philippe Streiff	Tyrrell-Ford Cosworth	11	8	9	r	r	6	r	4	9	r	12	12	7	8	12	r	4
16	Derek Warwick	Arrows-Megatron	r	11r	r	r	r	r	5	r	6	r	r	13	10	r	10	r	3
	Philippe Alliot	Lola-Ford Cosworth	–	10	8	r	r	r	r	6	r	12	r	r	6	6	r	r	3
18	Martin Brundle	Zakspeed	r	5	r	7	r	r	nc	nc	r	dq	r	r	11	r	r	r	2
19	René Arnoux	Ligier-Megatron	–	ns	6	11	10	r	r	r	r	10	10	r	r	r	r	r	1
	Ivan Capelli	March-Ford Cosworth	ns	r	r	6	r	r	r	r	10	11	13	9	12	r	r	r	1
	Roberto Moreno	AGS-Ford Cosworth	–	–	–	–	–	–	–	–	–	–	–	–	–	–	r	6	1
22	Yannick Dalmas	Lola-Ford Cosworth	–	–	–	–	–	–	–	–	–	–	–	–	–	9	14r	5	–(2)

Yannick Dalmas did not score points for the World Championship because his constructor had entered only one car for the season.

1988

Position	Driver	Car	Brazil	San Marino	Monaco	Mexico	Canada	USA	France	Britain	Germany	Hungary	Belgium	Italy	Portugal	Spain	Japan	Australia	Points total
1	Ayrton Senna	McLaren-Honda	pdq	p1	pr	p2	p1	p1	2	1	p1	p1	p1	p10r	6	p4	p1	p2	90 (4)
2	Alain Prost	McLaren-Honda	1	2	1	1	2	2	p1	r	2	2	2	r	p1	1	2	1	87(18)
3	Gerhard Berger	Ferrari	2	5	2	3	r	r	4	p9	3	4	r	1	r	6	4	r	41
4	Thierry Boutsen	Benetton-Ford Cosworth	7	4	8	8	3	3	r	r	6	3	dq	6	3	9	3	5	27
5	Michele Alboreto	Ferrari	5	18r	3	4	r	r	3	17r	4	r	r	2	5	r	11	r	24
6	Nelson Piquet	Lotus-Honda	3	3	r	r	4	r	5	5	r	8	4	r	r	8	r	3	22
7	Ivan Capelli	March-Judd	r	r	10	16	5	ns	9	r	5	r	3	5	2	r	r	6	17
	Derek Warwick	Arrows-Megatron	4	9	4	5	7	r	r	6	7	r	5	4	4	r	r	r	17
9	Nigel Mansell	Williams-Judd	r	r	r	r	r	r	2	r	r	r	–	r	2	r	r	r	12
	Alessandro Nannini	Benetton-Ford Cosworth	r	6	r	7	r	r	6	3	18	r	dq	9	r	3	5	r	12
11	Riccardo Patrese	Williams-Judd	r	13	6	r	r	r	r	8	r	6	r	7	r	5	6	4	8
12	Eddie Cheever	Arrows-Megatron	8	7	r	6	r	r	11	7	10	r	6	3	r	r	r	r	6
13	Mauricio Gugelmin	March-Judd	r	15	r	r	r	r	8	4	8	5	r	8	r	7	10	r	5
	Jonathan Palmer	Tyrrell-Ford Cosworth	r	14	5	nq	6	5	r	r	11	r	12r	nq	r	r	12	r	5
15	Andrea de Cesaris	Rial-Ford Cosworth	r	r	r	r	9r	4	10	r	13	r	r	r	r	r	r	8r	3
16	Satoru Nakajima	Lotus-Honda	6	8	nq	r	11	nq	7	10	9	7	r	r	r	r	7	r	1
	Pierluigi Martini	Minardi-Ford Cosworth	–	–	–	–	–	6	15	15	nq	r	nq	r	r	r	13	7	1

1989

Position	Driver	Car	Brazil	San Marino	Monaco	Mexico	USA	Canada	France	Britain	Germany	Hungary	Belgium	Italy	Portugal	Spain	Japan	Australia	Points total
1	Alain Prost	McLaren-Honda	2	2	2	5	1	pr	pl	1	2	4	2	1	2	3	r	r	76 (5)
2	Ayrton Senna	McLaren-Honda	pll	pl	pl	pl	pr	7r	r	pr	pl	2	pl	pr	pr	pl	pdq	pr	60
3	Riccardo Patrese	Williams-Renault	r	r	15	2	2	2	3	r	4	pr	r	4	r	5	2	3	40
4	Nigel Mansell	Ferrari	1	r	r	r	r	dq	2	2	3	1	3	r	r/dq	–	r	r	38
5	Thierry Boutsen	Williams-Renault	r	4	10	r	6	1	r	10	r	3	4	3	r	r	3	1	37
6	Alessandro Nannini	Benetton-Ford Cosworth	6	3	8	4	r	dq	r	3	r	r	5	r	4	r	1	2	32
7	Gerhard Berger	Ferrari	r	r	–	r	r	r	r	r	r	r	r	2	1	2	r	r	21
8	Nelson Piquet	Lotus-Judd	r	r	r	11	r	4	8	4	5	6	nq	r	r	8	4	r	12
9	Jean Alesi	Tyrrell-Ford Cosworth	–	–	–	–	–	–	4	r	10	9	–	5	–	4	r	r	8
10	Derek Warwick	Arrows-Ford Cosworth	5	5	r	r	r	r	–	9	6	10	6	r	r	9	6	r	7
11	Michele Alboreto	Tyrrell-Ford Cosworth	10	nq	5	3	r	r	–	–	–	–	–	–	–	–	–	–	6
		Lola-Lamborghini	–	–	–	–	–	–	r	r	r	r	r	r	11	npq	nq	npq	
	Eddie Cheever	Arrows-Ford Cosworth	r	9	7	7	3	r	7	nq	12r	5	r	nq	r	r	8	r	6
	Stefan Johansson	Onyx-Ford Cosworth	npq	npq	npq	r	r	dq	5	npq	r	r	8	npq	3	npq	npq	npq	6
14	Johnny Herbert	Benetton-Ford Cosworth	4	11	14	15	5	nq	–	–	–	–	–	–	–	–	–	–	5
		Tyrrell-Ford Cosworth	–	–	–	–	–	–	–	–	–	–	–	r	–	nq	–	–	
	Pierluigi Martini	Minardi-Ford Cosworth	r	r	r	r	r	r	r	5	9	r	9	7	5	r	–	6	5
16	Mauricio Gugelmin	March-Judd	3	r	r	nq	dq	r	nc	r	r	r	7	r	10	r	7	7	4
	Stefano Modena	Brabham-Judd	r	r	3	10	r	r	r	r	r	11	r	exc	14	r	r	8	4
	Andrea de Cesaris	Dallara-Ford Cosworth	13r	10	13	r	8r	3	nq	r	7	r	11	r	r	7	10	r	4
	Alex Caffi	Dallara-Ford Cosworth	npq	7	4	13	r	6	r	npq	r	7	r	11r	r	r	9	r	4
	Martin Brundle	Brabham-Judd	r	r	6	9	r	npq	npq	r	8	12	r	6	8	r	5	r	4
21	Christian Danner	Rial-Ford Cosworth	14r	nq	nq	12	4	8	nq	nq	nq	nq	nq	nq	nq	–	–	–	3
	Satoru Nakajima	Lotus-Judd	8	nc	nq	r	r	nq	r	8	r	r	nq	10	7	r	r	4	3
23	René Arnoux	Ligier-Ford Cosworth	nq	nq	12	14	nq	5	r	nq	11	nq	r	9	13	nq	nq	r	2
	Emanuele Pirro	Benetton-Ford Cosworth	–	–	–	–	–	–	9	11	r	8	10	r	r	r	r	5	2
	Jonathan Palmer	Tyrrell-Ford Cosworth	7	6	9	r	9r	r	10	r	r	13	14	r	6	10	r	nq	2
26	Gabriele Tarquini	AGS-Ford Cosworth	–	8	r	6	7r	r	r	nq	npq	npq	npq	npq	npq	npq	npq	npq	1
	Olivier Grouillard	Ligier-Ford Cosworth	9	dq	r	8	nq	nq	6	7	r	nq	13	r	nq	r	r	r	1
	Luis Sala	Minardi-Ford Cosworth	r	r	r	nq	r	r	nq	6	nq	r	15	8	12	r	r	nq	1
	Philippe Alliot	Lola-Lamborghini	12	r	r	nc	r	r	r	r	r	npq	16r	r	9	6	r	r	1

1990

Position	Driver	Car	USA	Brazil	San Marino	Monaco	Canada	Mexico	France	Britain	Germany	Hungary	Belgium	Italy	Portugal	Spain	Japan	Australia	Points total
1	Ayrton Senna	McLaren-Honda	1	p3	pr	pl	pl	20r	3	3	pl	2	pl	pl	2	pr	pr	pr	78
2	Alain Prost	Ferrari	r	1	4	r	5	1	1	1	4	r	2	2	3	1	r	3	71 (2)
3	Nelson Piquet	Benetton-Ford Cosworth	4	6	5	dq	2	6	4	5	r	3	5	7	5	r	1	1	43 (1)
	Gerhard Berger	McLaren-Honda	pr	2	2	3	4	p3	5	14r	3	16r	3	3	4	r	r	4	43
5	Nigel Mansell	Ferrari	r	4	r	r	3	2	p18r	pr	r	17r	r	4	pl	2	r	2	37
6	Thierry Boutsen	Williams-Renault	3	5	r	4	r	5	r	2	6	pl	r	r	r	4	5	5	34
7	Riccardo Patrese	Williams-Renault	9	13r	1	r	r	9	6	r	5	4	r	5	7	5	4	6	23
8	Alessandro Nannini	Benetton-Ford Cosworth	11	10r	3	r	r	4	16r	r	2	r	4	8	6	3	–	–	21
9	Jean Alesi	Tyrrell-Ford Cosworth	2	7	6	2	r	7	r	8	11r	r	8	r	8	r	ns	8	13
10	Ivan Capelli	Leyton House-Judd	r	nq	r	r	10	nq	2	r	7	r	7	r	r	r	r	r	6
	Roberto Moreno	EuroBrun-Judd	13	npq	r	nq	nq	exc	npq	npq	npq	npq	npq	npq	npq	npq	–	–	6
		Benetton-Ford Cosworth	–	–	–	–	–	–	–	–	–	–	–	–	–	–	2	7	
	Aguri Suzuki	Lola-Lamborghini	r	r	r	r	12	r	7	6	r	r	r	r	14r	6	3	r	6
13	Éric Bernard	Lola-Lamborghini	8	r	13r	6	9	r	8	4	r	6	9	r	r	r	r	r	5
14	Derek Warwick	Lotus-Lamborghini	r	r	7	r	6	10	11	r	8	5	11	r	r	r	r	r	3
	Satoru Nakajima	Tyrrell-Ford Cosworth	6	8	r	r	11	r	r	r	r	r	r	6	ns	r	6	r	3
16	Stefano Modena	Brabham-Judd	5	r	r	r	7	11	13	9	r	r	17r	r	r	r	r	12	2
	Alex Caffi	Arrows-Ford Cosworth	–	r	nq	5	8	nq	r	7	9	9	10	9	13r	–	9	nq	2
18	Mauricio Gugelmin	Leyton House-Judd	14	nq	r	nq	nq	nq	r	ns	r	8	6	r	12	8	r	r	1

1991

Position	Driver	Car	USA	Brazil	San Marino	Monaco	Canada	Mexico	France	Britain	Germany	Hungary	Belgium	Italy	Portugal	Spain	Japan	Australia	Points total
1	Ayrton Senna	McLaren-Honda	pl	pl	pl	pl	r	3	3	4r	7r	pl	pl	p2	2	5	2	pl	96
2	Nigel Mansell	Williams-Renault	r	r	r	2	6r	2	1	pl	pl	2	r	1	dq	1	r	2	72
3	Riccardo Patrese	Williams-Renault	r	2	r	r	p3	pl	p5	r	2	3	5	r	pl	3	3	5	53
4	Gerhard Berger	McLaren-Honda	r	3	2	r	r	r	r	2	4	4	2	4	r	pr	pl	3	43
5	Alain Prost	Ferrari	2	4	r	5	r	r	2	3	r	r	r	3	r	2	4	–	34
6	Nelson Piquet	Benetton-Ford Cosworth	3	5	r	r	1	r	8	5	r	r	3	6	5	11	7	4	26.5
7	Jean Alesi	Ferrari	12r	6	r	3	r	r	4	r	3	5	r	r	3	4	r	r	21
8	Stefano Modena	Tyrrell-Honda	4	r	r	r	2	11	r	7	13	12	r	r	r	16	6	10	10
9	Andrea de Cesaris	Jordan-Ford Cosworth	npq	r	r	r	4	4r	6	r	5	7	13r	7	8	r	r	8	9
10	Roberto Moreno	Benetton-Ford Cosworth	r	7	13r	4	r	5	r	r	8	8	4	–	–	–	–	–	8
		Jordan-Ford Cosworth	–	–	–	–	–	–	–	–	–	–	–	r	10	–	–	–	
		Minardi-Ferrari	–	–	–	–	–	–	–	–	–	–	–	–	–	–	–	16	
11	Pierluigi Martini	Minardi-Ferrari	9r	r	4	12	7	r	9	9	r	r	12	r	4	13	r	r	6
12	J.J. Lehto	Dallara-Judd	r	r	3	11	r	r	r	13	r	r	r	r	r	8	r	12	4
	Bertrand Gachot	Jordan-Ford Cosworth	10r	13r	r	8	5	r	r	6	6	9	–	–	–	–	–	–	4
		Lola-Ford Cosworth	–	–	–	–	–	–	–	–	–	–	–	–	–	–	–	nq	
	Michael Schumacher	Jordan-Ford Cosworth	–	–	–	–	–	–	–	–	–	r	–	–	–	–	–	–	4
		Benetton-Ford Cosworth	–	–	–	–	–	–	–	–	–	–	5	6	6	r	r	–	
15	Satoru Nakajima	Tyrrell-Honda	5	r	r	r	10	12	r	8	r	15	r	r	13	17	r	r	2
	Mika Häkkinen	Lotus-Judd	r	9	5	r	r	9	nq	12	r	14	r	14	14	r	r	19	2
	Martin Brundle	Brabham-Yamaha	11	12	11	exc	r	r	r	r	11	r	9	13	12	10	5	nq	2
18	Aguri Suzuki	Lola-Ford Cosworth	6	ns	r	r	r	r	r	r	r	r	r	nq	nq	r	nq	r	1
	Julian Bailey	Lotus-Judd	nq	nq	6	nq	–	–	–	–	–	–	–	–	–	–	–	–	1
	Emanuele Pirro	Dallara-Judd	r	11	npq	6	9	npq	npq	10	10	r	8	10	r	15	r	7	1
	Éric Bernard	Lola-Ford Cosworth	r	r	r	9	r	6	r	r	r	r	r	r	nq	r	nq	–	1
	Ivan Capelli	Leyton House-Ilmor	r	r	r	r	r	r	r	r	r	6	r	8	17r	r	–	–	1
	Mark Blundell	Brabham-Yamaha	r	r	8	r	nq	r	r	r	12	r	6	12	r	r	npq	17	1
24	Gianni Morbidelli	Minardi-Ferrari	r	8	r	r	r	7	r	11	r	13	r	9	9	14r	r	–	0.5
		Ferrari	–	–	–	–	–	–	–	–	–	–	–	–	–	–	–	6	

Half points were awarded in Australia where the race was stopped early.

1992

Position	Driver	Car	South Africa	Mexico	Brazil	Spain	San Marino	Monaco	Canada	France	Britain	Germany	Hungary	Belgium	Italy	Portugal	Japan	Australia	Points total
1	Nigel Mansell	Williams-Renault	pl	pl	pl	pl	pl	p2	r	pl	pl	pl	2	p2	pr	pl	pr	pr	108
2	Riccardo Patrese	Williams-Renault	2	2	2	r	2	3	r	2	2	8r	pr	3	5	r	1	r	56
3	Michael Schumacher	Benetton-Ford Cosworth	4	3	3	2	r	4	2	r	4	3	r	1	3	7	r	2	53
4	Ayrton Senna	McLaren-Honda	3	r	r	9r	3	1	pr	r	r	2	1	5	1	3	r	r	50
5	Gerhard Berger	McLaren-Honda	5	4	r	4	r	r	1	r	5	r	3	r	4	2	2	1	49
6	Martin Brundle	Benetton-Ford Cosworth	r	r	r	r	4	5	r	3	3	4	5	4	2	4	3	3	38
7	Jean Alesi	Ferrari	r	r	4	3	r	r	3	r	r	5	r	r	r	r	5	4	18
8	Mika Häkkinen	Lotus-Ford Cosworth	9	6	10	r	nq	r	r	4	6	r	4	6	r	5	r	7	11
9	Andrea de Cesaris	Tyrrell-Ilmor	r	5	r	r	14r	r	5	r	r	r	8	8	6	9	4	r	8
10	Michele Alboreto	Footwork-Mugen Honda	10	13	6	5	5	7	7	7	7	9	7	r	7	6	15	r	6
11	Erik Comas	Ligier-Renault	7	9	r	r	9	10	6	5	8	6	r	nq	r	r	r	r	4
12	Karl Wendlinger	March-Ilmor	r	r	r	8	12	r	4	r	r	16	r	11	10	r	–	–	3
	Ivan Capelli	Ferrari	r	r	r	10r	r	r	r	r	9	r	6	r	r	r	–	–	3
14	Thierry Boutsen	Ligier-Renault	r	10	r	r	r	12	10	r	10	7	r	r	r	8	r	5	2
	Johnny Herbert	Lotus-Ford Cosworth	6	7	r	r	r	r	r	6	r	r	r	13r	r	r	r	13	2
	Pierluigi Martini	Dallara-Ferrari	r	r	r	6	6	r	8	10	15	11	r	r	8	r	10	r	2
17	Bertrand Gachot	Venturi Larrousse	r	11	r	r	r	6	dq	r	r	14	r	18r	r	r	r	r	1
	Christian Fittipaldi	Minardi-Lamborghini	r	r	r	11	r	8	13r	nq	–	–	–	nq	nq	12	6	9	1
	Stefano Modena	Jordan-Yamaha	nq	r	r	nq	r	r	r	r	r	nq	r	15	nq	13	7	6	1

1993

Position	Driver	Car	South Africa	Brazil	Europe	San Marino	Spain	Monaco	Canada	France	Britain	Germany	Hungary	Belgium	Italy	Portugal	Japan	Australia	Points total
1	Alain Prost	Williams-Renault	p1	pr	p3	p1	p1	p4	p1	1	p1	p1	p12	p3	p12r	2	p2	2	99
2	Ayrton Senna	McLaren-Ford Cosworth	2	1	1	r	2	1	18r	4	5r	4	r	4	r	r	1	p1	73
3	Damon Hill	Williams-Renault	r	2	2	r	r	2	3	p2	r	15r	1	1	1	p3	4	3	69
4	Michael Schumacher	Benetton-Ford Cosworth	r	3	r	2	3	r	2	3	2	2	r	2	r	1	r	r	52
5	Riccardo Patrese	Benetton-Ford Cosworth	r	r	5	r	4	r	r	10	3	5	2	6	5	16r	r	8r	20
6	Jean Alesi	Ferrari	r	8	r	r	r	3	r	r	9	7	r	r	2	4	r	4	16
7	Martin Brundle	Ligier-Renault	r	r	r	3	r	6	5	5	14r	8	5	7	r	6	9r	6	13
8	Gerhard Berger	Ferrari	6r	r	r	r	6	14r	4	14	r	6	3	10r	r	r	r	5	12
9	Johnny Herbert	Lotus-Ford Cosworth	r	4	4	8r	r	r	10	r	4	10	r	5	r	r	11	r	11
10	Mark Blundell	Ligier-Renault	3	5	r	r	7	r	r	r	7	3	7	11r	r	r	7	9	10
11	Michael Andretti	McLaren-Ford Cosworth	r	r	r	r	5	8	14	6	r	r	r	8	3	r	–	–	7
	Karl Wendlinger	Sauber-Ilmor	r	r	r	r	r	13	6	r	r	9	6	r	4	5	r	15r	7
13	Christian Fittipaldi	Minardi-Ford Cosworth	4	r	7	r	8	5	9	8	12r	11	r	r	8r	9	–	–	5
	J.J. Lehto	Sauber-Ilmor	5	r	r	4r	r	r	7	r	8	r	r	9	r	7	8	r	5
15	Mika Häkkinen	McLaren-Ford Cosworth	–	–	–	–	–	–	–	–	–	–	–	–	r	3	r	4
	Derek Warwick	Footwork-Mugen Honda	7r	9	r	r	13	r	16	13	6	17	4	r	r	15r	14r	10	4
17	Philippe Alliot	Larrousse-Lamborghini	r	7	r	5	r	12	r	9	11	12	8	12	9	10	–	–	2
	Rubens Barrichello	Jordan-Hart	r	r	10r	r	12	9	r	7	10	r	r	r	r	13	5	11	2
	Fabrizio Barbazza	Minardi-Ford Cosworth	r	r	6	6	r	11	r	r	–	–	–	–	–	–	–	–	2
20	Alessandro Zanardi	Lotus-Ford Cosworth	r	6	8	r	14r	7	11	r	r	r	r	ns	–	–	–	–	1
	Érik Comas	Larrousse-Lamborghini	r	10	9	r	9	r	8	16r	r	r	r	r	6	11	r	12	1
	Eddie Irvine	Jordan-Hart	–	–	–	–	–	–	–	–	–	–	–	–	–	–	6	r	1

1994

Position	Driver	Car	Brazil	Pacific	San Marino	Monaco	Spain	Canada	France	Britain	Germany	Hungary	Belgium	Italy	Portugal	Europe	Japan	Australia	Points total
1	Michael Schumacher	Benetton-Ford Cosworth	1	1	1	p1	p2	p1	p1	dq	r	p1	dq	–	–	p1	p2	r	92
2	Damon Hill	Williams-Renault	2	r	6	r	1	2	p2	p1	8	2	1	1	1	2	1	r	91
3	Gerhard Berger	Ferrari	r	2	r	3	r	4	3	r	p1	12r	r	2	pr	5	r	2	41
4	Mika Häkkinen	McLaren-Peugeot	r	r	3	r	r	r	r	3	r	–	2	3	3	3	7	12r	26
5	Jean Alesi	Ferrari	3	–	–	5	4	3	r	2	r	r	r	pr	r	10	3	6	24
6	Rubens Barrichello	Jordan-Hart	4	3	nq	r	r	7	r	4	r	r	pr	4	4	12	r	4	19
7	Martin Brundle	McLaren-Peugeot	r	r	8	2	11r	r	r	r	r	4r	r	5	6	r	r	3	16
8	David Coulthard	Williams-Renault	–	–	–	–	r	5	–	5	r	r	4	6r	2	r			14
9	Nigel Mansell	Williams-Renault	–	–	–	–	–	–	r	–	–	–	–	–	–	r	4	1	13
10	Jos Verstappen	Benetton-Ford Cosworth	r	r	–	–	–	–	r	8	r	3	3	r	5	r	–	–	10
11	Olivier Panis	Ligier-Renault	11	9	11	9	7	12	r	12	2	6	7	10	dq	9	11	5	9
12	Mark Blundell	Tyrrell-Yamaha	r	r	9	r	3	10r	10	r	r	5	5	r	r	13	r	r	8
13	Heinz-Harald Frentzen	Sauber-Mercedes Benz	r	5	7	ns	r	r	4	7	r	r	r	r	r	6	6	7	7
14	Nicola Larini	Ferrari	–	r	2	–	–	–	–	–	–	–	–	–	–	–	–	–	6
	Christian Fittipaldi	Footwork-Ford Cosworth	r	4	13r	r	r	dq	8	9	4	14r	r	r	8	17	8	8	6
	Eddie Irvine	Jordan-Hart	r	–	–	–	6	r	r	r	r	r	13r	r	7	4	5	r	6
17	Ukyo Katayama	Tyrrell-Yamaha	5	r	5	r	r	r	6	r	r	r	r	r	r	7	r	r	5
18	Éric Bernard	Ligier-Renault	r	10	12	r	8	13	r	13	3	10	10	7	10	–	–	–	4
		Lotus-Mugen Honda	–	–	–	–	–	–	–	–	–	–	–	–	–	18	–	–	
	Karl Wendlinger	Sauber-Mercedes Benz	6	r	4	ns	–	–	–	–	–	–	–	–	–	–	–	–	4
	Andrea de Cesaris	Jordan-Hart	–	–	r	4	–	–	–	–	–	–	–	–	–	–	–	–	4
		Sauber-Mercedes Benz	–	–	–	–	–	r	6	r	r	r	r	r	r	r	–	–	
	Pierluigi Martini	Minardi-Ford Cosworth	8	r	r	r	5	9	5	10	r	r	8	r	12	15	r	9	4
22	Gianni Morbidelli	Footwork-Ford Cosworth	r	r	r	r	r	r	r	r	5	r	6	r	9	11	r	r	3
23	Érik Comas	Larrousse-Ford Cosworth	9	6	r	10	r	r	11r	r	6	8	r	8	r	r	9	–	2
24	Michele Alboreto	Minardi-Ford Cosworth	r	r	r	6	r	11	r	r	r	7	9	r	13	14	r	r	1
	J.J. Lehto	Benetton-Ford Cosworth	–	–	r	7	r	6	–	–	–	–	–	–	9	r	–	–	1
		Sauber-Mercedes Benz	–	–	–	–	–	–	–	–	–	–	–	–	–	–	r	10	

Additionally, Ayrton Senna † (Williams-Renault) started from pole position in the first three races of the season.

1995

Position	Driver	Car	Brazil	Argentina	San Marino	Spain	Monaco	Canada	France	Britain	Germany	Hungary	Belgium	Italy	Portugal	Europe	Pacific	Japan	Australia	Points total
1	Michael Schumacher	Benetton-Renault	1	3	pr	p1	1	p5	1	1	11r	1	r	2	1	1	1	p1	r	102
2	Damon Hill	Williams-Renault	pr	1	1	4	p2	r	p2	pr	pr	p1	2	r	3	r	3	r	p1	69
3	David Coulthard	Williams-Renault	2	pr	4	r	r	r	3	3	2	2	r	pr	p1	p3	p2	r	r	49
4	Johnny Herbert	Benetton-Renault	r	4	7	2	4	r	r	1	4	4	7	1	7	5	6	3	r	45
5	Jean Alesi	Ferrari	5	2	2	r	r	1	5	2	r	r	r	r	5	2	5	r	r	42
6	Gerhard Berger	Ferrari	3	6	3	3	3	11r	12	r	3	3	pr	r	4	r	4	r	r	31
7	Mika Häkkinen	McLaren-Mercedes Benz	4	r	5	r	r	r	7	r	r	r	r	2	r	8	–	2	ns	17
8	Olivier Panis	Ligier-Mugen Honda	r	7	9	6	r	4	8	4	r	6	9	r	r	r	8	5	2	16
9	Heinz-Harald Frentzen	Sauber-Ford Cosworth	r	5	6	8	6	r	10	6	r	5	4	3	6	r	7	8	r	15
10	Mark Blundell	McLaren-Mercedes Benz	6	r	–	–	5	r	11	5	r	r	5	4	9	r	9	7	4	13
11	Rubens Barrichello	Jordan-Peugeot	r	r	r	7	r	2	6	11r	r	7	6	r	11	4	r	r	r	11
12	Eddie Irvine	Jordan-Peugeot	r	r	8	5	r	3	9	r	9r	13r	r	r	10	6	11	4	r	10
13	Martin Brundle	Ligier-Mugen Honda	–	–	–	9	r	10r	4	r	–	r	3	r	8	7	–	–	r	7
14	Mika Salo	Tyrrell-Yamaha	7	r	r	10	r	7	15	8	r	r	8	5	13	10	12	6	5	5
	Gianni Morbidelli	Footwork-Hart	r	r	13	11	9	6	14	–	–	–	–	–	–	–	r	r	3	5
16	Jean-Christophe Boullion	Sauber-Ford Cosworth	–	–	–	–	8r	r	r	9	5	10	11	6	12	r	r	–	–	3
17	Aguri Suzuki	Ligier-Mugen Honda	8	r	11	–	–	–	–	–	6	–	–	–	–	–	r	ns	–	1
	Pedro Lamy	Minardi-Ford Cosworth	–	–	–	–	–	–	–	–	–	9	10	r	r	9	13	11	6	1

1996

Position	Driver	Car	Australia	Brazil	Argentina	Europe	San Marino	Monaco	Spain	Canada	France	Britain	Germany	Hungary	Belgium	Italy	Portugal	Japan	Points total
1	Damon Hill	Williams-Renault	1	p1	p1	p4	1	r	pr	p1	1	pr	p1	2	5	pr	p2	1	97
2	Jacques Villeneuve	Williams-Renault	p2	r	2	1	11r	r	3	2	2	1	3	1	p2	7	1	pr	78
3	Michael Schumacher	Ferrari	r	3	r	2	p2	pr	1	r	pr	r	4	p9r	1	1	3	2	59
4	Jean Alesi	Benetton-Renault	r	2	3	r	6	r	2	3	3	r	2	3	4	2	4	r	47
5	Mika Häkkinen	McLaren-Mercedes Benz	5	4	r	8	8r	6r	5	5	5	3	r	4	3	3	r	3	31
6	Gerhard Berger	Benetton-Renault	4	r	r	9	3	r	r	r	4	2	13r	r	6	r	6	4	21
7	David Coulthard	McLaren-Mercedes Benz	r	r	7	3	r	2	r	4	6	5	5	r	r	r	13	8	18
8	Rubens Barrichello	Jordan-Peugeot	r	r	4	5	5	r	r	r	9	4	6	6	r	5	r	9	14
9	Olivier Panis	Ligier-Mugen Honda	7	6	8	r	r	1	r	r	7	r	7	5	r	r	10	7	13
10	Eddie Irvine	Ferrari	3	7	5	r	4	7r	r	r	r	r	r	r	r	r	5	r	11
11	Martin Brundle	Jordan-Peugeot	r	12r	r	6	r	r	r	6	8	6	10	r	r	4	9	5	8
12	Heinz-Harald Frentzen	Sauber-Ford Cosworth	8	r	r	r	r	4	4	r	r	8	8	r	r	r	7	6	7
13	Mika Salo	Tyrrell-Yamaha	6	5	r	dq	r	5r	dq	r	10	7	9	r	7	r	11	r	5
14	Johnny Herbert	Sauber-Ford Cosworth	r	r	9	7	r	3	r	7	dq	9	r	r	r	9r	8	10	4
15	Pedro Diniz	Ligier-Mugen Honda	10	8	r	10	7	r	6	r	r	r	r	r	r	6	r	r	2
16	Jos Verstappen	Footwork-Hart	r	r	6	r	r	r	r	r	10	r	r	r	r	8	r	11	1

1997

Position	Driver	Car	Australia	Brazil	Argentina	San Marino	Monaco	Spain	Canada	France	Britain	Germany	Hungary	Belgium	Italy	Austria	Luxembourg	Japan	Europe	Points total
1	Jacques Villeneuve	Williams-Renault	pr	p1	p1	pr	r	p1	r	4	p1	r	1	p5	5	p1	1	pdq	p3	81
2	Heinz-Harald Frentzen	Williams-Renault	8r	9	r	1	pr	8	4	2	r	r	r	3	3	3	3	2	6	42
3	Jean Alesi	Benetton-Renault	r	p6	7	5	r	3	2	5	2	6	11	8	p2	r	2	5	13	36
	David Coulthard	McLaren-Mercedes Benz	1	10	r	r	r	6	7	7	4	r	r	r	1	2	r	10r	2	36
5	Gerhard Berger	Benetton-Renault	4	2	p6	r	9	10	–	–	–	p1	8	6	7	10	4	8	4	27
	Mika Häkkinen	McLaren-Mercedes Benz	3	4	5	6	r	7	r	r	r	3	r	dq	9	r	pr	4	1	27
7	Eddie Irvine	Ferrari	r	16	2	3	3	12	r	3	r	r	9r	10r	8	r	r	3	5	24
8	Giancarlo Fisichella	Jordan-Peugeot	r	8	r	4	6	9	3	9	7	11r	r	2	4	4	r	7	11	20
9	Olivier Panis	Prost-Mugen Honda	5	3	r	8	4	2	11r	–	–	r	–	r	6	r	7	6	7	16
10	Johnny Herbert	Sauber-Petronas	r	7	4	r	r	5	5	8	r	r	3	4	r	8	7	6	8	15
11	Ralf Schumacher	Jordan-Peugeot	r	r	3	r	r	r	6	5	5	5	r	r	5	r	9	r	r	13
12	Damon Hill	Arrows-Yamaha	r	17r	r	r	r	r	9	12	6	8	2	13r	r	7	8	11	r	7
13	Rubens Barrichello	Stewart-Ford Cosworth	r	r	r	r	2	r	r	r	r	r	r	r	13	14r	r	r	r	6
14	Alexander Wurz	Benetton-Renault	–	–	–	–	–	–	r	r	3	–	–	–	–	–	–	–	–	4
15	Jarno Trulli	Minardi-Hart	9	12	9	r	r	15	r	–	–	–	–	–	–	–	–	–	–	3
		Prost-Mugen Honda	–	–	–	–	–	–	–	10	8	4	7	15	10	–	–	–	–	
16	Pedro Diniz	Arrows-Yamaha	10	r	r	r	r	r	8	r	r	r	r	7	r	13r	5	12	r	2
	Shinji Nakano	Prost-Mugen Honda	7	14	r	r	r	6	r	11r	7	6	r	11	r	r	r	10	r	2
	Mika Salo	Tyrrell-Ford Cosworth	r	13	8	9	5	r	r	r	r	r	13	11	r	r	10	r	12	2
19	Nicola Larini	Sauber-Petronas	6	11	r	7	r	–	–	–	–	–	–	–	–	–	–	–	–	1
–	Michael Schumacher	Ferrari	2	5	r	2	1	4	p1	p1	r	2	p4	1	6	6	r	1	r	78

Michael Schumacher was stripped of his second place in the World Championship due to his move on Villeneuve in the European Grand Prix.

1998

Position	Driver	Car	Australia	Brazil	Argentina	San Marino	Spain	Monaco	Canada	France	Britain	Austria	Germany	Hungary	Belgium	Italy	Luxembourg	Japan	Points total
1	Mika Häkkinen	McLaren-Mercedes Benz	p1	p1	2	r	p1	p1	r	p3	p2	1	p1	p6	pr	4	1	1	100
2	Michael Schumacher	Ferrari	r	3	1	2	3	10	1	1	1	3	5	1	r	p1	p2	pr	86
3	David Coulthard	McLaren-Mercedes Benz	2	2	p6	p1	2	r	pr	6	r	2	2	2	7	r	3	3	56
4	Eddie Irvine	Ferrari	4	8	3	3	r	3	3	2	3	4	8	r	r	2	4	2	47
5	Jacques Villeneuve	Williams-Mecachrome	5	7	r	4	6	5	10	4	7	6	3	3	r	r	8	6	21
6	Damon Hill	Jordan-Mugen Honda	8	dq	8	10r	r	8	r	r	r	7	4	4	1	6	9	4	20
7	Heinz-Harald Frentzen	Williams-Mecachrome	3	5	9	5	8	r	r	15r	r	r	9	5	4	7	5	5	17
	Alexander Wurz	Benetton-Playlife	7	4	4	r	4	r	4	5	4	9	11	16r	r	r	7	9	17
9	Giancarlo Fisichella	Benetton-Playlife	r	6	7	r	r	2	2	9	5	pr	7	8	r	8	6	8	16
10	Ralf Schumacher	Jordan-Mugen Honda	r	r	r	7	11	r	r	16	6	5	6	9	2	3	r	r	14
11	Jean Alesi	Sauber-Petronas	r	9	5	6	10	12r	r	7	r	r	10	7	3	5	10	7	9
12	Rubens Barrichello	Stewart-Ford Cosworth	r	r	10	r	5	r	5	10	r	r	r	r	r	10	11	r	4
13	Pedro Diniz	Arrows	r	r	r	r	r	6	9	14	r	r	r	11	5	r	r	r	3
	Mika Salo	Arrows	r	r	r	9	r	4	r	13	r	r	14	r	r	r	14	r	3
15	Johnny Herbert	Sauber-Petronas	6	11r	r	r	7	7	r	8	r	8	r	10	r	r	r	10	1
	Jan Magnussen	Stewart-Ford Cosworth	r	10	r	r	12	r	6	–	–	–	–	–	–	–	–	–	1
	Jarno Trulli	Prost-Peugeot	r	r	11	r	9	r	r	r	r	10	12	r	6	13	r	12	1

1999

Position	Driver	Car	Australia	Brazil	San Marino	Monaco	Spain	Canada	France	Britain	Austria	Germany	Hungary	Belgium	Italy	Europe	Malaysia	Japan	Points total
1	Mika Häkkinen	McLaren-Mercedes Benz	pr	p1	pr	p3	p1	1	2	pr	p3	pr	p1	p2	pr	5	3	1	76
2	Eddie Irvine	Ferrari	1	5	r	2	4	3	6	2	1	1	3	4	6	7	1	3	74
3	Heinz-Harald Frentzen	Jordan-Mugen Honda	2	3r	r	4	r	11r	1	4	4	3	4	3	1	pr	6	4	54
4	David Coulthard	McLaren-Mercedes Benz	r	r	2	r	2	7	r	1	2	5	2	1	5	r	r	4	48
5	Michael Schumacher	Ferrari	8	2	1	1	3	pr	5	r	–	–	–	–	–	–	p2	p2	44
6	Ralf Schumacher	Williams-Supertec	3	4	r	r	5	4	4	3	r	4	9	5	2	4	r	5	35
7	Rubens Barrichello	Stewart-Ford Cosworth	5	r	3	9r	dq	r	p3	8	r	r	5	10	4	3	5	8	21
8	Johnny Herbert	Stewart-Ford Cosworth	r	r	10r	r	5	r	12	14	11r	11	r	r	1	4	7		15
9	Giancarlo Fisichella	Benetton-Playlife	4	r	5	5	9	2	r	7	12r	r	r	11	r	r	11	14r	13
10	Mika Salo	BAR-Supertec	–	–	7r	r	8	–	–	–	–	–	–	–	–	–	–	–	10
		Ferrari	–	–	–	–	–	–	–	–	9	2	12	7	3	r	–	–	
11	Jarno Trulli	Prost-Peugeot	r	r	r	7	6	r	7	9	7	r	8	12	r	2	r	r	7
	Damon Hill	Jordan-Mugen Honda	r	r	4	r	7	r	r	5	8	r	6	6	10	r	r	r	7
13	Alexander Wurz	Benetton-Playlife	r	7	r	6	10	r	r	10	5	7	7	14	r	r	8	10	3
	Pedro Diniz	Sauber-Petronas	r	r	r	r	r	6	r	6	6	r	r	r	r	r	r	11	3
15	Olivier Panis	Prost-Peugeot	r	6	r	r	r	9	8	13	10	6	10	13	11r	9	r	r	2
	Jean Alesi	Sauber-Petronas	r	r	6	r	r	r	r	14	r	8	16r	9	9	r	7	6	2
17	Pedro de la Rosa	Arrows	6	r	r	r	11	r	11	r	r	r	15	r	r	r	r	13	1
	Marc Gené	Minardi-Ford Cosworth	r	9	9	r	r	8	r	15	11	9	17	16	r	6	9	r	1